Second Language Learning and Teaching

Series Editor

Mirosław Pawlak, Faculty of Pedagogy and Fine Arts, Adam Mickiewicz University, Kalisz, Poland

The series brings together volumes dealing with different aspects of learning and teaching second and foreign languages. The titles included are both monographs and edited collections focusing on a variety of topics ranging from the processes underlying second language acquisition, through various aspects of language learning in instructed and non-instructed settings, to different facets of the teaching process, including syllabus choice, materials design, classroom practices and evaluation. The publications reflect state-of-the-art developments in those areas, they adopt a wide range of theoretical perspectives and follow diverse research paradigms. The intended audience are all those who are interested in naturalistic and classroom second language acquisition, including researchers, methodologists, curriculum and materials designers, teachers and undergraduate and graduate students undertaking empirical investigations of how second languages are learnt and taught.

More information about this series at http://www.springer.com/series/10129

Urszula Michalik · Paweł Zakrajewski ·
Iwona Sznicer · Anna Stwora
Editors

Exploring Business Language and Culture

 Springer

Editors
Urszula Michalik
Instytut Językoznawstwa
University of Silesia
Sosnowiec, Poland

Iwona Sznicer
Instytut Językoznawstwa
Wydział Humanistyczny
University of Silesia
Sosnowiec, Poland

Paweł Zakrajewski
Instytut Językoznawstwa
Wydział Humanistyczny
University of Silesia
Sosnowiec, Poland

Anna Stwora
Instytut Językoznawstwa
Wydział Humanistyczny
University of Silesia
Sosnowiec, Poland

ISSN 2193-7648   ISSN 2193-7656   (electronic)
Second Language Learning and Teaching
ISBN 978-3-030-58550-1   ISBN 978-3-030-58551-8   (eBook)
https://doi.org/10.1007/978-3-030-58551-8

This Springer imprint is published by the registered company Springer Nature Switzerland AG
The registered company address is: Gewerbestrasse 11, 6330 Cham, Switzerland

Preface

The highly complex nature of the contemporary business environment, approached from both the theoretical and practical standpoint, does not cease to prove that research into business studies cannot be dissociated from the cultural and linguistic context. Moreover, despite numerous studies, different approaches and classifications of English for Specific Purposes and Business English (they will henceforth be abbreviated as ESP and BE, respectively) offered so far, neither scholars for whom ESP and BE are the objects of linguistic and social analysis, nor professionals who treat ESP and BE as tools of communication within the scope of their activities, have come to a consensus on the coherent and transparent methodologies of ESP and BE research. Thus, the need for discussion about the developments of business language and other related disciplines, together with the presentation of current research trends and areas of interests, resulted in gathering scholars' reflections, expertise, and presentation of the results of their studies.

The main aim of this volume is to present the results of carefully selected academic research in the sphere of business language and culture, as well as the experience of pedagogical staff and practitioners concerned with broadly understood business. The contributors of the volume represent various fields of linguistic and literary studies; however, what makes their contributions unique is the interest, renowned research and investigation, as well as the ability of implementing various processes of the world of business into their studies.

The first part of this volume, *Developing Business English Competence*, consists of four chapters. The opening one by Anna Zelenková and Jana Javorčíková discusses teaching BE at universities in Slovakia. They postulate that teaching innovated ESP, known as English for Economic Disciplines (EED), should involve the development of students' intercultural competence owing to the internationalisation of both higher education and the labour market. Zelenková and Javorčíková therefore claim that the ESP and EED instructors should focus on integrating intercultural competence into traditional curricula, reorienting BE programs at universities so that students could acquire expertise on linguistic and cultural matters alike. That is why the emphasis is placed on suggestions concerning the content and methodology of EED, which ought to respond to the challenges of the globalised world of business.

Subsequently, Iwona Dronia intends to share the results of her study which was conducted among the students of the Business English Program and concerned the broadly understood nature of communication. In the discussion devoted to most common channels of students' communication, the scholar develops the approach to communication in L1 and L2 demonstrated by the representatives of Y generation. The study also explores the differences between various generations as regards lifestyle, values, and communication preferences, which impact on "soft" skills. Hence, it aims to raise awareness of changing communication patterns employed for L1 and L2 interactions.

The third chapter, authored by Anna L. Wieczorek and Maciej Mitręga, focuses on the topic of prosumption in postgraduate university education directed to students who already possess valuable professional experience. Wieczorek and Mitręga, therefore, stress the need for co-creation in university education, which assumes that the input from students—who, after all, are the consumers of knowledge—should play a central role in managing educational settings. The authors put forward a claim that education services at university level should strongly rely on postgraduate students' feedback concerning the quality of teaching, which may prove beneficial not only for the professional career of the teachers, but also for students, especially as regards their skills, engagement, and satisfaction with the academic experience.

Staying in the domain of teaching BE to postgraduates, a related chapter by Anna L. Wieczorek touches upon the problems encountered by the teachers of BE who happen to teach mixed groups of university postgraduates. Basing her observations on both satisfaction questionnaires administered to students and on interviews with their teachers (and with the heads of BE study programmes as well), Wieczorek draws the reader's attention to some problematic discrepancies between theory and practice, that is, between the lack of appropriate linguistic background and the lack of business experience. She argues convincingly that potential differences between the expectations of postgraduate students of BE from diversified educational backgrounds and between the capabilities of BE teachers may trigger teacher stress. Nonetheless, she sees the issue as a challenge, offering several useful suggestions on how to handle such situations and, hence, reduce teacher stress effectively.

The second part, *Values in the World of Business*, is made up of six chapters. It opens with the contribution by Ewa Wójcik, who discusses the issue of cross-generational differences in the perception of business ethics. These are outlined against a thoroughly presented social, historical, and demographic background, showing that the role of business ethics is fundamental since varying hierarchies of values and different perceptions of what is morally right or wrong in business can be the cause of cross-generational confrontations. In her paper, Wójcik attempts to explain why individuals belonging to different generations and coming from different cultural backgrounds differ in their perceptions of values and behaviours on corporate grounds. Her contribution is hence a voice in the discussion on the protection of the rights of stakeholders, that is, employees, consumers, and shareholders.

David Cole and Petra Strnádová work towards the elaboration of the notion of "good corporate citizenship". The authors look at the interaction of social responsibilities at the individual, corporate, and state level. They explain what it means to be fully in line with the concept of stakeholder corporate social responsibility, as well as how digital economy works in the globalised world of business. Concentrating on the region of Central and Eastern Europe (CEE), Cole and Strnádová explore the relationship between local national governments, along with their national responsibility, and important ethical issues. Thus, the multitude of perspectives on corporate social responsibility presented in the chapter allows new insights into the impact of different stakeholders and their responsibilities on the CEE region.

Cole and Strnádová's reflections are followed by Jolanta Łącka-Badura, who shares the results of a comparative analysis of the language of values, as reflected in online employee reviews and testimonials. The two types of electronic word of mouth studied demonstrate that values, expressed either explicitly or implicitly, can be divided into rational/functional, emotional/psychological, and higher-order benefits/brand values that, collectively, build the employee value proposition. Apart from studying the linguistic layer, Łącka-Badura points out that the non-identical nature of the two text types analysed stems from the functions they perform because testimonials usually foreground the persuasive/promotional function, whereas reviews tend to perform the evaluative one.

This chapter is followed by a comparative analysis conducted by Katarzyna Bańka-Orłowska, who addresses the topic of differences and similarities between Polish and Chinese business etiquette trends. The paper touches upon political and business relations between the two cultures and, most importantly, tries to answer the questions concerning proper behaviour in the context of Chinese culture. The author gives the reader several useful tips on how to prepare for a business meeting with Chinese entrepreneurs, remarks upon the appropriateness of certain acts, and explains two cultural phenomena known as "you mianzi" and "you guanxi", which are connected with losing face and with having contacts or influential relationships, respectively.

Bańka-Orłowska's considerations on business in intercultural environments are followed by the chapter prepared by Anna Stwora, who presents humour as a powerful managerial and communicative tool in business communication. She offers a short overview of the general theories of humour and sociologies thereof, dealing with both the universal and culture-specific aspects of the phenomenon in question. Then, Stwora introduces the most crucial sociopragmatic and strategic functions of humour with a view to checking how it is understood in business contexts across cultures. The paramount objective of her study was to conduct a comparative analysis of the results obtained from research participants from different linguistic and cultural backgrounds, i.e. from Polish and Taiwanese informants. Such a study makes it possible to capture the dynamics of humour, which is conditioned by various sociocultural factors, as well as compare value orientations among cultures so as to trace trans-cultural differences and similarities.

Anna Zelenková closes the second part of the volume with the summary of cultural taxonomies which are used in the process of understanding intercultural relations in business. The paper is a theoretical study which aims at exploring interconnections between culture and business. Moreover, the author takes into consideration the importance of culture and its impact on contemporary international business, thus supplementing theoretical frameworks with pertinent examples. Based on existing studies on cross-cultural business and communication, the chapter highlights the most important points to be taken into account in managing cultural diversity.

The third part of the volume, *Various Dimensions of Business Communication*, consists of five papers whose authors present different, very often unconventional, dimensions of communication in business world. Piotr Mamet offers a very thorough semantic investigation of the UK and US tank names from the LSP perspective. His study is particularly interesting because there has been little systematic research that paid attention to this topic. Thus, for the purpose of the analysis, Mamet applies semantic approach in order to identify and discuss both denotations and connotations of the names which are included in the corpus. Mamet's analysis is supported by the classification of names from business, in this case marketing, point of view. The combination of the linguistic and historical perspective on the development of tank names allows to see a variety of naming systems, making it possible to uncover both regularities and irregularities of various name components.

The chapter by Adam Pluszczyk is devoted to the phenomenon of small talk which takes place in the workplace. In his paper, the scholar focuses primarily on spoken discourse and the way it is reflected in various communicative exchanges in working environments. In order to demonstrate the interactions of Polish people during small talk in the workplace, the author conducted a study for which he implemented a questionnaire as his main tool of research. The responses provided by the informants helped the author determine the role, significance, and perception of, as well as attitudes towards small talk in professional settings.

Krystyna Warchał takes the readers to the world of academia, in particular written scientific discourse, and demonstrates that the two realms—business and academia—represent certain common discourse patterns. In her thorough investigation of the corpus of research articles, the scholar outlines selected communication practices and discourse mechanisms which are shared by these two domains which, as the scholar states, seem worlds apart. Drawing on shared rhetorical mechanisms, Warchał demonstrates that the origins, structures, and goals of both discourse types have several strong, though often overlooked, points of contact.

On the contrary, Anthony Barker reflects on the world of fiction, namely the film, and investigates the instances of doing business in selected American films which have been made since the 40s of the previous century. In his paper, the scholar clearly states that his main concern "is to review the films that deal with business as a legal and legitimate activity, even if there is often a fine line drawn, and some form of immorality is implicit". Thus, as a result of his observations, Barker proposes a very interesting classification according to which he discusses the selected material. In his in-depth discussion on the cinematic image of business people, Barker argues that a new film genre described as "the corporate scam exposure movie" has emerged in the last decade, presenting the viewers with more complete, and perhaps also more realistic, a picture of the world of business.

The volume closes with considerations by Anna Majer and Piotr Mamet on the language of M—a fictional character in Ian Fleming's *James Bond* series, as played by Judi Dench in seven *James Bond* movies. The main aim of the scholars' analysis is to answer a rhetorical—at first glance—question, namely whether M speaks like a man or woman. For the purpose of the investigation, the authors established a framework which is based upon previous research in the fields of discourse and gender and institutional discourse. They aim at checking whether the language of this particular female manager, who establishes her identity as the manager of MI6 and simultaneously enacts her gender identity, retains any characteristic features of institutional discourse, such as the managerial language specificity, and whether it reflects power relations in the workplace.

The book responds to the challenges of the modern, globalised world that induces cross-cultural cooperation, and thus communication, in business environments, offering invaluable insights into various aspects of business language and culture viewed from a number of perspectives. Given all the various strands of research surveyed in this book, the reader will surely find something interesting and inspiring in the chapters to follow that shed some light on various aspects of business language and culture. In closing, the editors would like to thank the contributors once again for their readiness to submit their papers and contribute to this collective volume, as well as for their collaboration in the process of preparing the manuscript.

Sosnowiec, Poland

Urszula Michalik
Paweł Zakrajewski
Iwona Sznicer
Anna Stwora

Acknowledgements We would like to express our gratitude to several people who offered their invaluable help at different stages of preparing this volume. We would like to thank Profs. Bożena Cetnarowska and Ewa Bogdanowska-Jakubowska from the University of Silesia in Katowice for reviewing this volume and sharing constructive and valuable remarks. We would also like to thank Prof. Mirosław Pawlak from the Faculty of Pedagogy and Fine Arts at the Adam Mickiewicz University in Kalisz for his scientific expertise and guidance. Finally, we owe our gratitude to Prof. Adam Wojtaszek from the University of Silesia in Katowice for his advice and support for our scientific projects.

Contents

Editors and Contributors

About the Editors

Urszula Michalik, Ph.D. is a senior lecturer at the Institute of Linguistics, Faculty of Humanities University of Silesia in Katowice, Poland. She received her M.A. in English Studies in 1997 and Ph.D. in Sociology of Communication from the University of Silesia in 2002. Her scientific interests centre on ESP-Business English and such related issues as corporate culture, cross-cultural communication in the world of business, marketing, advertising, and public relations. She has also devoted a lot of work and interest to such areas in business as negotiations, meetings, and presentations. Moreover, she is concerned with genre and register analysis of business texts and analysis of the language and cultural issues in the use of humour. Among her recent publications are *Cultural awareness as a vantage point for managers operating internationally—a case of American and Japanese managers* (2013), co-authored with Dr. Hab. Mirosława Michalska-Suchanek: *The word as a tool of persuasion in sales promotional letters in the light of the theories of needs and emotions* (2014), co-authored with Dr Hab. Mirosława-Michalska-Suchanek: *The Challenges of global marketing-cultural variables* (2014), *Język jako narzędzie budowania tożsamości produktu w promocyjnych listach sprzedażowych—Language as a tool of building company identity in Sales promotion letters* (2015), *Language of values-the core values of banks* (2017), and co-authored with Iwona Sznicer, *The Use of Humor in Cross-Cultural Business Environment* (2017).
e-mail: u.michalik10@gmail.com

Paweł Zakrajewski, Ph.D. is an assistant professor at the Institute of Linguistics, Faculty of Humanities University of Silesia in Katowice, Poland. He received his Ph.D. in Linguistics from the University of Silesia in May 2015. His scientific interests centre on discourse analysis, rhetoric, communication—especially new media, translation, and cross-cultural and cross-linguistic comparative studies. Recently, he has been involved in a number of projects related to genre and

linguistic analysis, effective communication, public relations, and ESP translation. He is also an assistant editor of *TAPSLA Journal* (*Theory and Practice of Second Language Acquisition*) and member of AEDEAN—Asociación Española de Estudios Anglo-Norteamericanos. Recent publications include *Researching Second Language Learning and Teaching from a Psycholinguistic Perspective. Studies in Honour of Danuta Gabryś Barker* (2016). Springer, (co-edited with Dagmara Galajda and Miroslaw Pawlak); *Young Scholars on Theoretical and Applied Linguistics: Research Projects* (2016). Oficyna Wydawnicza—Wyższa Szkoła Humanitas, (co-edited with Maria Wysocka, Dagmara Gałajda and Artur Kijak); *Multiculturalism, Multilingualism and the Self* (2017). Springer, (co-edited with Danuta Gabryś-Barker, Dagmara Gałajda and Adam Wojtaszek).
e-mail: pawel.zakrajewski@us.edu.pl

Iwona Sznicer, MA is a lecturer at the Institute of Linguistics, Faculty of Humanities University of Silesia in Katowice, Poland. Her academic interests focus on ESP-Business English and such related issues as corporate culture and cross-cultural business communication. She is also interested in genre and register analysis. Her experience includes teaching courses in, among others, specialised varieties of English and current economic and social issues. Among her recent publications are *Business Presentation. A Cross-Cultural Dimension* (2014), *Stereotypes in Cross-Cultural Business Communication* (2015), and co-authored with Urszula Michalik, *The Use of Humor in Cross-Cultural Business Environment* (2017). She is also a co-author of a textbook *English for Business Purposes-Finance and Politics* (under preparation).
e-mail: iwona.sznicer@us.edu.pl

Anna Stwora obtained her Ph.D. from the Institute of Linguistics, Faculty of Humanities of the University of Silesia in Katowice, Poland. She is also a Ph.D. student in linguistics at the Sapienza University of Rome, Italy. Her research interests oscillate around multimodal discourse of advertising, especially in its metaphorical and humorous dimensions, as well as around specialised registers viewed from the psycholinguistic and sociolinguistic standpoint. She is also interested in cognitivism, communication studies, and contrastive linguistics. In 2020, she took up a post as an editorial assistant at *The European Journal of Humour Research*. She has been involved in several projects including seminars, workshops, and conferences devoted to humour and contrastive studies, as well as to business language and culture. Her recent publications include *Humor Research Project: Explorations in Humor Studies* (2020). Cambridge Scholars Publishing (co-edited with Marcin Kuczok and Mariola Świerkot); "How to befriend an ad? A sociolinguistic and sociocultural inquiry into social media ads on Facebook" (2018); "Money Hanging in My Closet? Various Conceptualisations of Money in English" (2018); and "Language Change Through Ads: The Impact of Advertising Messages on Contemporary Idio- and Sociolects" (2018).
e-mail: anna_stwora@interia.eu

Contributors

Katarzyna Bańka-Orłowska Institute of Linguistics, Faculty of Humanities, University of Silesia in Katowice, Katowice, Poland

Anthony Barker University of Aveiro, Aveiro, Portugal

David Cole Department of Foreign Languages, Faculty of Economics, Matej Bel University, Banská Bystrica, Slovakia

Iwona Dronia Faculty of Humanities, Institute of Linguistics, University of Silesia, Katowice, Poland

Jana Javorčíková Department of English and American Studies, Faculty of Arts, Matej Bel University, Banská Bystrica, Slovakia

Jolanta Łącka-Badura University of Economics in Katowice, Katowice, Poland

Anna Majer Institute of Linguistics, Faculty of Humanities, University of Silesia in Katowice, Katowice, Poland

Piotr Mamet Silesian University of Technology, Gliwice, Poland

Maciej Mitręga VSB-Technical University of Ostrava, Ostrava, Czech Republic

Adam Pluszczyk Faculty of Humanities, Institute of Linguistics, University of Silesia in Katowice, Katowice, Poland

Petra Strnádová Department of Foreign Languages, Faculty of Economics, Matej Bel University, Banská Bystrica, Slovakia

Anna Stwora Faculty of Humanities, Institute of Linguistics, University of Silesia in Katowice, Katowice, Poland

Krystyna Warchał Institute of Linguistics, Faculty of Humanities, University of Silesia in Katowice, Katowice, Poland

Anna L. Wieczorek Institute of Modern Languages, University of Bielsko-Biala, Bielsko-Biala, Poland

Ewa Wójcik University of Economics, Katowice, Poland

Anna Zelenková Department of Professional Communication in Business, Faculty of Economics, Matej Bel University in Banská Bystrica, Banská Bystrica, Slovakia

Developing BE Competence

Business English Today: The Need for Intercultural Approach

Anna Zelenková and Jana Javorčíková

Abstract The paper explores the present state of teaching Business English (BE) at universities in Slovakia. BE is theoretically presented as a foreign language under the umbrella of English for Specific Purposes (ESP) which is generally based on students' needs. BE in economic disciplines should cover the present and future needs of students. These needs are evolving due to the advances in internationalization of higher education as well as the labour market and business in Europe and in the world. The paper defines specific purposes of teaching and learning BE at Slovak universities, its aims, priorities, and specific features in order to define the criteria for skills and intercultural competences required for today's globalized business world. Based on selected indicators in ESP, the theoretical study gives a rationale for intercultural directions in the teaching of ESP and BE. Historical insight helps to recognize the present state of BE teaching and learning and suggest the revision of future orientation of BE at universities towards a more inclusive subject integrating a broader scope of cultural competencies—English for Economic Disciplines (EED). The authors of the study explore the content, methods, and constraints of the proposed new approach to teaching ESP (BE).

Keywords English for specific purposes · Business English · Higher education · Intercultural competence

A. Zelenková (✉)
Department of Professional Communication in Business, Faculty of Economics, Matej Bel University, Banská Bystrica, Slovakia
e-mail: anna.zelenkova@umb.sk

J. Javorčíková
Department of English and American Studies, Faculty of Arts, Matej Bel University, Banská Bystrica, Slovakia
e-mail: jana.javorcikova@umb.sk

© Springer Nature Switzerland AG 2020   3
U. Michalik et al. (eds.), *Exploring Business Language and Culture*,
Second Language Learning and Teaching,
https://doi.org/10.1007/978-3-030-58551-8_1

1 Introduction

International business today and the labour market in Europe is characterised by cultural and linguistic diversity of the workforce and the workplace. Business operations get international dimensions and require from business professionals not only confident use of English and other foreign languages, but also mastering the cultural and intercultural aspects of business communication in order to establish themselves successfully on the international labour markets.

Studying foreign languages is part of the curricula at philological and also most non-philological faculties preparing graduates for various fields of economic disciplines, such as business management, banking, marketing, public economy, tourism, etc. Foreign languages are connected with the content of the subject study (foreign languages for specific purposes) to allow communication in a given field. The aims of developing foreign language competence (and specifically English language competence) are projected for the present study needs and future, professional, job-oriented needs of graduates. Therefore, it is essential to define the needs of the language users, establish the role of cultural and intercultural competence, and decide what role cultural studies play in the teaching of ESP and BE classes.

However, in terms of preparation of future business professionals, it is also essential to redefine the traditional concept of ESP in terms of the method of teaching which, since the 1960s (the 1990s in Slovakia) has inclined towards communicative language teaching. It is our assumption, as we will explicate in this study, that business professionals need to master the cultural as well as linguistic aspects of foreign language use and gain professional communicative competence, which, specifically in business life, guarantees effective communication in the intercultural business environment. In order to achieve this, it is inevitable to reconsider traditional ESP and BE and their constructive elements (goals, methods, and approaches).

2 Aims and Methods of the Study

The aim of this study is to present teaching ESP and its specifics in relation to the development of intercultural competences for future business professionals. The article outlines the development of ESP teaching in the context of Slovak university education. The authors attempt to define the factors that influence today's focus of cultural studies from the perspective of the learners' needs and teaching and learning objectives in various business-related academic and professional areas. The analysis of theoretical background and current methodology of teaching foreign languages and other related academic disciplines that have an impact on the content and focus of teaching ESP was taken for the starting point.

The general concept of this study lies in the assumption that traditional concepts of ESP and BE do not fully comply with the present-day requirements for real business life. Therefore, a new way of linguistic and cultural preparation of future business executives should be considered. For the purposes of this study, we suggest a more broadly organized denomination "English for Economic Disciplines"—methodologically and content-wise significantly different from ESP and BE in terms of integration of interculturality and communicative competence into traditional ESP and BE. To justify the establishment of EED, the authors will explore the discourse on the nature of General English, ESP, BE, and their hierarchy (with an insight into the historical development of these fields in Slovakia). Further, the study explores communicative and intercultural approaches to language teaching and their essential role in the preparation of future business professionals. Finally, we will analyse and evaluate three aspects of methodological praxeology of EED, which require innovation in order to integrate all the aforementioned elements into effective teaching: content, methods, and aims that affect EED. The authors postulate that teaching EED should involve developing students' intercultural competence.

2.1 Terminology Database: ESP, BE, and Intercultural Competence

ESP, emerging in the 1960s and developing across decades, has now entered a general academic lexicon. To define ESP, researchers have approached it from different points of view. Some of them tried to define it as a specific language (Strevens, 1988) and specific vocabulary development (Felices Lago, 2016; Kacetl & Klímová, 2015; Míšková, 2009); others focused on specific needs (Dudley-Evans & St John, 1997; Ellis & Johnson, 1994; Hutchinson & Waters, 1991; Jordan, 1997) and teaching methodology (Dudley-Evans & St John, 1997; Hanesová, 2007; Zelenková, 2010). We base our definition of ESP on Dudley-Evans and St John (1997) who suggest the absolute and variable characteristics. The absolute characteristics include:

1. ESP is defined to meet specific needs of the learners (e.g., English for chemists; business people, etc.; authors' note);
2. ESP makes use of underlying methodology and activities of the discipline it serves;
3. ESP is centred on the language appropriate to these activities in terms of grammar, lexis, register, study skills, discourse, and genre.

   The variable characteristics are:

1. ESP may be related to or designed for specific disciplines;
2. ESP may use, in specific teaching situations, a different methodology from that of General English;
3. ESP is likely to be designed for adult learners, either at a tertiary level institution or in a professional work situation. It could, however, be designed for learners at secondary school level;
4. ESP is generally designed for intermediate or advanced students;
5. Most ESP courses assume some basic knowledge of the language systems.

In their observations, Dudley-Evans and St John agree with the previous definition of Hutchinson and Waters (1991, p. 19): "ESP is an approach to language teaching in which all decisions as to content and method are based on the learner's reason for learning". Similarly, Ellis and Johnson (1994) and Donna (2000) stress the importance of the analysis of the needs of students and future users of the language.

Other authors addressed the teaching/learning aims of ESP in terms of competences, such as linguistic, communicative, and cultural competences (Hammerly, 1985) and were concerned with the pedagogic approach and principles to achieve these aims. According to Wang, Ayres, and Huyton (2010) it is necessary to improve practice-oriented competences to prepare students for the later job demands in the business sector, including language proficiency (problem solving in job-related situations in the business sector, such as handling customer relations and customer wishes). These requirements are in compliance with the linguistic competences in terms of "what can I do with the acquired language" as stated by the Common European Framework of Reference (CEFR) (Council of Europe, 2001, 2018).

BE thus might be considered one of the areas of application of ESP. BE (as defined by the British Council, for example) varies from General English in a broad sense, as the content is different—topics are related to the work place or world of business (Mehta, 2019, p. 1). The topic of business culture and cultural aspects of business, which is in our focus, is in most cases covered usually solely by one unit (e.g., Managing across cultures) introducing students only to a few rather contextless cultural differences.

Here, however, lies the core of the problem, regarding the scope and content of BE for the globalised business environment. Teaching ESP or, alternatively, BE, nowadays presents new challenges for teachers, course designers, curriculum planners, and course book writers, which lie in internalization of the study contents and approximating students culture as well as language or, in other words, language *as* culture. Anthony (2011) and Mehta (2019) anticipated the forthcoming shift of ESP (BE) towards interculturality:

> [Business English] is changing and very soon the difference between General English and Business English may not be so easily demarcated. With new General English course books coming out with titles like 'Natural English' and 'Skills for life,' the focus is changing as the role of English as a *lingua franca* is reaching new heights. Publishers recognise that the demand for English is now more than ever an instrumental demand. (Mehta, 2019, p. 1)

We agree with the view of Mehta and, in this study, we would like to expand this point to prove that there is a need for a thorough redefinition of the teaching contents of traditional BE and within the context of the analysis of the needs of students, integrating the communicative language teaching and intercultural CLT and ITC.

2.2 Historical Insight into the Teaching of ESP (BE) in Slovakia

In order to understand the developments in the teaching of ESP at non-philological faculties in Slovakia, it is necessary to take into consideration the continuum of development of ESP goals, methods, and procedures in the context of Slovak education system from the second half of the twentieth century up to the present. The milestones that were chosen include the time before 1990 (covering the years of former Communist system, detached from the world by the Iron Curtain), after 1990 (indicating the years of abrupt social changes and the opening towards the world and introducing CEFR), and after 2002 (the year when the Bologna declaration was adopted by the Slovak legal system and the process of internationalization of education started). The individual moves and related changes in diachronic perspective (including those of the cultural element) are illustrated on selected indicators in Table 1.

Table 1 shows that, prior to the 1990s, the cultural element in BE was represented mainly by the study of the so-called 'high culture' (literature, history, geography, social and political system, and other fact-based information, i.e., "realia" or "country studies") of a target country. ESP resembled the country studies taught at philological faculties, as then-popular assumption was; the study of culture was a part of the study of literature (Kačmárová, 2012). This concept of "realia" was effective until Williams and Hoggart proved the mutual influence of language and culture (Turner, 2005).

The 1990s were a significant milestone in teaching ESP; it has experienced a great boom and English became a universal *lingua franca* of business and communication. This cluster of linguistic and extralinguistic phenomena influenced the increasing inclination of ESP toward teaching cultural competences, as demonstrated by indicators selected in Table 1, resulting from two reasons:

1) practical professional reasons to study language (e.g., intercultural communication in practice),
2) academic reasons (e.g., opportunities for learning and student mobilities as a part of the European programmes framework).

Another reason that affected the global tendency toward intercultural approach in ESP teaching was plurilinguism, i.e., multilingual competences (Bírová & Bubáková, 2011) which are necessary for modern business.

2.3 Synchronic View of ESP (BE) at Non-philological Faculties in Slovakia

Having explained the historical shift of ESP (BE) in Slovakia, it is crucial to explain the core of the difference between ESP taught at philological (e.g., those preparing teachers and interpreters) and non-philological (business-oriented) institutions in Slovakia in terms of the cultural component. This difference dramatically affects

Table 1 Diachronic view of the development of the ESP goals, methods, and competences listed by indicators

Indicator	Prior to 1990	After the 1990s	After 2002
Entry level	Beginners, pre-intermediate	Pre-intermediate	Pre-intermediate, intermediate (B1, B2, C1); beginners excluded
Aims	Reading and translation of professional texts, mastering the vocabulary	Communication with professionals	Communication with experts in the intercultural (global) environment
Focus and content (including culture)	Teaching general English with partial focus on ESP and communication Fact-based studies of so-called "realia" of the target country (USA, UK; rarely Canada and Australia)	Teaching ESP; special emphasis on students' needs Rapid development of teaching ESP in specialised economic disciplines, such as business management, economics, tourism management, finance, and banking	Teaching ESP with special emphasis on academic and professional needs of students
Teaching method	Grammar-translation, direct method, infrequent attempts of communicative approach	Communicative approach, translation to mother tongue or vice versa minimised	Communicative approach, post-method, eclectic approach
Target skills	Mastering grammar, vocabulary, reading and translation of non-authentic texts (mostly produced by non-native speakers)	Teaching integrated skills necessary for effective professional communication (reading, writing, speaking, listening; translation to one's mother tongue is not taught as a special language skill)	Communication of professionals in the intercultural environment, intercultural communication, translation re-established as a core skill; translation and interpreting

(continued)

Table 1 (continued)

Indicator	Prior to 1990	After the 1990s	After 2002
Course books	Course books and study materials compiled by national authors	Foreign course books, authentic materials	International course-books, commercial course books, national course books (E-learning, dictionaries, online resources, the Internet)
Evaluation and assessment	Oral exams with little emphasis on writing skills (locally set assessment criteria)	Oral and written exams focused on four basic skills (regional criteria); first attempts to compare national and international standards	Testing of four/five integrated language skills, introducing international criteria (CEFR, UNIcert® (UNIcert®—international system of language education, assessment, and certification at non-philological faculties based on the document of leading German universities [used for ESP courses]), etc.)
Innovations of curricula		CLIL- and CBL-based teaching of specialised disciplines, beginnings of the intercultural direction of teaching ESP, formulating the need for intercultural communication and enhancing its role in ESP	Integration of the studies of culture as a distinctive phenomenon which affects international business communication Curricula and subjects taught via CLIL (CLIL—content and language integrated learning—learning a foreign language via content of a specific subject or vice versa: learning a specific content by the use of a foreign language; in American discourse, the term content-based learning/instruction is often used (CBL/CBI) instead) and CBL, study programmes and subjects taught in foreign languages as a result of the internationalisation of education (English-medium studies)

Source Adopted from Zelenková (2015), pp. 39–40

different students' needs that justify the inevitability of the shift in the ESP focus towards teaching language *as* culture.

Whereas language at philological faculties is *medium* per se (e.g., serves to explain a linguistic/cultural phenomenon), at non-philological faculties, it is an instrument to reach further goals, e.g., establish business contacts, give a presentation and, eventually, close a contract. Mastering the language thus means mastering the culture of one's economic partner. Major difference between the role language plays at philological and non-philological institutions thus lies in the needs of the end-user (speaker) to integrate the cultural component of the target language and target countries into discourse.

As a result, teaching ESP at business-oriented institutions has wider goals than mere linguistic and cultural ones; it focuses on the field of study or study programme in the given academic discipline and aims to prepare the graduate for smooth *functioning* in an international study environment and later in more and more internationalised work/business environment, which puts intercultural and communicative competencies at the forefront. Figure 1 shows specific goals of ESP and English for Occupational Purposes (EOP) versus English for Academic (EAP) and General Academic Purposes in specialised disciplines, such as economics, medicine, etc.

To specify the teaching of ESP for business and its cultural component, we can start with the two main strands of English for Specific Purposes as defined by Dudley-Evans and St John (1998, p. 6): English for Occupational Purposes (EOP) and English for Academic Purposes (EAP). These two strands differ mainly in learning objectives. English for Occupational Purposes focuses on skills needed to perform a certain job (such as language skills for future profession, professional jargon, or negotiation skills, customer orientation skills, etc.). English for Academic Purposes covers specific English studied for and in various specialized disciplines at the university, such as medicine, economics, engineering, technology, management, and others. Across all these specific fields of English, the general EAP plays a crucial role: teaching the integrated language skills of reading (academic texts), writing (for academic purposes—note-taking, summarizing, and mastering various genres), speaking (discussions, arguments), listening, and culture studies should be developed. As business is an international activity today, the cultural component that should be included makes the major difference between ESP for various disciplines and BE.

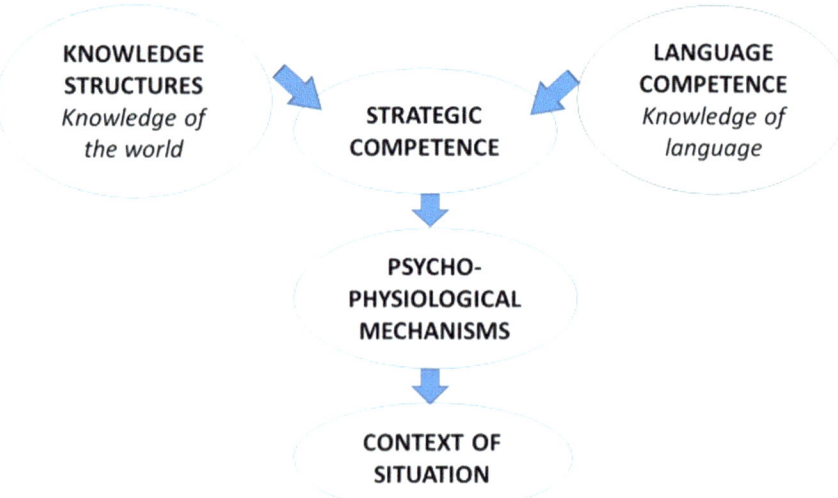

Fig. 1 Component of communicative language ability in communicative language use. *Source* Adopted by authors from Repka, Pčolinská, and Šipošová (2015), p. 73

To sum it up, the major difference in ESP (BE) lies in the necessity to master not only the language, but also the component of cultural awareness and competence. Such goals challenge traditional teaching of ESP and the place of intercultural competence between the target communication competencies. Moreover, successful graduates and future professionals should be able to cross cultures in intercultural communications and situations (Lustig & Koester, 2009, pp. 28–32). In the long run, a graduate of a non-philological programme focused on intercultural studies (unlike a graduate at philological faculties) will be prepared to communicate with experts in their professional field, to handle the situational use of language and the differences and similarities in communication at different levels and in different forms—written and oral, verbal and non-verbal, in a variety of culturally diverse environments. Traditional ESP and BE thus gain new constructive components—intercultural competencies and communicative competencies indispensable for successful business communication. What we mean is not just a minor extension of the original aims and procedures of ESP (BE) but a major revision of the very basic grounds of the fields in debate. Therefore, for the purposes of this study, in order to distinguish innovated approach to teaching ESP (BE), this new type of study will be denominated English for Economic Disciplines (EED).

3 Methodological Pragmatics of EED

In the next part of the study, attention will be paid to the practical methodological questions of how to implement EED effectively into the process of teaching English to future business professionals, in terms of teaching contents (Sect. 3.1), methods (Sect. 3.2), and EED syllabus design (Sect. 4).

3.1 Content of EED: Communicative Language Teaching Versus Intercultural Language Teaching

As stated before, except for traditional ESP and BE competence, EED requires implementation of two constructive components—intercultural competence and communicative competence. Communicative approach to language teaching, according to Richards (2006, p. 2), contains the following aspects of language use:

- knowing how to use language for a range of different purposes and functions,
- knowing how to vary our use of language according to the setting and the participants (e.g., knowing when to use formal and informal speech or when to use language appropriately for written, as opposed to spoken, communication),
- knowing how to produce and understand different types of texts (e.g., narratives, reports, interviews, comments),

- knowing how to maintain communication despite having limitations in one's language knowledge (e.g., through using different kinds of communication strategies) (Richards, 2006, pp. 2–3).

Professional educators, however, vary in their opinions on how to achieve maximum communicative competence and its constructive competencies. Many linguists (e.g., Bachman, 1990; Savignon, 2017, originally published in 1983) expanded the Hymes' model of communicative competence/performance (Hymes, 1972, pp. 269–93). For example, Scarcella and Oxford (1992, p. 63) distinguish four sub-competences of communicative competence:

1. Linguistic sub-competence, which refers to the knowledge of the linguistic code of a language (grammar, vocabulary, pronunciation).
2. Discourse sub-competence, which is concerned with the ability to generate not only individual sentences, but also connected texts.
3. Sociolinguistic sub-competence, which involves the knowledge of cultural and social context and communicative situations.
4. Strategic sub-competence, which generally refers to the strategies one uses to compensate for imperfect knowledge of language rules and breakdowns in communication due to performance variables. Interlocutors may sustain communication through paraphrase, circumlocution, repetition, literal translation, code switching (oral > written), generalization, and avoidance of difficult constructions.

In response to communicative theories of the 1980s, Bachman (1990, p. 85) developed a simplified model of communicative competence integrating five phenomena: knowledge structures and language competence enhancing strategic competence leading to the context of the situation via psychophysiological mechanisms.

The model of communicative competence by O'Grady, Dobrovolsky, and Aronoff (1997, p. 480) further distinguishes three fundamental sub-competencies of communicative competence: language competence, strategic competence, psychological competence, and their sub-specifications. Such a rapid development in the research of communicative competence proves its mutable and dynamic nature (Repka, Pčolinská, & Šipošová, 2015, p. 74) as well as its complex character.

The communicative approach deals with the method of teaching, whereas "interculturality" deals with the teaching contents. The intercultural language teaching focuses on teaching intercultural communicative competence which, according to experts, presents a number of "[new] challenges in the form of communication situations to which interlocutors ought to respond adequately" (Lustig & Koester, 2009, pp. 28–32). Intercultural competence is manifested by an acquisition of the summary of cultural information (cognitive component), new cultural patterns, and emotional skills (affective component) and behaviour, taking into account cultural differences and specificities of individual cultures (activity component, which means also intercultural communication). This triangulation framework is based on the pedagogical requirements for the development of the student's personality in the educational

Fig. 2 Components of
intercultural competence.
Source Developed by authors

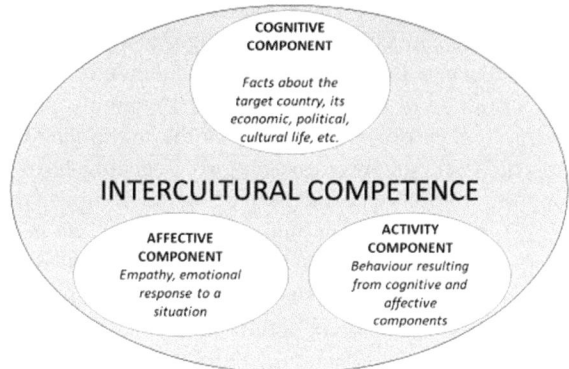

process. Figure 2 shows the set of intercultural competence components in ESP for business.

Communicative language teaching thus organizes the "how" of language teaching, whereas intercultural competences control the "what" of language teaching within EED. The idea of the implementation of more cultural components into preparation of future business professionals has resonated in the professional discourse. One of the supreme European institutions, the Council of Europe, formulated the need to develop intercultural competence in teaching ESP in the context of understanding the current model of skill competences, which represents not only the knowledge and control of language, but also includes "a component of cultural knowledge and awareness" (Council of Europe, 2001, p. 26, p. 104).

In teaching ESP at universities specialised in economics, this fact is even more significant as the students are trained to communicate with representatives of other cultures with the aim of building international business contacts. The correct use of language enhances effective communication, establishing and maintaining business contacts, while situation-bound and culture-bound, incorrect use of language (stemming from a different cultural background), ignoring the nuances of the language and culture, may lead to failure in closing a contract and, finally, be detrimental to the establishment of business partnership. In various cultures, people communicate politeness, demands, requests, and rejection in various ways, seen as polite in some cultures but impolite in other cultures (Hidasi, 2014). These differences can cause tensions, misunderstandings or even conflicts in international communication.

However, teaching intercultural competencies as a part of ESP at non-philological faculties is still far from common. A relatively common mistake in foreign language teaching is to assume that learning a foreign language automatically mediates intercultural competence, just because language inevitably carries certain crucial cultural phenomena. The current prevalent methodology still operates with a relatively narrow conception of the relationship of language and culture and is not quite clear in the case of the acquisition of intercultural competence (Lazár, 2015). Kramsch (1998, p. 12) also points out that language is still being taught as a fixed system of formal structures and universal linguistic features. Culture represents a kind of an "appendix", or, in other words an added element to language, to the extent that it further widens the gap between culture and language instead of approximating the two phenomena. Many teachers thus teach language and culture, not language as culture.

A solution is at hand: Kramsch, for example, proposes a framework for teaching culture which divorces itself from the traditional dichotomy between general and specific, i.e., language and culture. Teaching foreign language should serve as a platform for dialogue and joint efforts to minimize the differences (Kramsch, 1998, p. 12). In order to communicate effectively, we need not only good command of language (i.e., to become *languagewise*), but also we need to know how to use it appropriately according to the situation of the speaking activities and with respect to the cultural environment and its social context (Byram & Fleming, 1998). Zelenka defines the latter as becoming *culturewise* (Zelenka, 2007, p. 32).

3.2   Methodology of EED: Transformation of the Traditional ESP (BE) for the Purposes of Teaching Intercultural Communicative Competence

In order to answer the questions of methodological pragmatics how to achieve maximum communication and intercultural competence of students in EED, we need first to establish the basic goal of modern ESP for non-philological students. Generally, this goal relates to the general language skills as defined in CEFR (Council of Europe, 2001), including intercultural competence as a part of language capabilities. Based on CEFR, basic goals of ESP for non-philological students (or, alternatively, EED) may be stated as follows: Language users will reach the communication competence, which is adequate to specific social context in which they operate and communicate. First, emphasis should be put on acquisition of communication competence necessary for successful performance in academic (university) environment, i.e., to manage communication in students' educational context (such as studies, study skills, university, and mobility). Gradually, a wide range of fact-based information from various foreign sources expands these basic communication competences. Eventually, language users use and integrate their own expert opinion and expertise in oral and written speech and master four sub-competences, as defined by Scarcella and Oxford (1992, pp. 75–80):

1. Linguistic competence, which represents the control of the language system and the linguistic means typical of the professional language communication; in EED, linguistic competence means mastering of the following:

    • integrated skills: reading, writing, listening, speaking in professional (economic) situations,
    • individual skills: pronunciation: phonetic and phonological features, intonation, sentence and word stress,

- vocabulary register: specific economic and business vocabulary, idiomatic expressions, synonyms, antonyms, hyponyms, hypernyms, etc.

2. Sociolinguistic competence, which represents the modelling of speaking activities of the interlocutors who possess a spectrum of language resources and the ability to use them according to the communication context. Sociolinguistic competence presupposes awareness of the cultural context in which the user needs to know the language to use it properly in a given situation, and it represents the capability, which is now a component of intercultural competences. For example, a response to the question "how are you?" differs from country to country. In some countries, the only socially acceptable answer is simple and pre-formatted ("I'm fine"); in others, it is almost impolite not to go into great lengths, and not to mention individual members of one's family, their medical condition, job, and social life. Thus, proper functioning in the new culture might be even more important than mere mastering the linguistic rules of a foreign language.

   A so-called "culturewise" level of using a foreign language (Zelenka, 2007, p. 32) incorporates many verbal and non-verbal elements (including proximity, body language, social skills, codes and taboos, directness and indirectness, politeness, formality, and interpreting the meaning. For all the aforementioned data, Paige (1993, p. 171) introduces the term "cultural effectiveness", referring to one's ability to function in the foreign culture. Sociolinguistic competence is the key competence of students of EED, as lack of it may result in delays, injuries, and even deaths, and so it is detrimental to work progress. Future business professionals thus ought to be trained in sociolinguistic competences to foresee potential cross-cultural situations in which only the awareness of cultural differences helps to avoid misunderstanding.

3. Discursive competence, which is typical of the communication professionals, for a professional style, for instance:

   - mastering special economic and business-related language, such as business terminology: e.g., double entry book-keeping, single-entry book-keeping, protectionism, deregulation, economy of the gold standard, bear market, bull market, marketing,
   - mastering the general, culture-related vocabulary: *the V4, municipality, Department of Treasury, NYSE,*
   - mastering business jargon (business speak): buzzwords, vogue words, euphemisms, blends, abbreviations, e.g., *Brexit, infomercials, VAT, GDP, GDPR, GPO,*
   - mastering soft skills, such as presentation skills, management skills, business meetings skills, negotiations, discussions, interrupting or keeping silence— just to name those where cultural differences play an important role.

4. Strategic competence, which represents the ability to overcome the collapse of communication and other potential failures and hurdles that barrier effective communication, such as:

- the ability to overcome the collapse of communication (the right phrase of term) and replace it with a generic or general one (e.g., *first class flight ticket* vs. *business class flight ticket*),
- the ability to become aware of and anticipate potential intercultural differences, and behave with cultural sensitivity.

4 Discussion: Intercultural Competence and EED Syllabus Design

It is necessary to mention that all of the abovementioned sub-competences are a stable part of teaching EED. The problem lies in the depth or intensity of their representation in the syllabus. EED can be taught as topic-based (syllabus is organized around the topics, such as management, marketing, investments, shares, market structure, and many others), in which the focus is on the acquisition of the specific content of students' major studies in a foreign language. This content-based language learning is almost parallel to students' studies in their native language. In this type of syllabus, the development of communication in business situations is limited as the foreign language curriculum is usually determined by the school policy (the curriculum guarantors like to see the topics). Culture-specific topics are marginally covered, by one or two lessons, such as management across cultures, cultural differences in body language and some business activities. The learning outcome in this case is students' mastering of the specific content in terms of definitions of specific terms and performance of understanding of business/economic issues. Academic and generic skills (those which are transferable onto other context, for example in a future job, such as researching, note taking, listening to lectures, study skills, team work, cooperation with partners, negotiations, presentations, and academic writing skills) are developed.

We assume that if the syllabus is based on communication for business, a more communicative language is studied (revolving around business situations, such as dealing with clients, dealing with complaints, telephoning, ordering, delivering goods and services, etc.). This type of functional-notional syllabus allows for the inclusion of cultural aspects more than the content-based syllabus, but has little space for the development of cultural awareness and competences, as defined above. Cultural issues are often presented ad hoc, marginally, even in a grotesque way, which only contributes to the stereotyped perception of cultures instead of developing knowledge about culture, understanding of other cultures, or one's own culture and the attitudes to otherness (Byram, 1997). There is little space to teach culture as a phenomenon that determines our language and behaviour. In this case, the learning outcome is the acquisition of situational language and its (culturally) appropriate use. At this point, we agree that, for future jobs in business, it is necessary to acquire appropriate verbal and non-verbal communication. It is necessary to know certain usages and standards of conduct, as well as the use of specific means of communication—oral and written. The question is which language the course designers ought to choose, given there are many constraints concerning the attainment of the goals for professional and intercultural communication.

In order to set a concise set of educational aims for EED, it is necessary to identify potential constraints, i.e., external factors, such as the university educational policy controlling the scope and content of EED. Effectiveness of EED lies in the scope of the subject. It is a fact that university educational policy dramatically affects the number of teaching hours allotted to EED, which may depend on the study programmes, guarantors, and their understanding of the importance of modern language needs. The choice of content may well depend on the same factors. Thus, implementation of EED may depend on the autonomy of English teachers and their ability to implement real communication practice into the syllabus. There are also financial constraints to EED; the number of teaching units for foreign languages is limited and, usually, the first to be cut by management when introducing cost-saving measures at business oriented institutions. Thus, for lack of teaching time or finance, the teachers cannot address all the criteria set for EED, such as developing both the academic and professional language, communication skills, and intercultural awareness.

5 Conclusion

Europe has recently gained a profile of a multicultural society. On the one hand, this may bring an opportunity for cultural enrichment; on the other, it can lead to conflicts of different cultures and cultural misunderstanding. The perspective of cultural understanding and thread of cultural clashes clarify and justify the importance of intercultural competence as a means to communicate and act in intercultural situations in order to achieve mutual understanding of interlocutors.

Today, English, a new *lingua franca*, fulfils a very different role in international communication from English some 50 years ago. In the ethnic, social, and linguistic "superdiversity" (Morgado, 2017, p. 11) that we are witnessing today in cosmopolitan business encounters, English is used for communication in international and intercultural setting, where "communication constantly intersects other variables of ethnicity, cultures, mother tongues, and social status" (Morgado, 2017). Communicating in plurilingual and multicultural environment therefore requires other skills for intercultural dialogue (Council of Europe, 2016), such as accepting and valuing cultural diversity. For effective communication in this situation, modern English speakers (including business professionals) need to acquire skills to address, manage, and resolve conflicts that may arise between parties due to clashing worldviews, conflicting attitudes, different communication styles or verbal/non-verbal behaviour. As Morgado confirms, besides acknowledging cultural diversity, the intercultural communicative competence entails "knowledge and critical understanding of language and communication while new attitudes are added such as self-efficacy, civic mindedness, and tolerance for ambiguity" (Morgado, 2017, p. 10).

Business study programmes (including their language sub-programmes) ought to respond to the challenges modern times lie on pose for language users promptly and adequately. Internationalisation of education, increased cooperation of universities, and the mobility of students made possible by various EU programmes also bring new challenges; future business professionals study communication for an international environment (e.g., for mobilities) where they meet a diversity of cultural backgrounds. For such academic performance, they need to be prepared by a curricula programme of ESP (Camiciottoli Crawford, 2010).

Currently, the aforementioned international and intercultural links between professional and academic areas represent key factors for the transformation of ESP teaching. In the field of ESP, the academic focus and the building of intercultural competences have gradually gained their forefront position. As demonstrated by this study, the adoption of the Bologna declaration (1999) and adaption of its principles to the University Education Act in Slovakia (2002), which brought the implementation of the Bologna process in Slovakia enabled the internationalisation of university education in Europe and reinforced innovative approaches to teaching ESP.

One of the aims of the presented study was to clarify and justify the need for innovation of ESP. With regard to the political and social changes in Slovakia since the 1990s, teaching ESP dramatically changed its nature; currently, it is a dynamically developing didactic discipline that increasingly emphasizes the development of a cultural dimension of communication with the aim of developing intercultural competence for academic and non-academic purposes.

Moreover, innovated ESP (thus called by a new term English for Economic Disciplines—EED) uses the knowledge of a diversity of disciplines (such as economic and communication sciences, anthropology, cultural studies, sociology, and many others), which are incorporated directly into textbooks in the form of tasks developing cultural awareness. Examples are diverse—e.g., comparing intercultural differences, finding common features, solving intercultural problems and misunderstandings through case studies, critical incidents, individual or group projects, and intercultural web projects.

New globalised era also requires many more tasks from the ESP (EED) instructors. Integration of the diversity of disciplines into teaching requires extended linguistic-pedagogical education; teachers' professional profiles should include intercultural competences in a broader scope of disciplines. For example, in addition to their basic English language teaching, Slovak teachers provide CLIL/CBL-based courses in economic disciplines and their expertise represents added value in the overall foreign language profile of those philological and non-philological institutions that want to succeed in the international educational field. Academic and intercultural skills acquired in English-medium studies become beneficial for students' graduate profile; these skills are transferable onto the study of other subjects and to real-life situations.

To sum up, in global contexts, the transformation of ESP by integrating intercultural competence into traditional curricula (and thus creating a new concept of English for Economic Disciplines—EED) contributes to language users' expertise on linguistic and cultural levels; via these, it also enhances understanding and cooperation between diverse individuals and communities. In the era of globalisation (including both pre-Brexit and post-Brexit times), English serves and most likely will serve as common ground not only in *languagewise*, but, more importantly, also in the *culturewise* sphere, as a medium integrating many diverse cultures. It will mediate understanding between people and nations; and its users, if properly instructed on the intercultural potential of proper language use, will become cultural ambassadors in business and non-business discourse.

Acknowledgements This paper is one of the outputs of the research project *No. 033UMB-4/2017 (E)migration as a political, ethical, linguistic and cultural phenomenon in the era of globalization* supported by the Slovak Ministry of Education Scheme KEGA.

References

Anthony, L. (2011). English for specific purposes: What does it mean? Why is it different? In *Proceedings of the JACET 50th Commemorative International Convention (JACET 50)* (pp. 1–6). Retrieved from https://www.researchgate.net/publication/267631524_ESP_in_the_21_st_Century_ESP_Theory_and_Application_Today.

Bachman, L. (1990). *Fundamental considerations in language testing.* Oxford: Oxford University Press.

Bírová, J., & Bubáková, J. (2011). Multikultúra, plurilingvizmus a preklad Charty plurilingvizmu. *XLinguae: Trimestrial European Review, 3*(4), 51–58.

Byram, M. (1997). *Teaching and assessing intercultural communicative competence.* Clevedon: Multilingual Matters.

Byram, M., & Fleming, M. (1998). *Language learning in intercultural perspective.* Cambridge: Cambridge University Press.

Camiciottoli Crawford, B. (2010). Meeting the challenges of European student mobility: Preparing Italian Erasmus students for business lectures in English. *English for Specific Purposes, 29*(4), 268–280.

Council of Europe. (2001). *Common European framework of reference for languages: Learning, teaching and assessment.* Strasbourg: Council of Europe.

Council of Europe. (2016). *White paper on intercultural dialogue.* Strasbourg: Council of Europe. Retrieved from https://www.coe.int/t/dg4/intercultural/source/white%20paper_final_revised_en.pdf.

Council of Europe. (2018). *Common European framework of reference for languages: Learning, teaching and assessment: Companion volume with new descriptors.* Strasbourg: Council of Europe.

Donna, S. (2000). *Teach business English.* Cambridge: Cambridge University Press.

Dudley-Evans, T., & St John, M. J. (1997). *Developments in English for specific purposes.* Cambridge: CUP.

Dudley-Evans, T., & St John, M. J. (1998). *Developments in English for Specific Purposes. A multi-disciplinary approach.* Cambridge: CUP.

Ellis, M., & Johnson, C. (1994). *Teaching business English.* Oxford: Oxford University Press.

Felices Lago, Á. (2016). Tourism websites in English as a source for the autonomous learning of specialized terminology: A CALL application. *Iberica, 31,* 109–126.

Hammerly, H. (1985). *An integrated theory of language teaching and its practical consequences.* Michigan: Second Language Publication.

Hanesová, D. (2007). Prienik metodických prístupov v ESP. In R. Nedoma (Ed.), *Foreign language competence as an integral component of a university graduate profile* (pp. 104–115). Brno: CJP UO.

Hidasi, J. (2014). Cultural-mental programming and the acquisition of foreign languages. In A. Zelenková (Ed.), *Foreign languages: A bridge to innovations in higher education* (pp. 17–23). Banská Bystrica, Slovakia: Matej Bel University in Banská Bystrica.

Hutchinson, T., & Waters, A. (1991). *English for specific purposes.* Cambridge: Cambridge University Press.

Hymes, D. H. (1972). *On communicative competence.* Philadelphia: University of Pennsylvania Press.

Jordan, R. R. (1997). *English for academic purposes.* Cambridge: Cambridge University Press.

Kacetl, J., & Klímová, B. (2015). English vocabulary for tourism: A corpus-based approach. *Lecture Notes in Computer Science* 9405 (pp. 489–494).

Kačmárová, A. (2012). O kultúrnom kontexte: niektoré špecifiká slovenskej a americkej kultúry. *Jazyk a kultúra, 9.* Retrieved from https://www.ff.unipo.sk/jak/rus/9_2012/kacmarova.pdf.

Kramsch, C. (1998). *Language and culture.* Oxford: Oxford University Press.

Lazár, I. (2015). EFL learners' intercultural competence development in an international web collaboration project. *Language Learning Journal, 43*(2), 208–221.

Lustig, M. W., & Koester, J. (2009). *Intercultural competence: Interpersonal communication across cultures.* London: Pearson's.

Mehta, H. (2019). *Aspects of business English.* British Council Web. Retrieved from https://www.teachingenglish.org.uk/article/aspects-business-english.

Míšková, Z. (2009). Some specifics of teaching professional English in tourism. *Acta Linguistica 7—Language for Specific Purposes and Intercultural Communication,* 189–193.

Morgado, M. (2017). Intercultural communicative competence. In E. Císlerová & M. Štefl (Eds.), *Intercultural communicative competence: A competitive advantage for global employability* (pp. 10–12). Prague: Czech Technical University (in Prague).

O'Grady, W., Dobrovolsky, M., & Aronoff, M. (1997). *Contemporary linguistics.* New York: St. Martin's Press.

Paige, R. M. (1993). *Education for intercultural experience.* Yarmouth: ME Intercultural Press.

Repka, R., Pčolinská, M., & Šipošová, M. (2015). *An introductory course in English language didactics.* Bratislava: Z-F Lingua.

Richards, J. C. (2006). *Communicative language teaching today.* Cambridge: Cambridge University Press.

Savignon, S. J. (2017). *Communicative competence: Theory and classroom practice.* Wiley Online Library: Wiley.

Scarcella, R. C., & Oxford, R. L. (1992). *The tapestry of language learning: The individual in the communicative classroom.* Boston, MA: Heinle & Heinle.

Strevens, P. (1988). ESP after twenty years: A re-appraisal. In M. Tickoo (Ed.), *ESP: State of the art* (pp. 1–13). Singapore: SEAMEO Regional Language Centre.

Turner, G. (2005). *British cultural studies.* London: Routledge.

Wang, J., Ayres, H., & Huyton, J. (2010). Is tourism education meeting the needs of the tourism industry? An Australian case study. *Journal of Hospitality & Tourism Education, 22*(1), 8–14.

Zelenka, I. (2007). Languagewise or culturewise? *Pedagogické Rozhľady, 4*(16), 32.

Zelenková, A. (2010). *Interkultúrne vzdelávanie v cudzích jazykoch na vysokej škole: Metódy a ich reflexia.* Banská Bystrica: Ekonomická fakulta UMB.

Zelenková, A. (2015). *Interkultúrna kompetencia v kontexte vysokoškolského vzdelávania. Ekonómia, manažment a cestovný ruch.* Banská Bystrica: Belianum.

Anna Zelenková is Associate Professor at the Department of Professional Communication in Business, Faculty of Economics, Matej Bel University in Banská Bystrica, Slovakia. She has been teaching English for Specific Purposes, intercultural communication and managerial skills in English for more than 20 years. As a teacher trainer, she develops intercultural teacher training programmes and participates in educational projects. Her professional and research interests include pedagogic approaches to the teaching of foreign languages, intercultural competence in business, and teacher development. She is the author of six textbooks and two monographs on the methodology of intercultural education.

Jana Javorčíková has worked at the Department of English and American Studies in Banská Bystrica, Slovakia, since 1997. She specialises in cultures and literatures of the English-speaking countries (she currently teaches courses in American studies, Canadian studies, and selected courses in intercultural communication). Her recent publications include a coursebook of US studies entitled "Explorations in American Studies" (2019; co-authored with Michael Dove) and "A Modern Coursebook of Cultural Studies for Philologists" (2019). In 2010, she contributed to a two-volume reader on Canadian culture entitled "Slovak Immigration to Canada: Narrated Histories and Written Histories" (2010) integrating intercultural research of thirteen European countries. She has also published widely in the fields of American studies and literature. In 2005–2006, she spent a year teaching literature and culture at Minneapolis Community and Technical College in Minneapolis, Minnesota.

Millennials as Second Language Users. The Analysis of Communication Patterns Employed for L1 and L2 Interactions

Iwona Dronia

Abstract The character of global communication is changing due to multifarious reasons of social, technological or even political nature. The taxonomy created by Howe and Strauss (2000) and by Chester (2002) differentiates between various age generations—baby boomers, generation X, Millennials (generation Y), and Z generation, and each of them seems to constitute a unique group thinking, working, living, and communicating in its specific and age-appropriate way. Millennials have been labelled as those who adapt quickly to a world undergoing rapid technological changes. They are also the ones who have been called "Generation Me", as they follow self-centered life approach and are characterized by the rise of individualism in society. Although this generation has been greatly shaped by the technological advances, they are deficient in soft skills (Gibson and Sodeman, 2014) comprising the core of effective communication. The intention of this chapter is to describe a changing nature of communication of advanced young adults, students of English as a second language. The prime aim is to reveal most commonly used communication channels as well as to present various factors of sociopragmatic nature (e.g., their attitude to fluency and correctness in L1 and L2) that the respondents pay attention to. The article shall demonstrate the outcomes of a research study conducted among a cross-cultural millennial sample in order to verify typical attributes of generation Y concerning their approach to communication in general and L2 specifically.

Keywords Millennials · Communication preferences · Cross-cultural communication differences

1 Introduction

Millennials comprise one of few age groups commonly recognized by sociologists. It is not a coincidence that this particular cohort is commonly referred to as Digital Natives (Prensky, 2001), the "N-Gen" (for "net") or "D-Gen" (for "digital"), or Net

I. Dronia (✉)
Faculty of Humanities, Institute of Linguistics, University of Silesia, Katowice, Poland
e-mail: iwona.dronia@us.edu.pl

© Springer Nature Switzerland AG 2020   23
U. Michalik et al. (eds.), *Exploring Business Language and Culture*,
Second Language Learning and Teaching,
https://doi.org/10.1007/978-3-030-58551-8_2

Table 1 Generational personal and lifestyle characteristics

	Traditionalists	Baby boomers	Generation X	Millennials
Core values	Respect authority • Conformers • Discipline	Optimism • Involvement	Skepticism • Fun • Informality	Realism • Confidence • Extreme fun • Social
Family	Traditional nuclear	Disintegrating	Latch-key kids	Merged families
Education	A dream	A birthright	Way to get there	Great expense
Communication/media	Rotary phones • One-on-one • Write a memo	Touch-tone phones Call me anytime	Cell phones • Call me only at work	Internet • Picture phones • Email
Budget/money	Put it away • Pay cash	Buy now, pay later	Cautious Conservative	Earn to spend

Adapted from Hamill (2005), online (Published with the consent of Fairleigh Dickinson University)

Generation (cf. Jones, Ramanau, Cross, & Healing, 2010). Born between 1981 and 2005 (Howe & Strauss, 2000), this is probably the first generation (also known as Generation Y) that was immediately introduced to highly advanced, state-of-the-art technology being provided to them in the form of electronic toys, smart phones, smart watches and all the other possible gimmicks of the modern world. Being raised and brought up in such a "digital-friendly" environment pays off—Millennials are capable of surfing the net easily, they are computer-literate and know the ins-and-outs of all the incoming scientific improvements. Hamill (2005, online) characterizes them in the following way (Table 1).

As seen in Table 1, Millennials value self-confidence highly. They are also the ones who are sociable, easy-going and easy to spend what they earn. Employers commonly describe them as those that are not emotionally attached to one workplace and would often change their working environment. They are mobile, multitaskers and undeniably technology savvy. They also like taking an active role and initiative in various social campaigns.

2   Millennials and Their Communication Preferences

Millennials have already entered the workforce in significant numbers. Without a doubt, this is the most diverse and globally oriented, and IT knowledgeable cohort that any other preceding generation. However, being at the cutting edge of technology poses some threats, too. First of all, as Agrawal (2017, online) claims, Millennials are facing serious interpersonal problems, i.e., they are struggling with face-to-face communication:

Perhaps one of the biggest differences in why Millennials struggle with face-to-face communications is because they've always had the ability to edit a message. Even for the most mundane of conversations, younger generations have always had the time to think something over. This not only removes a sense of vulnerability but the raw emotion that could come with it.

This finding corresponds again to the one provided by Chester (2002) and the created hierarchy of communication. In his diagram, the bottom and the basic communicational expectations of Traditionalists, Baby Boomers and Generation X representatives are satisfied by personal meetings. However, only if all else fails, will they restore to texting. Millennials, on the other hand, will choose texting above all, placing personal encounters on the very last position. There is no denying that these discrepancies actually provide the argument for the existence of striking differences between the generations, and it seems that the only communication preference that is shared among all age groups is their neutral (in both cases occupying the third place in the ranking) attitude towards e-mails.

Face-to-face communication is employed by Me generation (Millennials) probably when anything else fails. The lack of the so-called "soft" skills, so necessary in maintaining spoken interaction, can contribute to their general negative attitude to this form of information exchange. It has been already stated that, in written communication, Millennials commonly come back to the text, edit it, correct it, and improve in any way possible. They may also rely on emoticons showing their emotions. Hence, it is logical to assume that in a real-life communication, one would have to look for WORDS to describe their feelings, and this may turn out to be difficult. Constant editing and a chance to paraphrase words so useful and handy in written communication may in turn have a debilitating effect on one's spoken mastery. Being engaged in a genuine interaction requires the ability to use the language on a here-and-now basis, in a spontaneous and immediate way. One is deprived of "thinking over" options and, in order to be understood, one has to communicate in a clear, concise and straightforward manner. It seems that, having grown up in a digital world, Millennials' biggest strength has actually become their biggest weakness. As Agrawal (2017) reminds, "the tough stuff (being it a breakup, getting fired, or handling a problem) has to be faced in person, even if one suffers from a lack of consideration from the medium".

Millennials communication preferences and their craving for social media has been reported by Pew Research Center and they conducted an extensive statistical analysis (2010, online). According to its findings, Me Generation outnumbers the other generations in their daily internet-oriented activities. The exact figures are displayed in Table 2.

Millennials are also more likely than older adults to use their cell phones to send and receive text messages: 88% use their cell phones to text, as do 77% of Gen Xers and 51% of Boomers. Undeniably, they are avid texters—not only do they do it much faster than any other generation, but they also frequently combine other activities to it (including a highly irresponsible match, such as texting and driving). Nearly two-thirds (64%) of Millennials say they have sent or received a text message while driving, compared with 46% of Gen Xers and 21% of Boomers (ibid.).

Table 2 Millennials versus technology use

Millennials outspace older Americans in technology use

	Millennial (18–29)	Gen X (30–45)	Boomer (46–64)	Silent (65+)
Internet behaviors	%	%	%	%
Created social networking profile	75	50	30	6
Wireless Internet away from home	62	48	35	11
Post video of themselves online	20	6	2	1
Use Twitter	14	10	6	1
Cell phones and texting				
Use cell to text	88	77	51	9
Texted in the past 24 h	80	63	35	4
Texted while driving	64	46	21	1
Have a cell phone/no landline	41	24	13	5
Median # texts in the past 24 h	20	12	5	–

Adapted from Taylor and Keeter (eds.), Pew Research Center Report, 2010, online (One should notice that the data displayed in Fig. 2 were published nine years ago, so the group of Millennials may be actually even in their late thirties now)
Note Median number of texts based on those who texted in the past 24 h

It can be concluded that generation Y is a brand new cohort following different standards and moral values as well as having a different outlook towards life, work and technology. Their communication preferences for particular modes make them the most digital-friendly group that, at the same time, suffers significantly from a certain form of interpersonal deficiencies.

3 Millennials as Second Language Users

Millennials' age ranges from 21 to 38 (people born from 1981 to 1998), so in terms of second language learning they may be defined as either young adults or adult learners. Hence, each of these age groups has its own unique characteristics and represents different levels of cognitive maturation or psychosocial development. Each of them would have to be approached differently in the second language classroom, as probably their motivation, needs and expectations towards the course vary significantly. As has been already mentioned, Millennials preferred communication modes rely mainly on the usage of social media and the Internet specifically. According to Prensky (2001), "today's average college grads have spent less than 5000 h of their lives reading, but over 10,000 h playing video games (not to mention 20,000 h watching TV). Computer games, email, the Internet, cell phones and instant messaging are integral parts of their lives". Thus it is safe to presume that only technology-oriented teaching resources would be able to cater for such "digital" requirements. As they comprise the most computer literate cohort, their learning and communication style should be through multi-media. As for the learning and teaching process, it should also be focused on web-based tools such as Web-CT, online courses, online journals and iPod downloads. Their daily need and use of podcasts and music, taking photos with their phones and texting messages one another in their created messaging language (McCasland, 2005) should be taken into account while planning classroom-oriented activities. Their style is high-tech and highly networked, and Millennials "will want to be able to work quickly and creatively, and they want to do it their way" (Zemke, Raines, & Filipczak, 2000, p. 143 in Nicholas, 2008). Their creativity and investigation with electronic media, free expressions, strong views and the need for independence without restraint are noted facets of their generation (Alch, 2000). Nicholas (2008) also stresses a big need for socializing and group-membership that the Millennials are known for. Moreover, they are accustomed to relating and collaborating with others through technology. They enjoy teamwork and prefer working with their chronological peers.

Generation Y comprises the learners belonging to the generation that enjoys the privilege of easily accessible second language education. This kind of education is commonly introduced even on kindergarten level (e.g., in Poland, it is a norm to introduce second language classes even to three-year-olds). As a result, this is probably the first generation (and this is definitely true for the post-communist countries) that may derive pleasure from unlimited and free choice of second language education, which is getting more and more accessible through web-based courses, programs, learners and teachers resources, etc. Thus, the average command of second language usage, and English specifically, is much higher than it used to be. Millennials seem to comprise a generation that is best educated (Taylor & Keeter, 2010, online), uses polite, respectful, motivational and electronic communication style (Howe & Strauss, 2000). Hence, while teaching them, as Prensky (2001) argues, one should take into account, e.g., the content, and especially its future-oriented type: "'Future' content is, to a large extent, not surprisingly, digital and technological. But while it includes software, hardware, robotics, nanotechnology, genomics, etc., it also includes the ethics, politics, sociology, languages and other things that go with them".

4 Research Questions

This paper will address the questions regarding communication preferences of the Millennial cohort. Its prime objective is to verify the communication channels Me Generation uses while interacting in their mother tongue as well as in the L2. An additional intention is also to assess their attitude towards language correctness and which of the aspects, such as fluency or accuracy, is of bigger prestige to them. The respondents were also asked to self-assess themselves in terms of feeling successful while communicating in L1 and L2. Last but not least, the research study aims at verifying Millennials' opinions referring to linguistic changes affecting their mother tongues and L2 (English) they use, respectively.

5   Data Collection

The instrument used for collecting data was a web-based questionnaire administered among 82 respondents: 52 female and 30 male students. The vast majority of the students filling in the questionnaire studies at the university of Silesia (these are the students of English philology department) either permanently or for some limited time, like, e.g., one semester in the case of Erasmus learners. Additional sample of respondents came from a private Humanitas University in Sosnowiec where the students of both English philology as well as Human Resource Management (studies run in English, European Union funded internationally-targeted projects) were asked to participate in the study. The remaining sample also comprised Dutch Radboud University students of International Business Administration.

The language of the questionnaire was English. A brief introduction informed participants what my aims are and assured students of their complete anonymity. The instrument consisted of two major sections spanned across 22 questions, preceded by some general questions about background variables of the participants: their sex, age, nationality, mother tongue and most frequently used L2. The respondents comprise a multinational group residing in many remote countries and representing 25 nationalities: British, Dutch, Polish, Ukrainian, Italian, Czech, American, Romanian, French, Moldavian, Luxembourgish, Kazakh, Tatar, German, Russian, Finish, Chinese, Australian, Russian, Belgian, Latvian, Irish, Colombian, Indian, and Bulgarian.

6   Results and Discussion

6.1   Mother Tongue Communication

All items included in the questionnaire were closed questions. The first section, referring to mother tongue communication, asked respondents to tick the communication channel that they use while using their mother tongue and indicate the frequency of using it by putting appropriate number where 1—means never; 2—hardly ever; 3—sometimes; 4—often, 5—always. The detailed distribution of the results is presented below (Fig. 1).

As seen from the diagram, still the most frequently applied mode is face-to-face communication, as almost 86% of the respondents ticked it to be the kind of interaction that they use, either always or often. For 68%, it is the telephone, for 34%—e-mail, for 72%—text and the remaining 54% communicate most often through social media. The SD of 1.74 indicates that the data points tend to be close to the mean of the set. If one looks at this data closely, it may be inferred that the difference between the frequency of face-to-face and text communication (in fact only 14%) is not as significant, and this can in turn imply that the thread of text

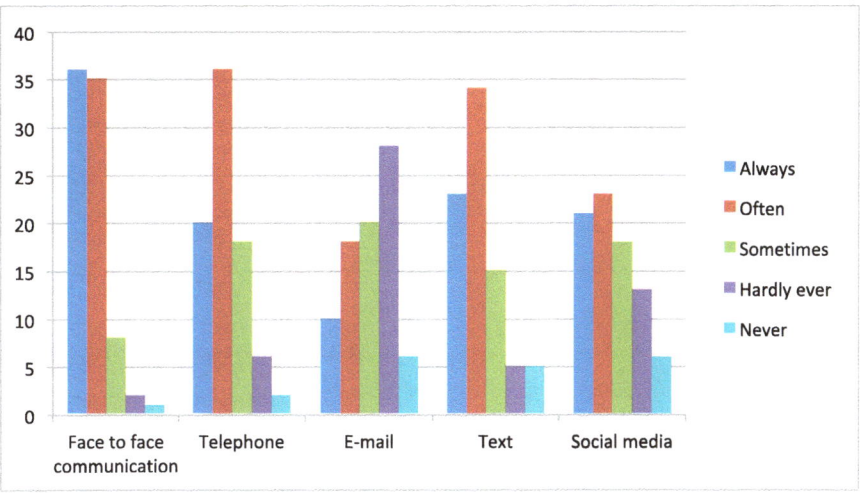

Fig. 1 The frequency of channels used for mother tongue communication

communication replacing the "natural" one is quite likely to occur in the incoming future.

When asked whether they feel successful while communicating in their mother tongue, the vast majority (94%) confirmed. The subsequent queries aimed at establishing Millennials approach towards the nature of communication, i.e., whether they take care of correctness and notice any disturbing trends happening in their L1 (Fig. 2).

As seen in the graph above, almost 54% of the Millennial cohort admit to having quite a "prescriptive" attitude towards their mother tongue and declare to actually take care of their language, at the same time paying attention to both oral and written forms of interaction. They also admitted that other people's negligence irritates them. However, the remaining sample is either neutral or even completely disinterested and does not care about the form of the language they produce. This finding goes in line with other observations made on the nature of contemporary communication (cf. Marcjanik, 2009, 2013; Dronia, 2014).

Another rather alarming discovery is that, for 41% of the sample, there is no upsetting or irritating language change affecting their mother tongue. Those, however, who are more observant and notice such changes, provided a list of a few irritating trends (Fig. 3).

According to the Millennial group, the most irritating is using less polite language. Surprisingly enough, this problem is also frequently noticed by older generations, i.e., the Generation X or Baby Boomers, but is typically ascribed as the negative attribute of Millennial cohort. More often than not, it is observed that the norms of polite communication have been lowered—there is lots of so-called "aggressive language" or taboo and intimate subjects eagerly discussed in the public, etc. Many (especially elder groups members) accuse younger generation of influencing, if not

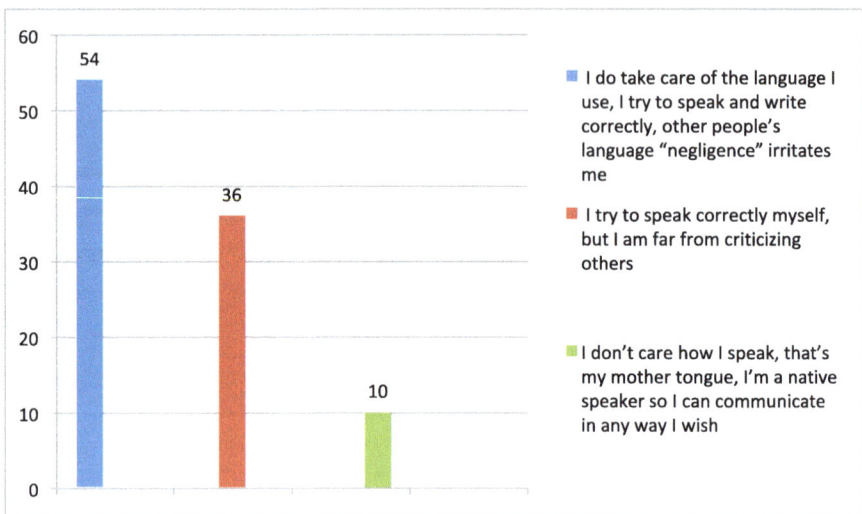

Fig. 2 Respondents' attitude towards communicating in their L1

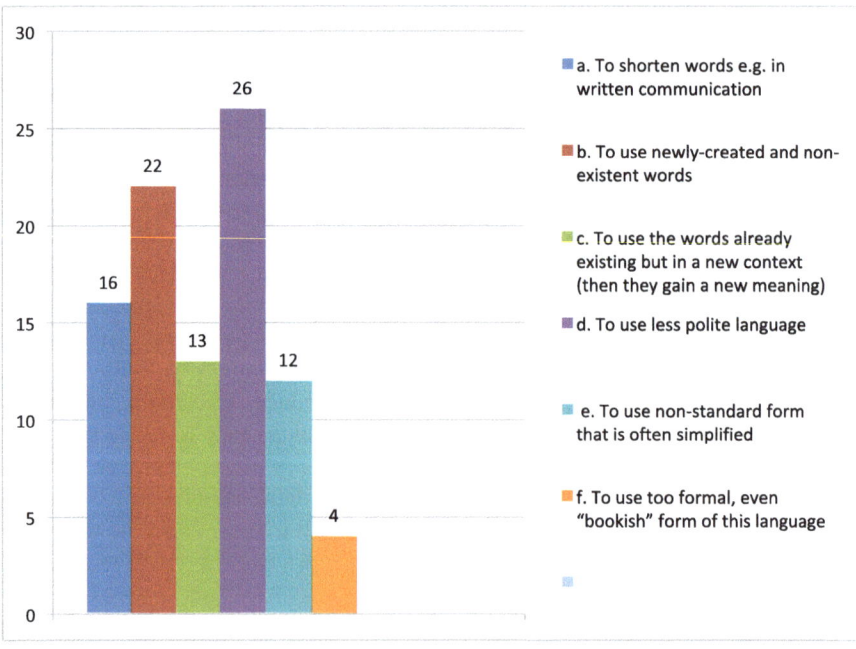

Fig. 3 Respondents' opinion on annoying changes happening to their mother tongue

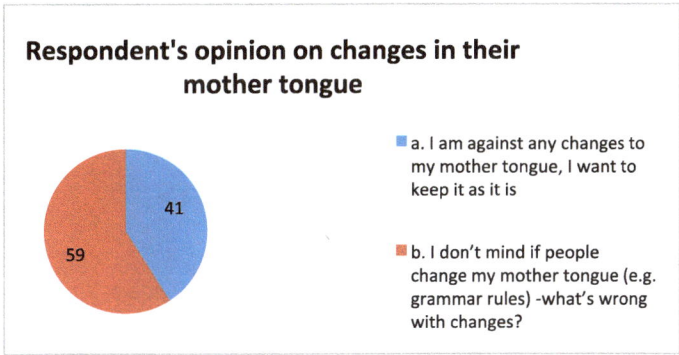

Fig. 4 Millennials attitude towards changes in their mother tongue

even imposing such changes on the discourse. It is them who are perceived as less polite, more straightforward and even pushy. Sadly, although the option "using less polite language" occupies the top position on the list of annoying language changes, still it is only 24% who actually notice such lowering standards. A common trend (visible especially in the language of advertising) such as using newly created and non-existing words that can remind of certain word formation processes is also found quite upsetting, together with shortening words, typical especially in written communication. Again, only 16% of the questioned poll admitted to being annoyed by such shortening but, for the vast majority of the Millennial cohort, such trends that are evident, blatant violations of grammar are totally acceptable. It appears that such language negligence does not seem to bother them. Millennials' attitude to preserving linguistic norms of their mother tongue is also revealed in the two subsequent questions. The first concerns their attitude to the introduction of changes to their mother tongue (Fig. 4).

The final query in the section devoted to their mother-tongue communication referred to Millennials' viewpoint on language correctness during interacting through various modes (Fig. 5).

The interpretation of this diagram leaves no doubts—maintaining correct communication (in terms of grammar and rules of politeness) is mostly significant in the case of written, e-mail communication (for 54% it is very important and for 22%—important). It is also worth noting that another form of written interaction, namely using social media, is also seriously treated here, as it scores 43% and 26%, respectively. A shocking conclusion that may be inferred is that, for the Millennial cohort, it is more important to communicate correctly while employing written form, and being accurate while communicating through social media is more significant than through face-to-face conversation (40% and 35%, respectively).

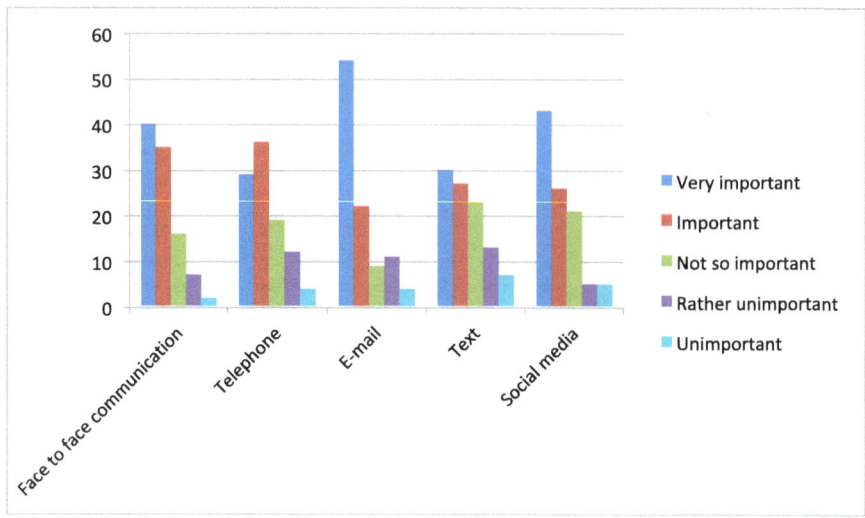

Fig. 5 Millennials' attitude to correctness during communicating through various modes

6.2 Second Language Communication

The second part of the questionnaire aims at collecting the responses concerning Millennials' second language communication characteristics. As has been already stated, Me Generation, on average, does not have any problem with developing their L2 ability—the idea of learning a second language is advocated worldwide.

It was none of surprise to learn that the most frequently learned L2 is English but, apart from it, other languages are also commonly taken up (Fig. 6).

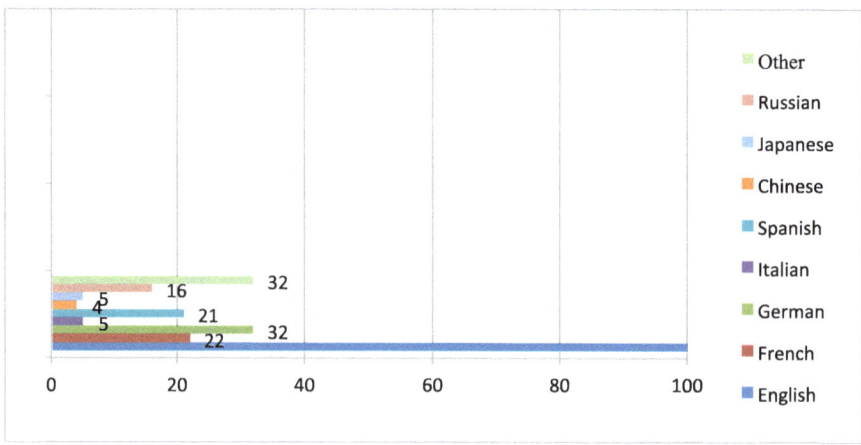

Fig. 6 Most commonly learnt L2

It has to be added, though, that many respondents chose more than one language and thus it may be stated that their average declared knowledge of learnt L2 equals 1.29. When asked to indicate the second language they most often communicate in, again, they pointed to English (100%). The next query referred to the most frequent way (oral or written) of this interaction. The detailed distribution of answers is presented in the graph below (Fig. 7).

As can be seen from the diagram, Millennials claim to use both, i.e., oral as well as written form of L2. When asked about the common situations for using an L2, they listed using it mainly for their personal needs (holidays abroad, meeting people, reading, etc.—73%), for work (61%) and for studies (49%). The respondents were also asked to verify the communication channels they use most often for L2 interaction. A detailed distribution of their answers is presented below (Fig. 8).

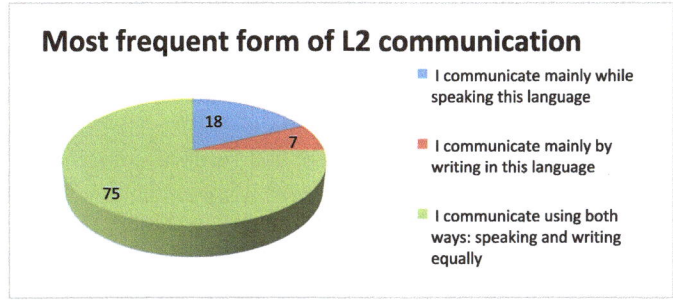

Fig. 7 Preferred form of communication

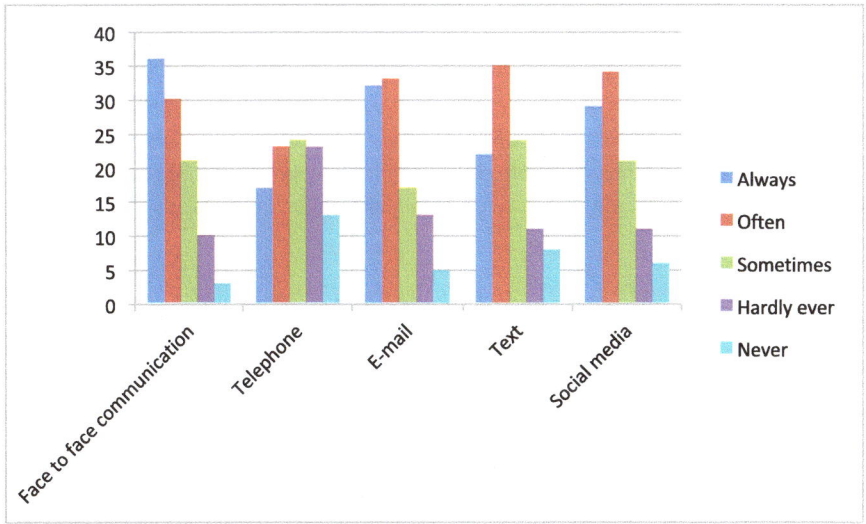

Fig. 8 The frequency of channels used for L2 communication

The results shown in the graph indicate that the Millennial cohort is quite diversified in their opinion, yet, for the vast majority, the most common modes for L2 interaction are face-to-face (66% uses it "always" and "often"), e-mail (65%) and social media (63%), and the difference between the answers is marginal. The least popular is a telephone, as it was indicated by not more than 40%. When asked whether they pay attention to the way they use an L2, the respondents provided the following opinion (Fig. 9).

It is clear that, for the vast majority of the Millennial cohort, it is important whether they are both fluent and accurate at the same time. However, there was one more option to be chosen from that was not indicated by this group, i.e., "I do not care if I make mistakes as long as I am understood". Bearing in mind that being correct is so significant for this age group (at least this is the image they want to display while presenting themselves in various social media), such a result is not really surprising. Again, when asked to provide the details concerning correctness involved in using various modes of communication, the group presented the following standpoint.

It seems that while communicating in the second language, it is most important for this group to produce correct emails. Knowing that 58% of this sample are in fact already working adults, it is not surprising to see such a declaration. Emails commonly comprise the most frequently applied form of corporate communication (cf. Fig. 10) and it is clear that employees do pay attention to their level of correctness. What may be quite astonishing, though, is the difference between the answers provided to the query concerning respondents' attitude towards correctness maintained in their mother-tongue communication. If one compares the results displayed in Fig. 7 to the ones provided in Fig. 11, they will see that the survey participants regard linguistic correctness to be more important in the case of emails in L2 (63% answers) than in the case of emails in L1 (54% of answers). Another, maybe not as sharp, difference may be observed between correctness maintained in telephone conversation (29% vs. 34%) and social media (5% difference). Generally, it is visible that Millennials pay more attention to being correct while communicating in the second language, with the exception of social media, as in this case it is more significant for them to remain correct while producing their mother tongue (43% vs. 38%). It can be also observed that both face-to-face as well as email communication comprise the most frequently employed means; however, in the case of the former, it

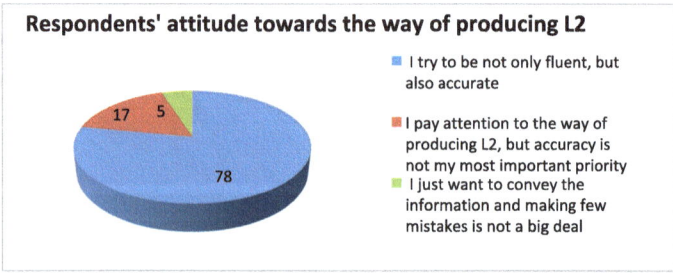

Fig. 9 Respondents' attitude towards the way of producing L2

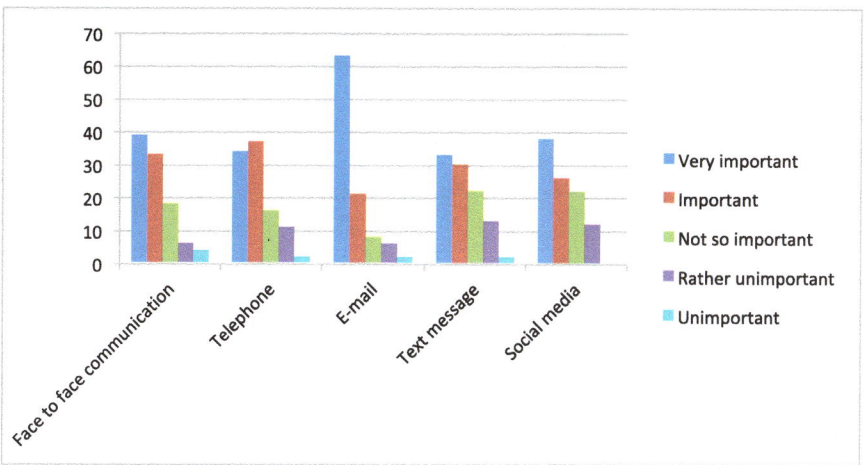

Fig. 10 Millennials' opinion on correctness involved in using various modes of L2 communication

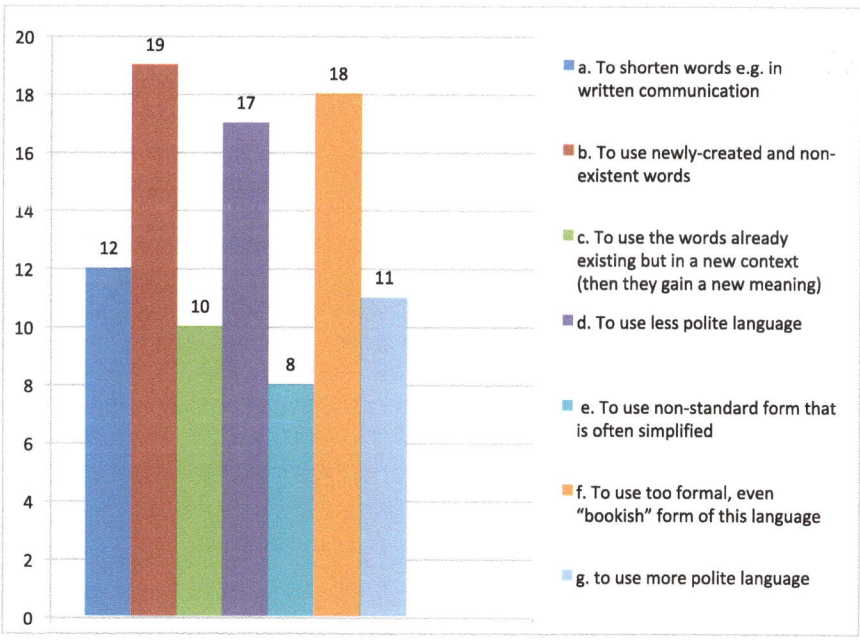

Fig. 11 Respondents' opinion on annoying changes happening to the L2

is not as important to speak correctly. In fact, being correct while communicating in L2 through face-to-face mode is as important as while implementing social media.

When asked whether they feel successful as L2 users, 88% of the sample confirmed. However, for only 52% of the sample, using the second language does not trigger the appearance of stress or tension. Many respondents actually admitted to having problems with foreign language anxiety manifesting itself mainly while speaking (indicated by 32%), writing and listening (13% and 12%). Reading in L2 was considered least stressful, as only 6% classify it to be a stress-provoking factor. The same, fairly positive outlook was presented in the next question where Millennials' task was to reveal their opinion on being successful in communicating with different age groups (older generations and their chronological peers) and nationalities (people of different or the same nationality). The following statistics display detailed distribution of their answers:

- 80% are very satisfied or satisfied while communicating with elder generations,
- 94% are very satisfied or satisfied while communicating with their chronological peers,
- 89% are very satisfied or satisfied while communicating with the same nationality,
- 83% are very satisfied or satisfied while communicating with different nationality.

One could not help but notice that this particular group holds a very optimistic outlook and perceives themselves as either very, or at least a successful group, able to communicate basically with everyone. It is not really surprising to discover that Millennials may find it a bit more difficult to communicate with people representing different age and ethnicity.

The last query concerned the existence of some irritating linguistic changes affecting English. Only 41% declared to notice such upsetting modifications and, out of few options possible, the respondents chose the following ones.

As shown above, what bothers Millennials in L2 communication most is the tendency to use newly-created and non-existent words as well as too formal, even "bookish" language. They also seem to object to applying less polite language.

7 Conclusions

The conducted research study aims at characterizing Millennials as language users. This particular cohort comprises people in their thirties and almost pushing forty, and thus, while analyzing behaviours of this group, one may get a relatively close glimpse into whole sample of working population. Undeniably, Me Generation stands out from all the others, including the way they communicate using both their first and second language. As the questioned group comprises 82 respondents residing in twenty-five countries, it may be deduced that their opinions in fact reflect the standpoint of the whole generation. Hence some of the responses, were they true and reliable, are thought-provoking and astonishing.

The first very visible difference between the way Generation Y communicates in L1 and L2 can be seen in their choice of communication modes. It is true that the most frequently applied channel for all types of interactions is still face-to-face communication (71% vs. 66 in L2). There is, however, a very significant (16%) difference in their preference for using telephones (56% vs. 40% in L2) and, above all, social media (44% vs. 63% in L2). Apparently, it is social media that are still gaining popularity and, at least when it comes to L2 communication, they are very likely to take over the role of face-to-face communication in the near future. Texting messages is equally attractive in both languages (57%). Thus, such a strong preference for smartphone-oriented communication may and should be taken into account while designing L2 courses, as this form of digital teaching and learning will be able to cater for Millennials' needs.

Another very sharp divergence may be observed in the attitude towards the way of producing the language. There is no doubt that Millennials especially take care of the "purity" of their second language rather than their mother tongues. For 78% of the respondents, it is very important to be both fluent and correct, but only 54% actually try to speak and write correctly in their L1. What is more, almost 60% of the questioned sample believes that introducing linguistic changes to their L1 and changing it is absolutely acceptable, and they do not see any problem openly stating "what is wrong with changes?" This "emotionless" attitude is not present while expressing their opinions on L2 and irritating changes happening to English. Here they show concern for "alarming" modifications, e.g., using newly-created and non-existent words or too formal, even "bookish" form of L2, as well as less polite language. What annoys them while using their mother tongue, however, is first and above all less polite language and newly-created and non-existent words. The most striking difference here is that too formal language belongs, among others, to the most annoying characteristics of L2 and, at the same time, is the least problematic in L1 communication. Such a huge divergence is quite difficult to account for, but may stem from the fact that acquiring L2 formal lexicon can be perceived as relatively difficult.

Millennials, asked to present their opinions on the attitude towards maintaining correctness while using various modes of communication, also provided different arguments, depending on the type of language (L1 vs. L2) they were to assess. Thus, while speaking both languages, it is most significant to keep it correct while writing emails, especially if one does it in L2 (76% in L1 vs. 84% in L2). Correctness should be also kept while using social media (69% in L1 and 64% in L2) as well as during face-to-face communication, again, especially if it is conducted in L2 (69% in L1 and 72% in L2). Moreover, the survey participants regard the linguistic correctness to be more important in the case of emails in L2 (63% answers) than in the case of emails in L1 (54% of answers). One may speculate about the cause of such discrepancies, but one of possible explanations is that, since many of them are already working (also in the places where English remains the official language of corporate communication), they want to be perceived as "professional" and "specialist" and poor language in terms of grammar or vocabulary would not help them in this respect.

It may be also observed that Generation Me is quite focused on their image and the way they present themselves. Thus, it is safe to guess why it is so vital for them to be correct while communicating through social media, as this is generally the most frequently applied channel enabling them to create the image they wish to project.

The conducted quantitative study setting out to investigate communication types employed by Millennials is not free from various limitations. Firstly, one may question whether the sample size is representative enough to enable drawing general conclusions applying to the whole Millennial cohort. As the respondents reside in 25 different and culturally as well as geographically distant countries, comparing them only in terms of age may be perceived as not sufficient and lacking credibility.

Another limitation may concern the lack of comparison of responses provided by participants representing particular ethnic and cultural groups (e.g., Polish respondents vs. Ukrainian respondents). However, such a comparison would be reliable and tenable assuming the sample was sufficiently numerous and hence statistically significant to observe some trends and, consequently, draw conclusions.

Thirdly, a qualitative approach employed through, e.g., a series of interviews will undeniably shed more light on this issue and, at the same time, help to understand this generation and their motivational drives.

References

Agrawal, A. J. (2017). *Millennials are struggling with face-to-face communication: Here's why.* Retrieved from https://www.forbes.com/sites/ajagrawal/2017/05/04/millennials-are-struggling-with-face-to-face-communication-heres-why/#4e60d94c26e8.

Alch, M. L. (2000). Get ready for a new type of worker in the workplace: The net generation. *SuperVision, 61*(4), 3–7.

Chester, E. (2002). *Employing generation why? Understanding, managing and motivating your new workforce.* Lakewood, Colorado: Tucker House Books.

Dronia, I. (2014). Dialogiczność relacji ze studentami a założenia grzeczności językowej. *Jak możliwy jest dialog? Księga jubileuszowa.* Sosnowiec: Wydawnictwo WSH.

Gibson, L., & Sodeman, W. A. (2014). Millennials and technology: Addressing the communication gap in education and practice. *Organization Development Journal, 32*(4), 63–75.

Hamill, G. (2005). Mixing and managing four generations of employees. *FDU Magazine Online.* Retrieved from https://www.fdu.edu/newspubs/magazine/05ws/generations.htm.

Howe, N., & Strauss, W. (2000). *Millennials rising: The next great generation.* New York: Vintage Books.

Jones, C., Ramanau, R., Cross, S., & Healing, G. (2010). Net generation or digital natives: Is there a distinct new generation entering university? *Computers & Education, 54*(3), 722–732.

Marcjanik, M. (2009). *Mówimy uprzejmie.* Warszawa: Wydawnictwo Naukowe PWN.

McCasland, M. (2005). Mobile marketing to millennials. *Young Consumers, 2,* 8–15.

Nicholas, A. (2008). *Preferred learning methods of the millennial generation.* Retrieved from https://www.academia.edu/21309870/Preferred_Learning_Methods_of_the_Millennial_Generation.

Prensky, M. (2001). Digital natives, digital immigrants. *On the Horizon, 9*(5). Retrieved from https://www.marcprensky.com/writing/Prensky%20%20Digital%20Natives,%20Digital%20Immigrants%20-%20Part1.pdf.

Taylor, P., & Keeter, S. (Eds.). (2010). *Millennials. A portrait of generation next. Confident. Connected. Open to change.* Pew Research Center Report. Retrieved from https://www.pew research.org/wp-content/uploads/sites/3/2010/10/millennials-confident-connected-open-to-cha nge.pdf.

Wrycza-Bekier, J. (2013). *Witam, Dzień dobry czy Szanowny Panie Profesorze? Etykieta w e-mailowej korespondencji studentów z wykładowcą.* Retrieved from https://www.kulturaihistoria. umcs.lublin.pl/archives/5121.

Zemke, R., Raines, C., & Filipczak, B. (2000). *Generations at work: Managing the clash of veterans, boomers, xers, and nexters in your workplace.* New York, N.Y.: American Management Association.

Iwona Dronia, Ph.D., is an assistant professor at the Institute of Linguistics, Faculty of Humanities, University of Silesia in Katowice, Poland. She received her Ph.D. in Linguistics from the University of Silesia in 2008. Her main areas of interest are SLA theory and research, discourse analysis (especially academic teacher discourse), rhetoric, sociopragmatics and cross-cultural communication.

Managing Prosumption in University Education—A Case Study Approach

Anna L. Wieczorek and Maciej Mitręga

Abstract The aim of this study is to discuss the role, multi-dimensionality and management of prosumption in educational settings, namely in university education. In the first part of the paper, the phenomenon of prosumption is briefly discussed and its different dimensions are elaborated on. Then its role in postgraduate university education is presented. The empirical research is based on a case study of postgraduate studies in the area of key account management, run for more than 10 years. We combined various data sources in this research: observation, survey and personal interviews. Our research identifies four dimensions of prosumption, namely: Enriching the quality of teaching process in action (1), Contributing to program improvement (2), Involvement in word-of-mouth marketing (3), and Contributing to scientific potential of service provider (4). While presenting dimensions of prosumption observed at university education, we also demonstrate how this prosumption is facilitated by the university and, especially, programme organizers and teachers. Thus, our study contributed also to better understanding of how prosumption may be managed in professional services area.

Keywords Prosumption · Education services · University education · Post-graduate

1 Introduction

The aim of this study is to discuss the role, multi-dimensionality and management of prosumption in educational settings, namely in university education. In the first part of the paper, the phenomenon of prosumption is briefly discussed and its different dimensions are elaborated on. Then its role in postgraduate university education

A. L. Wieczorek (✉)
Institute of Modern Languages, University of Bielsko-Biala, Bielsko-Biala, Poland
e-mail: awieczorek@ath.bielsko.pl

M. Mitręga
VSB-Technical University of Ostrava, Ostrava, Czech Republic

© Springer Nature Switzerland AG 2020
U. Michalik et al. (eds.), *Exploring Business Language and Culture*,
Second Language Learning and Teaching,
https://doi.org/10.1007/978-3-030-58551-8_3

41

is presented. The empirical research we conducted was based on a case study of postgraduate studies in the area of key account management, run for more than 10 years. We combined various data sources in this research: observation, survey and personal interviews.

Although prosumption is not a new phenomenon in business practice and not an entirely new academic concept, there are still some discrepancies concerning its definition and understanding. Therefore, we would like to briefly present main views on it and then discuss its role and facilitation in university education.

2   Understanding Prosumption

The term prosumption was at first proposed last century (in the 80s) with regard to post-industrial societies (Toffler, 1980). However, the empirical research on it emerged much later, as a response to changes in business environment and new paradigms in marketing theory. In the early marketing literature on prosumption, prosumers were proposed as one of emerging consumer segments which demand special managerial attention (Kotler, 1986). Later on, the new century brought significant shifts in the way that people communicate and build social ties. These changes were very much boosted by the popularization of information technology among individuals, especially WWW, smartphones, social media, etc. This new business environment triggered modification of consumer behaviour which allowed people to be more resourceful, or to exert more influence on companies' offerings as compared to the past. These all gave rise to collaboration of companies with customers on the mass scale.

The evolution of business environment went parallel with the emergence of some theoretical structures that focused on the intersection between production and consumption in human behaviour. These structures especially took the form of so-called service-dominant logic of marketing or service business logic (Gronroos, 2008; Vargo & Lusch, 2004), co-creation/co-production with customers (Payne, Storbacka, & Frow, 2008; Prahalad & Ramaswamy, 2004) and post-modern marketing (Cova & Dalli, 2009; Humphreys & Grayson, 2008). The empirically-grounded knowledge on prosumption, its antecedents and consequences is very fragmented, due to the fact that scholars have used different terms to describe the phenomena that fall within combining consumption with production, especially prosumption (Seran & Izvercian, 2014; Xie, Bagozzi, & Troye, 2008), value co-production/value co-creation (Ranjan & Read, 2016; Yi & Gong, 2013), customer participation in service (Ahn & Rho, 2016; Huynh & Olsen, 2015), and customer engagement (Dong & Sivakumar, 2017; Kumar et al., 2010). Dong and Sivakumar (2017) pointed out that extant literature lacks a clear and inclusive typology that describes the domain, scope and boundaries of consumer participation.

Hunt, Geiger-Oneto, and Varca (2012), on the other hand, claimed that prosumption's consequences have been thoroughly researched, whereas its antecedents still have not. Huynh and Olsen (2015) focused in their research on the antecedents of prosumption; however, they elaborated on a very extreme and the simplest, most widely-known dimension, which concerned producing some goods by the consumer (e.g., home meal preparation, clothmaking, etc.) instead of using services. It refers to consumer's involvement in the production of goods or services in collaboration with commercial providers indirectly via their input products that Xie et al. (2008) researched.

There is, according to Alves, Fernandes, and Raposo (2016), a gap in the literature with relation to exploration of such areas as, for instance, companies' strategies of organizing themselves to allow value co-creation, what resources companies need in order to boost co-creation, and what mechanisms companies should implement to learn about consumers' value co-creation processes. Further research is also necessary on the ways in which consumers interact among themselves to create value or even on understanding what kind of resources customers need to carry out these processes. Despite fragmented research on prosumption, there is quite consensus in the literature that co-production between consumers and companies is beneficial from a business perspective (Nishikawa, Schreier, Fuchs, & Ogawa, 2017). Hence, this process has some valuable consequences, like, for instance, the increase in customer satisfaction with offering, as a result of customer involvement in design and delivery of the offering (Hunt et al., 2012; Ranjan & Read, 2016).

Nowadays, the very term prosumption is broader than at the times of Toffler, and it is understood as any type of activity initiated by a consumer in order to add value to commodities and services purchased by them (Mitręga, 2013). According to Huynh and Olsen (2015), different terms have been used to examine the phenomena of consumer participation in value creation, such as self-service (after Curran, Meuter, & Surprenant, 2003; Dabholkar & Bagozzi, 2002), do-it-yourself (after Williams, 2008; Wolf & McQuitty, 2011), prosumption (after Witell, Kristensson, Gustafsson, & Lofgren, 2011; Xie et al., 2008), coproduction (after Etgar, 2008; Lusch & Vargo, 2006), and value cocreation (after Healy & McDonagh, 2013; Yi & Gong, 2013). Ranjan and Read (2016) distinguish two main types of modern co-creation: co-production and value in use. The former consists of direct or indirect "coworking with customers" (Ranjan & Read, 2016; after Hu & McLoughlin, 2012; Nuttavuthisit, 2010) or participation in the product/service design process (Ranjan & Read, 2016; after Auh, Bell, McLeod, & Shih, 2007; Dato-on & Beasley, 2005; Etgar, 2008; Fang, Palmatier, & Evans, 2008; Lemke, Clark, & Wilson, 2011), whereas the latter shows that value can be derived through interaction with the firm and its offerings; it can also arise through a process of consumption, which may be mostly independent of the company's intervention or exchange (Ranjan & Read, 2016).

Value in use, according to Vargo and Lusch (2004), is far more than just the co-production, exchange, and possession of a good or service, and it requires customers to learn how to use, repair, and maintain a product or service value proposition. Seran and Izvercian (2014) define prosumers as individuals that make a contribution (provide work to produce/create value) by getting engaged in a process for one's own use or for the use of others. According to Seran and Izvercian (2014), prosumption is not just a concatenation between production and consumption because we need a certain level of engagement and creativity alongside the "producer" and "consumer" equation for creating a prosumer experience. However, the majority of prior research does not differentiate prosumers from self-service users (Seran & Izvercian, 2014) or simple resource integrators for own consumption (Xie et al., 2008).

One's propensity towards prosumption is based on a certain state of mind (affective and cognitive spheres), but prosumption itself is expressed by certain behaviours (behavioural sphere). Additionally, prosumption, in its behavioural manifestation, does not have to be treated as a unidimensional phenomenon. One of many examples of prosumption would be, according to Mitręga (2013), informing a producer how to improve commodities they manufacture, and one of its determinants would be the level of one's self-confidence necessary to do it. The value created in the process of prosumption can be understood as a relation between costs and benefits associated with purchased goods and/or services. Nevertheless, prosumption is mainly interesting for academics for the cost factors, namely it is understood as a way to diminish costs.

The main benefit for the customer (increased value for the customer) that is stressed by researchers is the one connected with pleasure on the side of a customer, resulting from purchasing products that are, up to a point, tailor-made (Guido & Peluso, 2008; Hoyer, Chandy, Dorotic, Krafft, & Singh, 2010). Mitręga (2013) stresses that product customisation entails dialogue between customer and producer (e.g., at the product development stage), which means spending time on this discussion and losing some parts of customer's privacy, taking into consideration the nature of data processing. The price of a customized product does not necessarily mean it is cheaper; on the contrary, the end price is usually more expensive due to customization, its influence on the manufacturing process (producing short series) and higher costs of marketing and sales. The empirical study presented by Mitręga (2013) suggests that prosumption is a two-dimensional phenomenon, where one can distinguish Rationalistic Prosumption and Exhibitionistic Prosumption, where the former means lowering costs of purchasing and using products through taking in some tasks of the producer (e.g., furniture delivering and assembling on their own by the customer), whereas the latter concerns sharing knowledge and information with the producer in order to get customised products. Each aspect of prosumption is said to significantly influence the propensity towards dissemination of opinions on companies and their products. Therefore, prosumption is an important factor from the perspective of brand management (Mitręga, 2013). This means that the measurement of the tendency to prosume may be significant not only for the theory of marketing and consumer research, but for management practice as well.

3   Prosumption in Education Services

Since prosumption is multidimensional and it can be observed not only in the market of commodities, but also in services, it appears interesting and worthy to focus on prosumption and its dimensions in education services. Education in general means exchanging due to the nature of the process of learning and teaching and the dynamics between the teacher and students, and the students themselves, but, in this case, by exchange we mean the exchange between the service provider (organiser of the educational process) and the clients (which, in this case, are students). We focus on the teaching process happing mostly in traditional offline mode, although we acknowledge that online channels are increasingly important in education, especially in covid-19 pandemic realm (Bartosik-Purgat, Filimon, & Kiygi-Calli, 2017). Treating students as clients is not a new approach in teaching studies, as it was already used by Harmer (2000) nearly two decades ago while describing various roles that a contemporary teacher must play in the classroom (e.g., facilitator, partner, organiser, and provider) in order to satisfy the needs of students who, among others, also play a role of clients with certain needs and demands.

What is new in the concept of prosumption in education is treating students as clients that not only buy services from the provider (here the teacher/organiser of the educational process), but who may also contribute to the product (here: service) development, namely its quality; who may reduce marketing costs and contribute in a positive way to brand image of the service provided.

4 Prosumption at Postgraduate University Education—Case Study

The case study that we would like to present here is an ongoing (and longitudinal) one that has been carried out for more than 10 years already. The research area is the interactions between service provider and customers within post-graduate studies, namely: "Key Account Manager" (KAM) programme, held at a middle-size public university in Poland. The KAM customers (students) are usually people working in sales departments, mostly quite experienced business practitioners, who aspire for promotion at work, want to network with people from other companies within the same professional group, and intend to improve their professional skills. The studies are coordinated by the authors of the paper and it is already 13th edition of a two-semester course in 2018. A typical student group is composed of between 25 and 35 students. As the data collection was restricted to one Polish university only and we applied exploratory approach the results cannot be directly generalized into worwide context but they might be treated as quite universal with regard to university education at European transtional countries with similar level of socio-economic development (Mościbrodzka, 2014; Wronowska, 2015; Skare & Porada-Rochoń, 2019)

4.1 Research Approach

The research we present was generally qualitative in nature and the only quantitative elements incorporated was data obtained from student satisfaction surveys whose results were only used to validate the study programme in the light of students' opinion. Data in relation to prosumption for this case study was gathered between 2008 and 2018, mainly through participatory observation during classes and unstructured interviews carried out with some of the students, e.g., after individual examinations.

When it comes to the survey, a systematic study on student satisfaction was carried out twice each academic year from 2008. The student satisfaction survey contained a quantitative element—Likert scale measuring the performance of teachers in the following categories: expert knowledge, the proportion between theoretical and practical elements in each subject, the quality and usefulness of materials administered for students, the quality of teaching style of each teacher, and teachers' attitudes towards students. There were also open-ended questions—questions considered as more important for the purpose of our case study approach. The participants (students) were asked twice each year which elements of the offer and teaching they were most satisfied and dissatisfied with, and why and who their favourite and most disliked teachers were and why. They were also encouraged to give suggestions concerning the study concept, offer and programme, and many of them provided such information. Each year, the results were categorised and analysed, and some conclusions concerning the study programme and the quality of teaching were drawn. So far, 267 students have filled in the satisfaction questionnaire in total.

The next research method applied was a longitudinal, participatory observation (Clegg, 2013; Gebhard, 2006) carried out for 10 years by two heads of studies who are, at the same time, the authors of the paper, and who carried it out each year in order to improve the quality of their own teaching and the study programme, and, at the same time, to understand the interactions between teachers and students better, with special emphasis on the value co-created. The heads of studies observed interactions with students and they observed themselves each semester. At the end of each semester, the authors discussed together the tendencies emerging, problems to be solved and improvements to be made. They also wrote some memos with regard to the value co-creation, to keep the results categorised.

The third method and, at the same time, the most important one, in the context of this paper, was an interview method. In this paper, we present the results of semi-structured interviews carried out each year with some of the students (those who wanted to contribute and devoted some time to talk to the heads of studies). Those interviews revolved around the quality of teaching, study organisation and study programme. The co-creation manifestations were studied rather indirectly, i.e., the informants were not asked about how value was delivered and co-created, but they were asked about how they perceived various aspects of their involvement during classes and during post-classes interactions with teachers and university administration. As a result of those interviews, each year, if necessary, the programme was modified and teachers were instructed what to change in their teaching, or, in case of the teachers not appreciated by students, some new teachers were recruited. So far, 24 students have participated in the interviews and it resulted in resigning from 3 teachers, instructing 4 teachers how to improve their teaching, and in revising the general study programme significantly in 2016.

The results of the participatory observation were recorded each semester by two heads of studies in the form of memos (Konecki, 2000). The qualitative data obtained from 24 interviews was stored in the form of partial transcriptions, i.e., some main citations with memos were stored in the dataset, but full transcriptions and recording interviews on electronic devices were not applied in order to keep an informal atmosphere and due to resource limitations. This qualitative dataset was analysed in accordance with QDA (Qualitative Data Analysis) principles and, especially, the process of "noticing, collecting and thinking" (Seidel, 1998). This analysis resulted in formulating some general conclusions with regard to prosumption and identifying four main dimensions or four forms of prosumption in the context of educational services. The qualitative research approach we applied has some limitations, but it is well suited to complex social phenomena, especially while sensitive topics are in consideration (Kubacki, Siemieniako and Skinner, 2009). Next, we will elaborate on these research results.

4.2   General Feedback from Students and Its Utilization

Prosumption, in the context of managing postgraduate studies, was facilitated by the strong inclination of students towards providing the heads of studies with feedback about the teaching quality and study programme in general. The students were many times people with the same age and similar professional experience as the heads of studies themselves, which probably enabled more interactive and partnership atmosphere during classes and after classes ended. Thus, feedback with regard to postgraduate studies was not accessed only during interviews with students, but also during observing students' verbal and non-verbal communication and writing some memos with regard to this communication.

There were some general tendencies that emerged from the analysis of the empirical material, including insights from interviews and observations. Again, the satisfaction survey's results were treated only as supplementary material. First of all, the informants (students) appreciated most those lecturers who had great background knowledge with relation to the subject they taught and, at the same time, were very good teachers. To be a very good teacher, in the eyes of the study participants, meant to incorporate fun element into the teaching, facilitate soft skills of students (like, for instance, interpersonal communication skills) and foster student–student interaction to boost the exchange of good practices. The narrations below, which were taken from partial interview transcripts, portray what type of teacher was most appreciated by students, what students expected from the teaching process and what their needs concerning post-graduate teaching were.

> I appreciate the teachers here since I have fun during classes. It's important because I work more or less 10 hours a day for the whole week and here I feel I can relax while learning something valuable. Otherwise I would feel tired and discouraged. (Informant 4/2011, translation ours)

> I think you should hire more business practitioners, as we learn more from people really involved in business. They offer very interesting case studies to analyse, we speak about real cases and not about theory. Maybe they don't know sophisticated management terms, but they offer tacit knowledge, which is, in my opinion, most crucial in a job involving sales. I like when they tell stories about their career, especially about their ups and downs in sales and how they solved the problems. You definitely should have more teachers like X. (Informant 1/2013, translation ours)

> I like your classes and classes of X because you provoke students to think and exchange ideas with each other. You use coaching-like methods and I think they are very effective. I would like more classes conducted like that and fewer lectures. What we learn from lectures, we can learn from books or the Internet if we need it, and interaction teaches us some routines, lets us practice communication. (Informant 4/2017, translation ours)

As it can be seen, students appreciated teachers who used modern teaching methods (e.g., a coaching method) and who fostered interactions between fellow students and were able to conduct classes in a positive environment, letting students have fun while learning. As a result of the interviews, each academic year, some teachers were instructed how to alter their teaching in accordance with students' expectations. If a given teacher felt he/she was not able to change their teaching routines, new teachers were recruited. The study informants commented in the interviews not only on the teaching quality and their expectations in this area, but also on the general study concept and on study programme. They all liked the concept of the studies—the way the teaching process was organised and the organisation of exams, which were theoretical and practical (each time, after taking a test, they had to do a practical task in pairs or groups—for instance, present a product, prepare a marketing strategy in a context of a given industry, take a simulated job interview, etc.), but some of them were of the opinion that the studies should have a broader scope. This is explained by one of the narrations presented below.

> You should think about something more than just key-account management. The market is already saturated when it comes to key accounts and it helps us to get promotion if it is somehow indicated on our certificate that the study concerned something broader – like the skills of managing sales teams, designing sales strategies, etc. (Informant 2, 2015, translation ours)

Between 2013 and 2015, more and more students suggested broadening the scope of studies and implementing some major changes into teaching components. As a result, in 2016, the study programme went through a rebranding process that had an impact on many aspects of the study offer, including the studies' name. In general, the study programme was extended to embrace not only teaching skills relevant for key account managers, but skills relevant to sales directors as well. This way, students contributed in a very important way to the development of the study concept and programme. It was, in our opinion, a great example of prosumption in education services, which is going to be described in detail in the next section.

Before we do so, we would like to show more examples of the involvement of study informants (as a result of the interviews carried out) in the development of the studies. First of all, those students who were satisfied with the studies and talked about it to the interviewers offered to prepare recommendations for the teachers and for the studies. The recommendations were then uploaded to the studies' website. Moreover, some informants declared that they had already recommended the studies to some colleagues, which is an example of word-of-mouth marketing. Furthermore, while interviewing the students, the interviewers asked some of them if they could fill in questionnaires concerning their work in sales departments and this way obtained a source of research data in the field of management, which was treated as another form of prosumption.

4.3 Prosumption Manifestations in Post-graduate Education Services

All interactions with customers that contributed somehow to the value of the study offer, either by enriching the quality of teaching and study programme or by providing some valuable resources to the university and teachers employed at the university, were categorised into four main types of prosumption.

4.3.1 Enriching the Quality of Teaching Process in Action

The studies are organised in such a way so as to minimize lecturing and focus on practical aspects of managerial work, i.e., workshops. To do so, brainstorming sessions are organised, many case studies are discussed, students are provoked by their teachers to find answers and solutions to questions and problems they encounter at work. An exchange between them can be observed as they present cases from their professional life, share with their groupmates and with the teacher. This way, they not only remember better the learning material, but also minimize the costs of classes for the teacher since they produce case studies themselves and do not only rely on the teacher who does not need to gather all information relevant for teaching using only his or her own resources, e.g., invest into looking for the most updated case studies using general secondary sources of information.

Moreover, exams are organised as role-plays stressing managerial problems and proposing solutions, and here, again, efforts on the side of the teacher are minimised, but students' potential is utilised fully, their learning process is facilitated (Harmer, 2000) and their motivation is boosted because of their involvement in the process (Ur, 2012). They also practice soft skills, including body language, which is very much appreciated by them. This way, not only students get advantage because they really learn and not only copy theory like in many educational settings (i.e., taking tests only), but teachers and study organisers gain a lot—they save time and money due to some of their duties being done by the students, but they also build a portfolio of case studies for interactions with future generations of students. All these above examples are clear manifestations of prosumption since value is co-created for both parties each year and this process has even long-term effects on the quality of teaching.

4.3.2 Contributing to Program Improvement

The purpose of a student-satisfaction survey that is administered each year is to investigate if students are satisfied with the studies—if they think the program is relevant, if they are satisfied with teaching methods, their teachers and the service in general. However, again, feedback from students does not come only from the satisfaction survey, but it is provided systematically through observing interactions with students and the information they share spontaneously during classes and after them. The atmosphere during studies is created by the organisers and key teachers in such a way so as to encourage free exchange of opinions, not only between students, but between students and teachers as well.

Thanks to such an approach, students feel free to express their honest opinions about the quality of services not only in anonymous satisfaction surveys, but also on a regular basis with the organiser, i.e., in spontaneous conversations. This way, the staff that does not comply with students' needs is usually not invited to cooperate next semester. If students signal that some changes in the study programme are necessary, they are usually also implemented either in a given academic year or the next one. On the one hand, it may be viewed as stressful for the teachers and organisers due to the risk of losing face (Kyriacou, 2000); on the other, it helps to ensure high quality of the services provided. If a client is fast to report problems, they can benefit from the changes implemented during the studies e.g., already next semester; even if they are not fast, the next generation will benefit, and not only the organiser, which is, again, an example of the multidimensional character of prosumption.

4.3.3 Involvement in Word-of-Mouth Marketing

Due to high quality of services provided, the studies' organisers do not observe a need to use many marketing tools to promote the studies. In fact, there was never any significant budget for promoting these studies at all. For the past 13 years, generally only word-of-mouth marketing was enough to recruit new students. Taking into consideration product life cycle in education services, uncomfortable demographics in Poland, and growing competition in this market, it can be considered a great success.

Word-of-mouth marketing is an example of prosumption due to cost savings, as no money is spent on promotion (apart from general promotion for all post-graduate study programmes organised by the university, which, in many cases, does not help at all since many studies do not open), time of the organiser is saved, as well as energy that would be consumed by designing and implementing other promotional tools. The only promotional effort taken by the organiser is collecting letters of recommendation provided by volunteers graduating from the studies and uploading them to the website. Here, an obvious value is created for the organisers who save time and money, and energy, but value for clients also can be spotted, as they are better positioned as graduates of popular studies. Moreover, they can also get letters of recommendation from the service provider and sometimes they really ask for that, especially through social media like Linkedin.

4.3.4 Contributing to Scientific Potential of Service Provider

In services marketing, the image of service provider is crucial, so, in the context of post-graduate studies, the image of a university and some key-teachers involved in the programme is very important. By positive image here we understand, among other things, academic recognition and university's position, which is achieved by producing high-quality papers and publishing them in prestigious journals. To do so, teachers involved in postgraduate studies need empirical data. Students of post-graduate studies, especially due to the specificity of the teaching approach discussed earlier (encouraging exchange of opinions and experience), are seen as valuable sources of data since they are usually experienced business practitioners.

Again, not only service provider benefits here (because of having access to relevant data, e.g., by asking students to fill in questionnaires and administer them at work, by asking permission for using case studies they provide, etc.), but also the client since being involved in the process of data collection means sensitization to some phenomena that are hot topic in management at a given period of time. This, in turn, motivates students to broaden their knowledge and contributes to their development.

5 Conclusions

In the last decade, the idea of consumers becoming more active and resourceful in their relations with businesses has become very popular in academia, which resulted in research on such concepts as prosumption (Seran & Izvercian, 2014; Xie et al., 2008), customer engagement (Brodie, Hollebeek, Bilijana, & Ilic, 2011; Kunz, Aksoy, Barty, & Heinonen, 2017), and customer citizenship (Groth, 2005; Yi & Gong, 2013). In all of these streams of research, the value of the offer that a company provides to the market is somehow co-created in direct and indirect interactions between the company and its customers. This co-creation may take various forms and include multiple parties (Vargo & Lusch, 2016; Vargo, Maglio, & Akaka, 2008) but, in general, we may distinguish between two main aspects of value co-creation: VCC as value co-production and VCC as value in use (Ranjan & Read, 2016). "Co-production" refers to direct or indirect co-working with customers, e.g., during the product/service design process, whereas "value-in-use" goes beyond a firm-customer interaction and refers to value created during consumption, i.e., psychological and behavioural engagement with concrete products or services (Ranjan & Read, 2016).

Following this distinction, we may conclude that the case study we conducted illustrated that, in the context of commercial education at the university, both of these aspects of value co-creation are important. On the one hand, the students provide the university with feedback with regard to how teaching quality may be improved. As illustrated by our case study, such feedback may result in changes being implemented in the study offer year by year and can even motivate the major revision of the studies' programme, including rebranding, which happened in the case under consideration in 2016. The interactions that happen between students themselves and between students and teachers may strengthen the resources of the university, providing services in various ways, e.g., by providing the source for new teaching materials and academic research as well. Here the multiple roles that academic teachers are obliged to perform (i.e., teachers' role, researchers' role) may work as a personal incentive for teachers to get into in-depth interactions with students and value co-created this way is important from the perspective of all parties involved, i.e., improved teaching material is beneficial for the professional career of a teacher, but for training students' skills as well.

Thus, our case study provided empirical illustration towards the importance and multi-dimensionality of value co-production (Ranjan & Read, 2016) in a specific context of university teaching. On the other hand, our case study shows how prosumption or value co-creation may manifest through value in use (Ranjan & Read, 2016). In the period of time under investigation, except remarks that they made in order to revise some aspects of the programme, in comparison to other educational services they had experience with, students were very satisfied with the studies' programme and teachers themselves as well. Therefore, we may conclude that they became affectively engaged with the brand of the teaching programme, which, in turn, resulted in positive word of mouth creating market leverage for the studies through many years. We may even assume that without such student engagement, not only growth, but also the survival of the studies' offer would not be possible because it did not receive any special advertising support and the market conditions were visibly worsening in the analysed period of time.

This study has also contributed to the management aspects of prosumption, i.e., to the research problem of how prosumption may be managed from the perspective of running a company. This aspect is, to a large extent, neglected in the literature because even if there is growing evidence for the importance of value co-creation for various industries, our knowledge is especially weak with regard to how companies should manage co-creation (Alves et al., 2016; Hollebeek & Andreassen, 2018). Our case study suggests that organizations operating on the postgraduate-education market may facilitate value co-creation by applying appropriate teaching methods and stimulating appropriate atmosphere of interactions between teaching/management people and students. Among the available teaching techniques, group discussion, role playing, and case studies seem to be the most adjusted to creating potential for value co-creation and exploiting it. In general, these are very interactive or participatory teaching techniques, which enable, to a large extent, sharing experience and knowledge not only between teachers and students, but also between students themselves. As in the case of postgraduate studies, students usually possess valuable professional experience, they can present the advantages and disadvantages of applying the elements of the teaching programme in a rich context of organizations they were professionally involved with.

Moreover, in the case of role playing, they can also simulate how they would act in situations similar to their everyday work experience and such performance helps them, other students and teachers as well in understanding what works better or worse in such situations. However, applying appropriate teaching methods would not be enough if not supported by the atmosphere of interactions between teachers and students. Our case study suggests that, being confronted with students with rich professional experience, teachers must develop specific approach towards their teaching role. They must invest a lot in creating teaching materials that would enable student activation. Additionally, they must retain some distance towards any theories that are applicable to their teaching area because none of these theories is universal in the context of all industries and all organizations. Therefore, the role of a traditional lecturer that concentrates primarily on one-sided communication must be limited to the necessary minimum and the teacher must frequently act as a coach to students (e.g., by providing feedback towards students' performance during classes) and as a facilitator of communication (e.g., stimulating the group discussions, brainstorming, especially with regard to the most difficult teaching elements). Thus, stimulating value co-creation may be very challenging on a personal level and, as illustrated by our case study, not all people involved in professional services may be ready for combining all necessary roles in their actions. Even though the emotional cost of facilitating prosumption may be high on teachers' side, our case study demonstrates that business benefits are greater and also teachers themselves benefit from prosumption in short-term and in the long-run as well.

As in the case of a majority of qualitative studies, our study is not free from limitations and, in many aspects, it may be treated more as a call for more research in the area than as a conclusion to the ongoing dilemma on how prosumption works and may be managed in today's service-oriented economy. One should not neglect the fact that some people are more prone to prosumption than others (students who were oriented at exploring opportunities by their profession were a favourable and very specific target in this research). Therefore, our research results are not generalizable to the context of other industries, beyond the scope of university teaching. Postgraduate university teaching is a very specific business area so, in case of other forms of university teaching, e.g., teaching regular students at a Bachelor level, students may not have appropriate resources, e.g., knowledge and experience, to engage smoothly in prosumption at classes. Nevertheless, our research may work as an exploration on what prosumption in commercial education at universities may look like and how it can be managed. Further research in this area may apply other approaches, e.g., further research may incorporate insights from other forms of university teaching and apply other research techniques, including a large survey on how various aspects of value co-creation are perceived by students.

Acknowledgement The study by Maciej Mitręga was supported by the Grant Agency of the Czech Republic, grant GACR 19-10897S. The study by Anna Wieczorek was supported by Erasmus+ Project PIETE (Partnership for Initial Entrepreneurship Teacher Education), 2018-1-DE01-KA203-004276.

References

Ahn, J., & Rho, T. (2016). Influence of customer–firm relationships on customer participation in the service industry. *Service Business, 10*(1), 113–133.

Alves, H., Fernandes, C., & Raposo, M. (2016). Value co-creation: Concept and contexts of application and study. *Journal of Business Research, 69*(5), 1626–1633.

Auh, S., Bell, S. J., McLeod, C. S., & Shih, E. (2007). Co-production and customer loyalty in financial services. *Journal of Retailing, 83*(3), 359–370.

Bartosik-Purgat, M., Filimon, N., & Kiygi-Calli, M. (2017). Social media and higher education: An international perspective. *Economics and Sociology, 10*(1), 181–191.

Brodie, R. J., Hollebeek, L. D., Bilijana, J., & Ilic, A. (2011). Customer engagement: Conceptual domain, fundamental propositions, and implications for research. *Journal of Service Research, 14*(3), 252–271.

Clegg, J. W. (2013). *Self-observation in the social sciences.* New Brunswick, USA and London, UK: Transaction Publishers.

Cova, B., & Dalli, D. (2009). Working consumers: The next step in marketing theory? *Marketing Theory, 9*(3), 315–339.

Curran, J. M., Meuter, M. L., & Surprenant, C. F. (2003). Intentions to use self-service technologies: A confluence of multiple attitudes. *Journal of Service Research, 5,* 209–224.

Dabholkar, P. A., & Bagozzi, R. P. (2002). An attitudinal model of technology-based self-service: Moderating effects of consumer traits and situational factors. *Journal of the Academy of Marketing Science, 30,* 184–201.

Dato-on, M. C., & Beasley, F. (2005). A proposed cross-national study: The effects of self-serving bias and co-production on customer satisfaction. *Innovative Marketing, 1*(2), 40–48.

Dong, B., & Sivakumar, K. (2017). Customer participation in services: Domain, scope, and boundaries. *Journal of the Academy of Marketing Science, 45*(1), 1–22.

Etgar, M. (2008). A descriptive model of the consumer coproduction process. *Journal of the Academy of Marketing Science, 36,* 97–108.

Fang, E., Palmatier, R. W., & Evans, K. R. (2008). Influence of customer participation on creating and sharing of new product value. *Journal of the Academy of Marketing Science, 36*(3), 322–336.

Gebhard, J. G. (2006). *Teaching English as a foreign or second language: A teacher self-development and methodology guide.* Michigan, Ann Arbor: The University of Michigan Press.

Gronroos, C. (2008). Service logic revisited: Who creates value? And who co-creates? *European Business Review, 20*(4), 298–314.

Groth, M. (2005). Customers as good soldiers: Examining citizenship behaviors in internet service deliveries. *Journal of Management, 31*(1), 7–27.

Guido, G., & Peluso, A. M. (2008). Preconditions for the diffusion of prosumption among firms: A case study approach. *Problems and Perspectives in Management, 6*(4), 66–73.

Harmer, J. (2000). *The practice of English language teaching.* Edinburg: Longman.

Healy, J. C., & McDonagh, P. (2013). Consumer roles in brand culture and value co-creation in virtual communities. *Journal of Business Research, 66,* 1528–1540.

Hollebeek, L. D., & Andreassen, T. W. (2018). The SD logic-informed "hamburger" model of service innovation and its implications for engagement and value. *Journal of Services Marketing, 32*(1), 1–7.

Hoyer, W. D., Chandy, R., Dorotic, M., Krafft, M., & Singh, S. S. (2010). Consumer cocreation in new product development. *Journal of Service Research, 13*(3), 283–296.

Hu, Y., & McLoughlin, D. (2012). Creating new market for industrial services in nascent fields. *Journal of Services Marketing, 26*(5), 322–331.

Humphreys, A., & Grayson, K. (2008). The intersecting roles of consumer and producer: A critical perspective on co-production, co-creation and prosumption. *Sociology Compass, 2*(3), 963–980.

Hunt, D. M., Geiger-Oneto, S., & Varca, P. E. (2012). Satisfaction in the context of customer co-production: A behavioral involvement perspective. *Journal of Consumer Behaviour, 11*(5), 347–356.

Huynh, M. T. X., & Olsen, S. O. (2015). Personality, personal values, and consumer participation in self-production: The case of home meal preparation. *Psychology & Marketing, 32*(7), 709–724.

Konecki, K. (2000). *Studia z metodologii badań jakościowych: Teoria ugruntowana.* Warszawa: PWN.

Kotler, P. (1986). The prosumer movement: A new challenge for marketers. *Advances in Consumer Research, 13*(1), 510–513.

Kubacki, K., Siemieniako, D., & Skinner, H. (2009). Social aspects of alcohol consumption in Poland: an investigation into students' perceptions. *Worldwide Hospitality and Tourism Themes, 1*(2),133–148.

Kumar, V., Aksoy, L., Donkers, B., Venkatesan, R., Wiesel, T., & Tillmanns, S. (2010). Undervalued or overvalued customers: Capturing total customer engagement value. *Journal of Service Research, 13*(3), 297–310.

Kunz, W. H., Aksoy, L., Barty, Y., & Heinonen, K. (2017). Customer engagement in a big data world. *Journal of Services Marketing, 31*(2), 161–171.

Kyriacou, C. (2000). *Stress-busting for teachers.* Cheltenham: Stanley Thornes Publishers.

Lemke, F., Clark, M., & Wilson, H. (2011). Customer experience quality: An exploration in business and consumer contexts using repertory grid technique. *Journal of the Academy of Marketing Science, 39*(6), 846–869.

Lusch, R. F., & Vargo, S. L. (2006). Service-dominant logic: Reactions, reflections and refinements. *Marketing Theory, 6,* 281–288.

Mitręga, M. (2013). Czy prosumpcja w dobie kryzysu to zjawisko jednowymiarowe? Eksploracja wśród użytkowników portali społecznościowych. *Problemy Zarządzania, 11*(1), 40–63.

Mościbrodzka, M. (2014). The use of methods of multidimensional comparative analysis in evaluation of the standard of living of Poland's population in comparison with other countries of the european union. *Oeconomia copernicana, 5*(3), 29–47.

Nishikawa, H., Schreier, M., Fuchs, C., & Ogawa, S. (2017). The value of marketing crowdsourced new products as such: Evidence from two randomized field experiments. *Journal of Marketing Research, 54*(4), 525–539.

Nuttavuthisit, K. (2010). If you can't beat them, let them join: The development of strategies to foster consumers' co-creative practices. *Business Horizons, 53*(3), 315–324.

Payne, A. F., Storbacka, K., & Frow, P. (2008). Managing the co-creation of value. *Journal of the Academy of Marketing Science, 36*(1), 83–96.

Prahalad, C. K., & Ramaswamy, V. (2004). Co creation experiences: The next practice in value creation. *Journal of Interactive Marketing, 18*(3), 5–14.

Ranjan, K. R., & Read, S. (2016). Value co-creation: Concept and measurement. *Journal of the Academy of Marketing Science, 44*(3), 290–315.

Seidel, J. (1998). Qualitative data analysis. *The Ethnograph, 4,* 1–15.

Seran, S., & Izvercian, M. (2014). Prosumer engagement in innovation strategies: The prosumer creativity and focus model. *Management Decision, 52*(10), 1968–1980.

Skare, M., & Porada-Rochoń, M. (2019). Financial and economic development link in transitional economies: A spectral Granger causality analysis 1991–2017. *Oeconomia Copernicana, 10*(1), 7–35.

Toffler, A. (1980). *The third wave.* New York: Bantam Books.

Ur, P. (2012). *A course in foreign language teaching—Practice and theory.* Cambridge: Cambridge University Press.

Vargo, S. L., & Lusch, R. F. (2004). Evolving to a new dominant logic for marketing. *Journal of Marketing, 68*(1), 1–17.

Vargo, S. L., & Lusch, R. F. (2016). Institutions and axioms: An extension and update of service-dominant logic. *Journal of the Academy of Marketing Science, 44*(1), 5–23.

Vargo, S. L., Maglio, P. P., & Akaka, M. A. (2008). On value and value co-creation: A service systems and service logic perspective. *European Management Journal, 26*(3), 145–152.

Williams, C. C. (2008). Re-thinking the motives of do-it yourself (DIY) consumers. *The International Review of Retail, Distribution and Consumer Research, 18,* 311–323.

Witell, L., Kristensson, P., Gustafsson, A., & Lofgren, M. (2011). Idea generation: Customer co-creation versus traditional market research techniques. *Journal of Service Management, 22,* 140–159.

Wolf, M., & McQuitty, S. (2011). Understanding the do-it yourself consumer: DIY motivations and outcomes. *AMS Review, 1,* 154–170.

Wronowska, G. (2015). Welfare and higher education in EU member states–comparative analysis. *Oeconomia Copernicana, 6*(1), 33–45.

Xie, C., Bagozzi, R. P., & Troye, S. V. (2008). Trying to prosume: Toward a theory of consumers as co-creators of value. *Journal of the Academy of Marketing Science, 36*(1), 109–122.

Yi, Y., & Gong, T. (2013). Customer value co-creation behavior: Scale development and validation. *Journal of Business Research, 66*(9), 1279–1284.

Anna L. Wieczorek, Ph.D., is Assistant Professor, in the Institute of Modern Languages, at the University of Bielsko-Biala, Poland. She is a multidisciplinary scholar whose main interests revolve around academic teaching, FLT, business and academic productivity. Her doctoral dissertation and core publications concerned the affective aspects of teaching and teacher productivity in the field of foreign languages. She was a team-member of a research grant funded by the Ministry of Science in Poland that delivered comprehensive model of HR productivity in the area of university management in post-communist countries. Member of *PIETE—Partnership for Initial Entrepreneurship Teacher Education* Erasmus+ Project contributing to a new generation of entrepreneurial teachers in Europe. Head of 3 post-graduate studies in the area of Business English and sales management.

Maciej Mitręga is Associate Professor and Head of Organizational Relationship Management Department at the University of Economics in Katowice. Visiting Professor at Technical University of Ostrava, Szeged University and Wroclaw University of Economics. Devoted to high quality research with research papers published in *Long Range PlanningInternational Journal of Operations & Production Management* and *Industrial Marketing Management*. Prior Marie Curie Research Fellow and Honorary Research Fellow at Manchester Business School, UK. The member of the editorial review board in *Industrial Marketing and Management* and *Journal of Business & Industrial Marketing*. His area of expertise and research is interdisciplinary, focusing on business networking at inter-organizational and inter-personal level.

The Lack of Business Experience Versus The Lack of Appropriate Linguistic Background in Business English Teaching Context

Anna L. Wieczorek

Abstract Nowadays, in effect of globalisation, the development of international trade and need for employees with Business English background and good business communication skills can be observed. As a result, greater demand for advanced Business English courses and qualified Business English teachers can be observed. This, in turn, may be perceived as a challenge for English language teachers. In order to meet their students' expectations and fully develop their potential, the teachers do not only need to teach about "traditional" business language (e.g., vocabulary, writing, etc.), but they are also expected to teach business communication skills (Gibson, 2002) and soft skills in general (Sadaf, 2009), relevant for business purposes. The necessity to possess an appropriate linguistic background, as well as at least basic business-related knowledge, may be a great challenge for a language teacher and a school manager. The purpose of this paper is to elaborate on the dark challenges of Business English teaching in a specific context of post-graduate studies. In the paper, we call post-graduate students university's strategic customers since they bring direct income and they significantly differ from regular students when it comes to their (higher) expectations and (richer) business background, as compared to regular students. This research follows an explorative approach and we applied a longitudinal case study approach to identify specific interrelations between Business English post-graduate students and their teachers (by teachers we mean here teachers teaching Business English, as well as teachers teaching business-related subjects at post-graduate studies) and to deepen the existing knowledge on the dark side of Business English teaching.

Keywords Business English · Teaching · Post-graduate · Challenges

A. L. Wieczorek (✉)
Institute of Modern Languages, University of Bielsko-Biala, Bielsko-Biala, Poland
e-mail: awieczorek@ath.bielsko.pl

© Springer Nature Switzerland AG 2020
U. Michalik et al. (eds.), *Exploring Business Language and Culture*,
Second Language Learning and Teaching,
https://doi.org/10.1007/978-3-030-58551-8_4

1   Introduction

In the era of globalisation, employees with Business English background, experience and skills are looked for (Tang, 2015). As a result, more and more people prepare for a job in the business field nowadays and greater demand for advanced Business English courses can be observed. This, in turn, can be perceived as a challenge for Business English teachers and educators. In order to meet their students' expectations and fully develop their potential, teachers do not only need to teach about business language (e.g., vocabulary, writing, etc.), but they also need to teach business communication (Gibson, 2002), soft skills (Sadaf, 2009) relevant for business purposes (language of persuasion, stress management in business, public speaking and business presentations, business etiquette, etc.). Business English teachers are also expected to possess at least basic business-related knowledge (Tang, 2015). The teachers therefore claim that teaching Business English is much more difficult than teaching general English and they report great occupational stress due to the specificity of Business English teaching. The aim of the paper is to discuss the negative aspect of Business English teaching and propose potential solutions to the problems encountered by teachers. At first, however, Business English itself, its position in foreign language teaching and its specificity are going to be discussed.

2   The Role and Specificity of Business English Teaching

According to Zhu, Lin, and Zhu (2016), Business English at first developed from scientific English, and then (from the second half of the twentieth century) as a branch of English for Specific Purposes (ESP). Geng (2017) stresses that this area is attracting more and more attention and therefore deserves a considerate focus, especially in view of the fact that it is a comprehensive, interdisciplinary subject based on linguistics and applied linguistics (Zhu, 2010) rather than a simple addition of business and English. Geng (2017) calls it an organic integration of Business and English and an inevitable product of economic globalisation. Chuan and Zhu (2011) claim that Business English is a comprehensive subject based on linguistics and absorbing other research methods; it consists of three main elements: business background knowledge, the language used in a business context, and business communication skills. Many researchers in the field (i.e., Geng, 2017; Kustec, 2014; Mihaescu, 2013) unanimously agree that Business English is a very important and "hot" branch of ESP, but it still faces many problems and it needs a more systematic methodology of teaching (Sadaf, 2009) and, as a discipline, the development of theory system (Zhu et al., 2016). Business English teaching entails teaching business-related vocabulary, communication skills, business-related subjects, such as, for instance, marketing, sales techniques, EU funds, etc. Zhu et al. (2016) stress that:

> Business English is a system of communicative activities in which the business activity
> participants influenced by social elements obey the usage of trade and procedure, use

English vocabulary and grammar resources selectively, and apply pragmatic strategy and communicate orally or in writing. Now it has developed as a complete education system, including international trade, finance, marketing, management, e-commerce, cross-cultural communication, and so on. (p. 1)

It is visible that Business English teaching is much more than just foreign language teaching (Scrivener, 2005); it is, in view of Mihaescu (2013), teaching language and skills. According to Lang (1990), a demand for selecting business-related teachers who have a good or a very good command of English and willingness to teach in English, and who, at the same time, are ready to reflect on their own teaching, can be observed. Already knowing what Business English teaching is and what it entails, a question concerning the dark side of the process emerges. Is it only a problem of its complexity that teachers report, or are there some other factors contributing to teachers' negative feelings associated with BE (Business English) teaching?

3   Teachers' Dilemmas and Problems Concerning Teaching Business English

Taking into consideration the complexity of the scope of Business English teaching, it seems reasonable to assume that teaching it may trigger negative emotions of teachers. Before analysing those emotions, problems associated with Business English teaching should be discussed. First of all, the teaching goals for Business English students are not only to gain some knowledge about business (like, for instance, a business letter construction), but to learn how to use English to communicate flexibly and efficiently in a business environment and how to deal with real problems occurring in international business (Zhu et al., 2016). This is much more difficult for the teacher than teaching general English since it entails expertise in more than one field (e.g., linguistics and management).

Nowadays, according to Tang (2015), business teachers are required to have business background, and to constantly update teaching techniques, which, in turn, can offer their students a profound knowledge in this field. An average graduate of English Philology very rarely may boast about such expertise in both business and knowledge concerning modern teaching techniques that would be applicable in the context of Business English teaching. Kustec (2014; after Gibson, 2002) claims that newly-qualified teachers tend to lack a basic business awareness and an understanding of business life situations, and they are not familiar with the intercultural challenge, cultural dimensions, and the concept of business communication.

What is more, a problem frequently reported by Business English teachers is the one associated with teaching too heterogeneous groups. By heterogeneous we mean here vast differences with relation to students' linguistic background (mixed-ability groups), students' background business knowledge, their age and social status (Sadaf, 2009). Students enrolling for Business English courses that are not a part of a regular Bachelor or Master study programme usually represent very heterogeneous backgrounds. Ringler (1997) stresses that Business English students are, in the majority of cases, non-native speakers of English and they should be taught for service purposes. Teaching for service purposes means task-based learning (Sadaf, 2009) with emphasis on the acquisition of global requirements within Business English, together with language accuracy and proficiency. Such an approach to language teaching is, according to Ringler (1997), more practical than standard lecturing and it aims at empowering students to use Business English skills in practical business situations. It is all more difficult to design and implement for the teacher than typical, general foreign language content. Besides, task-based approaches to foreign language teaching are most often associated with private sector teaching services rather than public ones. The teachers providing business courses in public schools (like, for instance universities at Bachelor or Master programmes) would need to change their teaching completely if they wanted to meet the requirements of modern Business English teaching. Mihaescu (2013) claims that such problems as the ones discussed above cause teachers' dilemmas in relation to designing a course syllabus, especially in view of the fact that there is no standard description of what a Business English syllabus should be like, and most of the existent business coursebooks present a generally-accepted common core of vocabulary, structures and functions. Geng (2017) also stresses that Business English teachers should try to constantly adjust and perfect the curriculum in accordance with the changing business environment and students' changing needs, which, in turn, appears a very time-consuming and difficult task for teachers that generally are overloaded with work (Wieczorek & Mitręga, 2017).

The greatest challenge, though, seems the necessity to combine expertise from a variety of fields (e.g., linguistics and management) as, according to Łuczak (2012), Business-English-related classes should be taught by English teachers who also possess business knowledge. It may be perceived as a challenge not only for the teachers, but for school managers as well. For that reason, we decided that it would be worthwhile to have a close look at the negative aspects of the process of Business English teaching.

4 The Dark Side of Business English Teaching: Study Conceptualisation and Context

As mentioned earlier, the necessity to possess an appropriate linguistic background, as well as at least basic business-related knowledge, may be a great challenge for a teacher and a school manager. For that reason, we decided to elaborate on this issue and investigate if Business English teachers really perceive it as something negative and, if so, what the main reason for such feelings is. Additionally, we wanted to propose coping strategies which Business English teachers can use and we would like to discuss how the whole process of education is affected by all the Business

English teaching-related issues. The study context is post-graduate studies in the field of Business English organised at a middle-size public university in Poland, where all subjects—Business English, soft skills and business-related subjects (like, for instance, marketing strategies, sales strategies, negotiations, etc.)—are taught in English, by English teachers and teachers experienced in the area of management studies. It appears to be an underdeveloped research direction since the majority of research studies in the field were generally oriented at Business English teaching, without focusing on the specific context of post-graduate teaching.

Post-graduate teaching is specific due to a few reasons. First of all, taking into consideration rapid changes witnessed by contemporary academia (like, for instance, demographic crisis in the EU, changes in the financial system of universities resulting in stronger emphasis on scholars' finding financing outside university, e.g., grants, internships, etc.), universities now compete for students and take great care of extra income sources. By extra income sources we do not mean here money provided by the government for educating regular students, but money that students bring directly to the university, for instance by paying for extramural studies. Specifically, we call post-graduate students strategic or key customers at universities for the reason that they bring direct income and they significantly differ from regular students when it comes to their expectations and background knowledge. Post-graduate students tend to have different motivations for studying; as older and already involved professionally people, they know which pieces of knowledge they need to absorb to become better employees and to boost career. Therefore, they have clear expectations towards the lecturers and the learning-teaching process. Thus, they are relatively highly motivated but they also expect more, as compared to regular students. What is more, they tend to have much wider background knowledge of the subject matter since they very often are already specialists in the field they want to explore. They are really involved in classes, which creates an advantage but, at the same time, some of them may manifest wider practical knowledge than the academic teacher conducting a class and this may be perceived by some teachers as something difficult to cope with. Post-graduate students may also significantly differ as far as age, profile of education, etc. are concerned, and, this way, it may be more difficult to teach them, especially when it comes to foreign language teaching. For all those above reasons, we think that elaborating on the dark side of post-graduate Business English teaching may be a very interesting research direction and it may shed new light on various processes accompanying it that may be important not only for the teachers, but for studies' managers and university authorities as well since post-graduate students are nowadays perceived as university's key customers.

5   Research Approach

We applied a longitudinal case study approach to explore specific interrelations between Business English post-graduate students and their teachers (by teachers we mean here teachers teaching Business English, as well as teachers teaching business-related subjects at Business English-related post-graduate studies), and to deepen the existing knowledge on the dark side of Business English teaching. The case study method was often used in prior studies concerning business relationships (e.g., Pérez & Cambra-Fierro, 2015) and we can call the relationship between a university and its strategic customers a business-like one. Our study focuses on the dark side of a dyadic relationship between an organization and their key customers. The longitudinal case study method allowed us to observe which aspects of Business English teaching the teachers find most problematic, what is most difficult for foreign language teachers and what is problematic for teachers teaching other, business-related subjects in English to post-graduate students. The research was mostly qualitative in nature, which, taking into consideration the sensitivity of the issue under investigation (people's feelings and problems concerning Business English teaching), assured best results thanks to the closeness between the researcher and the investigated reality (Konecki, 2000).

5.1 Study Objectives

The main study objective was to explore specific interrelations between Business English post-graduate students and their teachers (teaching Business English, as well as other business-related subjects at post-graduate studies) and the dark side of Business English teaching. Detached objectives concerned deepening our existing knowledge in the area and discussion on the most problematic aspects of Business English teaching, specifically what is most difficult for foreign language teachers teaching Business English to post-graduate students with business background and what is problematic for teachers teaching business-related subjects in English to post-graduate students and how studies' managers should plan the educational process to achieve best results, taking into consideration the specificity of the student environment and expectations. Last but not least, we tried to look for benefits and threats of post graduate Business English and business teaching, and propose some solutions/coping strategies for teachers and studies' managers.

5.2 Profile of Informants

The informants were students of Business English-related post-graduate studies, their teachers and 2 study managers (heads of studies). The studies' offer was generally addressed to English Philology students/graduates who lacked business-related skills and to corporate workers who especially lacked linguistic skills in the area of Business English.

The students were, in the majority of cases, corporate workers from various business sectors who lacked linguistic knowledge with relation to Business English vocabulary and who lacked good English communication skills, and English philology graduates (mostly English teachers) who lacked business-related knowledge and Business English vocabulary. They chose that offer mainly for two reasons: first of all, acquiring a diploma in the area of Business English studies, nicely tailored to their career, and, secondly, they were looking for new knowledge and competencies with relation to business and business-related soft-skills area. They had clear needs and high expectations, and, at the same time, some of them had really significant knowledge in the area of sales, communication and sometimes middle-level management, as they were experienced employees. This way, they were valuable and demanding customers for the university and, especially, lecturers. Most of the students really wanted to contribute to the learning and teaching process and they took an active participation in shaping the course program for the next years. They also had a substantial impact on the attitudes of prospective customers (students) since their recommendations and word-of-mouth marketing played a significant role in promoting the studies.

Two heads of Business-English-related post-graduate studies also participated in the research; one of them was an expert in the area of English linguistics and had experience in Business English teaching, whereas the other one was an expert in the field of management and had some experience in teaching classes in which the language of instruction was English. They both were scholars. The two heads of studies were the initiators of the studies and authors of the study curriculum and syllabi.

Among the post-graduate teachers that participated in the research, there were 2 teachers of English that taught Business English and some business-related soft skills and 5 teachers of business-related subjects (e.g., sales strategies and negotiations, marketing, EU funds, etc.). Six of those teachers were scholars, whereas one was a so-called business practitioner (corporate top manager) teaching some business-related classes in English to post-graduate students.

5.3 Research Method and Tools

There were three main information sources that we used in the case study. Firstly, we used a survey method in which the research tool was an anonymous student satisfaction questionnaire administered twice per an academic year at post-graduate studies. The tool was not designed specifically for the purpose of this study because the heads of post-graduate studies have to administer questionnaires in order to measure satisfaction of students concerning the services provided and then report the results to university authorities. However, we realised that such questionnaires are an excellent source of information much beyond the quality of teaching–learning process and, for that reason, they were used for the purpose of exploring the specific interrelations between Business-English-related post-graduate students and their teachers (teaching business English, as well as other business-related subjects at post-graduate studies), especially with relation to problems encountered in the process of teaching, students' expectations towards teachers and the teaching–learning process. The student questionnaire aimed at measuring student satisfaction and extensive feedback with regard to various aspects of teaching/learning twice per academic year. This means that each group of students (each edition of studies) filled it in twice. In the questionnaire, there were close-ended questions designed in the form of a Likert scale which measured the performance of teachers in the following categories: expert knowledge, the proportion between theoretical and practical elements in each subject, the quality and usefulness of materials administered to students, the quality of teaching style of each teacher, and teachers' attitudes towards students. There were also open-ended questions that were more important for the purpose of our case study approach and there students were asked which elements of the offer and teaching they were most satisfied and dissatisfied with, and why, and who their favourite and most disliked teachers were, and why. They were also welcomed to give any suggestions concerning the concept of studies, offer and programme, and many of them provided such information. Each year, the heads of studies categorised and analysed the results and wrote down some conclusions concerning the study programme and the quality of teaching. In total, 127 informants participated in the survey within 5 years. We do not call it a longitudinal survey although the research lasted for 5 years for the reason that each year a different (new) group participated in the research.

The second method we used was a longitudinal interview carried out among post-graduate teachers. For the last 3 years, 7 teachers were asked to participate in personal unstructured interviews which concerned various aspects of teaching, including problematic situations experienced by them during the teaching process and interactions between students and themselves. The results of the anonymous student satisfaction questionnaires were also elaborated on during those interviews; the teachers got feedback and some solutions to potential problems were proposed.

The third method that we used was a longitudinal, participatory observation (Clegg, 2013; Gebhard, 2006) carried out for 6 years by two heads of studies. Every year, the heads of studies carried it out in order to make their teaching better and to improve the studies' offer, i.e.,—to adjust the syllabus and teaching methods to students' needs/expectations, and to reflect on one's own teaching. Observation included discussion on the teaching quality, study management and encountered problems and proposition of changes to be implemented in the course, if necessary, as well as changes in one's behaviour with relation to teaching and managing the studies.

In this paper, we try to analyse mostly qualitative data we gathered over the investigated time and try to interpret them in the context of the negative aspects of teaching Business English and business-related subjects in the context of post-graduate studies. The empirical material contained quantitative elements (Likert-scale-based information concerning performance of all academic teachers, usefulness of materials, teachers' attitudes towards students) and qualitative elements (open-ended questions referring to the advantages and disadvantages of the studies' programme, preferences with regard to the best and the worst academic teacher each year, etc.). In this case study, we were mostly interested in the qualitative data and only sometimes used quantitative information just to validate the qualitative results (e.g., checking if an academic teacher described in open-ended questions as the best one scored high on the Likert scale as one having great expertise, manifesting positive attitudes towards students, incorporating a good proportion of theory and practice into classes). To a large extent, with regard to results of personal, individual interviews, the qualitative data was double coded to avoid coder's bias (Krippendorff, 2004) and then it was analysed in accordance with the principles of QDA (Qualitative Data Analysis) (Seidel, 1998) and, especially, of the process of noticing, collecting and thinking. On the basis of the emerged theory, study objectives were addressed and they are going to be elaborated on in the next section of the paper.

6 Research Results and Discussion

The qualitative data that emerged as a result of applying QDA (Seidel, 1998) principles to data analysis revealed results that may potentially contribute to the still underdeveloped area of Business English teaching, especially in the very specific context of post-graduate teaching. Our results show problematic areas in teaching Business English and business-related subjects to people having background in linguistics and in business, and give an insight into the nature of an interaction between postgraduate students and their teachers, together with students' expectations towards the teaching process. The results have been grouped and they are presented below.

6.1 Students' General Expectations Concerning Business English and Business-Related Courses

When it comes to the expectations of students concerning the teaching process and the attitudes and expertise of teachers, English Philology graduates, as well as corporate workers, expected teachers who were able to provide a valuable course content, using modern teaching methods containing fun element. The teachers that achieved the highest score on the Likert scale were the ones that were reported by the students to implement games, role-plays and brainstorming sessions into their teaching. The informants (the students) indicated that they learnt faster this way and, at the same time, practiced communication and could perfect their soft skills due to constant interaction with the teacher and fellow students. Among the best teachers enumerated by the informants, teachers with linguistic background had higher scores. The differences were not substantial, but they gave a hint that probably teachers with linguistic (English) background were more at ease while conducting classes in English; besides, they were teachers of English by profession, so they had knowledge with relation to teaching methodology. Such teaching methodology is most likely helpful in achieving higher scores for innovative teaching methods. Incorporating elements of fun into post-graduate teaching also seems crucial in view of the specificity of such teaching—post-graduate students are extramural students and, in most cases, they have classes once per two weeks. The classes last the whole weekend (usually a given subject comprises 8 or 10 h per day) and here the entertaining element is very important to keep the students focused and motivated.

6.1.1 Differences of Expectations and Satisfaction Between Corporate Workers and English Philology Graduates

There were differences spotted in some expectations of corporate workers and English Philology graduates—both groups were generally satisfied with the quality of teaching and the studies' content, but they had contradictory expectations concerning some areas.

English Philology graduates were very satisfied with business-related subjects but expected a more advanced linguistic input. Some of them were even a bit disappointed when it comes to the scope of Business English classes. Those people were used to a very advanced linguistic input, taking into consideration their education and background knowledge, and this is the reason of their disappointment. Generally, they very rarely take it into consideration while enrolling for the studies that the group will be very heterogeneous with relation to linguistic competence. They were very satisfied with the services provided by Business English teachers but expected a broader scope.

When it comes to corporate workers, they were very satisfied with the linguistic input provided and generally satisfied with business-related subjects, but on condition that they could have fun while learning and could improve soft skills at the same time. This indicates that they were aware that they learnt best through interaction with teachers and colleagues, and that they found the development of business-related soft skills (e.g., business communication, social influence, public speaking, etc.) crucial for their overall linguistic and business development.

Corporate workers expected more case studies as a part of business-related subjects, whereas English Philology graduates found them boring and irrelevant to the course. This suggests that English Philology graduates were not fully aware of the importance of case studies within business theory and practice, whereas corporate workers were fully aware and expected more such elements incorporated into the teaching.

As far as language skills and students' needs with relation to them are concerned, corporate workers expected more speaking practice, whereas English Philology graduates—more classes devoted to written English. This shows the areas of students' needs concerning both groups: corporate workers knew that they had some lacks when it comes to speaking practice, whereas English Philology graduates, who were proficient speakers of English, needed more written practice, namely business letter and report writing practice. Corporate workers reported that they found it really difficult to spend 8 h speaking English and/or listening to teachers and colleagues speaking English.

All the differences of expectations and areas of satisfaction show that groups taught at post-graduate studies in the area of Business English are very heterogeneous. Such groups can be very problematic for students themselves and their teachers as well. Heterogeneity is not, of course the only problem observed in this context. All the problems reported by the investigated teachers are going to be discussed below.

6.2   Problems Reported by Teachers of Business English and Business-Related Subjects

The problems discussed in this section were reported by teachers of Business English and business-related subjects at Business-English-related post-graduate studies and by the heads of post-graduate studies who needed to solve some of the problems and adjust the teaching and the course content to students' expectations and teachers' capabilities. All the informants claimed that the most difficult and, at the same time, crucial thing about post-graduate teaching was to find balance between satisfying the needs of the two groups of students (corporate workers and English Philology graduates) and they all reported stress due to contradictory students' expectations and demands. This is compatible with the views of Kyriacou (2001) who discovered that student expectations, especially if they are contradictory, trigger teacher stress.

The lack of balance resulted in stress of all teachers and heads of studies, and they all stated that it was the most serious problem in the process of teaching. There were, however, other problems reported and there were some discrepancies visible between the teachers of Business English and teachers of business-related subjects. They are going to be discussed below.

6.2.1   Teaching Problems and Stressors Experienced by Business English Teachers and Teachers of Business-Related Subjects—Differences

The first problem to be discussed is an emotional one which concerns teachers of business-related subjects. Some of the teachers (and especially the so-called business practitioner) reported that they found it extremely stressful to speak English in the presence of English Philology graduates for fear of making mistakes, lacking fluency, bad pronunciation, etc. Those teachers did not have a formal linguistic background, although they had taught in English before and had produced papers in English. This suggests that the problem is rather emotional since it concerns the affective side of teaching and not real, serious lack of linguistic competence. The groups that they had previously taught were students other than English Philology graduates and they reported to have had better language skills than their students. In case of teaching Business-English-related post-graduate students, the situation was just the opposite, especially in the case of English Philology graduates, and the teachers found it problematic.

The teachers with English linguistic background reported other significant problems. First of all, they were aware (and as a result, stressed) that, while teaching Business English, they should teach not only about the language, but explain some business phenomena and give examples—some found it extremely difficult and stressful because of the presence of corporate workers who had a deeper business knowledge and understood some of the discussed phenomena better. Furthermore, Business English teachers reported some terminology problems—a discrepancy between theory and practice concerning some business vocabulary. In conclusion, some problems of Business English teachers were also of affective nature and they were similar to the problems reported by the teachers of business-related subjects; they all were stressed by the confrontation with students who had deeper knowledge and richer background than the teachers. The teachers with linguistic background feared corporate workers and their business expertise, whereas the teachers of business-related subjects feared the linguistic competence of English Philology graduates. We are inclined to think that the problems were emotional and did not show real lack of competence since all of the teachers scored high in student satisfaction questionnaires and students did not report the lack of competence of their teachers. The discrepancies between theory and practice concerning some business vocabulary were really problematic and forced the heads of studies to implement some changes in the way of delivering knowledge to students and in formulating teaching suggestions for teachers.

7   Conclusions and Teaching Implications

As discussed earlier, there were some significant problems reported by all the informants. Some of them resulted from low self-confidence of the investigated teachers, connected with teaching students who may have greater expert knowledge in some areas than the teachers. Those problems were mainly affective and we believe that they can be easily overcome and teacher stress resulting from them can be ameliorated if the teachers understand that they cannot be experts in all fields and, if they appreciate their students' expertise, let them actively participate in the process of teaching. The main problem, however, that is really the dark side of Business English teaching at post-graduate studies is the discrepancy between theory and practice (some vocabulary-related problems) and contradictory expectations of students who have very diversified educational backgrounds. Despite all the problems reported, we believe that the process of teaching can be improved if some practical solutions and coping strategies are implemented.

When it comes to coping strategies and solutions to the reported problems, the strategies proposed below may be applicable not only to post-graduate Business English teaching, but to all courses related to business and Business English teaching since they are universal and revolve around solving problems encountered by many teachers in the field of Business English.

First of all, the heterogeneity of business groups, especially in the context of post-graduate teaching, will always be observed and the key issue is to find balance between contradictory expectations of students and between these expectations and capabilities of teachers. The balance here means selecting an appropriate course content and teaching methods that would be suitable for all students (e.g., a little bit lowering the input for the most advanced students and increasing it for the less advanced ones). It is coherent with the suggestions of Geng (2017) who claimed that Business English teachers should try to constantly adjust and perfect the curriculum in accordance with the changing business environment and students' changing needs. In view of the fact that finding such a balance is very stressful for teachers, they should try to accept the situation and work out some coping strategies—for instance self-observation (Gebhard, 2006) followed by self-reflection (Łuczak, 2012) concerning their teaching that would help them to eliminate course content and activities which are not popular among students and improve their teaching. They should also be open to discussion and interaction with students and not afraid of those more competent ones. They should apply coaching methods of teaching which encourage student–teacher and student–student interaction, and which treat the teacher as a moderator in some teaching situations. This way, the teacher can facilitate some discussions and encourage competent students to share their knowledge with colleagues rather than treat them as competitors because of whom they may lose face.

Teachers of Business English can and, in our opinion, should gain at least basic knowledge in the field of management studies by, for instance, doing research and writing papers in the field; especially in view of the fact that Business English is a comprehensive subject, based on linguistics and absorbing other research methods, and it consists of three main elements: business background knowledge, the language used in business context, and business communication skills (Chuan & Zhu, 2011).

The studies' managers, in turn, should encourage their staff to use modern, activating methods of teaching, implement elements of coaching and case studies into their teaching. By implementing the proposed strategies, not only will the teachers feel better in their professional shoes, but the whole teaching process will improve and the image of studies will be more positive, so all the parties will get an advantage.

References

Chuan, P., & Zhu, W. (2011). Research on the CIPP evaluation model for the construction of the course system of Business English majors. *Chinese Foreign Language, 2*, 69–74.

Clegg, J. W. (2013). *Self-observation in the social sciences.* New Brunswick, USA and London, UK: Transaction Publishers.

Gebhard, J. G. (2006). *Teaching English as a foreign or second language: A teacher self-development and methodology guide.* Michigan, Ann Arbor: The University of Michigan Press.

Geng, Ch. (2017). On the teaching innovation of Business English teaching: A study on multimodal communicative competence of ethnic universities. *Theory and Practice in Language Studies, 7*(4), 322–326.

Gibson, R. (2002). *Intercultural business communication.* Oxford: Oxford University Press.

Konecki, K. (2000). *Studia z metodologii badań jakościowych: Teoria ugruntowana.* Warszawa: PWN.

Krippendorff, K. (2004). *Content analysis. An introduction to its methodology.* New Delhi: Sage Publications.

Kustec, A. (2014). The challenge of teaching Business English. *Letnik, 4,* 3.

Kyriacou, C. (2001). Teacher stress: Directions for future research. *Educational Review, 53*(1), 27–35.

Lang, D. (1990). A blueprint for teacher development. In J. Richards & D. Nunan (Eds.), *Second language teacher education.* Cambridge: Cambridge University Press.

Łuczak, A. (2012). O rozwoju zawodowym lektorów angielskiego języka prawniczego. *Języki Obce w Szkole, 4,* 36–41.

Mihaescu, C. (2013). Current issues in teaching Business English to university students. *Knowledge Horizons, 5*(1), 78–81.

Pérez, L., & Cambra-Fierro, J. (2015). Learning to work in asymmetric relationships: Insights from the computer software industry. *Supply Chain Management: An International Journal, 20*(1), 1–10.

Ringler, M. (1997). Business English. ETNI. Retrieved from www.etni.org/etnirag/issue6/marlene_ringler.htm.

Sadaf, F. (2009). The challenges of teaching Business English to multilingual audiences in Pakistan. In *Annals of Language and Learning, Proceedings of The 2009 International Online Language Conference* (IOLC 2009).

Scrivener, J. (2005). *Learning teaching.* Oxford, UK: Macmillan Education.

Seidel, J. (1998). Qualitative data analysis. *The Ethnograph, 4.* Retrieved from https://qualisresearch.com/.

Tang, Y. (2015). Reflection on Business English teaching and its future trend (published abstract). In *International Symposium on Social Science* (ISSS 2015).

Wieczorek, A., & Mitręga, M. (2017). *Academic teachers under stress in the publish or perish era.* Warszawa: CeDeWu.

Zhu, W. (2010). The context, characteristics and aging analysis of Business English teaching model. *Journal of Guangdong University of Foreign Studies, 7,* 22–27.

Zhu, Z., Lin, L., & Zhu, W. (2016). Research on the education system of Business English courses based on the case of GDUFS. *Higher Education Studies, 6*(2), 30–38.

Anna L. Wieczorek, Ph.D., is Assistant Professor, in the Institute of Modern Languages, at the University of Bielsko-Biala, Poland. She is a multidisciplinary scholar whose main interests revolve around academic teaching, FLT, business and academic productivity. Her doctoral dissertation and core publications concerned the affective aspects of teaching and teacher productivity in the field of foreign languages. She was a team-member of a research grant funded by the Ministry of Science in Poland that delivered comprehensive model of HR productivity in the area of university management in post-communist countries. Member of *PIETE—Partnership for Initial Entrepreneurship Teacher Education* Erasmus+ Project contributing to a new generation of entrepreneurial teachers in Europe. Head of 3 post-graduate studies in the area of Business English and sales management.

Values in the World of Business

Generational Values and Generational Confrontations: Ethical Challenges in the Light of Contemporary Economic and Social Trends

Ewa Wójcik

Abstract In economics, considered to be a moral science, the role of ethics is fundamental. Similarly, in today's business activity it is crucial in meeting the expectation that business activity should not be inimical to stakeholders' interests, in particular the public and employees. Morally right behaviour, which should derive from individual values or regulations, is believed to contribute to good business relations with the environment. The emergence of new models, such as the sharing economy, poses persistent questions of a regulatory nature because the pace of change is unlikely to be matched by slow-moving legislative procedures. According to the logic of the network economy, it is individuals, their personal connections and independent decisions that will shape contacts and relations within businesses which are increasingly less tied to discrete physical spaces and more dependent on staff working from different parts of the globe with varying values. Demographic changes and the altering age make-up of society will mean that different generations make their presence felt in changing proportions. The paper aims at discussing the sources of moral behavior as well as analyzing the background of different generations that shaped their attitudes and may have potential in solving moral dilemmas on corporate grounds.

Keywords Business ethics · Moral values · Demographic challenges · Economic trends · Generations

1 Introduction

Today's economy has witnessed profound changes in individuals' perceptions of ethical values. People are no longer passive recipients of values created and offered by companies, but engaged co-creators. This state of affairs is driven by different factors but technology and innovation seem to play the main part. The emergence of new generations, increasingly dependent on technology, now necessitates changes in

E. Wójcik (✉)
University of Economics, Katowice, Poland
e-mail: ewa.wojcik@ue.katowice.pl

© Springer Nature Switzerland AG 2020
U. Michalik et al. (eds.), *Exploring Business Language and Culture*,
Second Language Learning and Teaching,
https://doi.org/10.1007/978-3-030-58551-8_5

business. At the same time, aging societies need a particular focus to ensure that they are properly integrated into business and social systems. The changing age make-up of societies may require longer working lives and the co-existence of different generations in the workplace.

Globally, much attention is nowadays given to issues of social inclusion as well as the protection of vulnerable groups such as consumers and employees: there is legislation in the areas of basic consumer and employee rights, and codes of ethics exist in certain industries and companies to ensure that moral values are explicitly laid out. However, the issue of business ethics remains a vital one in our era of technological proliferation and with the emergence of new, less regulated business models such as the sharing economy and virtual organisations.

The purpose of the paper is to identify differences in attitudes to ethical issues among co-existing generations and to address the questions of (first) what ethical challenges businesses will have to face as a result of different generational pressures and (second) how businesses can deal with ethical deficiencies.

2   The Place of Ethics in Economics and Business

Ethics is understood as a set of principles relating to morals—that is, to right and wrong behaviour at once guiding and representative of a specific culture, society, group, or individual. Ethical norms are deeply rooted in culture and are mirrored in specific behaviour.

The issue of ethics in economics and business has long been one of the central topics addressed by researchers. Adam Smith in "An Inquiry into the Nature and Causes of the Wealth of Nations" (1776) defines economics as a moral science. His reasoning is based on the assumption that all market participants behave in a manner which will accrue to themselves the highest possible benefits, the sum of such effects benefitting the whole of society.

Economics dealing with human behaviour and its results has a definite social character and its bases are social customs, norms and moral values. This parallel focus on both economic performance and on social ties and morality was reflected in a discussion of human nature which led to the distinction between *homo oeco-nomicus* and *homo sociologicus*. The former term attributed to Smith (1776) and Mill (1848) implies that people make knowledgeable and rational decisions while the latter assumes that decisions are based on different premises such as behavioural factors and the effects of people's value systems and ethical norms.

The concept of *homo oeconomicus* refers to an individual, concentrated on his own good in pursuit of benefits, who contributes to the well-being of the whole of mankind by means of "the invisible hand of a market". *Homo oeconomicus* aims at the highest profit and efficiency. His rational activity consists in using all resources—financial, human and social, as well as his own knowledge, experience and skills—to obtain and process information, and to make reasonable choices for the allocation of scarce resources in the best possible way. Emotional behaviour driven by feelings is rejected in favour of cold, rational choices made to maximize the individual's own utility/satisfaction.

This dominance of rationality in human behaviour is opposed by the notion of *homo sociologicus*, which assumes that individuals are focused on the values and interests of the whole community rather than own wellbeing. Control over one's own resources can be forsaken for the benefit of an integrated community such as a nation or a local community. For *homo sociologicus*, it is the social group which dominates the individual, and evaluations are based on feelings, either positive or negative, and individual perceptions.

Today, the dominant opinion is that individual decisions are based on psychological and behavioural factors because the sheer complexity of tasks, and the increasing amount of information which individuals need to take into account, make rational decision-making challenging if not impossible—so one can only talk of "bounded" ("limited") rationality. This explains the increasing importance of values in human choices.

Such a social approach eschews the notion of external authority and sees moral behaviour as driven by one's absolute inner imperative: the ethical, practical brain. Kant's philosophy defines the categorical imperative as the determination of people's actions by good will itself rather than by the anticipation of outcomes. The categorical imperative derives from the objective rule of, and pure individual respect for, the law that governs the activity. In Kant's view, it is the motive behind the action, not the outcome of the action, that endows an action with moral value. He argues that the motive must arise from universal principles which are discovered by reason.

Thus ethics (deontological ethics) is connected with duty. Kant expresses this duty in the following way: "Act only according to that maxim by which you can at the same time will that it should become a universal law". He distinguished "positive" law—that is, law established and enforced by authorities and binding on individuals whose actions might be considered morally negative (1991, pp. 63–64)—from ethical rules that allow a subject to decide independently how to aim at morally valuable objectives or merits (1991, p. 194).

In today's globalised world, where companies contract work and compete in differing environments and employ people and serve customers from differing backgrounds, ethical values and norms have gained new dimensions. Attempts are made to standardize and give a fixed meaning to ethical behaviour. The International Organisation for Standardization, for example, defines it as "behaviour that is in accordance with accepted principles of right or good conduct in the context of a particular situation and is consistent with international norms of behaviour" (ISO 26000, 2.7), such norms in turn being understood as "expectations of socially responsible organizational behaviour derived from customary international law, generally accepted principles of international law, or intergovernmental agreement that are universally or nearly universally recognized" (ISO 26000, 2.11). The main concerns of the ISO are to ensure that such norms are incorporated into company activity as a response to the notion of Corporate Social Responsibility (CSR).

Economics as a social science focuses on many spheres of individuals' activity but it is business which is given particular attention in this context nowadays. According to this view, economic principles applicable in business practice should reflect scrupulous adherence to moral values, and any manifestation of business activity which might create precarious social conditions or negatively affect disadvantaged groups should be curbed.

An individual as *homo oeconomicus* should make rational decisions—so as a representative of an employer he should strive for maximization of profit, and as a consumer for maximization of utility. As *homo sociologicus*, he should ensure his actions are morally fair and aimed at the benefit of the group and the whole community. Thus, individuals should focus on the observance of ethical values and aim to root out ethically dubious behaviour.

In business activity, one of the areas where ethical values are in play is employer-employee relations. Ties between employees should be understood as an essential element of social capital within a company, which can contribute to meeting its economic goals as well as help establish norms of social responsibility.

All in all, in business activity the notion of "capital" plays a central part. For a business to operate and develop it is necessary to possess five types of capital: human, social, natural, infrastructural, and financial (Szczepański and Śliz, 2006, pp. 7–10). Kane (2001, p. 7) defines capital as "wealth in action" which is invested in order to generate future profits. Thus, moral capital is the moral prestige of people or institutions participating in economic activity.

Capital understood as company assets in this broader sense not only contributes to the development and expansion of business activity but is also reflected in a company's valuation and can, therefore, affect its image and ultimate success. The common trend nowadays is for company market valuations to be much higher than those recorded in company books and accounts. It can be argued that this discrepancy in valuation should be attributed to a company's intangible assets, among which human capital is core.

For Bordieu (1985, p. 248) and Coleman (1990, pp. 300–321), social capital is an important element among the intangible assets of an enterprise and a necessary complement to social networks and norms of reciprocation. Formal and informal norms and values shared by group members constitute a moral network, the value of which depends on members' readiness to give up the individual good for the good of the group. Trust is one of the forms of social capital that can lead to and encourage relationship building. Other elements include loyalty, reciprocation, solidarity, fairness, responsibility, and reliability.

According to Fukuyama (1997, p. 20) obligations, expectations and trust depend on the cultural heritage of a society and as such are independent of rational decisions but strictly connected and interconnected with social capital. Social relations in business are based on human capital and its elements, and social norms are needed for social interaction to take place.

Czapiński (2007, p. 264), who asserts that social capital is the key factor in building economic capital, sees its modern functions as much more far-reaching, i.e., as contributing to social integration and inclusion.

The notion of business responsibility, certain manifestations in the Middle Ages aside, first gained popularity in the 1990s, when it became too obvious that profit maximization by companies is mirrored neither by the profitability of the economy as a whole nor by the prosperity and wellbeing of society. Hence, it was argued, a society burdened with the costs and effects of detrimental company activity, such as environment pollution, should be given something in exchange.

Carroll (1991, pp. 39–48) defined the basic areas of responsibility that companies should take in the form of the Corporate Social Responsibility pyramid, with economic responsibility at the base and philanthropic activities aimed at members of the public at the apex, the intervening levels comprising legal and ethical responsibility. By legal responsibility is meant the observance of legal regulations, contractual obligations and consumer rights. Ethical responsibility involves the avoidance of undesirable behaviour and acting according to the law (the legal and ethical levels therefore being interdependent).

Although for a long time businesses concentrated primarily on generating profits and improving efficiency and economic ratios, at the end of the twentieth century a shift towards moral values was observed. Thus contemporary businesses have other responsibilities apart from meeting economic goals. Moreover, the relative importance of legal and ethical values is changing to the advantage of values rooted in human nature rather than those derivative of legal rules.

Too much regulation might imply that it is the role of regulators to ensure proper behaviour but such a mind-set results in diminished individual drive to assume control and responsibility. Similarly, the assumptions underlying the welfare state, however socially consequential, led to an excessive reliance on government to mitigate the consequences of the economic system of capitalism and the free market economy which, it was believed, inevitably generated differences between social classes, widening the gap between the rich and the poor. The state was expected to perform additional functions in protecting the poor and providing for equal opportunities and wealth distribution; but by taking on such responsibilities the state often exempted people from the duty to make their living from work. Instead, the sense of entitlement increased as did the group of beneficiaries of state welfare. Changed public perceptions of the governments' role resulted in a passive attitude and concentration on obtaining government aid rather than on searching for opportunities for employment. The role of entrepreneurship and resourcefulness diminished and an attitude of entitlement became common.

The obvious spin-off effect of this state of affairs was an ever-increasing pressure on the state to provide subsidies, which in turn inevitably meant an increase in the tax burden on the working population. A lack of motivation among the poor to seek additional or better employment for a higher standard of living, or to make efforts to improve working conditions, changed attitudes to work. Thus, an erosion of work ethics followed (Przybyciński, 2016, p. 32). A multitude of public programs with social security and progressive taxation systems proliferated across Western Europe in the 1960s and 70s (Karbownik, 2009, pp. 118–119, 171). By increasing social spending and assuming accountability for the fates of individuals, states dampened spirits, reduced motivation for self-development, and undermined morale.

Interestingly, too much protection, control and responsibility on the part of the state and its institutions is believed to lead to a poor level of economic education in today's society. Such systems as deposit protection funds are thought to diminish the alertness and care of individuals when choosing financial service providers and to alter perceptions of responsibility. It is commonly believed that it is the imperative of financial institutions and their regulators to guarantee the security of deposits. Case studies of financial scandals in which large numbers of people lost their savings demonstrated their unconcern, lack of care and awareness. It is assumed that poor financial education and confidence in state protection lead people to exonerate themselves from their duty of care as they take it for granted that government bodies will take over individual burdens of control and supervision. If the role of the state, its institutions and regulators is perceived as sufficiently protective, this can overwhelm the individual's sense of reasonable care.

Similarly, excessive regulation and codification of business activity is likely to result in a strong reliance on regulations, bylaws, rules of conduct and external bodies to provide not only protection but all sorts of standards, codes, procedures, templates or ready-to-use solutions. If this is the case, legal rules and regulations will be followed for the sake of compliance with the law rather than out of an inner imperative. Restricted freedom of choice and empowerment may lead to incapability, dependence, and helplessness. The question to be addressed, then, is what choices can be made in new, irregular or non-standard situations which demand innovative solutions.

3   Legal Regulations

There are various reasons why a certain degree of business regulation is required, such as the complex nature of human relations, the global nature of business activity, and the generational needs and expectations to be discussed later in this study. The most important reason, however, would seem to be the existence of vulnerable groups whose interests need to be protected so as to ensure that they are not disadvantaged. According to the ISO's definition, a vulnerable group is "a group of individuals who share one or several characteristics that are the basis of discrimination or adverse social, economic, cultural, political or health circumstances, and that cause them to lack the means to achieve their rights or otherwise enjoy equal opportunities" (ISO 26000, 2.26).

In business, two vulnerable groups should be distinguished: clients and employees. The recent trend towards relaxed employer-employee relations is connected with the fact that there are now fewer life-long jobs as professions disappear, while temporary employment is increasingly common and both job security and company loyalty diminish.

Polish regulations, in particular the Labour Code, constitute a source of law which defines the rights and obligations of the parties to an employment relationship and rules of conduct in cases of infringement. Recent changes in these regulations were intended to improve the situation of employees by ensuring that civil law contracts of mandate and contracts of work, widely referred to as "junk" contracts, are liquidated.

The intended results are improved morale and loyalty, greater security, and a shift in focus away from efficiency by means of reductions in the cost of employment and towards better employment relations.

Other internal regulations imposed by the Labour Code provide detailed prescriptions for the organisation and ordering of work and serve to define the related rights and obligations of the employer as well as employees. According to this regulation organisations employing over fifty employees must in principle adopt a bylaw document called "Work Rules and Regulations".

Statutory regulations, including the Labour Code, are concerned in large part with so-called "hard relationships", which manifest themselves in concrete actions or in failure to act. However, they also include references to ethical standards. For example, Section Four of the Code, which specifies the obligations of employers and employees, includes regulations pertaining to objectivity and fairness in the evaluation and remuneration of employees and so constitutes a basis for shaping ethical behaviour. Internal regulations may function not only to protect the employer against the violation of codified regulations in ethical respects, but also to maximize employee satisfaction, increasing commitment and, consequently, the efficiency of human capital.

Internal regulatory solutions implemented by employers can be wide-ranging in their freedom of scope, depth, and specificity. Depending on the nature and importance of the various factors influencing a good working environment, which may stimulate employee involvement, it is possible to limit or extend the scope of regulations. One of the factors that should be taken into account in the shaping of regulations is generational diversity, which may be expressed in contradictory approaches to work organisation or in differing expectations of employers and fellow employees. In order to facilitate internal integration and adaptation to the environment among members of an organization, a social and organisational culture of corporate activity—that is, a specific set of norms and values shared by all employees that influence their thinking, feeling and behaviour—is required (Schein, 1986, p. 12).

Global organizations and regional blocs also impose regulations or encourage certain business practices which ensure the protection of moral rights of stakeholders such as consumers, shareholders, and employees. Ethical responsibility has been discussed in different forums such as the United Nations (the Goals in the 2030 Agenda for Sustainable Development of the United Nations General Assembly). Directive 2014/95/EU of the European Parliament and of the Council of 22 October 2014, on the disclosure of non-financial and diversity information by certain large undertakings and groups, pointed to the need for increasing transparency of social and environmental information submitted by business entities in all member states. The updated OECD guidelines for multinational enterprises, the International Labour Organization (ILO)'s Three-Party Declaration of Principles for Multinational Enterprises and Social Policy, and the UN's Guiding Principles on Business and Human Rights are all documents with multidimensional guidelines that cover human rights, work and employment practices (e.g., training, diversity, gender equality, health, and wellbeing of employees), environmental issues, supply chains, life-cycle assessment, and the combating of bribery and corruption (European Commission, 2011).

In order to facilitate the implementation of universal principles in business practice, the United Nations Global Compact formulated ten principles based on the Universal Declaration of Human Rights, the International Labour Organization's Declaration on Fundamental Principles and Rights at Work, the Rio Declaration on the Environment and Development, and the United Nations Convention Against Corruption (UN Global Compact, n.d.).

4 A Business Entity as a Moral Subject

A business is a unit responsible *to* the environment (understood as stakeholders) as well as *for* the environment (in a broader meaning, comprising the whole of society and nature). As a moral subject it incorporates a culture derived from the moral standards of the individuals involved in its business processes, i.e., employers and employees.

For the system to be consistent, the cultural and moral values of both parties should be homogenous. For this reason, codes of ethics are issued, including rules and restrictions specific to the firm and its environment and reflecting both the value systems of employees and the organisational culture of the enterprise.

Ethics are concerned with morals, reflect conscious behaviours, and constitute the visible part of the "iceberg" which can be used to illustrate the relationship between *ethics* and *ethos*. *Ethos* (from the Greek word for "character") is used to describe the fundamental values, guiding beliefs or ideals that characterize a person, community, nation, or ideology. The ethos of an organisation thus refers to its subconscious culture, to those values which lie beneath the water-line and which, over time, are the critical determinants of how an organization will in fact behave. It is ethos that is referred to when describing core values and behaviour illustrative of employees' character within organisations.

It has been observed that over the years and with the succession of generations, the prevailing ethos has changed and taken on different forms, moving from a work ethos through a materialism and effectiveness ethos to a more contemporary, participative ethos incorporating eco-awareness.

For the post-World War Two generations, a work ethos was typical: engagement in company activity, company loyalty, and life-long employment were common. Then industrial and technological developments were accompanied by a surge in an effectiveness ethos characterised by greed and egoism and lack of moral scruples. Tasks were assigned to individuals without regard to the overall effects of the company's operations (including moral aspects) resulting in ethical alienation and the diminution of company loyalty among employees. However, devastation of the environment as well as intensified competition later brought about significant changes in attitudes towards and among business stakeholders. Ideas of Corporate Social Responsibility gained ground and eco-awareness became an important component of the business ethos. Contemporary business activity is therefore affected to a high degree by a new approach from consumers who want to participate in creating business offerings.

Moreover, young generations no longer attach so much importance to ownership and are more willing to share possessions. This trend towards a sharing economy is likely to strengthen in the future and is predicted to disrupt business activity in certain sectors.

A business unit as a moral subject should be scrutinised as such. Therefore, identification of areas of deficiencies should be the first step in remedying existing issues. In Poland, such research on the moral condition of business society was carried out by Dylus (2002). It revealed three main areas of deficiency:

1. Relations with competitors, unfair competition.
2. Clients and consumers being misled or cheated by producers/service providers.
3. Employee relations, discrimination, forms of slavery.

Moral deficiencies in companies operating in Poland included strong and constant pressure to increase sales, mobbing, frequent performance of actions which were morally questionable but in compliance with common practices, i.e., the adoption of "borderline" morality under pressure. This kind of ethos was defined as operating "in reverse", adopting behaviours with a view to outperforming competitors and pursuing success at any cost, and following economic principles of efficiency with the lowest possible "input of morality". It often took the form of a specific, distorted business culture or pseudo-culture which was then transformed into a pressure imposed on members of the organization (Dylus, 2002, pp. 273–303). In these circumstances, employees were treated as assets and a means to generate profit rather than as human beings whose ethical behaviour might add value. The fact that they deserved ethical treatment by employers was often ignored. Later research has shown that such practices have not yet been fully supplanted, despite that fact that CSR has been declared as a core value by a huge number of companies.

While a business entity as a moral subject should act ethically from inner imperatives, it is often argued that CSR activity is only undertaken in order to improve profitability—and indeed, research shows that social responsibility is very often treated as merely a way of building a company's image and strengthening its brand. Such motives were indicated by 76% of respondents in research (Menedżerowie 500, 2010). However, an equally important motivator was the need to build better relations with the local community, claimed by 74% of those surveyed.

Yet CSR initiatives seem to remain unnoticed by a vast majority of individuals. An online survey carried out by students of the Business, Finance and Administration Faculty of the University of Economics in Katowice in 2018 revealed that over 90% of respondents claimed not to know of any activities falling within the scope of CSR. The only recognized initiative was WOŚP (Wielka Orkiestra Świątecznej Pomocy), a countrywide charitable event aimed at collecting donations from the public in the streets, at internet auctions and concerts, through crowdfunding etc. in order to subsidize medical equipment for hospitals. This annual event, which takes place every January with the participation of numerous celebrities, gains wide publicity and is covered by the main TV channels.

It is also often claimed that today's increased corporate interest in ethics results from financial considerations as ethics become a less expensive substitute for regulation. For industries in most sectors—apart from those which positively require it—regulation is expected to reduce efficiency because of the expenses and time needed for its implementation.

The turn of the twentieth century saw the emergence of the expectation that business activity should not be inimical to stakeholders' interests or requirements. In this way ethics took on a "utilitarian" character to ensure good business relations with the environment. Attempts were made to organize and structure efforts to incorporate ethical issues into company strategy and operational activity. Over the first decade of the twenty-first century, the debate on the importance of Corporate Social Responsibility intensified, bringing to the public's attention the need to combine considerations of financial performance and market valuation with non-financial, environmental and social issues such as satisfaction of employees, contractors, investors, cooperating institutions, and customers (Wolska, 2013, pp. 45–53). Similarly, the ISO proposed that principles of ethical behaviour should be integrated into companies' core organizational decisions, and ISO 26000 suggests tools for achieving this.

As international guidelines are by their nature expressed in general terms while ethical dilemmas for businesses may be country- or region-specific, it should fall to organizational governance to ensure that leaders practice and promote ethical behaviour, accountability and transparency when operating in their specific environment, on both the micro and macro scales. The micro-environment consists of customers, suppliers, competitors, cooperating firms and the local community, while the macro-environment in this context comprises the natural environment, the national economy, and the whole of society.

In order to embody all national and international laws, accepted business practices and internal and professional standards in a business as a moral entity, the role of compliance officers was established. These were already in existence in heavily regulated industries such as healthcare and financial services but were expanded to other sectors at the turn of the century. The proliferation of Chief Compliance Officer (CCO) appointments in other industries is often attributed to the corporate and accounting scandals in the USA (e.g., the Enron affair).

Compliance officers have a knowledge of general business and industry-specific legal standards as well as their company's mission, goals and culture, which they utilize to set management standards, educate employees, and institute practices that ensure high standards of compliance with the rules. Their role is to ensure that business activity is ethically sound and that legally and corporately compliant behaviours and culture are built around the values of integrity, accountability, transparency, respect, and professionalism. Alongside the ethical aspects of the position there are also pragmatic elements of risk mitigation, avoidance of legal proceedings, and enhancement of company reputation.

5 Demographics and Generations

In the context of business ethics, a prime issue for consideration by business leaders is the significant changes in demography occurring now and in the near future. In 2015, there were 901 million people in the world aged 60 or above, accounting for 12% of the world's population. By 2100, that figure is projected to reach 3.2 billion. Within the European Union, the population of the very old (80 years or older) is projected to double from 5.3% in 2015 to 12.3% in 2080. The number of people aged 65 and above will grow by about 9 million, so that in 2020 every fifth person in the EU will be 65+ and in 2030 they are expected to account for a quarter of the population. This implies that the retirement-age population will be larger than the working-age population in coming decades.

Most importantly for the labour market, the working population (defined as people aged 20–64) is expected to continue to decline up to 2050 as a growing number of people born during the post-war boom reach retirement. The result of these changes will be a shrinking proportion of people of working age within the EU28 and an increasing percentage of people in retirement (Eurostat).

These demographic trends are mirrored in statistics such as the median age of workers, which in 2015 reached record high of 42.3 years (Eurostat). Such shifts in the age make-up of societies necessitate a variety of adjustments, particularly in social policies and social sectors, that will help lengthen working lives and avoid a "brain drain". Lifelong learning and activities within the scope of "edutainment" are areas which must catch up with the increasing demands of the silver economy.

For the labour market, the altering age make-up of society will also mean that different generations make their presence felt in changing proportions. As shown in Table 1, there are five commonly accepted generational labels defined according to year of birth, four of which are currently active on the job market.

Members of each cohort present differing views and behaviours which, as research proves, change over time. The changes are reflected, *inter alia*, in different perceptions and attitudes to moral values.

The presence of different generational cohorts side by side at work can lead to potential conflicts between staff who evince different ethical stances, moral values and tolerance of certain behaviours. Disagreement and lack of common ground

Table 1 The generations defined

Silent	Boomers	Generation X	Millennials	Generation Z
Born				
1928–45	1946–64	1965–80	1981–96	1997–2012
Age in 2019				
74–91	55–73	39–54	23–38	7–22

Source Own considerations based on: https://www.pewresearch.org/fact-tank/2019/01/17/where-millennials-end-and-generation-z-begins/Catalyst, *Quick Take: Generations—Demographic Trends in Population and Workforce* (August 20, 2018)

between generations may contribute to feelings of dissatisfaction among employees, which are evidently undesirable. Intergenerational conflicts were found to have been experienced by 60% of employees (Birkman International, 2019, p. 1). For company decision-makers, an understanding of intergenerational differences and relations is needed in order to be able to face such challenges.

At present the following generations co-exist on the labour market: Baby Boomers, Gen. Xers, Gen Ys (a.k.a. Millennials), and Gen Zs. According to projections from the U.S. Census Bureau (as of July 2016), the number of Generation Y representatives will likely surpass the numbers from previous generations on the labour market in 2019 and this will therefore become the most crucial group of employees. However, Generation Z has also been the focus of much attention of late as its oldest representatives have now reached maturity and started appearing on the labour market. From the perspective of the future of business, it seems, these two generations should attract the most interest.

Intergenerational differences are clear-cut in several ways, such as living and attaining maturity at varying times in history and being shaped by specific historical trends and spectacular events and influences. Another generation-shaping consideration is technological development, which defines the ways in which people communicate and interact. The key formative experiences which have helped shape the views of the various generations—world events and technological, economic and social shifts—are shown in Table 2.

Baby Boomers were raised by parents who lived through the Depression and World War Two, and these two experiences are mirrored in their thrift and hard work. They are more likely to refer to managers, follow management on ethical matters and follow ethics and compliance programs included in formal systems, more aware of corporate standards of accountability, and more responsive to signals from people in formal positions or in power. On the one hand they seem to pose less risk based on their innate characteristics but on the other hand they may, according to the National Business Ethics Survey in the U.S., make employers vulnerable to unethical conduct (Ethics Survey, 2013).

Generation X is often referred to as the link between Baby Boomers and Millennials, while Millennials themselves grew up in a period of unification in Europe, absence of military and ideological conflicts, borders or regional divisions, and hyper-intensive processes of integration. It is the first generation to disregard political divisions between countries or blocs and to have full, unrestricted access to common territories within the EU.

On the other hand, they share the experience of fear of terrorist attacks. They watched their parents build up capital and purchase goods to catch up with the rest of developed world. They mostly grew up in healthy economic times but are now poorer than their parents, possibly as a result of fewer working hours, more flexible schedules, or more prioritization of work/life balance. They came of age during a time of recession and their entrance to the workforce and the experience of earning a living was marked by a "slow start". Recollections of crises in which assets were lost and parents faced job losses affect their attitude to possessions.

Table 2 Formative experiences

Generation	Baby Boomers	Gen Xers	Millennials (Gen Yers)	Gen Zers
Defining events	Boom in post-war birth rate Space exploration	Fall of Berlin Wall Transformation of Central Europe	9/11 attacks Housing bubble collapse Recession of 2007 Internet expansion	Great recession (the oldest were 11 in 2008) Mobile internet and systems Social networks
Formative experiences	Western social values Idealism Environmental issues	Post-Boomers' recession, layoffs, saw parents fired after dedicating lives to company MTV HIV/AIDS	Globalisation Uncertain economic future Business agility	On-demand entertainment, communication Grew up learning how to be frugal
Technology/communi-cation and interaction	Television expansion changed lifestyle	Personal computers, computer revolution	Internet explosion, Google, Facebook, Twitter Video games	All inventions of previous generations from birth Facebook (broadly used after 2008) iPhone (first used in 2007) Mobile devices Wi-Fi High-bandwidth cellular services Social media

(continued)

Table 2 (continued)

Generation	Baby Boomers	Gen Xers	Millennials (Gen Yers)	Gen Zers
Characteristics	"Work to live" philosophy Redefinition of retirement Conservative Dedicated Experienced Knowledgeable Workaholics Desire quality Work efficiently Idealistic Competitive Consumerist	Tech-literate Focused on balance Flexi-time Telecommuting Job-sharing Collaborative Adaptable Structure and direction needed Sceptical Diverse Entrepreneurial Challenging Self-reliant Status-oriented	Tech-savvy Loyal to brands Smart Easily bored Short-term focus Individualistic Need constant variety of stimulation, feedback, guidance, challenge Tolerant Multitasking Goal-oriented Globally concerned Health conscious Adventurous Tenacious Environmentalist * "trophy generation", self- and experience-oriented, "me generation"	"Undefined" Radically "inclusive" Pragmatic Access instead of ownership Realistic and mindful of financial issues and future career Consumption as an expression of individual identity, a matter of ethical concern, Connected to interests and cultures around the world More about showing off their individuality
Communication and interaction	Written Formal Phone Personal interaction	Voicemail Email Direct Immediate Team player Love meetings Entrepreneurial	Text messages Blogs Emails Participative	True digital natives Communicate through social media and texts Constant connectivity

Source Own considerations based on: https://www.businessinsider.com/gen-zs-habits-different-from-millennials-2018-6?IR=T, https://www.mckinsey.com/industries/consumer-packaged-goods/our-insights/true-gen-generation-z-and-its-implications-for-companies

Millennials seem to observe fewer boundaries than previous generations and are more flexible about ignoring them and more likely to engage in or tolerate incorrect behaviour. They may question authority and demand meaningful work, challenges and a steep learning curve. They readily utilize the resources of ethics and compliance offices and respond to the elements of ethics and compliance programs that include social interaction and provision of support such as helplines, training, and mechanisms for seeking advice.

It should be stressed that, in the context of employment relations, Millennials are the first generation expected to operate in a multicultural work environment which is more internationally connected by proliferating technologies, and the first generation to coexist with older ones in the workplace for a longer period of time. Cross-cultural differences in a world of intensified migration call for greater understanding and tolerance.

Generation Z is the least thoroughly examined but researchers have already noted certain formative factors reflected in their characteristics, which are listed in Table 3.

Each generation seems to be more racially and ethnically diverse than its predecessor. Members of the same generation across the world are found to share most features but there are certain differences, and one area which can be most affected by such diversity is communication. According to Hall's Concept of Context, which defines the amount of shared versus transmitted information, cultures can be referred to as "low-context" or "high-context". In low-context cultures communication typically needs to be explicit, direct, formal and often written, while in high-context cultures it tends to be more indirect, informal and symbolic.

Table 3 Generation Z: characteristics and formative factors

• Oldest now turning 22, most still in their teens or younger
• 1996 a meaningful cut-off date between Gen Z and the previous generation in light of political, economic and social factors
• In recent years have taken hold in popular culture and journalism
• More diverse racially and ethnically than any other generation
• Growing up in an "always on" technological environment
• Shifts in youth behaviours, attitudes and lifestyles—both positive and concerning
• The first generation of true digital natives, with an unprecedented degree of connectivity
• Generational shifts and technological trends accelerated
• Search for "truth at the centre" is characteristic of behaviour and consumption patterns
• Around 70% of teens are self-employed, e.g., teaching piano, making money from a YouTube channel, or other creative ways of making money

Source Own considerations based on: Harvard Business Review, https://www.mckinsey.com/industries/consumer-packaged-goods/our-insights/true-gen-generation-z-and-its-implications-for-companies

In 1991, Hofstede, referring to Hall's Concept, concluded that individualism is very often connected to low-context cultures while low individualism (collectivism) is connected to high-context cultures. Lower-context cultures are typical for the USA (excluding the Southern States), Canada, Australia, England, Germany, Scandinavia, and Switzerland. Higher-context cultures prevail in Africa, Arab countries, Brazil, China, France, Greece, Hungary, Italy, Japan, Korea, Latin America, Spain, Portugal, Turkey, and Russia. Interestingly, Poland as a part of Central-Eastern Europe geographically, is located in between high- and low-context cultures.

In the era of globalized work and employment, conditions are likely to be heavily influenced by the unavoidable co-existence of representatives of different cultures, high- and low-context. It seems then that a challenge for businesses may lie in the need to mitigate potential misunderstanding and conflict in the course of communication between representatives of these differing cultural types.

6   New Models

Widespread trends in today's economy which impinge particularly on the role of the individual are liberalisation, the emergence of new business models, and changes in organisations from authoritarian pyramid structures to more dispersed structures in which employees seek autonomy, creativity and empowerment. The emergence of such new models is likely to pose persistent questions of a regulatory nature. In the sharing economy, vulnerable groups are not protected by law, and the pace of change is unlikely to be matched by slow-moving legislative procedures.

According to the logic of the network economy—an economy profoundly and to the highest degree ever based on human ties—it is individuals, their personal connections and independent decisions that will shape contacts and relations within businesses which are increasingly less tied to discrete physical spaces and more dependent on staff working from different parts of the globe. Therefore, cross-cultural analyses of values may make a helpful contribution to the understanding of different attitudes.

According to Castells, the network society is characterized by a breakdown in "rhythms" incorporated in the concept of the life cycle. Organisational and technological developments and cultural events typical of this newly emerging society undermine this ordered lifecycle but without offering any alternative. Castells claims that contemporary societies are organised around two opposing poles: the "Net" and the "Self" (1996). The former term refers to network organisations which have largely replaced vertically integrated hierarchies while the latter denotes the social identity of the individual in a constantly changing cultural environment.

7 Conclusion

Changes in the macro-environment, such as demographic transition or technological shifts as well as micro-environmental behavioural factors are affecting the global economy to a wide extent. Ethical issues, intangible, complex and difficult to standardize need to be given particular attention in the era of global business operating in different parts of the globe where attitude to values that derive from human nature can be diverse.

Since the trend of glocalization does not seem to be specifically considered in the capacity of human values, they are understood rather as universal ones, uniform and applicable all over the world in the same way.

However, ethical dilemmas and business solutions may be country- or region-specific. Individuals from different cultural backgrounds and belonging to different generations have certain features which determine not only their behavior, but also perception of ethical values. Cross-cultural analyses of values is needed to address the difference in attitudes typical for more individualist cultures, like the American one, and collectivist societies, or such as the Polish one which, according to researchers, is on the borderline between the two.

On top of that, further development of contemporary network economy together with social changes intensified by societal diversity, imply that cross-cultural issues will be gaining importance in business and the economy as a whole.

Today's global economy is bringing about new challenges and demands that the ethics of business activity are considered on an additional, multinational level.

New generations who are just about to assume control of the labour market will need to be given far more attention by employers and decision-makers. Their moral values are likely to shape future business to a much greater degree than hitherto, while legal systems may prove increasingly ineffective in the face of emerging challenges. Young generations, such as Z and Y, whose representatives are likely to predominate on the labour market very soon, with their specific stance and behavior seem likely to clash with the older ones. Conflicts, however detrimental, are unavoidable and they can multiply with much longer working lives expected and ageing societies. The only solution to mitigate such risks in business will be to recognise the specific features of all generations and understand that only their proper handling and utilization can bring potential to achieve synergy effect.

The importance of aspects of human behavior should not be underestimated by HR specialists, marketers, managers, business analysts and decision makers. Apart from ensuring legal framework to comply with, understanding of the specific features or requirements of the human component is indispensable for businesses to be successful and for the economy to grow in a sustainable way.

The contemporary trends imply that people are more prone to operate according to the rules of "social contract/agreement", ie acceptance of implicit norms rather than those worded explicitly in acts and other regulations. New generations' focus on self-driven solutions and more participative models is an evident reflection of their changing attitude to trust which is one of the most central ethical values.

The fiduciary role of the state and its institutions of public trust, such as banks with a social license to represent and protect the interests of the individual, is evolving and trust is shifting towards peer-to-peer model where the intermediary is eliminated. Instead of having confidence in institutions and activity protected and guaranteed by regulators, people are inclined to refer to own or peers' solutions. The new business models developing "from bottom up" prove that the role of individuals is unprecedented. The main principles on which such firms operate are peer-to-peer trust and lack of regulation or protection by law. This, in turn, signifies that regulatory environment may cease to have a dominant role in contemporary consumers' perceptions and evaluations, while decision-making process is likely to be reliant more on individual ethical values. The changing role of, and attitude to trust, may intensify the need to apply and encourage practices that society approves and expects businesses to comply with in order to protect the moral rights of stakeholders, such as consumers, shareholders and employees.

The dominance of new generations and changing position of different stakeholders necessitate comprehensive approach in the areas of behavioural factors. Therefore, a vast range of issues covering aspects of behavioral economics as well as interdependent and interconnected ethical, social responsibility and sustainability issues should be addressed in further research. The potential of individuals should be utilized and threats realized in order to be converted into benefits.

References

Birkman International. 2019. *How do generational differences impact organizations and teams?* Part 1, p. 1. Retrieved January 24, 2019 from https://brandmanvirtualteam1.weebly.com/uploads/7/5/8/7/7587559/generational_differences_article_706.pdf.

Bordieu, P. (1985). *The forms of capital.* In J. G. Richardson (Ed.), *Handbook of theory and research for the sociology of education* (pp. 241–258). New York: Greenwood.

Business Insider. 2019. Retrieved January 21, 2019 from https://www.businessinsider.com/gen-zs-habits-different-from-millennials-2018-6?IR=T.

Carroll, A. B. (1991). The pyramid of corporate social responsibility: Toward the moral management of organizational stakeholders. *Business Horizons, 34,* 39–48.

Castells, M. (1996). *The rise of the network society, the information age: Economy, society and culture* (Vol. I). Oxford: Blackwell.

Catalyst. (2018). *Quick take: Generations: Demographic trends in population and workforce.* Retrieved from https://www.catalyst.org/research/generations-demographic-trends-in-population-and-workforce/.

Coleman, J. S. (1990). *Foundations of social theory.* Massachusetts & London, England: The Belknap Press of Harvard University Press Cambridge.

Czapiński, J. (2007). *Kapitał społeczny.* In J. Czapiński & T. Panek (Eds.), *Diagnoza społeczna 2007. Warunki i jakość życia Polaków.* Rada Monitoringu Społecznego, Warszawa.

European Commission. (2011). *A renewed EU strategy 2011–14 for corporate social responsibility.* Retrieved from https://www.europarl.europa.eu/meetdocs/2009_2014/documents/com/com_com(2011)0681_/com_com(2011)0681_en.pdf.

Dylus, A. (2002). *Erozja standardów etycznych w biznesie.* In J. Mariański (Ed.), *Kondycja moralna społeczeństwa polskiego.* Kraków: WAM.

Ethics org. (2013). *Ethics and Compliance Initiative*. Retrieved January 25, 2019 from https://www.ethics.org/ecihome/research/nbes/nbes-reports/nbes-2013.

Eurostat. *Population structure and ageing*. Retrieved from https://ec.europa.eu/eurostat/statistics-explained/index.php/Population_structure_and_aging.

Francis, T., & Hoefel, F. (2018). *'True gen' Generation Z and its implications for companies*. Retrieved from https://www.mckinsey.com/industries/consumer-packaged-goods/our-insights/true-gen-generation-z-and-its-implications-for-companies.

Fukuyama, F. (1997). *Zaufanie. Kapitał społeczny a droga do dobrobytu*. Warszawa: PWN.

Hall, A. (1976). *Beyond culture*. New York: Anchor Books.

Institute of Business Ethics. *National business ethics survey 2013*. Retrieved January 21, 2019, from https://www.ibe.org.uk/userassets/survey%20summaries/nbes2013ibesummary.pdf.

ISO org. Retrieved January 21, 2019, from https://www.iso.org/iso-26000-social-responsibility.html.

Kane, J. (2001). *The politics of moral capital*. New York: Cambridge University Press.

Kant, I. (1991). *Metaphysics of morals*. New York, Melbourne: Cambridge University Press.

Karbownik, B. (2009). Analiza wydatków sektora finansów publicznych w krajach Unii Europejskiej. In D. K. Rosati (Ed.), *Europejski model społeczny. Doświadczenia i przyszłość*. Warszawa: PWE.

Mill, J. S. (1848). In W. J. Ashley (Ed.), *Principles of political economy with some of their applications to social philosophy*. Retrieved from https://oll.libertyfund.org/titles/mill-principles-of-political-economy-ashley-ed.

Pew Research Centre. (2019). Retrieved January 25, 2019 from https://www.pewresearch.org/fact-tank/2019/01/17/where-millennials-end-and-generation-z-begins.

Przybyciński, T. (2016). *Etyczne i ekonomiczne aspekty państwa dobrobytu*. In *Etyka w życiu gospodarczym*. Annales (Vol. 19, No. 3, p. 32). Łódź: Wydawnictwo Uniwersytetu Łódzkiego.

Raport Menedżerowie 500. (2010). Retrieved February 2, 2019 from https://odpowiedzialnybiznes.pl/wpcontent/uploads/2014/03/Raport_Menedzerowie500_LiderCSR_2010.pdf.

Schein, E. (1986). How culture forms, develops and changes. In R. Kilmann, M. Saxton, & R. J. Serpa (Eds.), *Gaining control of the corporate culture*. San Francisco: Bass Publishers.

Smith, A. (1776). *An inquiry into the nature and causes of the wealth of nations* (1st ed.). Retrieved from https://www.ibiblio.org/ml/libri/s/SmithA_WealthNations_p.pdf.

Szczepański, M. S., & Śliz, A. (2006). W kręgu kapitałów. In M. S. Szczepański & A. Śliz (Eds.), *Kapitały: ludzie i instytucje*. Studia i szkice socjologiczne, Tychy-Opole.

United Nations Global Compact. (2019). Retrieved January 25, 2019 from https://www.unglobalcompact.org/what-is-gc/mission/principles.

Wolska, G. (2013). Corporate social responsibility in Poland: Theory and practice. *Journal of International Studies, 6*(2), 45–53.

Ewa Wójcik, Ph.D., is a senior lecturer at the University of Economics in Katowice with research interests in the field of banking, marketing, micro and macroeconomics, business ethics, writing widely on savings market, competition in financial services market, value co-creation, consumer behaviour, business ethics and sustainability issues. She authors numerous scientific publications and co-authors numerous textbooks for learning English for students of economics, banking, finance. As a "reviewer of draft material" she cooperated with Pearson as well as the publishers of the IGI Global, an international academic publisher, and Journal of Sustainable Development (Integrated Business Faculty and Integrated Business Institute) Skopje, Macedonia reviewing papers submitted by authors and writing chapters for publication.

She participates in international conferences and international mobility programs giving lectures and running workshops in English at different academic institutions, e.g., the University of Technology in Gliwice, the University of Florence, Vilniaus Kolegija in Vilnus, Integrated Business Faculty in Skopje, Macedonia, University of Maribor in Slovenia, University in Asuncion in Paraguay, University of La Coruna in Spain.

An author of postgraduate programs of ESF and studies in the field of International Business of the Norwegian Funds and a lecturer, she was awarded many times for the achievements of students of the courses of the London Chamber of Commerce and Industry.

National Responsibility: The Missing Element of Business Ethics

David Cole and Petra Strnádová

Abstract In this paper we discuss the interaction of social responsibilities between the individual, state, and corporate level in the new global and digital era. It is built on the traditional shareholder and stakeholder models which are rather complementary than opposite, and is enhanced by Carroll's notion of "good corporate citizenship". The main concerns of the research, geographically based in the region of Central Europe (CEE), include the relationship of the local national governments to the western investors, particularly their generally low demands in return for often too generous incentives; the new trends in young generation's preferences and attitudes to less and less affordable housing within the corporate context; and the lack of the corporations' response to the exponential threat of negative externalities occurring as a result of dopamine-related digital and food products' abuse. The standard concept of CSR is thus further developed, with special attention to the key notion of responsibility on the part of different stakeholders and their mutual impact in the CEE region.

Keywords Corporate social responsibility · Stakeholder model · Business ethics · Nation · Digital economy

1 Introduction

Much has been written about the obligation of the corporations to think about the needs of both their employees and the community in which a company resides. It is almost a cliché that a company's impact on society and its employees does not end at the entrance gate. First and foremost, companies are profit-making entities with the express intent of creating wealth for the investors. It would be overly simplistic to

D. Cole (✉) · P. Strnádová
Department of Foreign Languages, Faculty of Economics, Matej Bel University, Banská Bystrica, Slovakia
e-mail: david.cole@umb.sk

P. Strnádová
e-mail: petra.strnadova@umb.sk

© Springer Nature Switzerland AG 2020
U. Michalik et al. (eds.), *Exploring Business Language and Culture*,
Second Language Learning and Teaching,
https://doi.org/10.1007/978-3-030-58551-8_6

state that the investors are so hell-bent on profit with untold riches being their main motivation. Few would want to be seen as the evil villains. Every person creates a "book-of-the-self" that can be seen as an epitaph for remembrance and this is also true of the corporate leader. As such, the leader would want to leave a legacy of being a good citizen in society. This greed vs. social standing forms the basis of the well-known diametrically opposed shareholder/stakeholder models. These two fundamental models are, however, largely a reaction to the state and its influence on corporate decisions. They overlook the fundamental basis for societal organization—a national identity. Even global companies are part and parcel to the nation upon which they find themselves in. Because of this, it is felt that a more holistic approach needs to be taken that goes beyond the immediate stakeholders.

In our paper, we have looked into how companies are dealing with positive and negative externalities of production. To borrow an analogy from quantum physics, corporate social responsibility (CSR) is local and global at the same time, depending on the viewpoint of the observer. Economists have long touted the benefits of globalization and to be fair, they are all around us, especially in terms of availability of consumer goods.

CSR can also be judged on a smaller individual level as society is a collective made up of individuals. Responsibility for the collective and the individual must be shared. Without a doubt, the new digital economy is affecting behaviour at this personal level as each year more of the economy is devoted to what can only be considered as excess and over-indulgence.

2 The Role of the State in CSR

The concepts of CSR have varied over the years, but it can be said that there are two poles representing two different thoughts. The first idea is that power belongs to the entrepreneur and owners of a company, with e.g., Friedman (1962) as its distinctive representative. On the second pole there is the concept that all actors involved in a corporation need to be considered and treated respectfully, as suggested by e.g., Freeman (1984). At the same time, governments have been both hands-on and hands-off in dealing with corporations. Throughout their history, the thought-pendulum has swung from one extreme to the other. This bi-polar view of the corporation as friend and foe was best summed up by a well-known Winston Churchill's observation presented in one of his 1950s speeches: "Some people regard private enterprise as a predatory tiger to be shot. Others look on it as a cow they can milk. Not enough people see it as a healthy horse, pulling a sturdy wagon".

Global competition cannot be viewed as a zero-sum game where, if someone wins, another person must lose. After all, the GDP of the world is ever growing. In the global context, though, not everyone can be a winner as there will be local jobs that are lost forever. The advantage of globalization is that it can raise living standards in developing countries by providing higher standard manufacturing jobs. Some types of work are no longer preferred in more developed countries, so the work is outsourced to countries where there is a desire for these occupations, e.g., textile, clothing, and shoes production. Offshoring certain skill sets to new countries allows for the development of higher-level skills in old countries, allowing them to move up to a higher level of value-added production.

There are, however, disadvantages within the global context. International companies move their operations to countries with low pay and lay off people in the higher paying countries. When offshoring certain occupations, the standards of worker safety and benefits are lowered, even when different standards of living are taken into consideration. As certain jobs are no longer performed in the country, these skills, especially in areas like research and development, are lost for good. Many have accused international corporations of starting a race to the bottom for the lowest production price and eventual lower living standards.

Currently, it can be said that CSR is an attempt to find a middle ground between extremes and this should be regarded in a new global context. For a modern version of CSR to be successful, it needs to consider the greatest possible good affecting the greatest possible number of people.

Carroll (1991) saw that CSR embraced four kinds of responsibilities: economic, legal, ethical, and philanthropic. For the conscientious businessperson, CSR must firstly be about making money. Profit, however, must be gained through legal means, thus obeying the law is paramount. Not all rules in society are specifically set out in law, thus ethical decisions that go beyond the law need to be considered. Lastly and dependent upon the success of the corporation, the final element is being a good corporate citizen and giving back to society. As a result, he envisioned CSR as a pyramid consisting of four levels, from bottom to top: (1) make a profit; (2) obey the law; (3) be ethical; and (4) be a good citizen (1991, pp. 39–48).

This pyramid should not be viewed with fixed layers or proportions. Obviously, some companies have more power to change the world for the better. Few people would argue that a chocolate company, a supplier of an indulgence, could be held to the same standard as Google with the ability to fundamentally change the world. The above pyramid also assumes that the laws are adequate. A simple way to put it is that CSR is not about how a company spends its money; it is about how a company makes its money.

3   CSR: The Interactions

Economics is a science that has long been divided into two competing philosophies that could be described as an individualist approach and a collectivist approach. The term that is most commonly used is the shareholder and stakeholder model. The shareholder model holds that the only social responsibility that a corporation has is to make a profit. The stakeholder model believes that long-term survival of a corporation depends on the satisfaction of other people or groups that have a legitimate interest in the company. In terms of the above pyramid, it could be said that the shareholder model forms the foundation while the stakeholder model, the top.

3.1   CSR: The Interaction of the Corporation and Society

Nobel Prize winner Milton Friedman (as cited in Wartick & Cochran, 1985) addressed the needs of the corporation by arguing that the corporation has only one social responsibility and that is to satisfy their owners, the shareholders. He went as far as to say that it was socially irresponsible for the corporation to divert time, money, and attention away from maximizing profits for social or charitable causes. Friedman believed that if a company spends money on social causes, they will have less money for quality materials or hiring talented workers, customers would find these products less desirable and choose a competitor. As such, spending money on social causes hurts all stakeholders. Friedman claimed that the corporation could not be asked to solve societal problems, as this was something best left for governments and their representatives by making appropriate laws.

The stakeholder theory attempts to address the morals and values in management by the identification of the interests of all groups that are necessary for the success of the company. The idea originated from Freeman (1984)[1] who believed it was necessary to find out which groups and what actions are really important in the success of an organization. The model is based on the idea that the company exists to serve the many stakeholders who have an interest in it or who, in some way, may be harmed or benefitted by it. These groups include employees, customers, suppliers, financiers, communities, governmental bodies, political groups, trade unions, and sometimes even the competitors.

There are some disagreements about who is considered a stakeholder, but we can generally divide them into two groups: primary and secondary stakeholders. The primary stakeholders are those whose participation is critical for the company's success (employees, shareholders, customers). Secondary stakeholders are those who are affected by the company (suppliers, government, even competitors). Apart from this general definition, stakeholders need to possess three characteristics: (1) legitimacy, i.e., having a legal claim to the company's activity; (2) power, i.e., having the ability to influence the company's decision-making process; (3) urgency, i.e., the ability to command attention from management (Mitchell, Bradley, & Wood, 1997).

Freeman (1984) suggests that a core competence of a manager is figuring out how the interests of the different stakeholders go in the same direction. The key question is finding out how each group is important to the business. It is all of the individual stakeholders that create a product together and it is something that not one of them can create alone. Therefore, it is important that each stakeholder group does not become totally self-interested.

According to Carroll's pyramid, the long-term existence of a corporation is dependent on the relevant stakeholders, who must receive some benefits from the top

---

[1] It is not much known, however, that the concept was originally developed by Ian Mitroff in his book "Stakeholders of the Organizational Mind", published in 1983. In R. E. Freeman's article on Stakeholder theory that appeared in the California Management Review in early 1983, there is no reference to Mitroff's work; Freeman claimed that the concept was the product of an internal discussion in the Stanford Research Institute.

echelon of the pyramid, both spiritually and economically. Very few companies manage to pass the test of time and fewer still have remained champions in their field: Ford, General Electric, Pfizer, Proctor and Gamble are just a few examples of companies that have managed to survive for over 100 years.

3.2 CSR: The Interaction of the Corporation and the State

The Central Europe region has become the "go to" region of Europe for new production facilities and this has provided opportunities for observation in negotiations of operational conditions. As a result of our previous research (Theodoulides, Kormancová, & Cole, 2019), we believe an ethics pyramid could be created based on three legs: transparency, accountability, and universality. Transparency refers to visibility or accessibility of information concerning business practices. Accountability is an obligation or willingness to take responsibility and to disclose results of an action in a transparent manner. Universality is the application of a rule to all and is based on Kant's (1993, 3rd Eng. Ed.) principle of *similarly situated persons*. The last leg of this triangle is sometimes being compromised in order to attract a large corporation to the community, i.e., the Kantian rule is not being applied evenly.

Some companies are able to negotiate favourable terms for their entry into the country. This includes tax holidays, loans, and infrastructure improvement. Other companies have complained that the tax holidays give the competition an unfair advantage. Part of this competition is for the limited talent in a country's labour force where the company with a tax benefit has an advantage over the other. This is especially true in manufacturing where many blue-collar workers can work across a wide range of jobs.

Infrastructure, especially in the form of highways, is a large factor that is indirectly violating the notion of universality among players. According to Camagni (2002), transport infrastructure is the competitive advantage that many businesses look for when deciding on where to invest. Cushman & Wakefield 20th Annual European Cities Monitor (2009) found that international links and connections to other major economic centres are the third most important criterion for determining the location of investment. The CEE region is considerably behind Western European nations in terms of highway construction.

Spatial evidence of regional inequality of infrastructure can be found in roadway construction, specifically 4-lane highways. This basic necessity for prosperity and the lack of balance can be seen in Fig. 1.

From the map of completed roadways above, it can be seen that the level of development in the Germanic countries (Germany, Austria, Switzerland) is much greater than in the so called Visegrad nations.[2] It can also be seen that the extreme

---

[2]Visegrad group, or V4, is a cultural and political alliance of four Central European countries—the Czech Republic, Hungary, Poland, and Slovakia.

Fig. 1 Completed 1st class highways for Germanic countries compared to Visegrad nations as of 7.2016. *Source* Own creation using available highway data

Eastern regions of the Visegrad countries have even less connection to the inter-European grid—a huge visual sign to the lesser status of the region. Moreover, with tension in Russia, Belarus, Ukraine, and Moldova, we believe that the economic push to the east has slowed considerably, adding to the negative expectation. In Slovakia, there is still no major highway connecting the two largest cities: the capital Bratislava in the west and Košice in the east. In 2018, not even a single kilometre of highways was built here. Even more abhorrent is the lack of north-south links, such as between Budapest and Warsaw.

The corporate need for infrastructure and the governments' ability to provide it are unwittingly creating regional winners and losers. A study by the German Federal Institute for Research on Building, Urban Affairs, and Spatial Development paints a very clear and disturbing picture, at least for Europe (2013):

- city regions are growing, in Central and Eastern Europe as well;
- half of Europeans live in shrinking regions;
- shrinking regions exist in nearly all countries.

The result is an expectation of further imbalances between the growing and shrinking areas. As infrastructural investment is seen as a duty of the government, corporations are not seen as being responsible, yet this is dodging the responsibility of causation, especially if the corporation is a recipient of a tax holiday or a government loan. By not building highways, the state is indirectly disadvantaging some regions. If tax and financial incentives are to be used by the government to entice business, it logically should be used to reduce regional disparities. As for highways, this should be a high priority from the EU. After all, highways do not stop at a country's border.

4   CSR: What It Means to a Company and the Individuals Within the Company

From our abovementioned research we have found in CEE region, the companies fully understand the optics of CSR, especially in terms of stakeholder support. Many of them do have initiatives designed to promote the company as being a good corporate citizen. As such, we find the companies of the CEE region to be fully in line with the concept of stakeholder CSR. This is rather unsurprising as, during socialism, the companies held a high social role in the community. Most of those we interviewed feel a deep connection with the local community and they are careful to nurture the image of positivity. Corporate leaders fully understand the need to have an image of benevolence.

The digital era has added a new layer of complexity to the notion of universality in terms of competition and also regional stability. It is assumed that all firms must keep reinventing themselves in order to stay relevant. Not doing so means that today's corporate leaders can become yesterday's horse and carriage in a heartbeat. This is a well-known Schumpeter's gale (2003), or a notion of creative destruction, i.e., the process of innovation where new products (and firms) replace old, outdated ones. It is considered standard dogma as the corporation and its competitors are seen to have the same universal rules and privileges.

New research from the OECD (Andrews, Cruscuolo, & Gal, 2015) suggests that Schumpeter's model is breaking down as frontier firms are growing much faster than the laggard firms. They define the frontier firms as companies in the top 5% of their industry, with laggards being the remaining 95%. They found that frontier firms tend to be global and part of a multinational group, and use other global frontier firms to provide the benchmark. What this means is that the gap between a frontier firm and other frontier firms in other nations is shrinking, while the gap between a frontier firm and a laggard within a nation is growing. The established notion that a market challenger may one day up-seat the market leader becomes questionable. This is especially true in services. The use of digital innovations of the frontier firms can lead to an incredibly fast scaling-up of networks and lowering of marginal cost, which means that the competition is overwhelmed with little time or resource to react. The productivity gains made by these firms stay at the frontier and do not trickle down to the rest of the economy. In the global context, a country can have a competitive leader that can take on the world. On the other hand, the countryside will be littered with national laggard firms that have no place in this modern utopia.

There is little consensus as to what should be done about this. Should governments support the laggards or should frontier companies give away their trade secrets? One thing is quite evident: the losers are crying foul at the voter box. From Europe, England, and the United States, marginalized people are voting for a dose of anarchy in hopes of shaking up the established order. There is also much disagreement as to why to engage in a protest vote other than a desire to get back at the leaders that are not listening to them. Corporate leaders in frontier firms are playing by the rules of the game defined by society, but are still creating the conditions where many are not benefitting, and this is very often geographically proximate, i.e., some areas grow stronger while others continue to decline.

4.1 CSR: Between the Corporation and the Individual

Classical economic theory suggests that man seeks to maximize his utility while a firm seeks to maximize its profit. What has been forgotten is that the above needs are as much rooted in the past (historical institutions, the national trait) as for future aspirations (modernity). This suggests that corporations must also consider other, more humanistic needs. Individuals strive to complete their 'life story' by choosing options that will leave them with a respectable legacy. All individuals in society are looking to find the best alternative for themselves and this desire can be expressed in terms of both material attainment and societal status.

The single largest purchase in an individual's life is a house, and, for the CEE region, homeownership is of high importance (over 90% in most CEE countries). According to the 'State of Housing in the EU' by the EU Urban Agenda Housing Partnership (Pittini, Koessi, Dijol, Lakatos, & Ghekiere, 2017), housing has become a problem due to the following:

- Buying a house is the highest expenditure for Europeans and remains stable at high level, hitting the poor disproportionly harder,
- House prices are growing faster than income in most Member States, while inequality and housing exclusion are mutually reinforcing,
- Territorial divide is alarming, as finding adequate and affordable housing in places with job opportunities is increasingly hard,
- As the level of housing construction is still low, especially major cities face a structural housing shortage,
- Political response to Europe's housing challenge remains poor.

For many of the larger firms, the importance of infrastructure exacerbates this problem. For management and corporate leaders, the decision to move to where housing is not readily available becomes ethically questionable, especially when a corporation seeks government funding. Even if a company is compensating their own employees fairly for a high-priced region, a knock-on effect can cause negative externalities for other firms.

In our on-going research conducted with EF UMB students since 2011, we have been able to define the expectations of work among the newer generation with over 1000 respondents so far. This evaluation consists of essays on future expectations (where do I see myself in 10 years?) and questionnaires on making choices between work and living options presented in a binary form. We have found that:

- students overwhelmingly wish to avoid a move to a large metropolitan area,
- houses are preferred overwhelmingly over flats, with bungalows being the most popular,
- students almost unanimously see themselves in some sort of desk job behind a computer, without any consideration of any other options,
- students will choose a desk job over a blue collar job even when the pay is one third less,
- female students would overwhelmingly choose a white collar worker over the blue collar worker for a husband, even when he is paid one third less,
- a change that has occurred recently is that newer students have a lower desire to go to another country for work opportunities.

For the new generation, there is a well-bounded definition of what work should be and, for most, a job in production does not create a good narrative to go into the book-of-the-self. The corporate leader would do well to increase the perception of work in production and to stress that the outcome of this work is stable, rewarding, and would help with the individual's legacy. A model for the specialist craftsman/technician can be found in Germany where work in production is still regarded highly by the government and also in society.

The digital economy has added to the uncertainty of long-term stability as companies can now quickly move and adapt to new environments, often more quickly than people. There is much cynicism among the young generation about companies having any long-term loyalty to its employees. As such, CSR between the corporation and employee must include long-term commitments to employees and, more importantly, a pathway to success that is defined by the individual and guided by the leaders.

5 Collective Versus Individual Responsibility

A main concept of Kantian theory is that individuals take responsibility for their actions and do not transfer these consequences to somebody else. This is a rather simple notion to follow on a personal level, as one's own action has direct cause and effect on others. Like Adam Smith, Emmanuel Kant lived in a time when basic survival was a challenge. They could not dream of a world with so much interconnection. It is this interconnection that has made life far more purposeful by allowing us to create the tools to overcome its challenges. Wars, famine, disease, though still in existence, have been tamed to such a point that human toil can now focus on pursuits other than basic survival. Now, a new concern is replacing the older ones. This can best be described as "too much of a good thing". We can refer to these good things as indulgences or engaging in activities more than what is good for you.

In the past, indulgence had its limits with alcohol and tobacco being a main concern. Shopping was functional rather than recreational. Hobbies were recreational rather than habitual. Now there is a growing area of the economy that is predisposed to the usurpation of individual responsibility. To put it bluntly, there are many economic agents who are prospering from addictions in its many forms. The big question is what is the responsibility of the corporation in regards to individualistic negative externalities?

Society and corporations have largely come to terms with alcohol/tobacco addiction, as there are many controls placed on their consumption and sale, e.g., taxes, warning labels, rules of sale. In psychological terms, addictive behaviour can be traced to brain chemistry, specifically dopamine. This neurotransmitter was found by Schultz (1998) to be a chemical reward for meeting the goals of an anticipated action. With this reward mechanism, an action can be habituated. Dopamine is a short-term experience with a need and a desire for more and higher levels of release. According to Lustig (2017), the corporation has learned to "hack" into this dopamine hit, presenting a growing list of problems such as obesity, consumer debt, and above all, the use of internet devices in its many forms. Few today could even consider purposely leaving home without the ubiquitous smartphone. For most individuals, a day does not go by without connecting to the internet. Food companies have gone from providing the basic staples to supplying added value processing and led to an abdication of the cooking responsibility to the food company.

All of the above has the risk of too much moralizing and chasing imaginary enemies. However, today's parents are constantly facing the threats posed by the smartphone, the internet, and food issues aimed at their children. Bad actors who can disseminate fake news, inflaming hatred, supply pornography, etc. have a platform that can reach millions with few limits. It needs to be asked if corporations have a responsibility to limit activities that are overly destructive to society, the collective, especially when it becomes all too apparent that their products are facilitating societal problem.

It would be hard to argue that firms should assume the obligation for individual responsibilities and few would relish living in a nanny state of government-imposed rules on commerce seen as a vice. On the other hand, it would be hard to call a corporation socially responsible if the end result is too many customers facing too many issues of addiction. This is especially true when the customer is a child.

The psychologist Leary (1983) famously evoked a previous generation to *tune in, turn on, drop out*. In order to meet the responsibility of today's world, the inverse of Leary's pronouncement may be more appropriate—to *tune out, turn off, drop back in*.

6   Conclusion

In this paper, the interaction of social responsibility was explored between the state and the corporation, the corporation and its stakeholders, and the collective and the individual. We have found the corporations to be engaged in the community and do their best to be seen in a positive light. Globalization has added a layer of complexity to CSR, as a company could be doing all the right things and still be contributing to negative externalities. We see a need for more open dialogue and cooperation between the state, corporate, and individual levels. Instead of focusing on legal obligations, the attention should turn to what is intuitively right. With a focus on what could be considered an intuitive good, it would be easier to come to agreements between all three levels of society, for example:

- Food industry: individuals are free to purchase their desire, but contents as to the amount of sugar and fat could be clearly and understandably marked on packaging.
- Car industry: cars should be marketed on their actual efficiency and emissions judged in real-world conditions rather than laboratory conditions.
- Children: companies need to be careful with supplying and marketing products that could be unhealthy to the body and the minds of children and should not engage in unscrupulous collection of their data (this is especially true of smart phones).
- All parties need to consider the individuals and regions that are being left behind, keeping in mind the principles of universality, i.e., equally situated people should have the same opportunities. This concept could be helped through the construction of adequate transportation infrastructure (highways) and through more equitable taxing and subsidy schemes.

The above examples are all instinctive in theory, but are often overlooked in the attempts to achieve greater short-term profit. Global companies have a special obligation to the nations they reside in. As frontier companies operating on the global level are pulling further away from their challengers, some are losing their sense of national obligation, as their focus is myopically on other global competitors. Too many governments see the frontier firms as 'white knights' and gift these saviour companies with infrastructure improvements and tax subsidies, yet the trickling down of technology is limited as the speed of the accumulative advantage has accelerated. Laggard firms and declining regions are truly at a disadvantage.

A common theme throughout this paper is the notion that individuals attempt to create a legacy that can be described in the book-of-the-self. One yardstick for success of an individual is the intergenerational comparison—am I better off than my parents when they were my age? This is a hard comparison, as the generations can be divided between pre and post internet. For Central Europe, where this research is focused, the generational differences are starker with the socialism/capitalism divide. In our gadget driven world, it is hard to imagine going back to a time of corded phones, limited TV, and information limited to books in libraries. On the other hand, it becomes harder to imagine affording a house or, even worse, affording children. These are the real canaries in the coal-mine that call into question long-term viability of some nations. CSR is more than just doing some good things for the immediate stakeholder: it is also a holistic interaction between all levels of society.

Acknowledgements This research is supported by the Scientific granting authority of the Slovak Republic-VEGA1/0786/18project: Abandoned Slovakia: Efficient solutions of creative use of abandoned buildings outside the bigger municipalities.

References

Andrews, D., Cruscuolo, C., & Gal, P. (2015). Frontier firms, technology diffusion and public policy: Micro Evidence from OECD Countries. *OECD 2015*. Retrieved October 10, 2018 from https://www.oecd.org/eco/growth/Frontier-Firms-Technology-Diffusion-and-Public-Policy-Micro-Evidence-from-OECD-Countries.pdf.

Camagni, R. (2002). On the concept of territorial competitiveness: Sound or misleading? *Sage Journals, 39*(13), 2395–2411.

Carroll, A. B. (1991). The pyramid of corporate social responsibility: Toward the moral management of organizational stakeholders. *Business Horizons, 34*(4), 39–48.

Cushman and Wakefield 20th Annual European Cities Monitor (EUR). (2009). *Europe Real Estate*. Retrieved October 19, 2018 from https://europe-re.com/cushman-wakefield-20th-annual-european-cities-monitor-eur-2/40379.

Federal Institute for Research on Building, Urban Affairs, and Spatial Development. (2013). *Growing and shrinking regions in Europe*. Retrieved June 10, 2018 from https://www.bbr.bund.de/BBSR/EN/SpatialDevelopment/SpatialDevelopmentEurope/AnalysesSpatialDevelopment/Projects/growing_shrinking/growing_shrinking.html.

Freeman, R. E. (1984). *Strategic management: A stakeholder approach*. Boston: Pitman.

Friedman, M. (1962). *Capitalism and freedom*. Chicago: University of Chicago Press.

Kant, I. (1993). *Grounding for the metaphysics of morals* (J. W. Wellington, Trans., 3rd ed.). Indianapolis: Hackett Publishing. (Original work published 1785).

Leary, T. (1983). *Flashbacks*. Los Angeles: G. P. Putnam's Sons.

Lustig, R. (2017). *The hacking of the American mind: The science behind the corporate takeover of our bodies and brains*. New York: Penguin Publishing.

Mitchell, R., Bradley, R., & Wood, D. (1997). Towards a theory of stakeholder identification and salience: Defining the principles of who and what really counts. *Academic Management Review, 22*(4), 853–856.

Pittini, A., Koessi, G., Dijol, J., Lakatos, E., & Ghekiere, L. (2017). *The State of Housing in the EU2017*. Brussels: Housing Europe.

Schultz, W. (1998). Predictive reward signal of dopamine neurons. *Journal of Neurophysiology, 80*(1), 1–27.

Schumpeter, J. A. (2003). *Capitalism, socialism and democracy*. London and New York: Routledge. (Original work published 1942).

Theodoulides, L., Kormancová, G., & Cole, D. (2019). *Leading in the age of innovations*. New York: Routledge.

Wartick, S., & Cochran, P. (1985). The evolution of the corporate social performance model. *Academy of Management Review, 10*(4), 758–769.

David Cole, Ph.D., is an Assistant Professor of the Department of Language Communication in Business at the Faculty of Economics, Matej Bel University in Banská Bystrica, Slovakia. Apart from the duties of language instruction, his research has focused on behavioural economics and its effect on regions outside of large metropolitan areas. This research deals with the question of what would be needed to stabilize rural and micropolitan areas, especially in small countries. This has led to the development of new social tools measuring sentimentalism as a counter-balance to second-modernity and its predecessor high-modernity in CEE countries.

Petra Strnádová, Ph.D., is an Assistant Professor at the Faculty of Economics, Matej Bel University in Banská Bystrica, Slovakia. The fields of her academic research include ESP/Business English (the main area of her teaching practice), discourse analysis and cross-cultural issues. She is currently involved in two international research projects; one is concerned with migration strategies of V4 countries' citizens after Brexit, and the other with perception of positives and/or negatives of EU membership in post-communist countries.

Online Word of Mouth as a Source of Employment Information: A Comparative Analysis of the Language of Values in Employee Reviews and Testimonials

Jolanta Łącka-Badura

Abstract The paper presents the results of a comparative analysis of the employee values reflected in two types of electronic word of mouth (eWOM): online employee reviews and testimonials. The two corpora comprise, respectively, 150 online employee reviews of 14 randomly selected companies and 270 employee testimonials extracted from the corporate websites of the same organisations. The analysis investigates what categories of employee values/benefits (rational/functional, emotional/psychological, higher order benefits/brand values) contributing to the EVP (Employee Value Proposition) are communicated in both text types and how those values are expressed linguistically. The results obtained indicate a large degree of similarity between the two sets of texts, yet they also reveal some interesting differences pertaining to the types of values and their linguistic expression; the differences can most probably be attributed to the location of the reviews and testimonials on the company-independent <<>> company-dependent continuum.While employee reviews clearly perform a (predominantly) evaluative function, employee testimonials seem to foreground the persuasive/promotional function, contributing to the creation of strong employer brands.

Keywords Employee reviews · Employee testimonials · Language of values

J. Łącka-Badura (✉)
University of Economics in Katowice, Katowice, Poland
e-mail: jolanta.lacka-badura@ue.katowice.pl

© Springer Nature Switzerland AG 2020
U. Michalik et al. (eds.), *Exploring Business Language and Culture*,
Second Language Learning and Teaching,
https://doi.org/10.1007/978-3-030-58551-8_7

1 Introduction

There is a broad spectrum of ways in which organisations may promote their employer brands and Employee Value Proposition, both internally and externally.[1] Advertising the EVP often involves making use of the same or similar methods and techniques that have been proven effective in consumer branding. Employee values and benefits can also be communicated by employees; the Internet provides almost unlimited opportunities for former and current staff members to share their experience of working for organisations, through reviews and comments posted in social media and review websites, or other forms of word-of-mouth communication.[2] In the recruitment context, word-of-mouth is seen as "interpersonal communication, independent of the organisation's recruitment activities, about an organisation as an employer or about specific jobs" (Van Hoye & Lievens, 2007, p. 373; see also Van Hoye, 2014). If favourable, such opinions can contribute significantly to the creation of strong employer brands; conversely, if critical comments prevail, the most valuable candidates may be discouraged and seek employment with competitors.

The paper presents the results of an analysis comparing the employee values reflected in two (closely related) types of electronic word-of-mouth: online employee reviews and testimonials. The aim of the study is to investigate whether and to what degree the value categories and the ways these values are expressed linguistically differ between the 'real' and company-dependent WOM.[3]

2 Theoretical Background

This section aims to provide a theoretical background for the analysis. It offers a short characteristic of the two related genres of employee reviews and employee testimonials; it also provides an overview of the nature and different categories of corporate and employee values; finally, it briefly summarises the approach to investigating the linguistic expression of values adopted for the purposes of the study.

---

[1]The concept of *Employee Value Proposition* (EVP), although not synonymous with the 'mainstream' marketing notion of *Unique Selling Proposition* (USP), has presumably been built on the latter (Barrow & Mosley, 2005; Hill & Tande, 2006; Martin & Hetrick, 2006).

[2]Basically, word-of-mouth is defined as person-to-person communication related to product, service or brand experiences (Godes et al., 2005; Sen & Lerman, 2007). Increasingly widespread *web-based word-of-mouth*, also referred to as *electronic word-of-mouth* (*eWOM*), makes use of chatrooms, electronic boards, and independent websites presenting interpersonal company information (Dellarocas, 2003).

[3]The paper is a continuation of an earlier study by the same author investigating employee values and their linguistic expression in a corpus of *employee testimonials* (Łącka-Badura, 2018). The present study compares the results with those obtained for 'real' word-of-mouth, i.e., *employee reviews*, using the same theoretical background and methodology.

2.1 Employee Reviews and Testimonials

In the employment context, *employee reviews* meet the definitional requirements of word-of-mouth entirely (cf. Van Hoye & Lievens, 2007, quoted in the introduction). They are typically anonymous and can contain positive as well as negative information about current or previous employers; they are generated by people who (at least theoretically) have no commercial interest in promoting the employing organisation.

Employee testimonials, i.e., official statements from employees which explain what they like about their job or company, are characterised by greater complexity.[4] They are predominantly persuasive and promotional, comprising texts of various lengths and level of elaboration, typically found under hyperlinks to career opportunities sections on corporate websites. They have gained significance in the last decades as an instrument used to convey (positive) information about employing organisations, the types of people potential applicants may encounter and work with if employed, quality of work life issues, organisational culture, values and image (Cober, Brown, & Levy, 2004; Kroustalis & Meade, 2007; Maagaard, 2014; Walker, Feild, Giles, Armenakis, & Bernerth, 2009).

Employee testimonials belong to the category of "company-dependent recruitment sources" of employment information (Van Hoye & Lievens, 2007, p. 373). Unlike job advertisements (seen as the most typical example of company-dependent source), employee testimonials combine the advantages of company-dependent and company-independent recruitment sources; the former can be directly controlled to promote a favourable image, while the latter share many characteristics with word-of-mouth as an interpersonal information source. The hiring organisation being the actual sender of the message conveyed in testimonials, they are nevertheless (at least partly) attributed to individual employees sharing first-hand experience of what it is like to be a member of a particular organisation; they provide a human touch to recruitment communication, thus facilitating identification with the potential employer (Cober et al., 2004; Maagaard, 2014). Consequently, employee testimonials can be seen as "company-controlled imitations of word-of-mouth" (Van Hoye & Lievens, 2007, p. 374). The success of the *imitations* depends, to a large degree, on how much of the experiences narrated in testimonials seem to originate in the employees themselves, and how much is attributable to the employing organisation.[5]

---

[4]Cambridge Business English Dictionary. https://dictionary.cambridge.org/dictionary/business-english/employee-testimonial.

[5]See Cable and Turban (2001), Maagaard (2014), Van Hoye and Lievens (2007), Van Hoye (2014), for a more detailed discussion on the credibility of employee testimonials as a source of employment information.

2.2 Linguistic Expression of Values

Although the concept of *value* (including business values) is very complex and multidimensional (see e.g., Bozeman, 2007; Fleischer, 2010; Frederick, 1995; Grunert-Beckmann & Askegaard, 1997; Hultman, 2005; Rokeach, 1973; Simons, 2001; Schwartz, 1992), its understanding is simplified for the purposes of this study and interpreted as overlapping with the notion of—broadly understood—*employee benefits*. The simplification seems justified in view of the conceptualisation of the EVP (Employee Value Proposition) presented briefly in the introduction, where the lexeme *value* is used synonymously with such lexemes as *benefit*, *reward*, and *reason* (for becoming or staying committed to an organisation).

In other words, the EVP contains the reasons for employees "to commit themselves to the organisation" (Hill & Tande, 2006, p. 19). Barrow and Mosley (2005) divide the EVP (or employer brand benefits) into three groups: (1) *functional benefits*, e.g., payment for the services rendered, a safe working environment; (2) *emotional (psychological) benefits*, i.e., people's emotional attachment to the employer, the extent to which they feel satisfied and valued; (3) *higher order benefits and brand values*—the core focus of the brand is shifted from the level of functionality towards a higher ground of brand values and image associations. Similarly, Adamczyk and Kubasiak (2009) divide the EVP elements into the categories of *rational*, *emotional*, and '*image*' benefits.

With regard to the *linguistic expression of values*, Puzynina (1992, 2003), seen in the Polish school of axiological linguistics as the advocate of the so-called pragmatic-residual approach to the language of values and evaluation (cf. Krzeszowski, 1997), emphasises that values are largely expressed by non-systemic (pragmatic) means. She differentiates between the direct (explicit) value judgements as 'systemic/semantic' means of expressing value, where the positive/negative value judgements are viewed as being embedded in the semantic structure of a linguistic entity, and the indirect (implicit, 'textual/connotative') means of expressing value, where the value judgement lies in the connotation motivated by speaker's/reader's general knowledge and cultural competences. It must be stressed that the distinction between *explicit* and *implicit* valuation is far from clear, and thus conveyance of attitudes and value judgements should probably be regarded as a *combination* of explicit devices and implicit strategies. The explicitness/implicitness seems to be a matter of *degree* in the continuum of scales of intensity (Bednarek, 2006; Puzynina, 1992, 2003).

3 Material and Methods

The analysis compares two corpora: the first one comprises 152 employee testimonials (ETs) extracted from the corporate websites of 14 randomly selected organisations[6]; the other corpus consists of 270 (five star) online employee reviews (ERs)

---

[6]The corpus of employee testimonials was extracted from the following corporate websites:

of the same companies, found on popular independent review websites: www.gla ssdoor.com and www.indeed.com (accessed on 5–8 February 2017). The decision to analyse almost twice as many reviews as testimonials stemmed from the fact that the number of reviews available on the two sites mentioned was far greater that the number of testimonials found on the corporate websites; insisting on an even number of texts in both corpora would thus limit the representativeness of the second corpus. Also, due to the fact that neutral or negative reviews are by nature very different form the positive ones, only the best (five star) reviews were taken into account, to make the review corpus more comparable with the sample of testimonials and, consequently, render the analysis more reliable. Therefore, the texts under comparison are, on the one hand, employee testimonials, and on the other—reviews by *happy/satisfied* employees. Table 1 presents the distribution of texts in both corpora.

As can be seen, different numbers of texts were available for different companies and no employee reviews were found for Bluearc. The analysis does not therefore compare texts evaluating particular employers, but rather investigates the samples as

---

ETs 122–131 KINDRED AT HOME.

https://www.kindredathome.com/careers/employee-testimonials/ [accessed 19.09.2014].

ETs 132–148 TELEPERFORMANCE.

https://teleperformanceukcareers.co.uk/testimonials/ [accessed 19.09.2014].

ETs 149–152 GENESIS SYSTEMS.

https://www.genesis-systems.com/how-we-do-it/company-info/employee-testimonials [accessed 19.09.2014].

ETs (Employee Testimonials) 1–10 CATERPILLAR.

https://www.caterpillar.com/en/careers/why-caterpillar/employee-testimonials.html [accessed 18.09.2014].

ETs 11–15 ICE.

https://www.iceenterprise.com/careers/testimonials.jsp [accessed 18.09.2014].

ETs 16–30 ALTISOURCE.

https://www.altisource.com/AboutUs/Careers/EmployeeTestimonials.aspx   [accessed 18.09.2014].

ETs 31–45 QUATRRO.

https://www.quatrro.com/employee-testimonials.html [accessed 18.09.2014].

ETs 46–49 LANDSCAPE STRUCTURES [accessed 18.09.2014].

https://www.playlsi.com/Learn-About-Us/Careers/Employee-Testimonials/Pages/Employee-Testimonials1.aspx
ETs 50–73 CALIBRE [accessed 18.09.2014].

https://www.calibresys.com/careers2/employee_testimonials.html [accessed 18.09.2014].

ETs 74 – 87 VICTAULIC.
https://www.victaulic.com/en/our-company/careers/employee-testimonials/   [accessed 18.09.2014].

Table 1 Distribution of texts in both corpora: Employee reviews and employee testimonials

Company	Employee testimonials (ETs)	Employee reviews (ERs)
CATERPILLAR	1–10	1–48
ICE	11–15	49–54
ALTISOURCE	16–30	55–72
QUATRRO	31–45	73–80
LANDSCAPE STRUCTURES	46–49	81–84
CALIBRE	50–73	85–110
VICTAULIC	74–87	111–128
NLIVEN SYSTEMS	88–91	129–137
ACCURATE HOME CARE	92–100	138–147
LOCKHEED MARTIN	101–116	148–197
BLUEARC	117–121	–
KINDRED AT HOME	122–131	198–220
TELEPERFORMANCE	132–148	221–269
GENESIS SYSTEMS	149–152	270

two wholes, aiming to examine potential differences between the employee values communicated in the two genres.

More specifically, the two corpora are analysed with a view to identifying the types of values expressed, both explicitly and connotatively, as well as their (mostly lexical) markers. The language of the texts constituting the corpora is thus treated predominantly as the *source* of information about the values/benefits as seen by the employees talking about their organisation; additionally, the language is viewed as an *instrument* of valuation and the *carrier* or *bearer* of the values communicated (cf. Bartmiński, 2003).

The framework for the study was created drawing on the classification of the EVP values/benefits proposed by HR scholars (Barrow & Mosley, 2005; Adamczyk & Kubasiak, 2009). In view of the fact that a lot of the higher order benefits and brand values found in the corpus are expressed indirectly through the emotional/psychological benefits and the (remarkably numerous) positive references

---

ETs 88 – 91 NLIVEN SYSTEMS.
https://www.nliven.com/careers/employee-testimonials/ [accessed 19.09.2014].
ETs 92–100 ACCURATE HOME CARE.

https://www.accuratehomecare.com/employee-testimonials.html [accessed 19.09.2014].

ETs 101–116 LOCKHEED MARTIN.

https://www.lockheedmartinjobs.com/testimonials.asp#tab1-anchor?personactive=eli [accessed 19.09.2014].

ETs 117–121 BLUEARC.
https://www.bluearcgroup.com/Employee-Testimonials.html [accessed 19.09.2014].

to employers' attributes, the framework was slightly adapted for the purposes of the analysis. Three categories of values/benefits are thus examined, encompassing

(1) functional/rational benefits,
(2) emotional/psychological benefits,
(3) employers' attributes.

As the demarcation line between explicit and implicit evaluation is far from clear (see Sect. 2.2), the explicitness/implicitness is treated in the analysis as being a matter of *degree*; consequently, the term 'explicit' is used to denote evaluation closer to the explicit pole of the explicit/implicit continuum, whereas the term 'implicit' refers to evaluation closer to the implicit pole of the continuum.

4 Results and Discussion

This section presents the results of the analysis of rational/functional and emotional/psychological benefits communicated in the corpora of employee testimonials (ETs) and employee reviews (ERs). It also provides extracts exemplifying how the values are expressed linguistically, both in a direct (explicit) and indirect (implicit) manner. Finally, employers' attributes as seen by the employees are presented, partially overlapping with the category of 'higher order' values (see above).

The first observation that emerges from the analysis is that the texts in the testimonial corpus communicate positive evaluation only. On the other hand, a significant 31% of the five star reviews include some sort of negative evaluation, for example:

(1) It's easy to get terminated (ER248).
(2) Lack of support (ER18).
(3) My contract ends (ER171).
(4) The elevator moving slow (ER79).

As can be seen, the unfavourable comments range from clearly negative evaluation of the employer in extracts (1) and (2), through extract (3) that can be interpreted as merely a statement of a fact, not directly related to the employer, to a complaint in (4) about an inconvenience that—under normal circumstances—would be regarded by most employees as insignificant.[7] The above difference is the first, easily observable indication that the communicative functions of employee reviews and testimonials, although overlapping to a large extent, are not identical.

The analysis of the broad categories of values, i.e. rational/functional versus emotional/psychological, reveals that the latter are communicated in both corpora in a significantly larger proportion of texts than the former. Also, as shown in Table 2,

[7]The results obtained for the ER corpus presented further in the analysis include those related to the critical/negative comments; even if the communicators complain about the *lack* or *deficiency* of particular rewards, it is interpreted as indicating that these benefits are highly appreciated.

Table 2 Rational/functional and emotional/psychological values

Type of values	% of ETs	% of ERs
Rational/functional	47	65
Emotional/psychological	89	85

the percentage of texts expressing the emotional/psychological values is very similar in the two samples (89% of ETs and 85% of ERs). On the other hand, a considerable difference has been found between the employee testimonials and reviews with regard to the rational/functional benefits, appreciated in 47% of ETs, and 65% of ERs.

The findings pertaining to the emotional/psychological values (Table 2) seem to confirm the great importance that employees attach to the emotional benefits associated with the job and the employing organisation, as indicated by HR scholars and practitioners (cf. Anderberg & Froeschle, 2006; Barrow & Mosley, 2005; Dobrowolska, 2009; Głowicka, 2009; Halvorson, 2013; Hill & Tande, 2006; Rynes & Cable, 2003). The relatively high percentage of ERs expressing appreciation for the rational/functional values (65%), if compared with the results obtained for ETs (47%), makes the observation somewhat less obvious; yet it must be noted that the degree to which employees recognise the worth of the rational/functional benefits is nonetheless lower in both corpora than the appreciation for the emotional rewards.

4.1 Employee Values Expressed Explicitly

A closer investigation shows a very strong tendency for both ETs and ERs to communicate employee values in a rather direct manner; 100% of the testimonials under study and 98% of the reviews include statements where positive value judgements related to the employment experience are embedded in the very semantics of the linguistic entities used.

Examples of the linguistic structures explicitly communicating rational/functional employee values include the following:

(5) Lockheed Martin values my efforts through <u>competitive compensation and benefits</u> like education assistance (ET111).
(6) Great place to work, <u>advancement, experience, competitive pay, benefits and pension</u> (ER39).
(7) CALIBRE <u>invests financially</u> in its employees' <u>professional development</u> (ET69).
(8) I'm <u>growing as a professional</u> more than ever (ET121).
(9) I gained so much <u>knowledge</u> and so much customer service <u>experience</u> and I also gained a lot of <u>friends</u> (ER233).

As can be seen from the above extracts, employees are very explicit when praising their remuneration and extra benefits (5, 6), or promotion prospects and professional as well as personal development (7, 8, 9).

Table 3 presents the percentage of ETs and ERs including explicit (or rather explicit) references to particular types of rational/functional benefits.

Table 3 indicates that promotion prospects and career development are the highest ranking values in both corpora, appreciated (almost equally) in 45% of ETs and 43% of ERs. Other rational/functional benefits are communicated in a markedly lower proportion of both sets of texts. However, significant differences have been found for some types of values, particularly remuneration and extra benefits; the former is communicated in merely 9% of ETs and 29% of ERs, while the latter in 2% of ETs and 14% of ERs. The results pertaining to work-life balance and job security/long-term career prospects also indicate that, apart from promotion prospects and career development, appreciation for tangible benefits is explicitly expressed in a markedly higher proportion of ERs than ETs.

The emotional/psychological benefits are also communicated rather directly. Examples of utterances explicitly expressing several types of these values are presented below:

(10)   ... the atmosphere within the company is a great factor (ET147).
(11)   a very collaborative workplace (ER105).
(12)   ... every day you come to work and you're doing something that helps support the country (ET113).
(13)   Great people who care about helping their customers (ER98).
(14)   I thoroughly enjoy working in Teleperformance (ET136).
(15)   I loved working there (ER 151).
(16)   ... the management team genuinely cares about the safety and well-being of employees (ET79).
(17)   They are so supportive of your life goals (ER 209).
(18)   ... keep my job fulfilling and interesting (ET15).
(19)   Challenging work with new experiences everyday (ER 80).
(20)   People feel appreciated and are recognized for their dedication and hard work (ET59).

Table 3 Rational/functional benefits expressed explicitly

Rational/functional benefits	% of ETs	% of ERs
Promotion prospects and career development	45	43
Extra benefits	9	29
Financial	7	26
Non-financial	3	10
Work-life balance	8	13
Remuneration	2	14
Job security/long-term career prospects	1	5

Table 4 Emotional/psychological benefits expressed explicitly

Emotional/psychological benefits	% of ETs	% of ERs
Work environment/atmosphere	52	53
Satisfaction/self-fulfillment/positive experience	34	31
Care/support (from employer)	31	39
Doing something for others	27	16
Professionalism/standards/ethics	21	8
Interesting/exciting/stimulating job/challenge	20	14
Respect/recognition/fair treatment	18	11
Prestige/pride	18	2
Importance/influence/impact	11	7
Fun/pleasure	10	10
Success/achievement	6	4
Responsibility/autonomy	4	3

(21) I'm treated with respect. (…) I am made to feel appreciated, always an open
      door policy (ER 79).

Different types of emotional/psychological values and the percentage of ETs and
ERs in which they are communicated explicitly are shown in Table 4.

Table 4 shows that by far the most valued emotional/psychological benefits are
good work environment and positive atmosphere, appreciated explicitly in an almost
identical number of texts in both corpora (52% in ETs and 53% in ERs). Very
strong similarity is also observed for the values of satisfaction, self-fulfillment, positive experience (34% of ETs and 31% of ERs), fun and pleasure associated with
the job and/or the organisation (10% of texts in each corpus), the feeling of being
successful in the job (6% of ETs and 4% of ERs), and satisfaction derived from the
fact that the position one occupies in the company involves a lot of responsibility,
allowing freedom, independence and autonomy (4% of ETs and 3% of ERs). The
results suggest that these values are appreciated to approximately the same degree
in both samples, irrespective of the source of information being company-dependent
or company-independent.

Some noteworthy differences have been found for several types of
emotional/psychological values, including care and support from employer (31%
of ETs and 39% of ERs), doing something for others (27% of ETs and 16% of ERs),
interesting, exciting, stimulating and challenging job (20% of ETs and 14% of ERs)
as well as respect, recognition and fair treatment (18% of ETs and 11% of ERs). The
findings may be interpreted as suggesting that—although the total percentage of
texts communicating emotional/psychological benefits is almost equally high in both
corpora—fewer reviews express highly intangible benefits, with the exception of care
and support from employer (which is very commonly and rather obviously associated with good employment conditions). This conclusion seems to be confirmed if
we consider the most significant difference between the two corpora observed in the

category of emotional/psychological benefits: the values of professionalism, standards and ethics (21% of ETs and 8% of ERs) as well as prestige and pride derived from working for the employing organisation (18% of ETs and 2% of ERs). These discrepancies may be indicative of the tendency for employee testimonials to foreground values that add to the prestige and reputation of the employer, rather than those naturally associated with the employees' self-interest.

4.2 Employee Values Expressed Implicitly

The first observation that emerges from the analysis of *implicit* ways of communicating employee values in both corpora is that such a mode of expression is used very rarely: in approximately 10% of testimonials and merely 3% of reviews.[8] Clear categorisation of values expressed implicitly (or rather implicitly) poses a bigger problem than classification of benefits communicated directly, as many instances of the linguistic structures analysed can be interpreted as expressing more than one value.

Among quite unambiguous references to the rational/functional benefits, instances of value expressions classified as (rather) implicit include the following:

(22) Excellent professional journey from an Associate to a Manager (ET26).
(23) … climb the ladder…(…) reach new heights (ET29).

The above extracts clearly express the employees' appreciation of the opportunity to make progress, develop professionally, and be promoted.

Some of the emotional/psychological benefits communicated indirectly are also rather easy to interpret, for example:

(23) … interact with a customer and see their smile (ET116).
(24) You are part of a big future for kids (ER84).
(25) They want you to go and take charge, and make something of yourself in this company (ET110).

Interacting with customers who *smile*, most probably showing their satisfaction (extract 23), as well as being a *part of a big future for kids* (24), can easily be associated with the emotional value derived from doing something for other people, particularly children. *Taking charge* in (25) implies the values of responsibility and autonomy, whereas *making something of yourself* is a popular idiomatic expression denoting an attempt to be successful on one's own initiative, clearly suggesting the value of success and sense of accomplishment, although it may also suggest the rational/functional benefit of professional development and advancement opportunities.

---

[8]References to *employers' attributes*, also classified as indirect communication of employee values (albeit of a different kind), are analysed as a separate category.

Yet, although no strongly implicit expressions have been found in the corpus of employee reviews, the corpus of testimonials does comprise instances of linguistic structures that do not render themselves to such clear interpretations and categorisations. Let's consider the following extracts:

(26)   … a corporation that gives back … (ET149).
(27)   This intangible quality called a 'fit' (ET52).

A *corporation that gives back* (26) and the good *fit* between the employee and their organisation (27) may plausibly be interpreted as encompassing *all* the possible benefits that employees can get in return for their commitment to the organisation.

4.3   Employers' Attributes

This sub-section summarises the results of the analysis concerning linguistic struc-tures found in both corpora which may logically be rephrased as [The employer is …/does …]. Extracts that refer to what the company *does for the employee*, or how *the employee* feels about working for the organisation, have been accounted for in Sects. 4.1 and 4.2, and have thus been excluded from this part of the analysis.

Examples of statements or phrases that can be classified as *praising employers' attributes* include the following:

(28)   CALIBRE is a strong, solid, stable company that withstood and excelled during a tremendous national economic downturn (ET65).
(29)   … a company that will never settle for mediocrity (ER71).

The above statements, if uttered by employees, and not the PR people repre-senting the organisations, appear to be (or are meant to sound) factual and objective. The employee values that are indirectly communicated through such acts of praising most probably include, in the first instance, the values of pride, prestige, and satisfac-tion derived from the company's market position, power, and constant development. These attributes may, however, bring associations with other values; the fact that the company in (28) *withstood and excelled during a tremendous national economic downturn* may imply the rational/functional values of job security (the job with this company is safe even in times of crisis, when lots of people working for different employers are made redundant) and stable remuneration (a company that *excels* when other businesses go down is not likely to reduce employees' wages even if the market is tough). Similarly, *a company that will never settle for mediocrity* (29) is associated with high standards of professionalism and quality, which may evoke the feeling of pride; additionally, the organisation may be perceived as maintaining high standards in all aspects of its activity, most probably including the standards of employee treatment.

Importantly, linguistic structures praising employers' attributes have been found in over a half of the testimonials (56% of ETs) and merely 5% of employee reviews. This is a remarkable difference that seems to confirm that the communicative function of testimonials, regarded as company-controlled imitations of 'real' word-of-mouth (cf. Sect. 2.1), is rather promotional than evaluative.

5 Summary and Conclusions

The present paper has sought to analyse two closely related types of electronic word-of-mouth, i.e., employee testimonials and reviews, with a view to investigating what employee values/benefits are communicated in both corpora and how these values are expressed linguistically. The results obtained indicate a large degree of similarity between the two sets of texts, yet they also reveal some interesting differences pertaining to the types of values and their linguistic expression.

The first observation that emerges from the analysis is that while all the testimonials communicate positive evaluation only, almost one third of the five star reviews include some sort of negative evaluation; this finding strongly suggests that the communicative functions of employee reviews and testimonials, although overlapping to a large extent, are not identical.

The analysis of the broad categories of values, i.e., rational/functional versus emotional/psychological, shows a great degree of similarity between ETs and ERs in terms of the percentage of texts expressing the emotional/psychological benefits, which is considerably higher (in both corpora) than the percentage of texts expressing the rational/functional benefits. On the other hand, a significant difference has been found between the employee testimonials and reviews with regard to the rational/functional benefits, appreciated in merely 47% of ETs, and 65% of ERs.

The comparative analysis of the ways values are expressed linguistically in the two corpora has demonstrated that in both testimonials and reviews the communicators tend to express employee values rather openly and directly, with positively charged lexical items denoting (or easily associated with) particular values. However, significant differences have been found for some types of explicitly expressed rational/functional values, particularly remuneration and extra benefits; the results clearly suggest that appreciation for tangible rewards is directly communicated in a markedly higher proportion of ERs than ETs.

As far as the explicit expression of emotional/psychological benefits is concerned, the most popular values of this kind (particularly good work environment/atmosphere) are expressed in an almost identical number of texts in both sets. However, a more detailed analysis of the less popular values shows that while employee testimonials tend to quite frequently express highly intangible benefits, the reviews focus more on the values that are naturally associated with the employees' self-interest. This is the second observation pointing to the difference between the communicative function of company-controlled versus 'real' word-of-mouth, with the former clearly foregrounding values that add to the prestige and reputation of the employer.

The corpus comprises some interesting instances of (rather) implicit expression of rational/functional as well as emotional/psychological values. It must be noted, however, that these instances are rare in the ETs corpus and extremely scarce in the ERs (only 3% of texts). This seems to confirm the openly evaluative character of the latter.

The non-identical nature of the two text types under analysis is further corroborated by the results pertaining to the "employers' attributes". Remarkably, such utterances are communicated in 58% of ETs, and merely 5% of ERs. Although potentially evoking the feeling of pride derived from working for a powerful and prestigious organisation, such statements can easily be interpreted as implicitly *promoting the employers*; their promotional appeal may actually be reinforced by the fact that, if uttered by former or existing employees, they sound far more factual, objective, and thus more credible than similar messages produced by PR or marketing people. This feature is probably the strongest signal found in the analysis, indicating that the voice that we hear in the company-controlled employee testimonials is not entirely the voice of employees.

In view of the above, it seems reasonable to conclude that although employee testimonials and reviews indeed demonstrate a large degree of similarity, both in terms of the types of values communicated and the way these values are expressed linguistically, the differences between the two text types can most probably be attributed to their location on the company-independent <<>> company-dependent continuum. While employee reviews clearly perform a (predominantly) evaluative function, employee testimonials seem to foreground (albeit indirectly) the persuasive/promotional function, contributing to the creation of strong employer brands.

References

Adamczyk, M., & Kubasiak, M. (2009). Employer Branding – budowanie pozytywnego wizerunku pracodawcy na rynku pracy. In U. Gołaszewska-Kaczan (Ed.), *Czas na EB*. Employer branding and corporate social responsibility* (pp. 139–151). Białystok: Wydawnictwo Uniwersytetu w Białymstoku.

Anderberg, M., & Froeschle, R. C. (2006). Becoming an employer of choice: Strategies of worker recruitment and retention. *Benefits and Compensation Digest, 43*(4), 1–8.

Barrow, S., & Mosley, R. (2005). *The employer brand. Bringing the best of brand management to people at work*. Chichester: Wiley.

Bartmiński, J. (2003). Miejsce wartości w językowym obrazie świata. In J. Bartmiński (Ed.), *Język w kręgu wartości. Studia semantyczne* (pp. 59–86). Lublin: Wydawnictwo UMCS.

Bednarek, M. (2006). *Evaluation in media discourse*. London: Continuum.

Bozeman, B. (2007). *Public values and public interest: Counterbalancing economic individualism.* Washington, DC: Georgetown University Press.

Cable, D. M., & Turban, D. B. (2001). Establishing the dimensions, sources and value of job seekers' employer knowledge during recruitment. In D. M. Cable & D. B. Turban (Eds.), *Research in personal and human resources management* (pp. 115–163). Bingley: Emerald Group Publishing Limited.

Cambridge Business English Dictionary. Retrieved from https://dictionary.cambridge.org/dictio nary/business-english/employee-testimonial.

Cober, R. T., Brown, D. J., & Levy, P. E. (2004). Form, content, and function: An evaluative methodology for corporate employment web sites. *Human Resource Management, 43*(2/3), 201–218.

Dellarocas, C. (2003). The digitization of word of mouth: Promise and challenges of online feedback mechanisms. *Management Science, 49*(10), 1407–1424.

Dobrowolska, J. (2009). Atrakcyjny pracodawca oczami studenta. In U. Gołaszewska-Kaczan (Ed.), *Czas na EB**. *Employer branding and corporate social responsibility* (pp. 175–180). Białystok: Wydawnictwo Uniwersytetu w Białymstoku.

Fleischer, M. (2010). *Wartości w wymiarze komunikacyjnym*. Łódź: Primum Verbum.

Frederick, W. (1995). *Values, nature, and culture in the American corporation*. Oxford, NY: Oxford University Press.

Głowicka, A. (2009). Przejawy Employer Branding w działalności firmy PriceWaterCoopers. In U. Gołaszewska-Kaczan (Ed.), *Czas na EB**. *Employer branding and corporate social responsibility* (pp. 73–79). Białystok: Wydawnictwo Uniwersytetu w Białymstoku.

Godes, D., Mayzlin, D., Chen, Y., Das, S., Dellarocas, C., Pfeiffer, B., ..., Verlegh, P. (2005). The firm's management of social interactions. *Marketing Letters, 16*, 415–428.

Grunert-Beckmann, S. C., & Askegaard, S. (Eds.). (1997). *"Seeing with the mind's eye": An exploratory study of the use of pictorial stimuli in value research*. Hillsdale, NJ: Lawrence Erlbaum.

Halvorson, C. (2013). What today's employees want from their managers. Retrieved from https://wheniwork.com/blog/what-todays-employees-want-from-their-managers.

Hill, B., & Tande, C. (2006). Total rewards. The employee value proposition. *Workspan, 10*(06), 19–22.

Hultman, K. (2005). Evaluating organizational values. *Organizational Development Journal, 23*(3), 39–48.

Kroustalis, C. M., & Meade, A. W. (2007). Portraying an organization's culture through properties of a recruitment website. Retrieved from https://www4.ncsu.edu/~awmeade/Links/Papers/Internet_Recruit(SIOP07).pdf.

Krzeszowski, T. (1997). *Angels and devils in hell. Elements of axiology in semantics*. Warsaw: Energeia.

Łącka-Badura, J. (2018). Building employer brands through employee testimonials: The linguistic expression of values. In G. E. Garzone & W. Giordano (Eds.), *Discourse, communication and the enterprise: Where business meets discourse* (pp. 320–342). Newcastle upon Tyne: Cambridge Scholars Publishing.

Maagaard, C. (2014). Employee testimonials: Animating corporate messages through employees' stories. *Discourse, Context & Media, 6*, 22–32.

Martin, G., & Hetrick, S. (2006). *Corporate reputations, branding and people management. A strategic approach to HR*. Oxford: Butterworth-Heinemann.

Puzynina, J. (1992). *Język wartości*. Warszawa: Wydawnictwo Naukowe PWN.

Puzynina, J. (2003). Wokół języka wartości. In J. Bartmiński (Ed.), *Język w kręgu wartości. Studia semantyczne* (pp. 19–34). Lublin: Wydawnictwo UMCS.

Rokeach, M. J. (1973). *The nature of human value*. New York, NY: Free Press.

Rynes, S. L., & Cable, D. M. (2003). Recruitment research in the twenty-first century. In W. C. Borman, D. R. Ilgen, & R. J. Klimoski (Eds.), *Handbook of psychology. Industrial and organizational psychology* (Vol. 12, pp. 55–76). New Jersey: Wiley.

Sen, S., & Lerman, D. (2007). Why are you telling me this? An examination into negative consumer reviews on the web. *Journal of Interactive Marketing, 21*(4), 76–94.

Simons, H. W. (2001). *Persuasion in society*. Thousand Oaks: Sage.

Schwartz, S. H. (1992). Universals in the content and structure of values: Theoretical advance and empirical tests in 20 countries. In M. P. Zanna (Ed.), *Advances in experimental social psychology* (Vol. 25, pp. 1–65). Orlando, FL: Academic Press.

Van Hoye, G., & Lievens, F. (2007). Investigating web-based recruitment sources: Employee testimonials vs word-of-mouse. *International Journal of Selection and Assessment, 15*(4), 372–382.

Van Hoye, G. (2014). Word of mouth as a recruitment source: An integrative model. In K. Y. T. Yu & D. M. Cable (Eds.), *The Oxford Handbook of Recruitment* (pp. 251–268). New York: Oxford University Press.

Walker, H. J., Feild, H. S., Giles, W. F., Armenakis, A. A., & Bernerth, J. B. (2009). Displaying employee testimonials on recruitment web sites: Effects of communication media, employee race, and job seeker race on organizational attraction and information credibility. *Journal of Applied Psychology, 94*(5), 1354–1364.

Jolanta Łącka-Badura, Ph.D., is a linguist and Business English lecturer, head of the Foreign Language Center at the University of Economics in Katowice. She also holds two postgraduate diplomas in Management and European Integration. Her research interests include business communication, teaching English for Business Purposes, discourse analysis, the language of persuasion and evaluation.

The Clash Between Polish and Chinese Business Etiquette Trends. The Differences, Similarities and Misunderstandings

Katarzyna Bańka-Orłowska

Abstract Is handing a business card appropriately towards the other, quite often international, business partner a key to a successful business meeting? Various countries follow individual approaches in terms of business and social interaction. To some, those approaches may seem absolutely incomprehensible or even shocking. The aim of the following article is the analysis of the differences and similarities in terms of Polish and Chinese versions of business meetings and their arrangement with some remarks on the appropriateness of certain acts and culture-based issues of two Chinese phenomena called: 'you mianzi'—'losing face' and 'you guanxi'—'having contacts/influential relationships'. Also, the author will provide a set of tips on how to prepare for a business meeting with Chinese entrepreneurs and how to improve business relationship with Chinese counterparts.

Keywords Chinese business etiquette · Losing face · You mianzi · Chinese culture · You guanxi

1 Introduction

The following chapter aims at verification of the specificity of conducting business in Poland and in China with emphasis on the different dimensions of business etiquette in both countries in question. At first, the author describes the most important changes in terms of Polish—Chinese economical and political areas, emphasizing the tightening of the relationship between the two countries in question.

The following part of the article describes the aim of the research and research questions that are going to be investigated in the analytical part of this paper. The author also introduces the research subjects and enumerates tools and methods used for the purposes of the further analysis. Then, the author explains the importance of China as a strategic partner for Polish entrepreneurs with a brief explanation

K. Bańka-Orłowska (✉)
Institute of Linguistics, Faculty of Humanities, University of Silesia in Katowice, Katowice, Poland
e-mail: katarzyna.banka@us.edu.pl

© Springer Nature Switzerland AG 2020
U. Michalik et al. (eds.), *Exploring Business Language and Culture*,
Second Language Learning and Teaching,
https://doi.org/10.1007/978-3-030-58551-8_8

123

of the necessity of acknowledging the complexity of the traditional Chinese culture (Chinese 'you mianzi' and 'you guanxi' phenomena) and the distinctness of the traditional Polish culture (post-communist society strongly influenced by Polish history) emphasizing the differences occurring in terms of the way of conducting business, communication and business etiquette in Poland and China.

In the later part of the article, the importance of business hierarchy, social and business status in Poland and China are examined as an introduction to the further analysis of the business meeting conduct in both Poland and China, focusing on the issues such as: arranging a business meeting, the course of events during such an event and the later culture-based elements occurring after the meeting, such as: business card handling or gift-giving ceremony.

The final part of the article is devoted to conclusions and final remarks. The author also provides a set of tips for Polish businessmen willing to do business with Chinese entrepreneurs, so that one could avoid 'losing face' in China.

2 Polish-Chinese Political and Business Relationship

Due to the fact that China has become a major player in global investments, the country started to look for new strategic partners to cooperate with. It could be one of the reasons why we can witness a tightening of the Polish-Chinese relationship in recent years. In 2011, the Polish-Chinese cooperation received a status of a 'strategic cooperation' implicating the significance of both countries' business relationship (based on: internet source 2).

There were numerous important projects launched in the recent years establishing the Polish-Chinese business relations and setting firm foundation for the future business cooperation initiatives, e.g., founding the Asian Infrastructure Investment Bank (AIIB) in 2014 (Poland became one of its founding members in 2015 (based on: internet source 3, 4)). Such step improved Polish balance of trade and helped Polish economy gain financial security. A vast majority of projects and business initiatives are and will be co-sponsored by AIIB. This initiative also creates a steady ground for gaining an easier access to the Chinese market by Polish entrepreneurs now and in the nearest future.

The following crucial date in history was Andrzej Duda's (Polish president) trip to PRC in 2015. This meeting helped to establish the political and economic cooperation between the new Polish government and the government of China, not only by meeting Chinese president Xi Jinping and the Prime Minister Li Keqiang, but also by attending Polish-Chinese Economic Forum (this event's importance for Polish-Chinese co-operation was strongly emphasized by the Polish Investment & Trade Agency PFR Group) and 20 the "16 + 1" initiative summit that took place in Suzhou (based on internet source 5). All these elements contributed to providing a chance for Polish entrepreneurs to establish trade cooperation with Chinese counterparts.

2.1 China: A Strategic Trade Partner for Polish Entrepreneurs

According to the Embassy of the Republic of Poland in Beijing, nowadays, Poland has become PRC's biggest and the most strategic trade partner in Central and Eastern Europe. Also, China's significance for Polish trade situation has increased, making China Poland's most important trade partner in Asia. Additionally, it is the second-biggest exporter of goods to Poland (11.6% of all imports to Poland) (based on: internet source 6).

In recent years, we can witness an increasing amount of Polish entrepreneurs trying to establish business relationship and business cooperation with Chinese counterparts. However, trading, negotiating, arranging a meeting, and meeting the demands of the Chinese businessmen tend to be tricky. Doing business with Chinese counterparts is a very difficult and time-consuming process. The way of business communication and etiquette in Poland and China are very distinctive, thus it is believed that this comparative analysis will provide a clarified view on how to prepare and perform an appropriate business meeting with Chinese counterparts, as each country has got its specific characteristics, which may deeply affect various aspects of business relationship, business conduct and communication between Polish and Chinese entrepreneurs.

3 Issues and Challenges

The following paragraph is devoted to the description of the study conducted for the purposes of this article. The author enlists the research questions she intends to answer. Also, the importance of the study is emphasized. Finally, the research subjects, methods and tools are explained.

3.1 The Importance of the Study

Although the issue of Western-Chinese business relations has been examined in details (e.g., Blackman, 1997; Chen, 1993; MacDougall, 1980), it is still considered to be a new field of research when investigated from the perspective of a Polish businessman. It is believed that this paper endeavours to provide basic guidelines for effective business meeting arrangements and negotiations with Chinese counterparts. Also, the presented material may be helpful in terms of performing further, more detailed analysis of the given subject set in Polish-Chinese business circumstances.

3.2   Research Questions

The article intends to answer the following questions:

What are the similarities and differences in terms of Polish and Chinese versions of business meetings and their arrangement?
How to behave properly in Chinese environment?
How to ease the process of doing business with Chinese?

3.3   Research Subjects, Methodology and Tools: Empirical Base

The empirical base for this article is author's investigation of Polish-Chinese business relationship of five large Polish companies employing at least 100 workers, five smaller companies employing 10–50 workers, and also some individual businessmen, small, family-run companies and one-person economic activities. All the companies and businessmen mentioned above requested to remain anonymous. The branches the research subjects may be associated with are connected with: electrical equipment, sports equipment, automotive, manufacture such as: clothing manufacture, toys production, etc.

Additionally, the author based her research on her working experience as a translator throughout the years, collecting empirical data enabling her to establish certain patterns and conclusions in terms of the Chinese-Polish business negotiation process, especially from the vantage point of the difference between Chinese and Western business culture.

The corpus data was collected by means of numerous tools and instruments, namely, a series of interviews conducted with the abovementioned subjects. Sometimes the discussion focused on a group interview (FGI), however, sometimes it was an individual in-depth interview (IDI).

Some other qualitative research methods were business meetings' observation (during the author's work as a translator—active participation), field notes, and the analysis of individually prepared written and audiovisual materials of Polish and Chinese companies used during business meetings. The quantitative research method was mainly administering, the questionnaires conducted on the above mentioned workers and entrepreneurs verifying their acknowledgement of the differences between Chinese and Polish business negotiation process and the culture-oriented issues concerning business meetings and challenges they encountered in their Polish-Chinese working relationships.

4 Business and Culture

"Culture is not a separate system alongside economics or politics; it constitutes (in the sense of both representing and composing) the social order" (Lipartito, 2008, p. 604). All the characteristics of culture in business are communicated through language, which is an integral part of culture.

It is necessary to understand the values and other symbolic systems that are specific for a particular society in order to succeed in any form of a business relationship (Kroeber & Kluckhohn, 1952). Hofstede (2003) claims that culture is a kind of software embedded inside one's mind, programming us to behave in a certain way through our personal experience, with members of our society, history, past experience, and everything that surrounds us. Culture, language and business are so much interrelated that, without proper understanding of cultural setting and social behaviour of a language use and culture-oriented elements, it may lead to misinterpretation and breakdown in communication. Thus, misunderstandings are bound to happen when two such distant groups of people (Polish and Chinese) decide to conduct business together.

4.1 The Complexity of the Traditional Chinese Culture, Chinese Entrepreneurs and Business Etiquette

Due to a great influence of Confucianism (儒家—rújiā) on Chinese people, Chinese companies (contrary to Polish business reality) tend to be both hierarchical and group-oriented. They tend to resemble families in their structure and emphasize group harmony ('yin yang') and loyalty. Also, Chinese deeply consider and emphasize their respect towards the most senior members of the company (and not only). In such a way, Chinese companies may resemble a very traditional, patriarchal scheme of a highly socially-structured organism (Seligman, 1999).

Before moving to a deeper analysis of an actual business meeting arrangement with Chinese counterparts, it is necessary to acknowledge and understand three distinctive cultural factors influencing the overall relationship with Chinese counterparts, namely:

- contacts—'you guanxi' concept,
- face—'you mianzi' concept,
- hierarchy—social and business status.

4.1.1 Contacts—'You Guanxi' Concept

Although a lot has changed over the years, there are still some factors, cultural traits, that influence Chinese people's decision-making processes. 'Guanxi' means in Chinese: 'connections' and 'relationships'; however, none of those translations describe the essence of this quite complex concept. It plays a fundamental role within the Confucian doctrine and it could be best defined as 'reciprocal favours' or assistance that two people can provide for each other. It defines the fundamental dynamics in personalized social networks of power (Yeung, 2007).

It is worth mentioning that Western expatriates who want to expand their business in China, or simply expand their careers in China, often miss this fundamental point, making their progress less efficient and definitely more time-consuming. However, the importance of 'guanxi' is quite relative and may sometimes depend on the geopolitical situation worldwide, industry, or the nature of the business itself. Nevertheless, business and societal relationships in China are still heavily influenced by networks of trust and mutual obligations rather than by strong, codified laws (Ostrowski & Penner, 2009). Seligman claims that: 'the key to getting anything important accomplished in China lies not in the formal order, but rather in who you know, and in how that person views his or her obligations to you' (Seligman, 1999, p. 180).

Building a good 'guanxi' may be a long and difficult process; however, after establishing trust, all the other steps leading to a successful business cooperation with Chinese counterparts seem easy. Polish businessmen often see the Chinese 'guanxi' concept as a tit-for-tat relationship between two people or business entities. Naturally, when necessary, Chinese companies turn to their 'guanxi' network seeking help, thus it is crucial to work hard on cultivating close relationships in high or strategic places. Chinese people also assume that all the rest of the world works on similar rules and principles, thus they sometimes 'view foreign friends as windows to benefits in the world outside China'; however, it is hard for them to differentiate between the personal and organizational sphere, and it may sometimes end up being awkward for foreigners when a personal Chinese friend asks for an organizational favour, and vice versa (Seligman, 1999, p. 195). Chinese believe that having 'guanxi' is a key to 'diminishing the danger of problems, and makes solving them much easier when they do arise' (Seligman, 1999, p. 196).

To some entrepreneurs, it may seem mildly like corruption or insider dealings, but in China, it is the natural way of doing things. Everything is done through connections. Certain issues we would consider unacceptable are sort of standard operating procedures over there. Some Polish businessmen even compared this system to Polish PRL style of doing business.

4.1.2 Face—'You Mianzi' Concept

A renowned Chinese writer and linguist Lin Yutang (1935, p. 199) once said that: 'Face cannot be translated or defined'. In some sense he was right because the concept of Chinese 'losing' and 'saving face' differs from the Western concepts acknowledged worldwide. In China this phenomenon deals not with the word '脸' ('liǎn') meaning literally 'face' as a body part, but with the word '面子' ('miànzi'). Chinese-English dictionaries translate this particular word mainly as: 'outer surface/outside/honor/reputation/feelings or even (medicinal) powder, and of course as: face (as in "losing face")/self-respect (www.mdbg.net). Thus 'you mianzi' ('to have face') is a concept of Chinese social psychology, emphasizing the importance of personal esteem, appearance, respect, and sense of shame (Bogdanowska-Jakubowska, 2010). Simply speaking, to Chinese, 'you mianzi' means avoiding disgrace or humiliation by any means possible. Hu (1944) claims that: 'it is built up through initial high position, wealth, power, ability, through cleverly establishing social ties to a number of prominent people, as well as through avoidance of acts that would cause unfavourable comment'. Seligman (1999, p. 209) emphasizes that although 'mianzi' is an abstract concept, it is a deadly serious issue for Chinese people and that 'mianzi, money and power are the three key motivators in China today' (ibid., p. 209).

It is one of the most significant concepts of living life in harmony with one another in China. Knowing and understanding its depth enables us to comprehend numerous situations and Chinese people's behaviour which may later help in addressing certain business situations without making anybody 'lose their face'.

4.1.3 Hierarchy—Social and Business Status

As stated above, there is a strong influence of Confucius' teaching on Chinese people's everyday life. Chinese people emphasize hierarchical relationships and each person shows certain respect for others, depending on their position in the hierarchy. There is a specified social order. Confucius spoke of *Five Constant Relationships*—between parent and child, elder sibling and younger sibling, husband and wife, elder friend and junior friend, and ruler and subject. Depending on one's place in the hierarchy, s/he is expected to behave in a certain way and is being treated in correspondence to his/her social status (Kaplan, 2015; Seligman, 1999; Yu, 2005).

Contrary to Western business hierarchy, Chinese business hierarchy can be called 'a triangular set with a genre of top-down pattern, which can be seen in the picture below, based on the webpage: www.hierarchystructure.com (Fig. 1).

As we can see above, the leaders (Higher level management) are responsible for the organization's direction making. They are in charge of the middle level management's work and set goals that are later carried out by the lower level management on command of the middle level management. All in all, there is a strict business and administration level hierarchy in most Chinese companies. Sometimes even the simplest issue must first be examined by each member of a particular group of management before being processed to the next stage of execution. The progression of a particular goal strictly depends on the verification by all the experts and cannot be outrun. Hierarchical structure of Chinese business management is sacred, even though it takes twice as much time to execute things than in Western companies. Such a system would be unacceptable in Poland firstly because of the fact that the companies usually do not employ so many workers, and, secondly, because Polish people cherish quick conduct and fast reaction more than careful and time-consuming double verification of each process.

What is more, it was emphasized by numerous of my research subjects during our group and individual discussion that, contrary to Western promotion standards, in

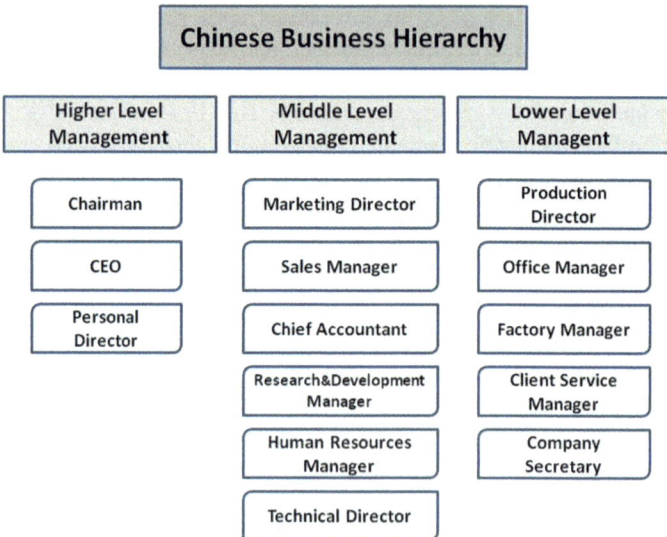

Fig. 1 Chinese business hierarchy (based on: https://www.hierarchystructure.com/chinese-bus iness-hierarchy/)

Chinese companies, promotions are based on age and length of employment rather than abilities and working results, although younger workers are often more talented than the older workers. Additionally, the younger workers must show more respect towards their elder colleagues than the other way around. In terms of Polish business area, seniority is taken into consideration usually in nationally run companies, such as Police Department, Fire Department, etc. In family run companies or Western companies, promotion depends on the overall results of a particular employee and progression of his/her work. It was considered much more efficient by the research subjects I have discussed this issue with.

4.2 The Distinctness of the Traditional Polish Culture, Polish Entrepreneurs and Business Etiquette

In order to understand the issues and challenges Polish entrepreneurs undergo during the business meetings with Chinese counterparts, one has to understand the uniqueness of Polish people's way of thinking and behaviour mechanisms, which will be explained in the following section.

Poland underwent a variety of historical events shaping its today image. Due to hundreds of years of wars, disappearing from the map of the world, and numerous, political engagements, defeat and deception, Poles have a strong memory of humiliation affecting their perception of themselves and, most importantly, others (Sztompka, 2002).

In 1989, as a post-communist society of Central and Eastern Europe, Poland's economy has transformed from a centrally-planned to the free-market economy. Sztompka (2002) claims that, aside from the change of the political and economic system in Poland, such an economic shift was also responsible for Poles' perception of values, norms, sense of self and their identity. She even called this new social, economic and political style of living being a cultural trauma for Poles. The transition period lasted until 2004, when Poland joined the EU (Klimczuk, 2010).

Höhmann et al. (2002) claims that people living in countries with transition economies, such as Poland, belong to 'low-trust' societies. Contrary to China, social trust in Poland is on a very low level. More and more Poles declare lack of trust in legislative and executive powers (over 60%), creating a general lack of trust leading to a consistent lack of cooperation what would be unacceptable in China.

The way in which we function within society, how we perform daily chores and preserve business relationships, strongly depends on our religious beliefs. Aside from the historical factors affecting Poles' way of living and perception of reality, Catholicism is also one of the key elements to understanding Polish people. Contrary to Confucianism, Catholicism is not promoting the entrepreneurial attitude, equality and harmony. It influences the power distance and emphasizes the social and economical inequality (Sztompka, 1996). Although, taking into consideration the power distance issue, it may seem similar to the Chinese business hierarchy, the Chinese structure is more stabilized, the power distance results from the level of seniority and working position rather than from economical inequality.

Due to Pole's strong attachment to the Polish history (especially the 19–20th Century) and the influence of the Catholic church, Polish people are very patriotic and have a strong sense of the national spirit and pride. However, it has been verified that over 51% of Poles see themselves as pessimist and admit taking pleasure in complaining about their underachievement, which is at odds with the Chinese 'you mianzi' concept, where pride and pessimism are seen as 'loss of face' (Rabczuk & Kuś, 2015). On the other hand, pessimism does not dim Polish people's strong need to strive for success, trying to be the best at everything. They often become unhealthily ambitious and hard-working, which leads to depression and overwork, which can be also seen in terms of Chinese people.

Contrary to Chinese entrepreneurs, Polish businessmen like to see the results of their actions quickly. They prefer shortcuts and situations leading to a quicker success, even if it means a short-term success. Whereas, as stated above, Chinese businessmen carefully consider all the possible implications of a particular decision, they are always taking their time in considering most favourable option in order to avoid 'losing face' in the process. 'Chinese spend far more time thinking about 'face', and see its relevance in far more situations than foreigners do (Seligman, 1999, p. 210).

Although Polish economy has grown impressively over the last two decades and Polish living standards (GDP per capita) have doubled (European Commission 2017),

Poles still fear for their working and living conditions, wages and overall well-being; thus, they are reluctant to share knowledge, believing that, by doing so, they create potential competition. Also, Polish managers' short-term orientation, high expectations and demand of quick results do not enhance business relations. It may lead to the end of a partnership at any time. All the above factors alter Polish way of conducting business.

4.2.1 Hierarchy—Social and Business Status in Poland

It is very difficult to introduce one unified vision of Polish business interaction and conduct. All in all, contrary to Chinese preference for establishing large companies employing more than 200 workers, Polish entrepreneurs prefer, as stated above, a 'family-run' businesses or small enterprises. There are over 1.8 million of such active companies in Poland employing less than 9 workers (Lewenstein, 2006). The smaller the company, the less trust issues it brings to the Polish owner or manager.

In Poland, we can also witness a form of 'guanxi' relationship between business entities. As stated above, Polish businessmen also see foreign cooperation as a window to benefits. Such a business relationship with foreign entrepreneurs is often strengthened by having well established connections or contacts in 'high places'. Additionally, Polish entrepreneurs also prefer handing over small gifts to their business partners. They believe that, by doing so, they tighten the relationship with one another and it is not treated as corruption. However, building up the relationship and business partnership never takes as much time as in the case of Chinese businessmen (Sztompka, 2002).

Above, I have mentioned four main cultural and social aspects influencing Chinese style of doing business. Also, I have introduced the most important, distinctive features of Polish people in general, emphasizing their influence on certain aspects of conducting business by Polish entrepreneurs. Having such knowledge enables the comprehension of the following material concerning the analysis of the arrangement of business meetings in China by Polish businessmen. Lack of such knowledge leads foreign businessmen to confusion and misunderstanding, which later often leads to business failure on the Chinese market.

5   Research

Both, Polish and Chinese perspectives of conducting business vary a great deal from one another. The following section is devoted to a comparative analysis of business meeting proceedings in Poland and China, enumerating the most prominent differences occurring in the entire process.

5.1 Business Meeting: Chinese Versus Polish Perspective: Comparative Analysis

Business meetings in China and Poland are proceeded in an entirely different way. It is necessary to emphasize that, due to two various dimensions in which Polish and Chinese entrepreneurs were bought up, and various cultural backgrounds they lived in, the arrangement and proceedings of business meetings both in Poland and China differ immensely. The following paragraphs are devoted to the comparative analysis of the abovementioned issues, with the emphasis of the culture-oriented background influencing the process of doing business in Poland and China.

5.1.1 Arranging a Business Meeting: Chinese Versus Polish Procedures

In Table 1, there are presented all the necessary actions that need to be arranged or are needed to take place in both China and Poland, respectively, before setting a date of a business meeting (Table 1). However, the data introduced in the following part of the article cannot and should not be treated as the only way in which business is proceeded. The following data is only a summary of the results I have gathered during my research conducted for the purposes of this article.

The analysis of the empirical data of my research enabled me to create Table 1 and led me to the conclusions that arranging a business meeting with Chinese

Table 1 Arranging a business meeting: Chinese versus Polish procedures

Arranging a business meeting	
Chinese perspective	Polish perspective
– Telephone/fax/email/wechat contact – Verification of the potential business partner (recommendations, reference, past working experience)—'guanxi' verification – Introduction of the reasons for the meeting – Justification of the meeting's necessity and verification of potential advantages to the Chinese company – If all the points are accepted—Issuing a date of the meeting – Preparation of the team of the Chinese experts needed for the purposes of the meeting (Chinese business hierarchy) and difficulty of setting a fixed date, due to experts' time limitations often arranged after the foreign delegation arrives to China) – Preparation of counterarguments for the meeting and negotiations – Written form of every single document	– Telephone/fax/email contact – Introduction of the reasons for the meeting – Issuing a date of the meeting – Written form of every single document

counterparts is a tiresome, confusing and time-consuming activity. Arrangement of a business meeting in Poland is limited to only three general actions: contacting the company one wants to make an appointment with, during which the introduction of the reason of the meeting is explained. Next, if the addressed company is interested in potential cooperation, both sides issue a date of the meeting during which everything else will be discussed in details. Each decision and procedure must be presented in a written form (just like in China), however, in Poland, e-mails often tend to be sufficient enough; in China, all the documents must usually be prepared in the form of paper documents with signatures and stamps on them, and even these documents are often being not taken under consideration by the Chinese party as sufficient enough. All in all, written agreements have priority over verbal agreements.

In addition, due to the strong influence of 'guanxi' on Chinese business conduct, Chinese counterparts need to verify their potential business partners, searching for recommendations and past experience a particular company had with others. Thus, it is wise to be prepared in advance, and have such documents ready for the 'needy Chinese'. This stage of verification is being processed by lower class management which decides if the offer is attractive enough to be presented to the higher level management or company officials ('Chinese business hierarchy'). This process takes time, all the pros and cons have to be analyzed in details, and only then will the date be issued. The delegation of Polish businessmen is usually limited to only two or three company members (usually because of financial reasons and time away from the office), but the Chinese side will never limit themselves to two or three people, no matter if the business meetings takes place in China or abroad. There are always at least 4–5 expert members aside from the CEO or a direct manager participating in the meeting. Arranging one fixed date suitable for everyone is often a very demanding task. After gathering all the experts and scheduling the date of the meeting, the Chinese side also needs some additional time to prepare themselves for negotiations, so that they would 'not lose their face' by being surprised with a question they did not expect.

Another issue is that although more and more Chinese speak fluent English, the company officials still know it quite poorly or not at all, thus each document must be translated into English either by the Polish company beforehand or by the Chinese party. This part, yet again, takes additional time. Thus, as illustrated above, business meetings with Chinese seem to be a daunting task before they even start.

5.1.2   Business Meeting in China. The Course of Events

When it comes to face-to-face business meeting and communication, both Polish and Chinese businessmen share some similar features. Both parties are considered to be formal, moderately quiet and likely to be reserved, especially when a particular meeting is the first one without prior cooperation and past experience. Additionally, in both countries jokes are rather not welcomed and are not well perceived during first contacts. They are usually reserved for more social occasions, rather than at important business meetings.

However, sometimes, in China, the host company arranges a lunch or dinner often served with alcohol prior to the business meeting in order to get familiarized with one another. Such meetings tend to be an 'incognito' examination of the potential business partner's behaviour, especially when it comes to the traditional style of drinking a considerate amount of alcohol 'ganbei' style—bottoms up. Only 5 out of all my research subjects were invited to the dinner prior to the business meeting, thus it cannot be considered being an organizational rule.

The data collected for the purposes of this research helped me enumerate the most important issues which are necessary to be considered in the process of the business meeting.

As can be seen in Table 2, there are many more stages occurring during a business meeting in China. Chinese people value punctuality. It is rude to come to a business meeting too early because it may stress the host that they did not prepare themselves for such circumstance. However, it is even worse to come late to the meeting. Although Chinese people are rather self-contained and avoid physical contact with strangers, Chinese hosts who had prior experience with foreigners usually prefer a handshake as a first physical contact with the Western Company representatives welcoming them in the hosts' company.

Usually, Polish company members know English at least on a communicative level, thus they rarely arrange for translators or interpreters to travel with them around China. However, as I emphasized in the previous sections, Chinese hosts (high level

Table 2 The course of a business meeting: Chinese versus Polish perspective

The course of a business meeting	
Chinese perspective	Polish perspective
– Punctuality – Special conference room – Greeting style – Special sitting arrangement – Introduction of each party member – Business card handing tradition – Waiting for the guest businessmen to start the Conversation/negotiation – Polite discussion of potential disagreements ('you mianzi') – Introduction of the host's demands – English-Chinese translator (always necessary) – Revision of the meeting process – Documents signing – Picture time – Gift giving ceremony – End of the meeting – Dinner or lunch together (a meal often organized before the meeting to get familiarized with the potential business partner)	– Flexibility – Rather free sitting arrangement – Standard welcoming – Host starts presenting the company – Start with the relevant issues of the meeting

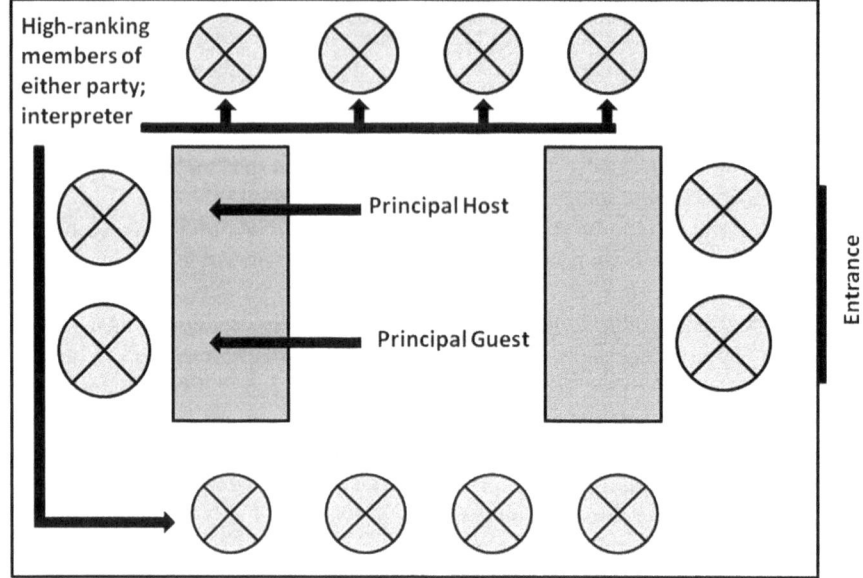

Fig. 2 Sitting arrangement during business meetings in China. 1 (based on: Seligman, 1999, p. 94)

management members) quite often have problems communicating in English, thus the English-Chinese translator's presence is always necessary during the meeting.

When a Chinese company is a host of the meeting, there are usually special conference rooms provided for the meetings. Also, there are certain sitting arrangements that need to be followed. They are best represented by the two pictures that can be seen in Figs. 2 and 3. It is necessary to mention that, depending on the rank of a particular worker, Chinese usually enter the room in a fixed order, first the boss enters with the guests, then other company members enter the room in the order of their experience and qualification level.

Figure 2 introduces a conference room in which there are three sitting spaces, one or two sofas and chairs on both sides of the sofa. The principal guest is always seated at the principal host's right side on a sofa opposite the door, so that they would always see people coming in and out of the room. Other high-ranking guests are seated in the immediate vicinity. Chinese workers are seated in a certain order, depending on their working status and company hierarchy status, only the translator must be seated next to the host of the meeting regardless of his/her business status.

In the following picture of the conference room sitting arrangement (Fig. 3), there is a big table in the middle of the room. In this configuration, the individuals are seated around this table in such a way so that the principal guest would be seated opposite the principal host. Additionally, the principal host should be seated back to the door so that any message from the offices outside the conference room could be quickly provided to the host without interruption of the meeting. It is also influenced by 'feng shui'; however, due to the space limitations of this article, I will not go

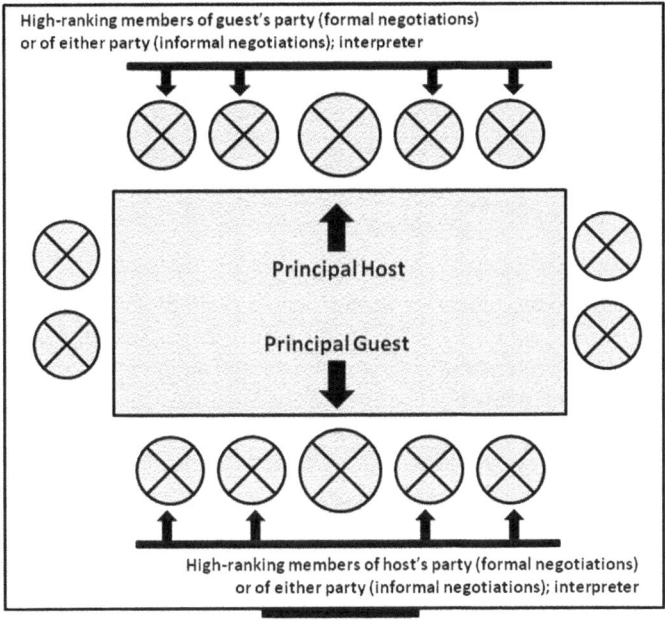

High-ranking members of guest's party (formal negotiations) or of either party (informal negotiations); interpreter

Principal Host

Principal Guest

High-ranking members of host's party (formal negotiations) or of either party (informal negotiations); interpreter

Entrance

Fig. 3 Sitting arrangement during business meetings in China. 2 (based on: Seligman, 1999, p. 95)

into more details. As can be seen in Fig. 3, the interpreters are, yet again, seated in the immediate vicinity of the principal host and guest. Sometimes, in this table arrangement, the name cards placed around the table ease the seating arrangement issue.

After the seating arrangement is finally fixed, each party member introduces themselves. Afterwards, business card handling occurs. It is followed by a set of rules. In China, one may disrespect a Chinese businessman when handing a business card using inappropriate manners. It is worth mentioning that business cards are sometimes being handed right after the primary introduction, sometimes, however, they are exchanged after the entire meeting. Nevertheless, it is necessary to hand a business card to a Chinese businessman with both hands, with the name directed towards the Chinese partner. While handing the business card, one should slightly bow towards the recipient of the card, but not too much. Contrary to Japanese businessmen's bow, the slight bow towards Chinese counterparts is rather delicate and limited to a head nod rather than a full upper body movement. After the Western guest receives the Chinese party's business card (also with both hands), one should take a moment to take a look at it, acknowledging the whole process and hide it either inside a business card case or a pocket of the upper part of the suit closer to your heart, never inside the trousers' pocket because that would be treated as a disrespectful act ('you mianzi').

After the acknowledgement of a business card, the Chinese host is waiting for the guest businessmen to start the conversation and negotiations. Due to the previously discussed 'you mianzi' concept, Chinese lead a rather formal and polite discussion. Poles, contrary to Chinese, are considered to be rather self-confident and decisive when it comes to business. They prefer maintaining direct eye contact, get straight to the point and say what they think (Table 2). Whereas Chinese businessmen rarely maintain direct eye contact and, in order to prevent 'losing face', they rarely directly issue statements which are contrary to the other party's goals, arrangements or ideas. They prefer 'going around the subject', which can often be seen by Polish people as suspicious.

After the negotiation process and reaching some kind of an understanding, Chinese business partners tend to prepare a written summary of all discussed matters so that everyone would make sure they understood the other party correctly. Afterwards, the document signing is being held with a commemorative photo.

In the end of the meeting, right before the closing dinner, the gift giving ceremony occurs. Chinese people are very superstitious; thus, there is a potential risk of handing the wrong type of present to Chinese hosts, which may result in hurting their feelings (and 'losing their face'). Thus, one should take a closer consideration towards this issue. The gifts, similarly to name cards, should be handed with both hands and should not be too expensive or in the amount of four because this number is treated as unlucky due to the fact that it sounds similar to the word 'death'. One should avoid giving watches, umbrellas, knives, and scissors as presents to Chinese people because they are all connected with negative emotions and will be treated as highly offensive gifts. It is best to choose something rather symbolic, connected with one's company or country of origin, a small souvenir, like sweets or some local symbolic souvenirs. After receiving a gift, it is important not to open it immediately, unless the person who gives it to you requests that you open it right away.

Before going to China, it is important to think about all the abovementioned tips so that no one would feel disappointed or disrespected. 100% of my research subjects stated that, before going to China, they had no prior knowledge about the abovementioned rules upon gift-giving tradition, thus most of them were prone to commit faux pas.

After the gift giving ceremony, everybody gathers around and goes for a meal together (if there was not one prior to the meeting); however, due to space limitations, I will not go into details because it is yet another very complicated topic.

6   Conclusions

The article introduced and analyzed the differences in terms of Polish and Chinese versions of business meetings and their arrangement with detailed analysis of the subject. The data was based on numerous empirical materials collected over the years of working with Polish and Chinese businessmen both in Poland and in China.

Despite the differences, Chinese also bare certain similar traits in terms of social interaction, such as keeping distance with the interlocutor. Both Polish and Chinese businessmen tend to be more formal than, for instance, American businessmen, and they rarely joke during the official part of the meeting, establishing a rather professional contact with one another (Table 3).

Polish entrepreneurs whom the author investigated also emphasized the fact that Chinese cherish the cultivations of the relationship and that Chinese companies spend heavily to establish and maintain relationships with influential people. However, sometimes all it takes to establish that connection is a conversation, a meal, or a favour. Thus, there could be found certain similarities in terms of 'guanxi' in Poland and China due to the fact that Poland, as one of post-communist countries, is included into collectivist, particularistic culture, moderately oriented to relationships (Gesteland, 2012; Glińska-Neweś, Escher, Brzustewicz, Szostek, & Petrykowska, 2016).

Table 3 Similarities and differences between Polish and Chinese entrepreneurs and business conduct

Polish perspective	Chinese perspective
Economy and social attitude	
Low trust economy	High trust economy
Low social trust	High social trust
People	
High self-esteem	Modest ('you mianzi')
self-confident, decisive	Indecisive, never refusing anything and polite ('you mianzi')
Pride, patriotism and a strong national spirit	Modest ('you mianzi')
A resemblance of 'you guanxi' in Polish business conduct	'You guanxi' concept
Pessimism	Positive, rarely complaining ('you mianzi')
Constant fear for one's welfare	–
Trust issues towards potential business partners	–
Religion	
Catholicism—mild influence	Confucianism—strong influence
Business conduct	
No unified business hierarchy	Fixed Chinese Business Hierarchy (triangle shaped business structure)
Promotion depending on working progress and results	Promotion by seniority
Quick response to any issue	Time-consuming response to any issue
Noticeable importance of 'guanxi'	Significant (strong) importance of 'guanxi'
Formal interaction	Formal interaction
Distance between the interlocutors	Distance between the interlocutors
Small amount of jokes (if any)	Small amount of jokes (if any)
Quick relationship development	Cultivation of the relationship
Small gift giving	Large gift giving ceremony

However, there are definitely more diversities concerning the specificity of Chinese business conduct, namely: the specificity of the triangle-shaped business hierarchy, the specificity and lengthy performance of each task being overanalyzed by each layer of the management structure, the significant influence of 'you guanxi' on the effectiveness of projects' performance, the concept of seniority over talent in terms of promotion, Polish and Chinese character traits' diversity, and, of course, culture-based differences (Table 3).

Polish businessmen must learn a significant amount of patience towards their Chinese business counterparts because the 'you mianzi' and 'you guanxi' concepts may cause numerous misunderstandings, especially when rather self-confident and decisive Polish businessmen expect results immediately, whereas Chinese businessmen must analyse everything with every business member (Table 3).

In the following, and last part of the article, the author provides a summarized set of tips on how to ease the process of doing business with Chinese, which was also analyzed and described in details in the previous sections of the article. The author also explains how to behave properly in the Chinese environment in order to avoid misunderstandings. Fortunately, nowadays, Chinese businessmen, especially the younger generation, are accustomed to the Western style of 'doing business', thus they are more understanding and respectful towards cultural differences. They do not expect foreigners to be entirely accustomed to Chinese traditions. However, knowing basic Chinese words, addressative forms and having a basic grasp of Chinese business etiquette and culture will not only impress future Chinese partners and clients, but will also enable building stronger foundation towards closer and more stable working relationships without misunderstandings and gaps in communication.

7 Final Remarks

Conducting business in China may give a company a chance to expand and grow rapidly. However, one has to take into consideration the cultural differences which were analyzed in details in the article. Below, I have enlisted a set of 10 helpful tips which would enable Western businessmen to succeed when discussing business matters with Chinese.

Tips for Polish businessmen willing to conduct business with Chinese entrepreneurs

1. Perform a solid market assessment in order to find a business area which would be attractive for both parties to collaborate.
2. Collaborate with long-term goals in mind.
3. Be prepared. Prepare your company's reference, especially from some actual business partners or the one's from the past.
4. Make good quality materials, best in both English and Chinese (if possible).
5. Be patient when arranging a meeting with Chinese counterparts.
6. Be punctual.
7. Conduct in formal introductions.

8. Consider the big cultural differences, so that you know how to behave properly in the Chinese environment.
9. Learn how to address Chinese business partners.
10. Learn some basic words in Chinese in order to impress the Chinese business partners.

Internet Sources

1. https://www.mylifeelsewhere.com/country-size-comparison/china/poland [last access date: 20.04.2019]
2. https://pl.china-embassy.org/pol/xwdt/t888992.htm [last access date: 20.04.2019]
3. https://www.scmp.com/comment/insight-opinion/article/3005496/why-austra lia-could-be-big-loser-us-china-trade-deal [last access date: 20.04.2019]
4. https://europe.chinadaily.com.cn/business/2016-03/12/content_23836397.html [last access date: 20.04.2019]
5. https://www.paih.gov.pl/index/?id=55053683268957697aa39fba6f231c68 [last access date: 20.04.2019]
6. https://pekin.msz.gov.pl/pl/wspolpraca_dwustronna/wspolpracagospodarcza/ wymianahandlowa/
7. https://warsaw-beijing.pl/intro-to-polish-chinese-relations/ [last access date: 20.04.2019].

References

Blackman, C. (1997). *Negotiating China: Case studies & strategies.* Australia: Allen & Unwin Pty Ltd.
Bogdanowska-Jakubowska, E. (2010). *Face. An interdisciplinary perspective.* Katowice: Wydawnictwo Uniwersytetu Śląskiego.
Chen, M. (1993). Tricks of the China Trade. *The China Business Review, 20*(2), 12–16.
Gesteland, R. R. (2012). *Cross-cultural business behavior: A guide for global management.* Copenhagen: Copenhagen Business School Press.
Glińska-Neweś, A., Escher, I., Brzustewicz, P., Szostek, D., & Petrykowska, J. (Eds.). (2016). *Relationship focused or deal-focused? The changing framework of building business relationships in Poland.* Poznań: 32nd IMP Conference.
Hofstede, G. (2003). *Cultures and organizations: Software of the mind.* London: Profile Books.
Höhmann, H. H., Kautonen, T., Lageman, B., & Welter, F. (Eds.). (2002). *Entrepreneurial strategies and trust: Structure and evolution of entrepreneurial behavioural patterns in East and West European environments; concepts and considerations.* Bremen: Forschungsstelle Osteuropa an der Universität Bremen.
Hu, H. C. (1944). The Chinese concepts of face. *American Anthropologist, 46,* 45–64.
Kaplan, R. D. (2015, February 6). Asia's rise is rooted in Confucian values. *The Wall Street Journal.* Retrieved from: www.wsj.com.

Klimczuk, A. (2010). Bariery i perspektywy integracji międzypokoleniowej we współczesnej Polsce. In D. Kałuża & P. Szukalski (Eds.), *Jakość życia seniorów w XXI wieku z perspektywy polityki społecznej* (pp. 92–107). Łódź: Uniwersytet Łódzki.

Kroeber, A. L., & Kluckhohn, C. (1952). *Culture. A critical review of concepts and definitions.* Cambridge, MA: The Museum.

Lewenstein, B. (2006). Społeczeństwo rodzin czy obywateli - kapitał społeczny Polaków okresu transformacji. *Societas/Communitas, 1*(1), 163–196.

MacDougall, C. (1980). *Trading with China: A practical guide.* London: McGraw-Hill.

Ostrowski, P., & Penner, G. (2009). *It's all Chinese to me: An overview of culture & etiquette in China.* North Clarendon, VT: Tuttle Publishing.

Lipartito, K. (2008). Business culture. In G. Jones & J. Zeitlin (Eds.), *The Oxford handbook of business history* (p. 604). United Kingdom: Oxford University Press.

Rabczuk, A., & Kuś, K. (2015). Pogoda jest obrzydliwa, dzieci chorują, a szef się na mnie wyżywa, czyli o tym, jak narzekać po polsku. *Kwartalnik Polonicum, 20,* 26–34.

Seligman, S. (1999). *Applause for Chinese business etiquette.* New York: Grand Central Publishing.

Sztompka, P. (2002). *Socjologia. Analiza społeczeństwa.* Kraków: Znak.

Sztompka, P. (1996). Trust and emerging democracy lessons from Poland. *International Sociology, 11*(1), 37–62.

Yeung, H.W.-C. (2007). *Handbook of research on Asian business.* United Kingdom: Edward Elgar Publishing.

Yutang, L. (1935). *My country and my people.* New York: Reynal & Hitchcock.

Yu, Y.-S. (2005). Confucianism and China's encounter with the west in historical perspective. *Dao, 4*(2), 203–216.

Katarzyna Bańka-Orłowska, Ph.D., received numerous scholarships and grants founded by the Chinese Embassy and the HANBAN institution, enabling her to participate in Chinese language classes and Chinese methodological training courses in China over the years 2007–2015 (Beijing Language University, Shanghai Normal University, etc.). She is a winner of the second prize in national part of the Chinese Bridge Competition, 2010 and a finalist of the national contest— Chinese Language Knowledge Contest, Warsaw 2012. In 2012, she became a permanent faculty member of the Institute of Linguistics, University of Silesia in Katowice. In 2016, she became a coordinator of the Chinese-English programme at the Institute of Linguistics. Her main interests concern: Chinese language acquisition and teaching, Chinese business culture and multilingualism.

Sociopragmatic and Strategic Functions of Humour in Intercultural Business Contexts

Anna Stwora

Abstract Humour plays an important role in corporate cultures and its sociopragmatic functions are already evidenced by ample research. This paper aims at supplementing the existing studies on this issue, presenting the results of a cross-cultural survey on humour in business context. The emphasis is placed on checking the awareness of the workings of humour in intercultural business contexts among Polish and Taiwanese respondents. Furthermore, the paper will focus on basic considerations related to humour, as well as on the universal and culture-specific aspects of humour. Is there a place for humour in business, in negotiations or in one's workplace? Is more humour associated with more risk in intercultural communication? Which strategic functions of humour seem crucial to the informants? These are the research questions the author will try to answer.

Keywords Humour studies · Functions of humour · Culture · Intercultural communication · Business context · Negotiation · Workplace

1 Introduction

Humour is all-pervasive a phenomenon which exerts significant influence on every aspect of human life, including workplace and business. Therefore, in the context of growing globalised communication and inter-cultural interaction, business people, including not only managers, but also grassroots employees, should know how to use it in multicultural communication on a daily basis. Humour is indeed a powerful managerial and communicative tool which may be used in various business contexts but, simultaneously, constitutes a double-edged weapon since, if the producer and receiver of the joke, for instance, happen to represent different cultures, a humorous attempt may simply fall short of the mark or even worse—sour the atmosphere of the workplace or ruin negotiations. If used with moderation and consideration, however,

A. Stwora (✉)
Faculty of Humanities, Institute of Linguistics, University of Silesia in Katowice, Katowice, Poland
e-mail: anna_stwora@interia.eu

© Springer Nature Switzerland AG 2020   143
U. Michalik et al. (eds.), *Exploring Business Language and Culture*,
Second Language Learning and Teaching,
https://doi.org/10.1007/978-3-030-58551-8_9

it can serve as an icebreaker, as a means to persuading others, motivating, facilitating change or saying the unspeakable (Barsoux, 1993).

It is widely acknowledged that humour plays an important role in corporate cultures and its sociopragmatic functions are already evidenced by ample research. This paper aims at supplementing the existing studies on this issue, presenting the results of a cross-cultural survey on humour in business context. The emphasis is placed on checking the awareness of the workings of humour in intercultural business contexts among Polish and Taiwanese respondents. In order to gain a deeper under-stating of how people representing these different cultures understand the notion of appropriateness of humour in business life, a qualitative study of two groups of respondents was undertaken and set against existing literature on the subject matter.

Furthermore, the paper will focus on basic considerations related to humour, as well as on the universal and culture-specific aspects of humour. Is there a place for humour in business, in negotiations or in one's workplace? Is more humour associated with more risk in intercultural communication? Which strategic functions of humour seem crucial to the informants? These are the research questions the author will try to answer. Numerous works cited in this paper will put current research into a larger context concerning humour in intercultural contexts, highlighting the significance of the sociologies of humour and cultural insider-knowledge (Critchley, 2002), which is vital not only in business, but also in general communication across cultures.

2   Humour Across Cultures in Business Contexts

As a field of study, intercultural business communication is located at the confluence of discourse, culture, communication, and business studies (Vuorela, 2005), which is why it requires comprehensive knowledge. Likewise, humour in multicultural busi-ness environments is complex an issue since it must take cognisance of numerous culture-specific tastes, possible taboo topics that vary across cultures or the very appropriateness of joking behaviours in specific contexts. Given its complexity and hence perilousness, "humour in the workplace has not always been considered desir-able. (…) However, the approach to humour and its role in the workplace has changed over the years" (Michalik & Sznicer, 2017, p. 23) because of its valuable sociateprag-matic functions. Thus, once avoided, humour is now invited in the workplace and negotiation as well so as to serve as an icebreaker, for instance. Naturally, this does not mean spontaneous going for the jocular, as each intercultural context of business communication, humorous or not, requires thorough consideration and preparation through "partnership research between business practitioners" (Vuorela, 2005, p. 14) or between co-workers; "it is important to move beyond within-culture comparisons as a basis for predicting intercultural negotiation processes" (Drake, 1995, p. 72) or conversations, to open one's mind to other cultures and their idiosyncrasies, as well as to rise public awareness of possible effects of varying cultural backgrounds in business and everyday communication in general.

Owing to their being related to the psychological and social well-being, performance, cooperation, and job satisfaction, "humour, joking, and shared laughter are basic and fundamental parts of human interaction, especially in the workplace (Morreall, 2008)" (Vivona, 2014, p. 1; cf. Scheel, Putz, & Kurzawa, 2017) since they can bring advantage to individuals and groups alike. "From a functional perspective, humour performs important cultural roles, such as enforcing social norms and defining cultural identity (…) (Duncan, 1985)" (Kim & Plester, 2014, p. 3), which encompasses both individual and in-group identities. This and many more sociopragmatic and strategic functions of humour will be described in this paper, with emphasis placed upon humour in multicultural workplace. Nonetheless, it seems advisable to provide the reader with a short overview of the general theories of humour and sociologies of humour beforehand so as to offer some background knowledge that is indispensable while discussing the topic. The following discussion will focus on literature concerning the notion of humour; then it will centre on the said sociopragmatic and strategic functions of humour, as well as on the universal and culture-specific aspects of the jocular.

2.1 Basic Considerations Related to Humour

While a plethora of definitions has been put forward to describe the notion of humour, the very construct of humour still poses some theoretical problems since it may refer to "(…) a feeling of amusement, a response of laughter, and a disposition to engage in a humorous or good-humoured manner. Therefore, conceptually, humour can be viewed in the forms of a stimulus, response or a disposition (Plester, 2007)" (Kim & Plester, 2014, p. 2). What is more, it should be remembered that humour is always in the eye of the beholder, so to speak, for it is not an intrinsic property of people, situations or things, as follows from the citation below:

> We may or may not "see the humour in the situation" depending on the contents of our mind at the time. This is not like failing to appreciate the size or shape of something we see because we are distracted. The joke, rather than being funny intrinsically, can be seen as an object that reliably provokes the sense of humour in a mind. (Hurley, Dennett, & Adams, 2011, p. 36)

Although things, people or situations are subject to individual perception, and in spite of the fact that humour is a matter of cognition, some stimuli are still more likely to produce humour than others, which is neatly captured by three general theories of humour known as incongruity, superiority, and relief theory of humour. While it is not the author's intention to provide an exhaustive review of literature on the topic, a set of representative sources will be cited with the aim of adumbrating the said theoretical frameworks and the sociologies of humour as well.

2.1.1 General Theories of Humour and Sociologies of Humour—A Short Overview

In contemporary humour studies, one can differentiate three basic theories of humour, namely the incongruity-resolution, superiority, and relief theory of humour. The INCONGRUITY- RESOLUTION THEORY rests upon discrepancies between the concepts contrasted that, once comprehended by the perceiver thanks to a conceptual shift, yield humorous effects (Attardo, 1994). The SUPERIORITY THEORY, on the other hand, says that people in general experience humour once they feel superior to someone who happens to be less fortunate as a result of an amusing mistake or mishap (Kim & Plester, 2014). Lastly, the RELIEF THEORY suggests that "humour reduces psychological tension (…). Nervous energy is released through laughter, where the suppressed desires (that individuals fear to express out in the open) are indirectly revealed to relieve the tension" (Kim & Plester, 2014, p. 5). Therefore, under this framework, humour functions as a valve that lets people vent emotions through joking, laughing or entertaining a humorous thought and hence get rid of stress.

As far as the sociologies of humour are concerned, one can point out to various social actions performed by humour. "According to sociologists, the social impact of joking and humour is very important in our everyday life and there are many different theories on the social impact of humour" (Mulder & Nijholt, 2002, p. 6), a division of which was proposed by Rutter (1997) and comprises three groups he calls maintenance theories, negotiation theories, and frame theories. To begin with, MAINTENANCE THEORIES, as the very name suggests, say that humour helps to maintain established social roles, order, and hierarchies both in private life (e.g., within the family) and within a given working environment. It can bond group members or, conversely, become a tool to point out one's mistakes or even punish him through making him the butt of a joke, for example. When it comes to NEGOTIATION THEORIES, they "focus on the role of humour as a means of interaction, pastime, and an event where more than one person is involved. The hearer decides if a joke is funny or not, depending on the social and cultural context of the joke and its environment" (Mulder & Nijholt, 2002, p. 7; cf. Rutter, 1997). In formal discussions aimed at reaching some kind of agreement, these theories are particularly crucial, for they revolve around contextual and cultural conditioning in an exchange of thoughts that should always take any intercultural differences into account. Last but not least, FRAME THEORIES "tend to see joking as a break from the everyday serious life. The joker makes a shift from the serious frame to the humorous frame and is allowed to present criticism without fear for retribution" (Mulder & Nijholt, 2002, p. 7; cf. Rutter, 1997). Such humour helps not only to reduce stress or weariness through having a break, but also to share thoughts in an open manner, thus being conductive to enhanced and uninhibited creativity. More details on the sociologies of humour introduced herein will be provided in the section devoted to the sociopragmatic and strategic functions of humour.

2.1.2   Humour in Its Universal and Culture-Specific Aspect.

Being embedded in all cultures, humour is a universal aspect of human experience (Kim & Plester, 2014; Martin, 2007), as people all over the world are reported to share similar basic cognitive structures when it comes to humour appreciation (Alden, Hoyer, & Lee, 1993); consequently, numerous cultures refer to the three rudimentary theories of humour outlined in the preceding section, which testifies to the fact that humour can be viewed as universal a phenomenon. As a matter of fact, people think alike when it comes to detecting incongruities, laughing at specific targets or feeling some kind of a relief once nervous tension is released through humour. This line of thought is supported by Goldstein, cited below:

> One might best make the assumption of cultural universality when dealing with the most fundamental sorts of behaviour. Physiological processes, for example, are quite likely to be trans-cultural, as are basic perceptual-cognitive principles and certain structural features of social interaction. (Goldstein, 1976, p. 167)

Nevertheless, it seems difficult to search for general principles of humour as the assumption of cultural universalism often becomes less tenable with regard to cultural remoteness. As a result, people are partial to certain jokes while others do not amuse them whatsoever and can even simply backfire (Barsoux, 1993).

> What is funny for the French may be anathema to an Arab; your very best story may be utterly incomprehensible to a Chinese; your most innocent anecdote may seriously offend a Turk. Cultural and religious differences may make it impossible for some people to laugh at the same time. (Lewis, 2006, p. 15)

In the light of the foregoing, "apparently all cultures use humour, but humour is often context-specific" (Vuorela, 2005, p. 15) because of the fact that "humour is local and a sense of humour is usually highly context-specific and is a form of cultural insider-knowledge" (Critchley, 2002, p. 67). Hence, it is culture that provides the behavioural framework within which humans happen to interact (Neuliep, 2016) and it is the sociocultural context that underlies the perception and appreciation of humour (cf. Michalik & Sznicer, 2017) (for a more comprehensive discussion of various dimensions and theoretical frameworks of cultures see Liu, 2015). If predicted, however, cultural differences may not even emerge in the course of an interaction between culturally different, or even discrepant, business environments (Drake, 1995). In human communication, especially in formally constrained contexts, humour is usually instantiated verbally, which is why the notion of the language of humour is perhaps as vital as the very theory behind it.

> Jokes are important not because of their consequences but as a phenomenon in their own right, as a favourite pastime of many people and a great source of popular enjoyment and creativity. Also, jokes provide insights into how societies work – they are not social thermostats regulating and shaping human behaviour, but they are social thermometers that measure, record, and indicate what is going on. (Davies, 1990, p. 9)

It is important to remember that humour has both its advantages and drawbacks. First of all, one should be aware of the way humour is understood by different people, which entails being sensitive to cultural and religious differences, for instance. If ill-timed, aggressive or confusing, humour can have a detrimental effect on interpersonal relations, one's self-esteem or negotiation processes (cf. Romero & Cruthirds, 2006). In a nutshell, it can be concluded that humour should be used with moderation and mindfulness since going for the jocular can be tricky indeed, especially that "the social context in which the joke is presented should be appropriate in order to enhance humour appreciation (Staley & Derks, 1995)" (Vuorela, 2005, p. 15).

> We must bear in mind that humour is a double-edged sword. Therefore, what some consider humorous may elicit contradictory, if not conflicting, emotions from others. (…) Humour has to be geared to the audience and occasion, otherwise it can have a damaging effect. (Michalik & Sznicer, 2017, p. 25)

2.2   Sociopragmatic and Strategic Functions of Humour

As far as the advantages of humour in workplace are concerned, they are captured by the sociopragmatic and strategic functions thereof, which are closely related to the sociologies of humour already adumbrated in the previous section (for an interesting pragmatic study on the strategic potential of humour see, e.g., Vuorela, 2005). As evidenced by ample research in the field, the most commonly recognised sociopragmatic and strategic functions of humour are "alleviating tension in stressful situations, communicating face-threatening messages, increasing one's persuasiveness, building solidarity, [and] boosting likeability" (Dynel, 2017; cf. Attardo, 1994; Martin, 2007), to name but a few.

Humour in professional contexts is generally purposeful (Vivona, 2014) but its purposes vary. First and foremost, humour in workplace and in corporate cultures contributes to the creation of TEAM SPIRIT through BUILDING SOLIDARITY (Dynel, 2017), as it reinforces group identity and cohesion (Michalik & Sznicer, 2017; Romero & Cruthirds, 2006; Vivona, 2014), as well as "the feelings of togetherness of a group" (Vuorela, 2005, p. 15; cf. Critchley, 2002). "Relationships can be built between individuals using humour as a medium of connection, as humour itself can create positive affect between different people" (Kim & Plester, 2014). It is a well-known fact that shared laughter or jokes requiring some insider knowledge make it possible to build group solidarity, bonding group members through in-group humour.

> Shared laughter and the spirit of fun generates a bonding process in which people feel closer together - especially when laughing in the midst of adversity. This emotional glue enables team members to stick together on the tough days, when members of the team need each other to complete a project and assure quality customer service. (McGhee, 1999)

Such bonding can even conduce to a considerable reduction of barriers that separate management from other employees, resulting in a SHORTENING OF THE DISTANCE between people; consequently, humour may lead to more open communication and frankness, working towards BUILDING TRUST (McGhee, 1999; Romero & Cruthirds, 2006), BOOSTING LIKEABILITY towards group members (Martin, 2007;

Dynel, 2017) or improving relations with partners and customers (Morreall, 2008; Michalik & Sznicer, 2017). Furthermore, the persuasive potential of humour is not to be underestimated either since it can serve to better one's argumentation and increase one's PERSUASIVENESS (Dynel, 2017), thus facilitating serious business confrontations (Barsoux, 1993), helping to boost morale, manage people in general or communicate ideas. In this context, "humour forms an important part of organisational culture. It is a means of communicating and maintaining organisational values and norms of behaviour. It also serves to punish and ridicule those who fail to observe them" (Michalik & Sznicer, 2017, p. 25; cf. Kim & Plester, 2014), thus, in fact, operating as a managerial tool.

Another aspect to be mentioned here is the one of creating a pleasant, more RELAXED ATMOSPHERE which can effectively counter any tension that builds up thanks to shared laughter or a note of levity introduced (Bullmore, 1991). This is particularly important as far as the maintenance of psychological well-being and work performance of the staff are concerned because humour can fulfil stress-relieving functions through introducing an air of detachment and countering ego depletion (Scheel et al., 2017). Humour can furthermore "help the employees to relax, inspire creative thinking, and thus improve their performance (Morreall, 2008, p. 460)" (Michalik & Sznicer, 2017, pp. 23–24), ENCOURAGING them to work and providing them with new, broader perspectives. Besides encouragement, humour can BREED CREATIVITY (cf. Barsoux, 1993; Morreall, 2008; Romero & Cruthirds, 2006) because it "opens up new ways of viewing things, and stimulates innovative ideas for solutions to difficult problems. This effect is especially important in team settings, where the ideas of one person can serve to trigger novel ideas for resolving problems in someone else" (McGhee, 1999). Therefore, the positive energy that comes along with humour opens space for creativity, for proposing, pondering over, and accepting new solutions.

"Humour, then, provides a channel for introducing new ideas on to the agenda and testing their validity. (…) All this is possible because the normal rules governing serious interaction are momentarily suspended when a remark is signalled as being humorous" (Barsoux, 1993, p. 49). In this way, "humour can pave the way for innovation" (Barsoux, 1993, p. 48) because it involves creative thinking and putting forward ingenious solutions. In fact, researchers point out to interestingly similar mechanics of problem solving involved in humour and problem solving in general (see: the incongruity-resolution theory), for both "Ha ha!" and "Aha!" (Hurley et al., 2011, p. 401) rely on finding solutions so as to fill in the gaps in comprehension; "the newly added jigsaw puzzle pieces from problem solving may complete a part of the puzzle, and at the same time add a new contradiction which helps to pinpoint a mistaken belief - a previously misplaced piece of the puzzle - thus causing mirth" (Hurley et al., 2011, pp. 401–402; cf. Koestler, 1964; Barsoux, 1993).

Apart from COMMUNICATING LEVITY or sprouting creativity, humour may also help in stressful or difficult situations when negative emotions arise since it "plays a role in how workers select and retain interpretations of work events" (Vivona, 2014, p. 3). Specifically, "it helps one to face threat rather than succumb to it. It can also serve to deflect criticism, cope with failure, and defuse conflict" (Michalik & Sznicer,

2017, p. 30) because it provides a sense of detachment, helping to distance oneself from problems and arguments (Barsoux, 1993), thus being an asset while HANDLING CONFLICTS or socially awkward situations through triggering laughter. Moreover, humour may also be used to COMMUNICATE FACE- THREATENING MESSAGES that may seem to violate the principles of politeness, give negative feedback or express mixed emotions (Dynel, 2017; Liu, 2015). In addition to maintaining face in communication, it can also serve to COMMUNICATE BAD NEWS in a manageable way, so to speak; as maintained by Barsoux, for instance, "confrontation in negotiation is more about *how* things are said than *what* is said" (Barsoux, 1993, p. 57), so, in this context, humour may be treated as a way out of thorny issues and as a means to stress reduction. The ALLEVIATION OF TENSION IN STRESSFUL SITUATIONS (Dynel, 2017) is perhaps the most central sociopragmatic function of humour; humour mitigates stress (Michalik & Sznicer, 2017; Morreall, 2008) and, what is more, is capable of changing stress perception (Romero & Cruthirds, 2006). Humour may serve as a tool to reconstruct or reframe situations for them to seem more bearable and less stressful, which testifies to the fact that humour can be used as a coping strategy (Abel, 2002).

Strategically beneficial as it is, though, one can never take humour for granted and expect it to bring positive results at all times since "the main problem is how individuals perceive humour and what they associate with it" (Michalik & Sznicer, 2017, p. 25). Because no topic or thing is humorous per se, humour is the function of perceptual processing (Hurley, Dennett, & Adams, 2017, p. 72), and perceptions differ across cultures, resulting in different realisations of humour. "The linguistic component cannot be isolated from the cultural one. In fact, humour is constrained by these two components, which indicates that there must be some common knowledge or experience (…)" (Fuentes Luque, 2010, p. 392) that is shared by the addressor of the humorous message and by its recipients. In business contexts, this poses a serious dilemma for both managers and employees, forcing them to decide whether to adopt a more global and universal perspective or the one centred on intercultural dissimilarities in communication, humorous or not. It is vital to bear in mind that "culture may predispose certain strategies over others but does not determine them. Rather, the choice would be made in the context of the interaction at hand" (Vuorela, 2005, p. 14), thus making it impossible to offer any solutions that would be applicable to all cases.

3   Survey on Humour in Business Contexts

In order to gain an understating of how humour in business contexts is understood across cultures, a quantitative study was undertaken based on a Google Docs survey conducted among two groups of respondents, namely Polish (60 informants, Business English students of the Institute of English, University of Silesia, Poland) and Taiwanese (45 informants, mostly students of the National Taiwan Normal University and graduates thereof that already have some job experience). The questionnaires were distributed online between March and September 2018. The respondents from each cultural group were exposed to the following set of questions:

Is there a place for humour in business?
Is there a place for humour in business negotiations?
Is there a place for humour in the workplace?
Can you name any constraints imposed on humour in the contexts listed above?
Choose 6 strategic functions of humour that seem the most important to you.

- *alleviating tension in stressful situations/stress reduction*
- *communicating face-threatening messages (that may seem impolite or express negative emotions)*
- *communicating bad news*
- *increasing one's persuasiveness/bettering one's argumentation*
- *building solidarity/team spirit*
- *boosting likeability*
- *breeding creativity/positive energy*
- *encouraging to work*
- *building trust*
- *handling conflicts*
- *creating pleasant/more relaxed atmosphere*
- *shortening the distance between people*

Is it okay to be humorous in intercultural/multicultural business/negotiations? Why? Why not?
Is there any aspect of humour you should avoid in multicultural contexts at all costs?

3.1 Polish Versus Taiwanese Perspective

First, the respondents were asked if there is a place for humour in business at all and they were unanimous in saying so, irrespective of the nation represented. The question concerning humour in the workplace yielded identical results, but when it comes to business negotiations, the author gathered only 75% of positive answers from Poles and 90% of positive answers from the Taiwanese group. As far as the main constraints imposed on humour in the abovementioned contexts are concerned, Polish informants listed cultural and religious aspects, differing senses of humour among people, and the specificity of the in-group sense of humour, as well as the offensive potential of humour; furthermore, some of them were concerned about increased tension caused by failed humour and about humour being unprofessional in certain formal contexts. The constraints mentioned by the Taiwanese included cultural differences and the provenience of business counterparts, mood and attitude, context, and the face-threatening use of potentially abusive or vulgar language. Having answered these preliminary questions, the informants were requested to look at the list of twelve strategic functions of humour and choose six that seemed the most important to them.

The most popular sociopragmatic functions of humour selected by Polish respondents (see Fig. 1) encompassed (1) breeding creativity and positive energy (80%), (2) creating pleasant atmosphere (80%), and (3) building solidarity or team spirit (75%). Most of them also claimed that humour contributes to (4) the shortening of the distance between people (70%) and (5) alleviating tension in stressful situations (70%), as well as helps to (6) encourage people to work (55%). Polish informants were therefore focused on the power of humour to make their working environment more relaxed, pleasant, and manageable. It is worth noting that they placed the playful aspect before the social one; the ability to boost likeability (50%) was considered relatively important, then followed handling conflicts and building trust (45% each), the remainder was marginal.

Taiwanese informants (see Fig. 2), on the other hand, placed (1) stress reduction first (90%). In the respondents' view, (2) shortening the distance between people (80%) and (3) creating pleasant atmosphere (80%) were equally important. Interestingly, their responses turned out to be very similar and, furthermore, four of them were consistently chosen by 50% of the respondents; these encompassed: (4) building

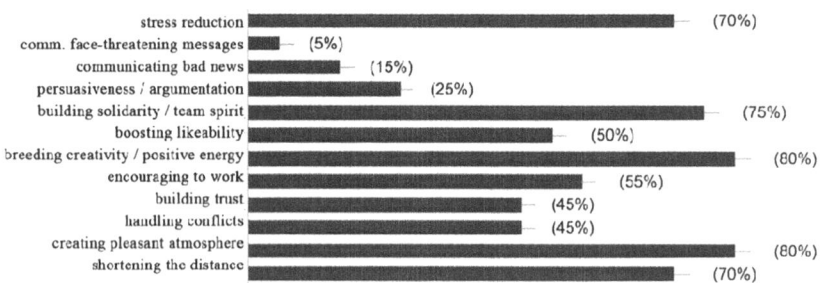

Fig. 1 Strategic functions of humour chosen by Polish respondents. Designed in Google Docs by A. Stwora

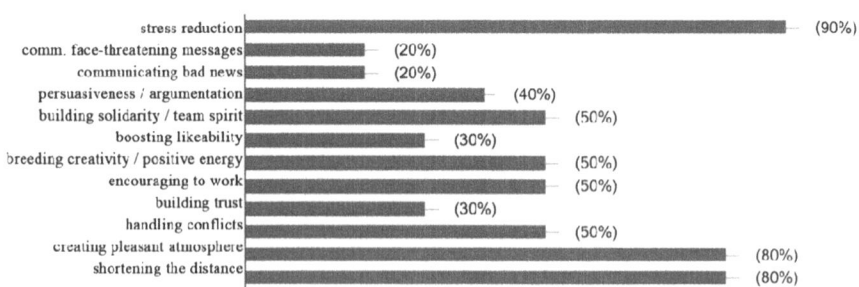

Fig. 2 Strategic functions of humour chosen by Taiwanese respondents. Designed in Google Docs by A. Stwora

solidarity and team spirit, breeding creativity and positive energy, encouraging to work, as well as handling conflicts. Thus, for the Taiwanese respondents, going for the jocular in professional contexts is also connected with the issue of playfulness, well-being, and maintaining good relations with others, which is particularly important for this pro-partner and relationship-focused culture (Gesteland, 2002). Unlike Poles, Taiwanese informants also acknowledged the role of humour in increasing one's persuasiveness and bettering one's argumentation (40%).

Subsequently, the informants were requested to answer the following question: *Is it okay to be humorous in intercultural/multicultural business/negotiations?* 75% of Polish respondents agreed, saying that "as long as you know the cultural boundaries and move within them, there is no reason to limit your scope of expression" (anonymous survey respondent). Nonetheless, many of them claimed that negotiations should be kept serious, for one should be aware of the threats of failed humour. According to the Taiwanese, humour in intercultural business context is allowed (80% of the respondents agreed) as long as the counterparts are respectful, aware of the cultural differences, and do not overuse humour. Given their cultural profile, they were probably centred on these issues because they value harmony with others, observation of social rituals, kindness, moderation, and courtesy (Neuliep, 2016).

The last query in the survey was aimed at getting the respondents opinions on the aspects of humour that should be avoided in multicultural contexts at all costs. Thus, Polish informants listed black humour, racist jokes, jokes about sex, religion or sensitive cultural topics, as well as jokes addressing personal issues; moreover, they also suggested that one should abstain from telling jokes about history, bombs or terrorist attacks. Taiwanese respondents, in turn, said that it would be advisable to refrain from jokes about religion or sex, racist jokes, gender-related jokes, and jokes addressing personal or political issues.

4 Conclusions

Having surveyed the participants from two linguistic and cultural backgrounds, it appears that their responses overlap to a certain extent despite cultural remoteness. As far as the sociopragmatic functions of humour are concerned, the results obtained show that Polish respondents indicated that humour-induced playfulness and well-being thanks to positive energy and good team spirit at work were most valued; then followed the social aspect responsible for bonding people and making them less worried. Being representatives of a variably expressive culture, Poles claimed that it is good to use humour, but with moderation and consideration. Taiwanese informants, on the other hand, placed emphasis on such sociopragmatic functions of humour as stress reduction, shortening the distance between people, and creating a more relaxed atmosphere, yet their main concern was avoiding face-threatening situations that humour may engender. This culture is known for treating humour with ambivalence and reserve, for being humorously serious even, which may be attributed to Confucianism that upholds social order and hierarchy (Drozd, 2020; Neuliep, 2016).

Both cultural groups surveyed were for the use of humour in business and in one's workplace but had some misgivings when it comes to humour in business negotiations. As can be observed, the results of the survey were a touch contradictory since, on the one hand, the informants were positive about using humour but, simultaneously, seemed to be driven by fear and the more they thought about the topic, the more reservations they voiced about the appearance of humour in formal contexts. Naturally, it is not the author's intention to generalise from the student population to non-students since they lack certain professional experience that would have helped them handle the topic. Rather, choosing this particular age group was aimed at sensitising them to the workings of humour, as they will sooner or later enter the business market and thus will need to develop their sociopragmatic knowledge of humour in business situations. Obviously, humour is used differently in different workplaces, which results from different cultures, values, specialisations, etc. (Holmes & Marra, 2002); in such contexts, if one decides to go for the jocular, he should remember about the multicultural nature of the modern world and business contacts, as well as that humour has to be inclusive. If used properly, it can become an important source of strategic advantage, for "humorous interaction is bracketed off from normal interaction" (Barsoux, 1993, p. 50), inviting more ease, creativity, relaxation, and levity to mundane activities. "Simply speaking, humour makes working life more liveable (…) [but] one must bear in mind that although the ability to appreciate and enjoy humour is universal and shared by all people, each culture has a different perception of what constitutes humour" (Michalik & Sznicer, 2017, p. 30).

Humour has its own dynamics conditioned by the language, community, culture, and context factor, which is why cross-national comparisons are so valuable: they enable to compare value orientations among cultures and trace trans-cultural differences or similarities. Consequently, further research on the topic should certainly cover more cross-cultural studies on humour in professional contexts, as well as possible analyses that would, for example, take into account the scale of business (e.g., by means of comparing results for big and small companies). All in all, only cross-cultural studies can provide profound and invaluable insights into the dimensions of cultural variability of the modern world.

References

Abel, M. H. (2002). Humor, stress, and coping strategies. *Humor—International Journal of Humor Research, 15*(4), 365–381.

Alden, D. L., Hoyer, W. D., & Lee, C. (1993). Identifying global and culture-specific dimensions of humor in advertising: A multinational analysis. *Journal of Marketing, 57*(2), 64–75.

Attardo, S. (1994). *Linguistic theories of humor*. Berlin and New York: Mouton de Gruyter.

Barsoux, J. L. (1993). *Funny business: Humour management and business culture*. London: Cassell.

Bullmore, J. (1991). *Behind the scenes of advertising*. Henley-on-Thames: NTC Publications.

Critchley, S. (2002). *On humour. Thinking in action*. London: Routledge.

Davies, C. (1990). *Ethnic humor around the world: A comparative analysis.* Bloomington and Indianapolis: Indiana University Press.

Drake, L. E. (1995). Negotiation styles in intercultural communication. *International Journal of Conflict Management, 6*(1), 72–90.

Drozd, I. (2020). Analysis of humour translation from Chinese to Polish in "Balzac and the little Chinese seamstress." In M. Kuczok, A. Stwora, & M. Świerkot (Eds.), *Explorations in humor studies: Humor research project* (pp. 31–49). Newcastle upon Tyne: Cambridge Scholars Publishing.

Duncan, W. J. (1985). The superiority of humor at work: Joking relationships as indicators of formal and informal status patterns in small, task-oriented groups. *Small Group Research, 16*(4), 556–564.

Dynel, M. (2017). *Seeking the truth about humour: Humour and (un)truthfulness.* Paper presented during the seminar Humor Research Project, University of Silesia in Katowice, November 30, 2017.

Fuentes Luque, A. (2010). Shopping around: Translating humour in audiovisual and multimedia advertising. In C. Valero-Garcés (Ed.), *Dimensions of humor: Explorations in linguistics, literature, cultural studies and translation* (pp. 387–406). Diazotec: Universitat de València.

Gesteland, R. R. (2002). *Cross-cultural business behaviour. Negotiating, selling, sourcing and managing across cultures.* Gylling: Copenhagen Business School Press.

Goldstein, J. H. (1976). Cross cultural research: Humour here and there. In A. J. Chapman & H. C. Foot (Eds.), *It's a Funny Thing, Humour: Proceedings of the International Conference on Humour and Laughter* (pp. 167–174). Oxford etc.: Pergamon Press.

Holmes, J., & Marra, M. (2002). Having a laugh at work: How humour contributes to workplace culture. *Journal of Pragmatics, 34*(12), 1683–1710.

Hurley, M. M., Dennett, D. C., & Adams, R. B., Jr. (2011). *Inside jokes. Using humor to reverse-engineer the mind.* Cambridge, MA and London: The MIT Press.

Hurley, M. M., Dennett, D. C., & Adams, R. B., Jr. (2017). *Filozofia dowcipu. Humor jako siła napędowa umysłu* (R. Śmietansa Trans.). Kraków: Copernicus Center Press.

Kim, H., & Plester, B. (2014). *Ironing out the differences: The role of humour in workplace relationships.* Paper presented during the Australian and New Zealand Academy of Management Conference (ANZAM 2014), Australian and New Zealand Academy of Management in Sydney, Australia, December 3–5, 2014.

Koestler, A. (1964). *The act of creation.* London: Hutchinson.

Lewis, R. (2006). *When cultures collide. Leading across cultures.* Boston/London: Nicolas Brealey Publishing.

Liu, Y. (2015). *A Paradigm for business communication across cultures: Theoretical highlights for practice.* Tsinghua: Tsinghua University Press.

Martin, R. A. (2007). *The psychology of humour: An integrative approach.* Burlington: Elsevier Academic Press.

McGhee, P. E. (1999). *The laughter remedy.* Retrieved from https://www.laughterremedy.com/humor.dir/humor7_99.html.

Michalik, U., & Sznicer, I. (2017). The use of humor in the multicultural working environment. In D. Gabryś-Barker, D. Gałajda, A. Wojtaszek, & P. Zakrajewski (Eds.), *Multiculturalism, multilingualism and the self: Studies in linguistics and language learning* (pp. 19–32). Berlin: Springer.

Morreall, J. (2008). Applications of humor: Health, the workplace and education. In V. Raskin (Ed.), *The primer of humor research* (pp. 449–478). Berlin: Mouton de Gruyter.

Mulder, M. P., & Nijholt, A. (2002). Humour research: State of the art. *CTIT Technical Reports Series, 2*(34), 1–24.

Neuliep, J. W. (2016). *Intercultural communication: A contextual approach.* Thousand Oaks: SAGE Publications.

Plester, B. (2007). *Laugh out loud: How organisational culture influences workplace humour.* (Unpublished doctoral thesis). Albany, New Zealand: Massey University.

Romero, E. J., & Cruthirds, K. W. (2006). The use of humor in workplace. *Academy of Management Perspectives, 20*(2), 58–69.

Rutter, J. (1997). *Stand-up as interaction: Performance and audience in comedy venues.* (Unpublished doctoral thesis). University of Salford.

Scheel, T., Putz, D., & Kurzawa, C. (2017). Give me a break: Laughing with colleagues guards against ego depletion. *European Journal of Humour Research, 5*(1), 36–51.

Staley, R., & Derks, P. (1995). Structural incongruity and humor appreciation. *Humor—International Journal of Humor Research, 8*(2), 97–134.

Vivona, B. D. (2014). "To laugh or not to laugh": Understandings of the appropriateness of humour and joking in the workplace. *European Journal of Humour Research, 2*(1), 1–18.

Vuorela, T. (2005). *Approaches to a business negotiation case study: Teamwork, humour and teaching.* Helsinki: Helsinki School of Economics Print.

Anna Stwora obtained her Ph.D. from the Institute of Linguistics, Faculty of Humanities of the University of Silesia in Katowice, Poland. She is also a Ph.D. student in linguistics at the Sapienza University of Rome, Italy. Her research interests oscillate around multimodal discourse of advertising, especially in its metaphorical and humorous dimensions, as well as around specialized registers viewed from the psycholinguistic and sociolinguistic standpoint. She is also interested in cognitivism, communication studies, and contrastive linguistics. In 2020, she took up a post as editorial assistant at *The European Journal of Humour Research*. She has been involved in several projects, including seminars, workshops, and conferences devoted to humour and contrastive studies, as well as to business language and culture. Her recent publications include *Humor Research Project: Explorations in Humor Studies* (2020). Cambridge Scholars Publishing (co-edited with Marcin Kuczok and Mariola Świerkot); "How to befriend an ad? A sociolinguistic and sociocultural inquiry into social media ads on Facebook" (2018); "Money Hanging in My Closet? Various Conceptualisations of Money in English" (2018); and "Language Change Through Ads: The Impact of Advertising Messages on Contemporary Idio- and Sociolects" (2018).

Using Cultural Taxonomies to Understand Intercultural Relations in Business

Anna Zelenková

Abstract The relations between culture and business have been explored by many disciplines, which resulted in the creation of cultural theories and cultural taxonomies. The cultural taxonomies provide us with the insights into how cultures are manifested, how they are associated with social groups, or how they influence people's behavior and interaction. Our paper is a theoretical study aimed at exploring interconnections between culture and business and the impact of culture on the way international business is done today. For this purpose, the paper presents four selected theories of culture and cultural taxonomies which are applied in business studies in order to raise the intercultural competence of (future) workers in a culturally diverse business world. Firstly, the paper gives the background to the concept of culture. Secondly, it explores four selected cultural taxonomies relevant to international business. Thirdly, it specifies some areas in which the knowledge of cultural taxonomies and cultural characteristics can help raise awareness of intercultural relations in business. We focus on the cultural knowledge and skills which are necessary for avoiding misunderstandings in intercultural communication in business situations.

Keywords Cultural taxonomies · Culture studies · Business studies · Culture and business

1 Introduction

The beginning of the twenty-first century is marked by increased connectivity and interdependence of markets, which has made the world of business more complex than ever before. Space has opened up for the mobility of ideas, goods, businesses, and the work force. For many people and companies, a location in a foreign country has become a must. Companies are trying to maintain their competitive advantage either by hiring skilled and educated professionals from abroad, or by using cheaper

A. Zelenková (✉)
Department of Professional Communication in Business, Faculty of Economics, Matej Bel University in Banská Bystrica, Banská Bystrica, Slovakia
e-mail: anna.zelenkova@umb.sk

© Springer Nature Switzerland AG 2020
U. Michalik et al. (eds.), *Exploring Business Language and Culture*,
Second Language Learning and Teaching,
https://doi.org/10.1007/978-3-030-58551-8_10

foreign labour force of less developed countries. While these practices bring many advantages to the company, they also bring problems. The more cultures are present in a company, the higher the chances for cultural conflicts in communication, managerial approaches, organizational cultures, and other issues that affect the way business is done today.

This is why intercultural issues have been the focus of many researchers, anthropologists, linguists, and psychologists. Studies in intercultural communication and intercultural management have been undertaken as a result of the increasing demand of multinational companies for better understanding of cultural differences. One of the outputs of intercultural research are the cultural theories which categorize various cultures into certain groups according to the features they share. The knowledge of these categorizations can help business people around the globe to face differences in the ways business is conducted in different parts of the world. There are many cultural theories and taxonomies, but, in our paper, we have decided to present four selected taxonomies of cultures that can be applied in international business relations and used as guidance for intercultural understanding, effective communication, and adequate behaviour.

2   Theoretical Background to Culture in Business

When studying the relations between culture and business, it is necessary to understand the concept of culture. The traditional distinction is between *high culture* and *low culture*. Under high culture (also called "Olympian culture" (Brooks, as cited in Omaggio-Hadley, 1993, p. 361)) we understand the cultural representation, such as great literature, music, arts, and architecture of a given country, while under low culture other aspects and the patterns of everyday life of a culture-bound group of people are included. Another distinction points out the *material culture* (products and artefacts of culture, institutions, and systems) and the *non-material, spiritual culture* (way of thinking, beliefs, behaviour, and values) as the distinctive achievements of human groups (Kroeber & Kluckhohn, as cited in Adler, 2008, p. 18). In late 1960s, the shift in cultural studies changed focus. They moved from the study of formal aspects of a civilization to an emphasis on anthropological or sociological concerns, including intercultural communication (Hall, 1966; Seelye, 1987).

Culture is a complex phenomenon and carries many different meanings. It has been defined in many ways, depending on the discipline it is studied by, such as anthropology, sociology, linguistics, psychology, communication science, and others. The beginnings of theoretical studies can be set in the 1950s when Parsons (1951) designed his theory of culture as a social system, which is, on the one hand, the product of, and on the other—a determinant of systems of social interaction. As a social system, culture presents an institutionalized system of beliefs and values (Parsons, 1951, pp. 56–58) which is learned, shared, and transmitted, and constitutes a heritage or a social tradition (Geertz, 1973). Other anthropologists see culture as all acquired knowledge, beliefs, art, law, morals… and "any capabilities and habits acquired by a person as a member of a society" (Symington, as cited in Adler, 2008, p. 18), or as more or less stereotyped patterns of learned behaviour. Kroeber and Kluckhohn (as cited in Adler, 2008) defined culture as patterns of and for behaviour, acquired and transmitted by symbols; the core of any culture consists of "traditional ideas and beliefs and their attached values" (Adler, 2008, p. 18). Another, if not the most important, element of any culture is language and communication, both verbal and non-verbal. The way people communicate reflects their cultural reality. Language expresses how people view the world around them. Its omnipresent quality makes it one of the most powerful stimuli behind human behaviour (Samovar, Porter, & McDaniel, 2006). This point was also underlined by Hall (1966) when he concluded that "there is not one aspect of human life that is not touched and altered by culture" (p. 169). According to his studies, culture is perceived as a "set of subconscious incentives and mechanisms which lead to specific behaviour of members of a given culture" (Hall, 1997, p. 15). We can see that culture is defined as a broad concept which embraces all aspects of human life. A Dutch social anthropologist and sociologist Geert Hofstede (2001) defines culture as deep values which are surrounded by more visible practices. He also suggests that culture is the "software of the mind... it is the collective programming of the mind which distinguishes the members of one group or category of people from another" (Hofstede, Hofstede, & Minkov, 2010, p. 6). Hence, culture is the unique lifestyle of a particular group of people.

Psychology defines culture as "a way of thinking, feeling, believing. It is the group's knowledge stored up (in memories of people; in books and objects) for future use. A culture constitutes a storehouse of the pooled learning of the group" (Adler, 2008, p. 18). On the other hand, communication sciences and linguistics study culture as the way of communication of a certain group of people (Kramsch, 1993). They assert that "culture is communication and communication is culture" (Ramírez, 1995, p. 59). The basic characteristics which are repeatedly mentioned in these definitions are as follows: culture is passed and transmitted from one generation to the next through the process of inculturation; culture is shared—members of a given culture share their beliefs, communicate and develop their knowledge about attitudes towards life; culture is symbolically expressed; and, culture is adaptive—societies are constantly adapting to the environment in order to survive. As Maude (2011) concludes, underpinning most definitions of culture is the concept of culture as "a system of beliefs, values, and practices which enable particular cultures to solve universal problems" (Maude, 2011, p. 4). Among universal problems she includes the relations to age, the relations within a family, or relations between men and women. Maude's model of culture, as a closed system of interrelated cultural values, basic beliefs, and cultural practices (p. 5), may be a good outset for understanding the nature of intercultural relations in business.

We can conclude that the culture we talk about in a business context is mainly defined by social sciences (culture as learned group-related perceptions), communication sciences influenced by anthropological studies (culture as contextual, symbolic patterns of meaning, involving emotions), and interdisciplinary cultural studies (culture as a heterogeneous, dynamic and contested zone) (Martin & Nakayama, 2010).

All the mentioned aspects of culture, such as values, beliefs, patterns of behaviour, ways of thinking, language, material objects and artefacts, social patterns for living, social systems and rules, deep and inherited knowledge are the factors around which various taxonomies of cultural groups have been developed by various scholars and researchers. The knowledge of these taxonomies, their identification and application in business context lead to better understanding of the ways business is conducted in international contexts.

3 Cultural Taxonomies

Cultural taxonomies present the output of practice of classifying world cultures based on theoretical concepts of cultures delivered by scientific disciplines. Cultural taxonomies are based on certain principles underlying these classifications. The classifications are done from different points of view, in which such factors as national characteristics, attitudes to various aspects of life, ways of thinking or communication, and behavioural patterns play a role.

In the following part of the paper, we shall present selected cultural taxonomies whose characteristics are reflected in business practices and applied in business studies in order to prepare future businesspeople for effective functioning in today's business world. The only criterion for selecting these theories is their impact on cultural studies and intercultural communication studies, and their relevance for international business.

3.1 Edward Hall's Taxonomy: Basic Cultural Factors

The first taxonomy to discuss is the taxonomy of cultures based on the concept of key cultural factors defined by the American anthropologist Edward Twitchell Hall (1966). According to this scholar, the key cultural factors making difference between cultures are context, time, and space. These factors also have an impact on intercultural communication in business. Hall's theory influenced further development of intercultural communication studies.

Context (contextual dimension) as a cultural factor distinguishes between *high-context* and *low-context* cultures. People tend to express their thoughts and feelings in different ways. In high-context cultures, there are many contextual elements that help people understand the rules. Much is taken for granted, so, for the outsider, it may be difficult or confusing to understand the "unwritten rules". People in high-context cultures are generally not direct in their expressions, use a lot of non-verbal communication, and many covert and implicit messages, with the use of metaphors where reading between the lines is required. In the case of international business, the process of doing business, negotiating or making a contract is more important than the product of this process (signing a contract).

Low-context cultures are more direct, strict, and organized in their time schedules. Overt and explicit messages, which are simple and clear, dominate interaction. They tend to be more specific and expressive in behaviour. During conversations or negotiations, they tend to go straight to the point without any unnecessary talks. Fulfilment of the task is more important than the process and relationships.

Space factor (spatial dimension) laid foundation of proxemics, the study of space and relations within it. Hall found out that, in some cultures, people need more space in all areas than people in other cultures. Hall described four main types of personal distances for different situations: intimate, personal, social, and public distances, which change depending on culture. For instance, an Argentinian person who needs less space will stand closer to a Canadian, which will make the Canadian feel uncomfortable.

The time factor (temporal dimension) described cultural differences in the perception of time and divided cultures into two main groups: *monochronic* and *polychronic* cultures. Monochronic orientation means doing one thing at a time, concentrating on the job at hand. It also assumes careful planning and scheduling. Polychronic time orientation, on the other hand, means the ability of doing several activities at once. It may also involve easy distraction from the job to be done. Human interaction is valued over time, leading to a lesser concern for getting things done.

Hall's research and work (done in the 1950s and 1960s) remained influential for the years to come and laid foundations for the study of intercultural communication.

3.2　Hofstede's Taxonomy: A Model of Dimensions of Culture

The second taxonomy of cultures is based on Hofstede's analysis of national cultures in work context (Hofstede et al., 2010). As the research was conducted in business context (employees of IBM in more than 50 branches around the world), it is valuable for understanding interaction in international business and management. Business-people working internationally use this classification today and find it a good guideline for intercultural interaction, as it provides the characteristics of national business cultures. According to Hofstede's dimensional model of culture, each culture can be analysed according to six different dimensions. Hofstede developed such categories as individualism and collectivism, power distance, masculinity and femininity, long-term and short-term orientation, uncertainty avoidance, and indulgence versus restraint. These differences in cultural values influence communication, interaction, and business behaviour.

The dimension of *individualism vs. collectivism* explains how people see themselves: either as independent individuals or as members of a group. Individualistic societies see people as single, independent actors, not as group members at a deep level, as people in collectivistic societies do. In individualistic cultures, people are supposed to look after themselves and their close relatives. In collectivistic societies, people feel they belong to in-groups (or larger collectives) which are supposed to look after them in exchange for loyalty. Being a group member is a natural thing and is a matter of identity. Dependency on the group's decision is stronger than any individual wish or goal.

Masculinity versus femininity dimension gives insight into which values prevail in particular societies. In masculine societies, the dominant values are achievement and success. Masculinity is demonstrated by such values as: strength, achievement, competition, assertiveness, and performance. On the other hand, femininity is demonstrated by kindness, building relationships, caring for people and the environment, sharing, and reaching agreement through communication. In a culture with a low masculinity dimension, men also share the values connected with women and there is more equality between men and women.

Power distance dimension shows the gap between people who have power and those without power in a group (which can be a community, a company, or the whole society). It explains how the less powerful members of a society (or organization) accept that power is distributed unequally. *High-power distance* cultures are hierarchical, with power concentrated on a small number of people at the top who make most of the decisions. In this type of cultures, the gap between those with a lot of power and those with little power is wider. *Low-power distance* cultures expect power to be earned and the power relations are more democratic than those in a high-power distance society.

Uncertainty avoidance dimension puts societies into two groups: those with high uncertainty avoidance and those with low uncertainty avoidance. In high uncertainty avoidance cultures, people prefer to have everything presented in details without any surprises or shocks in order to avoid uncertain or risky situations. In low uncertainty avoidance societies, people are more relaxed about the unknown, unexpected or new situations and do not worry if they do not have all the details. Unclear situations are not seen as a problem, but as a challenge.

Long-term versus *short-term* orientation is the dimension explaining which perspective prevails in a society. In long-term oriented cultures, people exhibit a future-oriented perspective and pragmatism, while in short-term cultures, past or near-term perspective and conventional, normative views prevail: respect for tradition, social obligation, protecting ones face, etc.

The sixth dimension added to the original Hofstede's five-dimensional model of cultures is that of indulgence versus restraint. Indulgent societies take gratification of basic desires, wishes, and natural human needs for granted. Enjoying life and having fun is a natural component of life. People in these societies feel free to pursue their happiness and are healthier and happier. They know how to use and organize leisure time, participate actively in sports, are optimistic, and have a sense of personal life control. Restrained societies, on the other hand, suppress gratification of desires and needs, and regulate them by means of strict social norms. People feel less happy and less healthy, are more pessimistic, cynical, and introverted personalities with stricter moral discipline.

Hofstede's theory has been criticized by many scholars (Essays, UK, 2018; McSweeney, 2002) because the dimensions are attached to national characters and can produce national stereotypes. It is important to remember that these dimensions are tendencies, not rules. They just explain how members of particular cultures tend to behave and can give important insights for someone wishing to enter a new culture for business or other purposes. The knowledge of this typology can help us predict action or behaviour of groups, societies, or nations, but we should take into account that there will always be different individuals.

3.3 Trompenaars and Hampden-Turner's Business Cultures Taxonomy

Trompenaars and Hampden-Turner (1997) defined business culture as "the way in which a group of people solves problems and reconciles dilemmas" (p. 6). They have defined seven fundamental dimensions of culture and cultural typologies accordingly. The classifications of five of them are based on the relationships with other people and include such categories as universalistic or particularistic cultures. In universalistic cultures rules prevail, while in particularistic cultures relations and particular interests prevail above keeping the rules. Another category includes communitarian versus individualistic cultures, which shows the difference in how people primarily regard themselves: as individuals or parts of a group. The dimension of neutral versus emotional is about the range of feelings which are acceptable to be displayed in an interaction. Neutral cultures do not display emotions as often as emotional cultures. The category of specific versus diffuse explains the difference in how much a person is involved in a business relationship—allowing either for a real and personal contact or following a very strict, specific relationship prescribed by a contract. The achievement versus ascription dimension distinguishes between the ways people are judged and rewarded in an organization: either according to their performance or achievements, or according to the status that is attributed to them (by birth, kinship, age, or personal connections).

Besides these cultural dimensions regarding the relationships between people, the authors also look at other dimensions, such as attitudes to time (time perceived as passing in a straight line, a sequence of events, or time perceived more as moving in a circle, the past and present interwoven with future possibilities) and attitudes to the environment (how much an individual can affect the environment).

3.4 Lewis' Taxonomy of Cultural Communication Styles

Lewis (2003) presented a typology of cultures which is based on the way people communicate and behave. He distinguishes three types of cultures that we come across in business situations and management styles. His famous triangle graph shows the distribution of these styles across cultures, where blue coloured cultures are called *linear-active* cultures, red coloured represent *multi-active* cultures, and yellow coloured cultures are indicated as *reactive* cultures. While blue indicates cool, factual and decisive planners, red indicates warmness, emotionality, and impulsiveness of the members of these cultural groups. The yellow cultures represent courteous, amiable, accommodating compromisers and good listeners.

People in a linear-active culture are highly organized and deal with daily problems in a very rational way. They tend to act logically, without emotions, and usually do one thing at a time. As a result, they like scheduling, planning, and organizing so that they can move from one thing to another, step by step, like on a line (linear thinking and doing). To sum up, business people in this type of culture are polite but direct, results- and job-oriented, and written word is important for them.

In multi-active cultures, emotions, feelings, and intuition play an important role. They approach daily problems in a more emotional way than the linear-active cultures. Therefore, they tend to do many things at a time (multi-activities), not concentrating solely on one problem. They are good at improvising and approaching the situation as it comes (without much planning). They also tend to be flexible in changing business strategies. To sum up, in this type of culture, we can expect businesspeople to be relationship-oriented, placing feelings before facts, and putting emphasis more on spoken than written word.

Members of reactive cultures predominantly do not act in business situations. As they prioritize courtesy and respect, they would listen quietly and calmly to their interlocutors. They tend to react carefully to the other side's proposals, listening before making decisions. In business meetings, they are likely to get the other side to talk first so that they can react to what was said (reactive). They also tend to avoid confrontation and find suitable ways for both parties to make an agreement. In this type of culture, businesspeople tend to react to partner's action and are good listeners, as harmony-orientation comes first.

Of course, many nations are combinations of two or three of these types, but one of them is dominant. While the three types are distinctive, each possesses behavioural elements from the other two categories. It is a question of which one is dominant. Many individuals deviate from the national type in a work situation, e.g. engineers and accountants tend to be linear, salespeople are multi-active, while lawyers and doctors may be more reactive. Nevertheless, the use of Lewis' model can help international companies organize communication within and performance of multinational teams (Gates, Lewis, Bairatchnyi, & Brown, 2009).

4 Implications for International Business

In this part of the paper, we explore some areas of international business where inter-cultural differences play a crucial role. To demonstrate the real impact of intercultural differences coined by the typologies, we examine the encounters and interplay of contrasting approaches to dealing with selected business issues. The selection of examples was made simply according to the criterion of adequacy for the illustration of these different approaches. It should be clear that examples in all spheres of business are many and a lot of research has been conducted in order to advise business people on solving the cultural clash within organizations (Adler & Gundersen, 2008; Dersky, 2011; Gibson, 2000), help them understand the features of individual cultures (Borec, 2009; Mešková, 2016; Olejárová, Benčiková, Friedová, Mešková, & Vetráková, 2007; Tomalin & Nicks, 2010), or prepare them for communication pitfalls and adequate communication with foreign business partners (Dignen, 2011; Gudykunst, 2003; Lewis, 2003; Maude, 2011). The authors of cultural typologies (Hampden-Turner & Trompenaars, 2000; Hofstede et al., 2010; Lewis, 2003) actually provide the extract of cultural characteristics, and illustrate them with examples and case studies. Thorough knowledge of these characteristics, along with some reflection of one's own culture and critical thinking, allow to prepare businesspeople for adequate handling of intercultural situations. The knowledge about the variety of factors impinging on any international business encounter can help to avoid the culture clash in the boardroom or at the workplace.

4.1 Reflection of Cultural Taxonomies in International Business

In today's international business, there are many areas in which culture is present and may affect the success or failure. The awareness of intercultural differences in the way business is done in various cultures is therefore important (DEW Project Partnership, 2010). Businesspeople or negotiators tend to be more conscious of the impact of culture when the deal, contract or talks fail than when they succeed (Cohen, 2007, p. 18).

Cultural differences in business interaction may be based on the country of origin, world regions or on the culture of individual jobs (Trompenaars & Hampden-Turner, 1997). The decisive factors to which attention should be paid, according to Tomalin and Nicks (2010), are cultural values and attitudes.

Values and attitudes create the essence of cross-cultural communication and are reflected in business behaviour. Values may range from believing in the system, clarity, directness, and organisation up to believing in friendship and relations, which may stay above the system, rules, and directness. Values are behind the misunderstandings which arise when representatives of two different value orientations meet in a business interaction. For example, the value of time/the time dimension (coined by Hall, 1966, and extended for business by Trompenaars & Hampden-Turner, 1997) causes problems in situations like arriving on time for a meeting, business dinner, interview, or business event. Another situation may be the use of time in monochronic cultures, where time is perceived as passing in a straightforward manner. Things are done in a rather scheduled and planned manner, organised, moving from one step to another. Strict time-keeping, thorough planning, organising, and punctuality are a must. A clash arises when business people from monochronic cultures have to deal with people from polychronic cultures, which seem to prefer doing many things at one time, such as making telephone calls during negotiations, not concentrating solely on the task or changing plans unexpectedly. Unpunctuality and flexibility are common and accepted. This may seem a distraction from the job or even an offence in the eyes of "monochronic" partners.

The prevalence of masculine values is expressed, for example, in such management issues as rewarding employees, which is based on competition, assertiveness, and looking out for the number one employee. These attitudes do not work in feminine societies, which care for the well-being of all members, are based on relationships (rather than competition), and reach agreement through communication and discussion. Finding agreement is more important than "winning" a discussion.

The value of individualism is expressed in the freedom to make one's own decisions, following one's own personal goals. A company in an individualistic society values and supports this approach. On the other hand, the collective or communitarian societies do not accept the approach of rewarding individual workers, as the primary goal of these societies is the success of the whole group (team, department, or company). Rewarding the best salesperson would be seen as humiliation of the rest of the group.

Another Hofstede's dimension, uncertainty avoidance, is exemplified by the situation of introducing a change in a business. High-uncertainty avoidance cultures are resistant to changes and any change (imposed by the managers from the low-uncertainty avoidance cultures) will be introduced more slowly than expected and in a complicated way. Embracing change, taking risk, and experimenting with new organisational methods is a natural part of the low-uncertainty culture, while defence of the status quo and resistance to change is part of the high-avoidance culture.

Power distance in business may be illustrated by the approach to authority (DEW Project Partnership, 2010). The behaviour towards those in authority is diametrically different across cultures and may be a frequent source of misunderstandings. In high-power distance cultures, the boss is the highest authority employees rely on and they never challenge the boss's decisions. In low-power distance cultures, the boss's decisions may be challenged, the decisions are made after a discussion. More relaxed relations between the boss and workers prevail.

This is also connected with the way respect is displayed in business structures. In a flat matrix management environment, people communicate directly with other departments, make community decisions, and get two-way feedback, while in the vertical structures communication happens through hierarchy and decisions are made by the leader.

In conclusion, we can see that business behaviour depends on the cultural style of those involved in business. Besides the values orientation and organisation structures, as exemplified above, this cultural style of doing business depends on the other components, such as communication style, working style, discussion style, leadership style, decision-making style, attitude to time, and work-life balance (Tomalin & Nicks, 2010). Among the most important cultural aspects in diplomatic negotiations, Cohen (2007) includes the following:

- low-context (individualistic and result-focused) versus high-context (relationship-oriented),
- monochronic versus polychronic concept of time,
- directness versus indirectness,
- reluctance to say no.

These cultural aspects may apply well to business negotiations, as they constitute the factors influencing intercultural communication in any context.

4.2 Reflection of Cultural Taxonomies in Intercultural Business Communication

The language of international communication in business is English. English functions as a general means of communication for people who do not speak it as their mother tongue, but their proficiency in English does not necessarily mean they will be able to communicate without problems. There is clear evidence that the use of English as a lingua franca may hide the underlying culture-based concepts (Mader & Camerer, 2010). Many misunderstandings in communication happen not because of poor language proficiency, but because of lack of knowledge of cultural differences in communication situations (DEW Project Partnership, 2010; Kramsch, 1993).

There are different ways of expressing politeness, gratitude, disagreement, thanks, etc.—for example, people use different words, different accent, intonation, behave differently when speaking, asking, and replying. This is because language expresses the cultural reality (Mader & Camerer, 2010). The way in which people use the spoken, written or visual language creates meanings which are understandable to the group they belong to, but their meaning may be hidden for members of other culture. As culture penetrates the language system, every aspect of communicative competence acquires a cultural dimension. In various cultures, people communicate demands, requests, and rejections in various ways. These ways can be seen as polite in some cultures but impolite in other cultures (Hidasi, 2014). These differences can cause tensions, misunderstanding, or even conflicts in international communication.

For example, when greeting other people, in some cultures you shake hands, in other cultures you also kiss; and in other ones you do not shake hands, you do not kiss, you do not touch the person, you simply bow. In high-power distance cultures, greetings and relations to the people with power (boss or manager) will be expressed through formal language. In low-power distance culture, the language is informal (addressing the boss by first name), the relations are more relaxed; even the boss's decisions may be challenged by the subordinates.

Expressing disagreement (saying no) is another example of the cultural use of language connected with what is considered polite, impolite, honest or dishonest. In Slovak, we simply say *no* or *I don't agree* (*I disagree*) if we really disagree. If we communicate in English, we use the same words (*no, I disagree*), or more polite *I am afraid I do not agree*. Germans also say *no* and disagree directly, considering it to be the most honest way. But, in some cultures, for example the Japanese (reactive cultures), people are reluctant to say no directly, as it could be considered a disturbance to the harmony of the group. The harmony of the group is more valuable than the opinion of the individual. Instead, *no* can be indicated by a non-verbal gesture, by silence, by asking a question, or simply by changing the subject or saying *yes* (meaning *no*). The British express disagreement in different ways which indicate more politeness, for example: *I agree, up to a point, I am afraid I can't..., Let's agree to disagree* (less direct, avoiding open conflicts), *That's not always true...* (less direct), *No, I' m not sure about that* (careful disagreement). Arabic speakers often say *insha'allah* meaning *if God wills it* to say *no* in a very polite way, which is something that non-Arabic speakers always think means *yes*, but it does not! We can see that it is not enough to know the little word *no* in English. It is important to understand the context of disagreement in different cultures.

Intercultural communicative competence includes knowledge of linguistic-cultural and socio-cultural contexts, and the use of appropriate situational language—when to say what and how to express oneself in various situations. Spencer-Oatey and Franklin (2009) assert that the intercultural communicative competence should be studied not only as linguistic competence but—in its cultural complexity—as intercultural interaction competence (pp. 50–80). According to Hidasi (2014), the Hungarian expert on European-Japanese intercultural communication, it is necessary to learn how to manage various communication situations and be prepared to express politeness, demand, request, wish, refuse or assert in a culturally appropriate way. In some cultures, these things can be expressed in a direct manner, while in other cultures expressing them indirectly, being ambiguous, silent, and expressing oneself vaguely is regarded as perfectly correct. Therefore, communication in a foreign language should be mastered not only "languagewise", but also "culturewise" (Zelenka (2007), as cited in Javorčíková & Dove, 2013, p. 13).

5   Conclusion

All the abovementioned cultural aspects of international business are more recognizable when they are related to the cultural characteristics stated by the taxonomies of cultures. We have introduced four selected taxonomies and illustrated their application in the real-life business interaction and company culture in some selected examples. Based on the examples, we can summarize the areas of business where the characteristics of cultures must be taken into account in order to avoid misunderstandings, problems in communication, or failure of business activities. Mainly, multinational companies must ask a question and make decisions about:

- applying either a set of rules in any business situation or relying on relationships to people,
- adapting management styles and considering the boss's and manager's role,

- using time—either by fixed planning, scheduling, programming or by flexible changes,
- rewarding employees—either by achievements and performance or by the status that is ascribed by age or experience,
- rewarding employees—either an individual or a team,
- recruiting staff and giving preference—either to individual performance or work in a team (fostering team building, co-operation, and collaboration),
- developing relationships and socializing, or focusing solely on fulfilling the task and doing the job,
- adapting appropriate communication styles,
- introducing and managing change,
- achieving status within a company—either through performance or through ascription,
- adapting organizational structure—either flat or vertically hierarchical.

As we can see, this is only a short list that must be taken into account when managing international business. Because the international dimension of business becomes an intercultural or cross-cultural issue, multinational companies consider cultural competence an important management requirement. It is management that is responsible for managing cultural diversity and reconciling the differences arising from diverse cultural backgrounds of the workforce, but the employees should also be led and trained towards the understanding of their diverse cultural origins. As Bennett and Bennett (2003) conclude, global business is recognizing that international effectiveness depends on an "intercultural mindset and skillset" (p. 163) and, therefore, the need for the development of intercultural sensitivity and intercultural competence will be increasing.

Acknowledgements This paper is one of the outputs of the research project No. 033UMB-4/2017 (E)migration as a political, ethical, linguistic and cultural phenomenon in the era of globalization supported by the Slovak Ministry of Education Scheme KEGA.

References

Adler, N. J., & Gundersen, A. (2008). *International dimensions of organisational behavior* (5th ed.). Mason, OH: Thomson South-Western, Thomson Learning.

Bennett, J. M., & Bennett, M. (2003). In D. R., Landis, J. M., Bennett, & M. Bennett (Eds.), *Handbook of intercultrual training* (3rd ed., p. 168). Thousand Oaks, CA: Sage.

Borec, T. (2009). *Manažéri na cudzom parkete*. Bratislava: Neopublic Porter Novelli.

Cohen, R. (2007). *Negotiating across cultures. International Communication in an interdependent world*. Washington, DC: United States Institute of Peace Press.

Dersky, H. (2011). *International management. Managing across borders and cultures*. Boston, MA: Pearson.

DEW Project Partnership. (2010). *Diverse Europe at work*. Sibiu, Romania: Editura Etape Sibiu.

Dignen, B. (2011). *Communicating across cultures*. Cambridge, UK: Cambridge University Press.

Essays, U. K. (2018, November). *The Criticisms of the Hofstede's model.* Business Essay. Retrieved from https://www.ukessays.com/essays/business/the-criticisms-of-the-hofste des-model-business-essay.php?vref=1.

Gates, M. J., Lewis, R. D., Bairatchnyi, I. P., & Brown, M. (2009). Use of the Lewis model to analyse multicultural teams and improve performance by the World Bank: A case study. *The International Journal of Knowledge, Culture & Change Management, 8*(12), 53–59.

Geertz, C. (1973). *The interpretation of cultures.* New York, NY: Basic Books.

Gibson, R. (2000). *Intercultural business communication.* Oxford, UK: Oxford University Press.

Gudykunst, W. B. (2003). Intercultural communication: Introduction. In W. B. Gudykunst (Ed.), *Cross-cultural and intercultural communication* (pp. 163–190). Thousand Oaks: Sage.

Hall, E. A. (1997). *Beyond culture.* New York, NY: Anchor Books.

Hall, E. T. (1966). *The hidden dimension.* Garden City, NY: Doubleday.

Hampden-Turner, C., & Trompenaars, F. (2000). *Building cross-cultural competence. How to create wealth from conflicting values.* New Haven and London: Yale University Press.

Hidasi, J. (2014). Cultural-mental programming and the acquisition of foreign languages. In A. Zelenková (Ed.), *Foreign languages: A bridge to innovations in higher education* (pp. 17–23). Banská Bystrica, Slovakia: Matej Bel University in Banská Bystrica.

Hofstede, G. (2001). *Culture's consequences: Comparing values, behaviors, institutions and organizations across nations.* London, UK: Sage.

Hofstede, G., Hofstede, G. J., & Minkov, M. (2010). *Cultures and organisations. Software of the mind.* New York, NY: McGraw Hill.

Javorčíková, J., & Dove, M. (2013). *Explorations in American life and culture.* Banská Bystrica, Slovakia: Belianum, Vydavateľstvo UMB.

Kramsch, C. (1993). *Context and culture in language teaching.* Oxford, UK: Oxford University Press.

Lewis, R. D. (2003). *When cultures collide. Leading across cultures.* London, UK: Nicholas Brealey Publishing.

Mader, J., & Camerer, R. (2010). International English and the training of inter-cultural communicative competence. *Interculture Journal, 9*(12), 97–116.

Martin, J. N., & Nakayama, T. K. (2010). *Intercultural communication in contexts* (5th ed.). New York, NY: McGraw Hill.

Maude, B. (2011). *Managing cross-cultural communication.* New York, NY: Basingstoke Palgrave Macmillan.

McSweeney, B. (2002). Hofstede's model of national cultural differences and their consequences: A triumph of faith—A failure of analysis. *Human Relations, 55*(1), 89–118.

Mešková, Ľ. (2016). Cultural differences between Western Europe and the former Eastern Bloc. In A. Stoica (Ed.), *Culture and paradiplomatic identity: Instruments in sustaining EU policies* (pp. 168–189). Newcastle upon Tyne, UK: Cambridge Scholars Publishing.

Olejárová, M., Benčiková, A., Friedová, A., Mešková, L., & Vetráková, M. (2007). *Charakteristika vybraných krajín z pohľadu interkultúrnej komunikácie.* Banská Bystrica, Slovakia: Matej Bel University in Banská Bystrica.

Omaggio-Hadley, A. (1993). *Teaching language in context.* Boston, MA: Heinle & Heinle Publishers.

Parsons, T. (1951). *The social system.* London, UK: The Free Press of Glencoe, Collier—Macmillan Limited, 1964.

Ramírez, A. G. (1995). *Creating context for second language acquisition: Theory and methods.* White Plains, NY: Longman Publishers USA.

Samovar, L. A., Porter, R., & McDaniel, R. (2006). *Intercultural communication. A reader.* Belmont, CA: Thomson/Wadsworth.

Seelye, N. H. (1987). *Teaching culture. Strategies for intercultural communication.* Lincolnwood, IL: National Textbook Company.

Spencer-Oatey, H., & Franklin, P. (2009). *Intercultural interaction. A multidisciplinary approach to intercultural communication.* New York, NY: Palgrave Macmillan.

Tomalin, B., & Nicks, M. (2010). *The world's business cultures and how to unlock them.* London, UK: Thorogood Publishing.

Trompenaars, F., & Hampden-Turner, C. (1997). *Riding the waves of culture. Understanding cultural diversity in business.* London, UK: Nicholas Brealey Publishing.

Zelenka, I. (2007). Languagewise or culturewise? *Pedagogické rozhľady, 4*(16), 32.

Anna Zelenková is Associate Professor at the Department of Professional Communication in Business, Faculty of Economics, Matej Bel University in Banská Bystrica, Slovakia. She has been teaching English for Specific Purposes, intercultural communication and managerial skills in English for more than 20 years. As a teacher trainer, she develops intercultural teacher training programmes and participates in educational projects. Her professional and research interests include pedagogic approaches to the teaching of foreign languages, intercultural competence in business, and teacher development. She is the author of six textbooks and two monographs on the methodology of intercultural education.

Various Dimensions of Business Communication

Naming the Weapon: A Study of UK and USA Tank Names

Piotr Mamet

Abstract A thorough investigation on tank names seems to be non-existent especially when compared with the research on the tank design and history. The article analyses the names of UK and USA tanks since their first appearance to the present day. Its aim is to identify the naming systems and their components. The semantic approach is applied in order to identify the denotations and connotations of the names. It is combined with the classification of names from the marketing point of view. The paper starts with a theoretical investigation of the name, the brand name, and their linguistic dimension. Then follows a brief discussion of tank, its origin, and development. In the research part, a corpus of UK and USA tank names is analyzed in order to identify the name components together with regularities and irregularities of their occurrence. The analysis indicates the variety of the naming systems. Their obligatory, i.e. almost always used elements include alfa-numeric and generic names. Other components range from names of famous people (warriors, tanks designers or politicians), warlike occupations, animals and objects. They usually have the connotation of power and danger and/or indicate the features of the tank.

Keywords Tank · Brand name · Connotation

1 Introduction

Compared with the research on the tank design and history, any investigation on tank names seems to be non-existent. Research books, encyclopedias, and other reviews of tank models, like the ones quoted in this paper, occasionally explain some tank names. This, however, can hardly be called a systematic research.

It is the aim of this paper to research into the names of UK and USA tanks since their first appearance to the present day. The study aims at the identification of what it calls the naming systems and their components. The semantic approach is applied

P. Mamet (✉)
Silesian University of Technology, Gliwice, Poland
e-mail: p.mamet@gmail.com

© Springer Nature Switzerland AG 2020
U. Michalik et al. (eds.), *Exploring Business Language and Culture*,
Second Language Learning and Teaching,
https://doi.org/10.1007/978-3-030-58551-8_11

in order to identify the denotations and connotations of the names. It is combined with the classification of names from the marketing point of view.

The paper starts with a theoretical investigation of the name, the brand name, and their linguistic dimension. Then follows a brief discussion of tank, its origin, and development. In the research part, a corpus of UK and USA tank names is analyzed in order to identify the name components together with regularities and irregularities of their occurrence.

2   Name and Brand Name

More than one hundred years ago, the tank came into being as a result of human ingenuity, manufacturing capabilities, and the desire to satisfy military needs. The invention had to be provided with a name to denote both the type of product and its different models.

The concepts of name and brand name form the background of the linguistic analysis in this paper.

From the linguistic point of view, a name may be defined as an acoustic, graphic, etc. symbol of a notion (Polański, 1999, p. 388). Alternatively, one may say that "things and categories of things have individual and unambiguous names" and that "language appears … to provide neat, clear labels for everything we might want to talk about (even *think* about)" (Hall, 2001, p. 49, brackets and italics in the original text).

Zboralski maintains that naming is a basic psychological need, an absolute necessity of both the developing civilization and daily life. Nothing can exist in the human mind without a name. The author makes reference to Hegel's ontological concept and the assumption that whatever cannot be named cannot exist (2000, p. 14). The motto to Zboralski's book on business names is taken from Stanisław Lem, a famous Polish science-fiction writer, and it says: "in order to conquer the world, one has to name it first" (trans. PM).[1]

Kotler and Armstrong (2001) provide the following, well known, definition of brand: "a name, term, sign, symbol, or design, or a combination of these, that identifies the maker or seller of a product or service" (p. 301). In this definition, the name functions as a part of the brand, hence the concept of brand name. The American Marketing Association defines brand in a similar way.

A *brand* is a name, term, design, symbol or any other feature that identifies one seller's good or service as distinct from those of other sellers (American Marketing Association, AMA Dictionary).[2]

Moreover, according to the Common Language Marketing Dictionary,

ISO brand standards add that a brand "is an intangible asset" that is intended to create "distinctive images and associations in the minds of stakeholders, thereby

---

[1]"Żeby opanować świat trzeba go pierwej – nazwać" (S. Lem, on the cover of Zboralski, 2000).
[2]https://marketing-dictionary.org/b/brand/.

Table 1 Types of brand names (own study based on Zboralski, 2000, p. 80, verified and quoted from Mamet, 2008, p. 55)

Brand name	Brand character Method of transferring the message	Examples
Descriptive (semantic)	Direct motivation in the meaning of words	Lux
Suggestive (relative)	Allusion, connotation, suggestion	Dr Witt, Mustang
Symbolic (emblematic)	Symbol contents	Gold, Ivory
Arbitrary (speculative)	Motivation hidden from the receiver, accidental, image based	Hit, Renault
Artificial (non-semantic)	No motivation	Adidas, Kodak

generating economic benefit/values" (International Organization for Standardization).[3]

Brand name, in turn, is: "that part of a brand that can be spoken. It includes letters, numbers, or words".[4]

There are different classifications of brand names. The simplest one is the division into:

- Transferred names based on the lexemes catalogued in the system of a language, e.g., (VW) *Passat.*
- Invented names, e.g., *Kodak* (Zboralski, 2000, pp. 138–139).

Another classification is presented in Table 1, which contains the type of name, its character, and examples. The method of transferring the message is used as the criterion to identify five types of names.

The classifications and examples quoted in Table 1 indicate that brand names have a linguistic dimension and may be analyzed from the linguistic perspective.

3 Linguistic Aspects of a Brand Name

Brand is a marketing term, and its equivalent in linguistics is *chrematonym.* Kosyl (2001) indicates the Greek origin of the term, i.e., *chrema, chrematos* stand for thing, object, or commodity (p. 447). The term comprises proper names of all material products of human activity. These include products of craft or manufacturing industry, single specimens, and mass-made products, and they are not connected with a given geographical landscape (p. 447).

The role of linguistics in the creation and evaluation of a brand name is obvious both for linguists (e.g., Kosyl, 2001) and for marketing researchers (Altkorn, 1999, pp. 89–118, Kall, 2001, pp. 150–171, Zboralski, 2000, pp. 100–142). Usunier and Shaner claim that "the value analysis of a brand name must be assessed

---

[3] Ibid.

[4] https://marketing-dictionary.org/b/brand-name/.

using several different branches of linguistics (phonetics, phonology, semantics, etymology, rhetoric and semiotics)" (2002, pp. 212–213, brackets in the original text).

The analytical tool used in this study is semantics, i.e., "the study of meaning" (Richards, Platt, & Platt, 1999, p. 329), and it involves the investigation of the denotations and connotations of words. Semantics is also a suitable tool to explain the meaning hidden behind abbreviations and numbers in alpha-numeric names, which appear very often in tank names.

Pavia and Costa (1993) provide a neat definition of alpha-numeric brand names as "brand names with numeric components" or "a name that contains one or more numbers either in digit form (e.g. '5') or in written form (e.g. 'five')" (p. 85, examples, brackets, and quotation marks in the original text). The authors admit this kind of brand names received little attention and the term itself is not well defined (p. 85).

Boyd claims that "more and more products are becoming identified and named with nonsense mixtures of letters and figures rather than with proper names" (Boyd, 1985, p. 48). For the author it is the fulfillment of the science-fiction world dominated by technology, in which proper names of individuals are replaced with code numbers (p. 48).

4   The Named Object: Definition and Development of the Tank

Collins Cobuild Dictionary (2001) defines tank as: "a large military vehicle that is equipped with weapons and moves along on metal tracks that are fitted over the wheels" (p. 1594). *Encyclopedia Britannica* gives the following definition:

> Tank, any heavily armed and armoured combat vehicle that moves on two endless metal chains called tracks. Tanks are essentially weapon platforms that make the weapons mounted in them more effective by their cross-country mobility and by the protection they provide for their crews. Weapons mounted in tanks have ranged from single rifle-calibre machine guns to, in recent years, long-barreled guns of 120- or 125-mm (4.72- or 4.92-inch) calibre (Ogorkiewicz, 2019).

The idea of a tank is probably as old as the history of warfare. *Encyclopedia Britannica* indicates that the concept may be traced back to the ancient Egyptians, who used horse-drawn war chariots. Hittite fighters with bows and arrows used mobile platforms, and wheeled siege towers were used by the Assyrians in the 9th century B.C. Guide de Vigevano constructed battle vehicles as early as in 1335, followed by Leonardo da Vinci in 1484. In 1855, James Cowen patented armed, armored, and wheeled vehicle on the basis of the steam tractor (Ogorkiewicz, 2019). Antal summarizes the factors that finally gave rise to the construction and military use of the tank in the following way: "tank was the fusion of several emerging commercial technologies, primarily a continuous track system to replace wheels and the gasoline engine … [The] first serious "tank" prototypes were developed in 1915 and the first significant use of tanks in battle occurred in 1916 during the Battle of the Somme" (2014, p. 112).

The development of the tank involves the design of its varieties in terms of weight and mode of application. The issue will be addressed in the section analyzing the generic name of the tank.

5 Corpus Description and Methodology

There does not seem to exist any research, available to a non-military researcher, that might provide the full list of tanks that have ever been made.

For the purpose of this research, it has been decided that the tank name is the one that appears in printed sources and web pages devoted to tank history and description. Several major sources were studied to provide the corpus for the analysis. The basic one is *The World Encyclopedia of Tanks & Armoured Fighting Vehicles* by Forty and Livesey (2017). The authors state that it "contains a wide selection of tanks through the ages … deliberately confined (…) to the more important and interesting models worldwide, so while it is not an exhaustive encyclopedia, it will give the reader a good indication of what the tank is all about" (p. 13). Two more encyclopedic publications and two internet sources were used to complement and verify the data. Appendix 1 includes all the names analyzed in this paper together with their sources. The number of names is 97; 7 countries are represented. Most of the names come from UK (55 names), and US tanks are the second largest group (54 tank names). The corpus also includes a few tanks from British dominions: Australia (1), Canada (3), and New Zealand (1). Three joint projects are analyzed: UK/India (1) and UK/USA (2), the latter providing two names for analysis. The corpus thus collected may be said to be nearly complete and representative in terms of gathering all the names that contribute to the analytical classifications.

As said above, the study is limited to semantics, which is a tool to explain the denotation (including that hidden behind alpha-numeric names) and connotations of a name. The analysis also involves classification of the tank names according to the brand name types specified in the section entitled "Brand names" (see Table 1).

Taking into consideration the history of the tank (over 100 years), the diachronic approach is used to provide data for the introduction, continuation, or discontinuation of a naming system.

The names in the main text are listed in the Appendix and quoted without references. The latter ones are used when any names not included in the Appendix are mentioned.

6   The Analysis

The analysis uses the methodology and corpus presented above. The starting point is the study of the generic name of the vehicle. It is followed by the identification and discussion of other systems identified.

6.1   Tank—The Generic Name

It is held that the name "tank" was used for secrecy reasons (e.g., Ogorkiewicz, 2016, p. 35, Trewhitt, 2006, p. 6A). Deighton is more precise when he indicates that: "The army ordered 100 of them, describing them as water tanks for safety reasons. The name stuck" (p. 126). The generic name is often complemented with a modifying component, which classifies the tank using various criteria, such as:

- Weight:

    - light tanks e.g., *Mark IV Light Tank* [UK 1934];
    - medium tanks, e.g., *Mark I Medium Tank* [UK 1924];
    - heavy tanks, e.g., *M26 Pershing Heavy Tank* [USA 1944].

- Mode of application:

    - amphibious tank, e.g., *Vickers-Armstrong Amphibious Tank Model 1931* [UK 1931];
    - cruiser tanks, e.g., *A27L Cruiser Tank Mark VIII Centaur* [UK 1942];
    - infantry tanks, e.g., *A12 Infantry Tank Mark I* [UK 1938];
    - general – purpose/Main Battle Tank, e.g., *Chieftain Main Battle Tank* FV 4202 [UK 1963];
    - tank destroyers, e.g., *M10 Wolverine Tank Destroyer* [USA, 1942];
    - test vehicle, e.g., *High Mobility Agility Test Vehicle* [USA, 1978];
    - *A1 E1 Independent* [UK, 1926]—The name *Independent* may, according to Forty and Livesey (2017, p. 54), stand for a tank "designed … for independent actions". Other connotations of this name are discussed in the section entitled "Features of tanks—adjectives".
    - *Challenger 2 MBT* [(UK, 1994], MBT stands for *Main Battle Tank*.

Using the criteria set out in Table 1 above, one may classify the generic names as descriptive (semantic) ones because their main function is to inform about the features and mode of application of the named fighting vehicle.

6.2   British Problems with Tank's Gender

In the period from the first use of the tank till WWII, it may be observed that tank designers in Britain could not make up their minds whether tanks were male or female beings. Originally, they referred to the construction as a land cruiser ship or a battleship (Ogorkiewicz, 2016, p. 35). The names related to sea vessels carry female connotations in the British culture and language (Barder, 2013). However, the name of the prototype made in 1915 was *Little Willie* (David, 2014), which suggested its being a male creature. Another machine, the prototype of British Heavy tanks, originally named Wilson's machine (1915), started to be known as *Big Willie, His Majesty's Land Ship Centipede*, or *Mother* (Little Willie, n.d.). This suggests that the tank changed its gender, together with its name, several times.

The concept of *male/female* tanks was very short lived and occurs only in a few cases of British prototypes. The gun equipped tanks were called *male tanks*, possibly because such an armament suggested and connoted more strength than the machine gun in *female* tanks.

A12 Infantry Tank Mark I Matilda I [UK, 1939]/*A12 Infantry Tank II Mark II Matilda II* [UK, 1940] carry a female name. Forty and Livesey (2017) state that: "There are a number of stories as to how the tank got the nickname *Matilda*, one being that when General Sir High Ellen saw the tank's comic, duck-like appearance and gait, he named it after a cartoon series of the day. In fact, the codeword 'Matilda' appears on the original proposal for the A11 in John Carden's handwriting" (p. 56). John Carden is the tank's designer (p. 56).

The male name of another British design, *Mark III Valentine Infantry Tank* is connected with the fact that its prototype was presented on February 14, 1940, i.e., on St. Valentine's day (Forty and Livesey, 2017, p. 98).

The data suggest that the selection of *Matilda* and *Valentine* names was accidental or arbitrary. The connotations of male strength and female weakness may be difficult to escape; however, one must not forget that personifications of countries in female forms have been extremely popular over the years, especially in the context of wartime propaganda and patriotism: Brittania, Germania, Mother Russia, Marianne (for France), and Italia Turrita are but a few examples (Barder, 2013).

An illustration of problems with gender may be found in the name *Mark I Medium Tank ("Mother") Male* [UK, 1916]. The connotations of mother's care and delicacy contrast with the masculine character implied by another part of the name.

6.3   Manufacturers' Naming Systems

For the purpose of this paper, the term "manufacturers' naming systems" stands for the name used by the manufacturers, armies, or governments. Each of these institutions has its reasons to develop a name that would classify the vehicle. The government may invent names used in the bidding or ordering system. The manufacturer, in turn, may use its own nomenclature or use the names suggested by the army.

The naming system analyzed here is far from clear and concise and may differ among particular countries. While admitting that the system is complicated, Cidlinský (2018a, p. 84) lists the following components of a tank name in the British system:

- the formula: *a letter + Arabic number*. This naming tradition is connected with the vehicle's technical data specification, and it is used in the government tendering documentation. The vehicle which is ordered by the government uses this mark, e.g., *A9*. Roman number is added if there are any other manufactured vehicles with the same technical specification. Letter *A* may be followed by the subsequent letter in the alphabet, which thus stands for another series. The author seems to overlook the fact that the additional Roman number is preceded with *Mk/Mark* item, indicating a subsequent version of the original design, e.g., *A15 Cruiser Tank Mark VI Crusader*.
- tank category (*fast, light, support*), e.g., *Cruiser Mk IV*, *Infantry Mk. IV*;
- acronym related to the weapon carried and the doctrine of use, e.g., *CS* for *close support*;
- "Fight names" only, e.g., *Covenanter* or *Churchill*.

Cidlinský's explanation does not seem to be clear and exhaustive. It does not exactly explain how A series ends and B series starts. The appearance of *Mk/Mark* is not explained, either. Nevertheless, one may agree with Cidlinský that the system produced lengthy names, such as *A13 Mk.III Cruiser tank Mk. V*. A simpler name of the same vehicle is *Covenanter II CS* (Cidlinský, 2018, p. 84). Regardless of the discrepancies in Cidlinský's explanation, one must admit that the system was far from being simple and clear.

Cidlinský (2018b) also analyzes the US naming system. The author observes that the US system is less complicated than the British one but still lacks consistency. Its principles may be listed in the following way:

- T + number (Arabic), denoting subsequent prototypes, e.g.. *T24*;
- E + number (Arabic) denoting versions with a variety of components, e.g., *T24E3*[5];
- M + (Arabic) number used in vehicles ordered by the army, e.g., *M4*;
- A + (Arabic) number denoting the particular version manufactured, e.g., *M4A1*;
- "Fight names", gradually introduced to simplify the system at the end of WWII. Cidlinský (2018b, p. 37) does not quote any example for this name component.[6]

Several observations have to be made with reference to the naming principles outlined above:

---

[5]One may guess that E stands for extension, i.e.; extended version.

[6]Cidlinský does not define the concept of fight names, however, the examples provided seem to make it possible to distinguish it from other systems mentioned.

(1) The UK and USA systems are good examples of alpha-numeric system;
(2) The systems are sophisticated, produce lengthy names, and are understood by a narrow group of specialists;
(3) The systems are gradually, but not totally, abandoned.

The last issue requires some more attention:

(4) Alpha-numeric symbols co-exist with fight names, e.g.,

- *A 33 Heavy Assault Tank Excelsior* [UK, 1943];
- *A27 M Cruiser Tank Mark VIII Cromwell* [UK, 1943];
- *A30 Cruiser Tank Challenger* [UK, 1943];
- *M24 Chaffee Light Tank* [USA,1944];
- *A 41 Centurion Medium Tank* [UK, 1945].

(5) Even well-known fight names are accompanied with numbers, in connection with the development of the model, e.g.,

- *Stingray I* [USA, 1965] and *Stingray II* [USA, 1996];
- *M1/A1 M1/A2 Abrams* [USA, 1995];
- *Challenger I MBT* [1982] and *Challenger II MBT* [UK 1994].

A lot of specialized knowledge is necessary to decipher the names, which may be classified as arbitrary/speculative, their motivation hidden from the receiver and inaccessible to a non-specialist.

6.4 Manufacturer in the Name

The occurrence of the manufacturer's name in the brand is quite natural, and it is recognized as a branding strategy. It is applied in the UK/USA names, such as:

- *No.1 Lincoln Machine* [UK, 1915] (William Foster and Co. Ltd of Lincoln—"the firm that would build the first tanks"; Forty and Livesey, 2017, p. 17);
- *Vickers,* e.g.; *Vickers 6 Ton Tank* [UK, 1928], *Vickers Valiant MBT* (UK, 1985), *Vickers Mark 3 MBT* [UK, 1997];
- *Ford,* e.g., *Ford 6 ton Tank* (USA, 1917) and *Ford 3 Ton Tank* (USA, 1918);
- *Holt-Gas Electric Tank* [USA, 1918].

One may see that the USA tradition started in the WWI period continues in Britain after WWII, e.g.:

- *Alvis Scimitar Combat Vehicle Reconnaissance* [UK, 1973];
- *Alvis Scorpion Combat Vehicle Reconnaissance* [UK, 1973];
- *Vickers Mark 7 Valiant MBT* [UK, 1985];
- *Vickers VFW Mark 5 Light Tank* [UK, 1987];
- *Vickers Mark 3 MBT* [UK,1997].

6.5 People

People's names appeared for the first time in tank brands in 1915 in the UK—*The No.1 Lincoln Machine "Little Willie"* and *"Tritton Machine"* [UK, 1915] (Forty and Livesey, 2017, p. 17)—and have functioned until the present day, e.g., *M1/A1 M1/A2 Abrams MBT* [USA, 1985], also on the international scale, e.g., *Leclerc MBT* [France 1992].

A large group of tank names in the analyzed corpus consist of the names of especially famous US generals, heroes, and politicians. This group also includes tank designers' names and names of managers, as well as names of people connected with warfare and a few names that escape classification.

6.6 Heroes, Leaders and Politicians

The names of many famous USA generals were used to name tanks. The most famous one is *M4 Sherman Medium Tank* [USA, 1941], one of the best known tanks of WWII.

During WWII, the United States of America supplied a considerable amount of military equipment to Britain. A major part of the supplies consisted of one of the most famous model of tanks, i.e., the *Medium Tank M4*. According to Oliver (2011), it was Winston Churchill's idea to give the tank the name *Sherman* (p. 3). General William T. Sherman was one of the prominent generals in the victorious Union Army during the American Civil War 1961–1865.

Oliver claims that giving names to particular types of tanks has been a British tradition (2011, p. 3). This latter statement holds true as far as the names of the US tanks used in the British Army in WWII are concerned. The British habit was taken over by the Americans, who started to give names of famous generals of the US Army to the US made tanks. Thus, apart from *Sherman,* one may mention:

- The Civil War generals:

  - *Light Tank M3 General Stuart* [USA, 1940], named after the Civil War General J.E.B. Stuart;
  - *M 551 Sheridan* [USA, 1968], named after Philip Sheridan, a Civil War General (Blumberg, 2019).

This group includes a tank with two names:

- *Medium Tank M3 General Lee* [USA, 1941] (in the original US version);
- *Medium Tank M3 General Grant* [UK, 1941] (the British version of the tank) (Trewhitt, 2006, pp. 24–25, Forty and Livesey, 2017, p. 111).

General Lee and General Stuart were commanders in the Confederate Army in the American Civil War, which fought for the case of secession of the southern states and the maintenance of slavery. In terms of the functions of the tank name, their military achievements and skills were considered to be more persuasive than their political points of view.

- Other famous generals:
- *Light Tank M24 Chaffee* [USA, 1944], named after General Chaffee, the "Father of the US Armored Force" (Forty and Livesey, 2017, p. 118);
- *M26 Pershing* [USA, 1944] after John J. Pershing, the general who commanded the American Expeditionary Force (AEF) in Europe during WWI (Pershing, 2018);
- *M 46 Patton* [USA 1952] after George Patton, "the famous US WWII General" (Forty and Livesey, 2017, p. 200);
- *M1/A1 M1/A2 Abrams MBT* [USA, 1985] after Creighton Williams Abrams, Jr., "one of the most aggressive and effective tank commanders during World War II" and a commander of "all U.S. forces in Vietnam during the latter stages of the Vietnam War" (Sorley, 2018).

The names designed in this way are eponyms and, using the criteria set out in Table 1, they may be classified as suggestive ones. The names of efficient generals bear the connotations of bravery and efficiency in the military trade. The features may be referred to both the fighting vehicles and their crews.

Apart from the recognized generals, tank names carry the names of famous leaders, politicians, and heroes. The British system again provides many prime examples, such as:

- *A27 M Cruiser Tank Mark VIII Cromwell* [UK, 1943], named after Oliver Cromwell, one of the leaders of Britain's republic (1649–1660), in fact, a powerful and severe ruler (lord Protector 1653–1658). Cromwell was also a good military leader who "created a new 'model' army, the first regular force from which the British Army of today developed" (McDowall, 1991, p. 92, inverted commas in the original text).
- *Mk IV Churchill* [UK,1941], an infantry tank that started to be supplied to the army in 1942 and was named after Winston Churchill, the living Prime Minister actively leading the nation during WWII (Zasieczny, 2006, p. 103).
- *A 43 Infantry Tank Black Prince* [UK, 1945] (Forty and Livesey, 2017, p. 63), named after "Edward … the eldest son of Edward III … created prince of Wales in 1343 …. The title of Black Prince developed after his death and may refer to black armour that he wore" (Edward, the Black Prince, n.d.).

Both Cromwell and Churchill were famous and efficient leaders and politicians. Both of them had enormous influence upon the functioning of the army. Their names may be said to connote the same features as those of the USA generals discussed above.

Cromwell may be said to be a controversial person. However, just like in the case of USA generals fighting for the case of the Confederate states in the Civil War, his name is used to connote the desired features of a soldier-leader, not the case he fought for.

Black Prince was a victorious fighter, who won the Battle of Poitiers on September 19 and took John II of France into captivity. His achievements and image supported with the black armor he wore were good reasons to give his name to a fighting armored vehicle.

The dates of introduction of the UK and US tanks mentioned above indicate that the tradition has been continued since WWII till modern times.

The group of tank names analyzed here contains the names of politicians who are known to a limited number of people, as can be seen in the following examples:

- *A25 Light Tank Mark VIII Harry Hopkins* [UK, 1944], named "after the American President Roosevelt's confidential advisor" (Forty and Livesey, 2017, p. 61);
- *The "Semple" Tractor Tanks* [New Zealand, 1942], named after Bob Semple, a gold miner and then a union leader and the Minister of Public Works in New Zealand (Hickey, 2010).

6.7 Tank Designers and Engineers

Some of the tanks are named after the engineers who designed them or their mechanisms, or who defined tank development policies. The tradition begins with one of the first prototypes. It carried many names, e.g., *Little Willie* (see above) or *Tritton Machine* (UK, 1915). William Tritton was one of the designers and the manager of the manufacturer of first tanks (Forty and Livesey, 2017, p. 17). Other examples include:

- *M 1931 Christie* [USA, 1931], named after John Walter Christie, the designer of the suspension system, also bearing his name (Ogorkiewicz, 2016, p. 77).

People in this group may be anonymous and hidden behind the alpha-numeric system:

- *TOG 1/TOG 2 Heavy Tanks* [UK, 1940], where TOG—"stands for 'The Old Gang' and refers to the team set up on the outbreak of World War II to find solutions to UK tank needs" (Forty and Livesey, 2017, p. 71).

6.8 Matilda and Valentine—Exceptional Cases

A12 Infantry Tank Mark I Matilda I [UK, 1938]/*A12 Infantry Tank II Mark II Matilda II* [UK, 1939] complement the list of people's names together with another British design, *Mark III Valentine* [UK, 1940]. The names are discussed in the section entitled "British problems with tank's gender".

6.9   Groups of People: Warlike Jobs and Trades

People appear in the names of tanks not only as individuals but also as groups connected with military activities.

This group contains names like:

A24 Cruiser Tank Mark VII Cavalier [UK,1941] or *Challenger 2 MBT* [(UK, 1994].
These names will be discussed in the section entitled "The initial letter system", where names starting with C are analyzed.

- *A17 Light Tank Mark VII Tetrarch* [UK, 1942], in which the lexeme "tetrarch" is of Greek origin and stands for the "ruler of a quarter" or "in Greco-Roman antiquity the ruler of a principality, one of them being Herod Antipas' (Tetrarch, 1998).

This naming principle is also used in Australia, as the following example demonstrates:

- *Sentinel AC1, AC2, AC3, AC 4 Cruiser Tank* [Australia, 1942)], which stands for "sentry".[7]

It can also be found in Austrian names referring to cavalry soldiers, such as[8]:

- *ASCOD 105 Light Tank Ulan*[9] [Austria, 1996];
- *SK 105 Kürassier Light Tank*—cuirassier [Austria, 1965].

One should add another name here, i.e.:

- *M18 Hellcat Tank Destroyer* [USA, 1943].

  Its connotations are not strictly military but aggressive, i.e. of a mysterious danger.
  The concept of naming tank models after the names of particular people or groups of people may be classified as arbitrary. People who designed the names, however, must have been aware of the connotations that lie behind the names and which, as mentioned above, include features very much sought for in the battlefield.
  A diachronic study indicates that people's names occur in the names of tanks throughout its history, from the first designs till the post-WWII period. The first name of a person appeared in *The No. 1 Lincoln Machine "Little Willie", "Tritton Machine"* [UK, 1915]; then, the names of famous generals appeared, starting with *M4 Sherman Medium Tank* [USA, 1941], and this practice continues until the present day, as can be seen in *M1/A1 M1/A2 Abrams MBT* [USA, 1985].
  Warlike jobs and trades started to appear in tank names during WWII with *A13 Mark III Cruiser Tank Mark V Covenanter* [UK, 1940] and continue to be used today, e.g., *Challenger 2 MBT* [UK, 1994].

---

[7]https://www.merriam-webster.com/dictionary/sentinel.

[8]http://www.kuerassierregimenter.de.

[9]https://www.dictionary.com/browse/ulan.

6.10 Animals

The best known examples of the use of animal names come from Germany, e.g., *Panther, Tiger,* or *Leopard.* The names of UK/USA tanks include no wild cats, except two British tanks manufactured for Iran, namely:

- *Shir 1 (FV4030/2)* [UK, 1979];
- *Shir 2 (FV 4030/3)* [UK, 1979].

Forty and Livesey (2017, p. 190) indicate that "shir" stands for "lion", and the tanks were improved versions of British *Chieftain* tank.

Animal names started to be given to UK tanks nearly from the beginning of the tank's history. One of the first prototypes, *Wilson's machine* [UK, 1915], started to be known *as Big Willie, His Majesty's Land Ship Centipede,* or *Mother* (Little Willie, n.d.). A *centipede* may hardly match a panther or a tiger in terms of connotations of skill and aggressiveness. The British name is less suggestive than descriptive and refers to the tank's tracks.

This tradition was continued in the UK and USA and involves the use of the names of aggressive animals. Examples include:

- *Medium B Whippet* [UK, 1917] and *Medium A Whippet* [UK, 1918];
- *Medium C Hornet* [UK, 1918];
- *M22 Locust Light Tank* [USA, 1941];
- *M10 Wolverine Tank Destroyer* [USA, 1942];
- *Stingray I Light Tank* [USA, 1953];
- *M 56 Scorpion Tank Destroyer* [USA, 1953];
- *Alvis Scorpion Combat Vehicle Reconnaissance* [UK, 1973].

Scorpion is the name used by both UK and USA designers. *Stingray* is the only fish in the group. It may possibly be perceived as a dangerous one or some symbolic meaning may be attributed to it: In this case, stingray symbolism is letting you know that everything is now in place (…) your stingray meaning is telling you that everything you have worked toward is open to you. Therefore, you must stop hesitating. Furthermore, have faith in your abilities and follow your inner guidance. Alternatively, stingray symbolism is asking you to stay on course and keep moving forward. Henceforth, you must not allow distractions or drama to sway you from your journey. In fact, protect your path if you need to (Stingray symbolism, 2015).

Possibly the most fearful animal in the group occurs in the name of the Canadian version of *Sherman* tank, that is:

- *Grizzly* [Canada, 1943].

Another animal in a Canadian tank name is much less fearful, but it is still known for its horn-supported fighting spirit:

- *Ram Mark I Cruiser Tank* [Canada, 1941].

One must also mention *A39 Heavy Assault Tank Tortoise* [UK 1946]. Forty and Livesey (2017, p. 70) comment on it in the following way: "a 799,252 kg/78 ton monster appropriately called Tortoise". Thus, the shape and weight of the animal is the motivation for the tank name. The authors do not mention the fact that tortoise, or *testudo*, was one of the major military tactics of the ancient Roman army. The formation of soldiers indeed resembled a tortoise. Their large shields allowed them to present a 360-degree wall of wood to opponents. The front rank of the formation would kneel behind their interlocked shields, over a metre in height. The second rank would hold their shields above the heads of the men in front, and so on (Ricketts, 2018).

Starting with *centipede* in 1915 and *ending* with elephant in 1980 [*Olifant*, South Africa 1980], the tradition continues from WWI till the present day.

Animals as names of tanks are suggestive and they allude to the design (centipede) or to the dangerous nature of the vehicle (scorpion). One cannot escape noticing the similarity of names like *Alvis Scorpion* and *Ford Scorpio*.

6.11 Objects

Another group covers a variety of objects, whose military connotations are of different nature and sometimes difficult to trace, as in:

- *Alvis Scimitar Combat Vehicle Reconnaissance* [UK, 1973]

The name denotes a weapon, since "scimitar" may be defined as a saber having a curved blade with the edge on the convex side, used chiefly by Arabs and Turks.[10]

Some other names in this group have limited, if any, connections with fighting. This is the case with the following example:

- *A34 Cruiser Tank Comet* [UK, 1945]

The name may denote both a guiding star in the Biblical sense or the danger of a global destruction caused by a comet's tail hitting a planet (for the discussion of the *Comet* name, see also the section entitled "The initial letter system").

One name in the corpus suggests the desired outcome of military operations, namely:

- *Vickers Mark I MBT Vijayanta* [UK-India, 1964] (Forty and Livesey, 2017, p. 201).

Vijayanta stands for "victory" (Forty and Livesey, 2017, p. 252), a name component used earlier in the USSR:

- *JS-2 Heavy Tank*, known also as *Victory* [USSR, 1944].

In the analyzed corpus, one may also find the following name:

---

[10]https://www.merriam-webster.com/dictionary/scimitar.

- *M 50 Ontos Tank Destroyer* [USA, 1955].

Ontos in the name stands for "thing" in Greek (Forty and Livesey, 2017, p. 214). It seems a good idea to employ a foreign equivalent of an ordinary noun to give the named product an aura of sophistication.

Objects in tank names represent a variety of features and applications. They range from weapons (*Scimitar*) to abstract nouns (*Vijavanta–Victory*), include astronomic phenomena (*Comet*), or denote any existing object (*Ontos*). *Scimitar* is a suggestive name, in which an old weapon stands for the name of a modern one. *Victory* is a speculative name, as suggested above, while *Ontos* may possibly be classified as an arbitrary name. The Greek lexeme also has the connotations of extensive education and sophistication. *Comet*, the name analyzed in more detail in the section entitled "The initial C", has symbolic content.

The examples quoted above show that names of this type are seldom used and appear in the period of WWII and after.

6.12   Features of Tanks—Adjectives

The corpus includes three names in which adjectives are used, namely:

- *A1 E1 Independent* [UK, 1926];
- *A 33 Heavy Assault Tank Excelsior* (UK, 1943);
- *FV4401Contentious Air Portable Tank Destroyer* [UK, 1956].

The first name is descriptive and stands for a tank "designed … for independent actions" (Forty and Livesey, 2017, p. 54), which fits the classification presented in Table 1. It may, however, also be treated as a suggestive name, because it denotes the way of living—or living conditions—sought by people whom the weapon is supposed to protect.

Collins English Dictionary gives the following meaning of "excelsior":

1. excellent: used as a motto, in the names of hotels, and as a trademark for various products, esp. in the US for fine wood shavings used for packing breakable objects.
2. upwards.

It also indicates the Latin origin of the word, i.e., higher.[11] Moreover, the word may refer to the famous massive rough diamond weighing 995 carats.[12] A possible military connotation of the name is roughness, a desirable feature of any tank. A more general connotation is that of top quality and performance.

The meaning of "contentious" is discussed in the section entitled "The initial C".

---

[11]https://www.collinsdictionary.com/dictionary/english/excelsior.

[12]https://www.internetstones.com/excelsior-diamond-famous-jewelry.html.

Names in this category appear very seldom. The time span ranges from the pre-WWII to post-WWII period.

6.13 Alpha-Numeric Systems

Alpha-numeric systems appeared in large numbers in the section entitled "Manufacturers' naming systems". The data presented above indicate that the alpha-numeric component occurs in all categories of names. Indeed, a detailed presentation of the data would involve quoting almost all the names from Appendix 1.

A comprehensive explanation is beyond the capacity of a single researcher, especially an outsider to the military community. Outsiders may perceive the names as arbitrary, while for the military, they may function as descriptive ones, with letters and symbols conveying some relevant information.

On the other hand, insiders may also face some problems in understanding and using the alpha-numeric system. This is confirmed by Bates (2004), a retired officer and logistician of the US Army. The author describes problems with finding a model of a military vehicle across different types of computerized data bases. The author indicates the incompatibility of "nomenclature" and "item name" based systems (p. 21).

The system may be classified as arbitrary, and it has accompanied the development of tanks throughout their history.

6.14 The Initial Letter System

In the names of British tanks, two other systems may be observed. They cut across the systems discussed above and may be labeled as the initial C and the initial S systems, respectively.

The initial C

This tradition started in the WWII period. Originally, the "initial C names" were just one of the many types of names given to tanks. However, since the introduction of *Centurion* in 1945, the system presented below has prevailed.

The list of UK tanks within the system, in the chronological order of their introduction, is presented below:

- *A13 Mark III Cruiser Tank Mark V Covenanter* [UK, 1940];
- *A15 Cruiser Tank Mark VI Crusader* [UK, 1940];
- *A24 Cruiser Tank Mark VII Cavalier* [UK, 1941];
- *A22 Infantry Tank Mark IV Churchill* [UK, 1941];
- *A27 L Cruiser Tank Mark VIII Centaur* [UK, 1942];

- *A30 Cruiser Tank Challenger, Challenger I MBT, Challenger II MBT* UK, 1943, 1982, 1994];
- *A 41 Centurion Medium Tank* [UK, 1945];
- *A34 Cruiser Tank Comet* [UK, 1945];
- *FV 4101Charioteer Tank Destroyer* [UK, 1954];
- *FV 214 Conqueror Heavy Tank* [UK, 1956];
- *FV4401Contentious Air Portable Tank Destroyer* [UK, 1963];
- *FV 4202 Chieftain MBT* [UK, 1963].

A summary of the data may be presented as follows:

- Eight names in the list above may be classified as names of rulers, warlike jobs, and tradespeople: *Cavalier, Centurion, Challenger, Charioteer, Chieftain, Conqueror Covenanter,* and *Crusader*;
- One of them may classified as a famous person's name: *Churchill*;
- One represents a dangerous mythical creature: *Centaur*;
- One refers to an object: *Comet*;
- One represents a feature of the bearer: *Contentious*.

What all of them share is the sense of fighting spirit (or at least danger in *Comet*). In six of them, one may find the element of leadership (or guidance, as in *Comet*), and seven have historical, war-connected connotations, plus, in the case of *Comet*, the Biblical associations with guided travel to newborn Jesus.

The features discussed above, represented by a variety of symbols, make it possible to classify the names as both suggestive and symbolic.

The initial S

Forty and Livesey (2017) present some British fighting vehicles the names of which start with the letter "S". These include:

- *FV 603 Saracen Armoured Personel Carrier* (UK, 1953) (p. 488-489);
- *FV 601 Saladin Mk Armoured Car* [UK, 1959] (p. 487);
- *Alvis Scimitar Combat Vehicle Reconnaissance (Tracked)* [UK, 1973] (p. 164);
- *Alvis Scorpion Combat Vehicle Reconnaissance (Tracked)* [UK, 1973] (p. 165);
- *(FV 102) Striker Self-Propelled Tank Guided Weapon Vehicle* [UK, 1975] (p. 196);
- *Spartan Armoured Personel Carrier* [UK, 1978] (p. 494);
- *Stormer Armoured Personel Carrier* [UK, 1983] (p. 495).

One can see that S-initial names are common not only in the tank naming systems discussed in this paper but also in different types of weapons. The names of tanks (*Alvis Scimitar* and *Alvis Scorpion*) in the list above have been discussed in previous sections, while the names of other vehicles are beyond the scope of this study.

The system, as the dates indicate, is a post-WWII one. One can hardly find any equivalent in other countries. The Soviet-Russian system of T-34, T-54, T- 62, and T-90 (Forty and Livesey, 2017) may be classified as an alpha numeric one, where T stand for the generic name. The initial letters in the UK names are connected with the connotative "fight" names.

6.15   Obligatory and Non-obligatory Components

The generic name of the vehicle is an obligatory element in the analyzed corpus. It involves the lexeme *tank*, which may occur together with other constituents, called in this study "modifying components", e.g., *cruiser tank* or *light tank*. The components may be hidden in an abbreviation, mainly *MBT—Main Battle Tank*.

The alpha-numeric component is another major element in terms of occurrence. The few cases in which there are no digits, abbreviations, letter symbols, or any combinations of these include prototypes:

- *Vickers Commercial Dutchman Light Tank* [UK, 1936],
- *The "Semple" Tractor Tank* [New Zealand, 1942].

Provided that the generic name is hidden in an abbreviation, we can assume that the alpha-numeric names are the only ones that may function without any other components, as in M60 MBT, and MBT 70. These are, however, exceptional rather than typical cases.

The remaining components are transferred names, and they include famous people (e.g., *Abrams, Churchill, Sherman*), classes of people (e.g., *Challenger, Chieftain, Crusader*), animals (e.g., *Grizzly, Stingray, Scorpion*), objects (*Comet, Scimitar*), and abstract concepts (*Independent, Excelsior*).

Another component of the name is the name of the manufacturer, e.g., *Alvis, Vickers*.

Except very few cases of the alpha-numeric name standing alone, the tank name includes minimum two components, e.g., *M6 Heavy Tank*.

7   Conclusion

Taking into consideration the data presented above, one may conclude that there is an unquestionable British input into the tank history, not only in terms of tank's design and application but also in terms of its name. First of all, the British provided the generic name of the invention, which covers not only the basic concept but also its varieties, subject to different doctrines and modes of application (*cruiser tank, heavy tank*, etc.).

The UK designers developed unique initial C and initial S name systems that cut across other naming systems and, as in the case of the initial S system, extend to other types of fighting vehicles. The initial S system is recent (developed after WWII), while the initial C system started to be used during WWII and has been continued till now. Also, it is in the UK that the tradition of naming tanks after famous generals started during WWII (*Sherman*) and has continued till now (*Abrams*).

There is an unquestionable British contribution, if not pioneering work, to the development of the practice of using terms denoting warlike groups of people and occupations in tank names.

The naming systems identified in the UK/USA corpus involve obligatory components, i.e., the generic name (also in an abbreviated form) and the alpha-numeric component (in one of its varieties).

There are other components, which are interchangeable and include names of people (*Christie, Matilda, Churchill*), especially of famous generals (*Grant, Patton*), names of groups of people involved in war trade, or types of warriors (*Crusader, Centurion*).

Another naming component is based on the names of species of animals (*Centipede, Scorpion, Grizzly*) and is followed by names of different objects, abstract or concrete ones (*Victory, Comet, Ontos*). There is also a small group of names which are based on adjectives describing features of the bearer (*Contentious, Independent*). Finally, there is a group of names which involve the name of the manufacturer (*Alvis, Ford, Vickers*).

Some of the naming components, namely, the obligatory ones and the names of people or animals, have functioned since the birth of the tank till now. The small group of feature-based names originated in the interwar period and has continued to be used after WWII. Some other naming traditions, such as using names of famous generals or the initial C names, started during WWII and have been continued till now.

In a historical perspective of the tank name development, one can observe that nearly all types of names analyzed in this project have been in use since the emergence of the tank. Still, the WWII period added some dynamism to the development. This is connected with the introduction of the names of generals and the beginning of the initial C system. The design development, represented by the introduction of the Main Battle Tank (MBT), has reduced the number and length of the names. The generic name is hidden in the MBT acronym, and the fight names continue the naming tradition, especially the famous generals line (USA), as in *M1/A1 M1/A2 Abrams MBT*, and the warlike people line (UK), as in *Challenger 2 MBT*.

The only change that seems to be settled is the abandonment of female elements, which have not appeared in tank names in Britain since WWII. However, the diversity of the systems brings to mind the title of a subchapter in Bates' article: "Military Names Have Not Been Yet Standarized" (2004, p. 21).

Appendix 1

Names of UK and USA tanks analyzed

No.	Name	Country	Year	Source (listed below)
1	*The No.1 Lincoln Machine* *"Little Willie"* *Also "Tritton Machine"*	UK	1915	S1: 87

(continued)

(continued)

No.	Name	Country	Year	Source (listed below)
2	*Mark I Medium Tank ("Mother")* *Male*	UK	1916	S1: 92/93
3	*Mark I Medium Tank ("Mother")* *Male*	UK	1916	S1: 92/93
4	*Ford 6 Ton Tank (M1917)*	USA	1917	S1: 81
5	*Mark I and Mark III Heavy Tanks*	UK	1917	S1: 95
6	*Mark IV Heavy Tank*	UK	1917	S1: 100
7	*Medium A Whippet*	UK	1917	S1: 90
8	*Ford 3 Ton Tank*	*USA*	*1918*	S1: *81*
9	*Holt Gas-Electric Tank*	USA	1918	S1: 83
10	Mark V Heavy Tank	UK	1918	S1: 102
11	Mark VIII Heavy Tank	UK	1918	S1: 106/7
12	*Medium B Whippet*	UK	1918	S1: 89
13	*Medium C Hornet*	UK	1918	S1: 89
14	*War Tank America Steam Tank* *Experimental Combat Vehicle*	USA	1918	S3
15	*Mark I Medium Tank*	UK	1924	S1: 94
16	*Mark II Medium Tank*	UK	1925	S1: 96
17	T1 and T2 Medium Tanks	USA	1925	S1: 146
18	A1 E1 Independent	UK	1926	S1: 54
19	Vickers 6 Ton Tank	UK	1928	S1: 155
20	M 1931 Christie	USA	1931	S1: 19
21	*Mark I and Mark III Light Tanks*	UK	1931	S1: 97
22	*Mark I and Mark III Light Tanks*	UK	1931	S1: 97
23	*Vickers-Armstrong Amphibious* *Tank Model 1931*	UK	1931	S4: 126
24	*Mark IV Light Tank*	UK	1934	S1: 99
25	M1 and M2 Combat Cars	USA	1935	S1: 108
26	*Mark V Light Tank*	UK	1935	S1: 99
27	Vickers Commercial Dutchman Light Tank	UK	1936	S1: 154
28	Mark VI Light Tank	UK	1937	S1: 104/5
29	A12 Infantry Tank Mark I Matilda I	UK	1938	S1: 56
30	A13 Cruiser Tank Mark III	UK	1938	S1: 58
31	A12 Infantry Tank II Mark II Matilda II	UK	1939	S1: 57
32	A13 Mark II Cruiser Tank Mark III	UK	1940	S1: 58

(continued)

(continued)

No.	Name	Country	Year	Source (listed below)
33	A13 Mark III Cruiser Tank Mark V Covenanter	UK	1940	S1: 59
34	A15 Cruiser Tank Mark VI Crusader	UK	1940	S1: 60
35	M2 Light Tank series	USA	1940	S1: 109
36	M3 Light Tank series (M3 A Light Tank Stuart Mk III)	USA	1940	S1: 114
37	*Mark III Valentine Infantry Tank*	UK	1940	S1: 98
38	TOG 1/TOG 2 Heavy Tanks	UK	1940	S1: 70
39	A22 Infantry Tank Mark IV Churchill	UK	1941	S1: 62
40	A24 Cruiser Tank Mark VII Cavalier	UK	1941	S1: 64
41	M22 Locust Light Tank	USA	1941	S1: 118
42/43	M3 General Lee Medium Tank (also: Grant)	Joint UK/USA	1941	S1: 110/1
44	M4 Sherman Medium Tank	USA	1941	S1: 112/3
45	Ram Mark I Cruiser Tank	Canada	1941	S1: 134
46	A17 Light Tank Mark VII Tetrarch	UK	1942	S1: 61
47	A27L Cruiser Tank Mark VIII Centaur	UK	1942	S1: 64
48	M10 Wolverine Tank Destroyer	USA	1942	S1: 116
49	M5 Light Tank	USA	1942	S1: 114
50	M6 Heavy Tank	USA	1942	S1: 115
51	Ram Mark II Cruiser Tank	Canada	1942	S1: 134
52	The "Semple" Tractor Tank	New Zealand	1942	S2
53	Sentinel AC1, AC2, AC3, AC 4 Cruiser Tank	Australia	1942	S1: 137
54	A 33 Heavy Assault Tank Excelsior	UK	1943	S1: 67
55	A27 M Cruiser Tank Mark VIII Cromwell	UK	1943	S1: 65
56	A30 Cruiser Tank Challenger	UK	1943	S1: 66
57	M4 Grizzly Medium Tank	Canada	1943	S3 S2
58	A38 Infantry Tank Valiant	UK	1943	S1: 67
59	M18 Hellcat Tank Destroyer	USA	1943	S1: 117
60	A25 Light Tank Mark VIII Harry Hopkins	UK	1944	S1: 61

(continued)

(continued)

No.	Name	Country	Year	Source (listed below)
61	M24 Chaffee Light Tank	USA	1944	S1: 118
62	M26 Pershing Heavy Tank	USA	1944	S1: 115
63	M36 Gun Motor Carriage	USA	1944	S1: 117
64	M4A3E2 Sherman Jumbo Assault Tank	USA	1944	S2
65	Sherman VC Firefly Tank Destroyer	US	1944	S2
66	A 41 Centurion Medium Tank	UK	1945	S1: 58/9
67	A 43 Infantry Tank Black Prince	UK	1945	S1: 63
68	A34 Cruiser Tank Comet	UK	1945	S1: 68/69
69	A39 Heavy Assault Tank Tortoise	UK	1946	S1: 70
70	M 44 Walker Bulldog Light Tank	USA	1951	S1: 198/9
71	M 47 Medium (Patton Tank)	USA	1952	S1: 200/201
72	M 48 Patton MBT	USA	1953	S1: 201/3
73	M 56 Scorpion Tank Destroyer	USA	1953	S1: 205
74	FV 4101Charioteer Tank Destroyer	UK	1954	S1: 180 S2
75	M 50 Ontos Tank Destroyer	USA	1955	S1: 204 S2
76	FV 214 Conqueror Heavy Tank	UK	1956	S1: 181
77	M60 MBT	USA	1960	S1: 206/7
78	Chieftain MBT (FV 4202)	UK	1963	S1: 178/9
79	FV4401Contentious Air Portable Tank Destroyer	UK	1963	S3
80	Vickers Mark I (Vijayanta) MBT	UK/India	1964	S1: 252
81	Stingray I Light Tank	USA	1965	S1: 222
82	MBT 70	UK/USA	1967	S1: 212
83	M 551 Sheridan Light Tank	USA	1968	S1: 208
84	Alvis FV 107 Scimitar Combat Vehicle Reconnaissance (Tracked)	UK	1973	S1: 164 S2
85	Alvis FV 101 Scorpion Combat Vehicle Reconnaissance (Tracked)	UK	1973	S1: 165 S2
86	High Mobility Agility Test Vehicle HIMAG	USA	1978	S1: 185
87	High Survivability Test Vehicle (Lightweight) HSTV(L)	USA	1980	S1: 185
88	Shir 1 (FV4030/2)	UK	1979[a]	S1: 190
89	Shir 2 (FV 4030/3)	UK	1979[a]	S1:190

(continued)

(continued)

No.	Name	Country	Year	Source (listed below)
90	Challenger 1 MBT	UK	1982	S1: 174/5
91	AA1 Rapid Deployment Force Light Tank	USA	1983	S1: 162
92	M1/A1 M1/A2 Abrams MBT	USA	1985	S1: 160/161
93	Vickers Mark 7 Valiant MBT	UK	1985	S1: 255
94	Vickers VFW Mark 5 Light Tank	UK	1987	S1: 254
95	Challenger 2 MBT	UK	1994	S1: 176/7
96	M8 Ridgeway Armoured Gun System	USA	1995	S1: 191
97	Stingray II Light Tank	USA	1996	S1: 222
98	Vickers Mark 3 MBT	UK	1997	S1: 253

Sources
S1 Forty, G., Livesey, J. (2017). *The World Encyclopedia of Tanks*. London: Lorenze Books
S2 www1 http://www.tanks-encyclopedia.com/modern/Egypt/Ramses-II.php
S3 www2 https://www.militaryfactory.com/armor/detail.asp?armor_id=934
S4 Zasieczny, A., (2006). *Czołgi II wojny światowej*. Warszawa: Oficyna Wydawnicza Alma-Press
[a]Date of cancellation of the contract by Iran. Tanks bought in 1981 by Jordan and named *Khalid Shir*

References

Altkorn, J. (1999). *Strategia marki*. Warszawa: Państwowe Wydawnictwo Ekonomiczne S.A.
Antal, J. (2014). Armour forward! The evolution of tanks since World War I. *Military Technology, 6*, 112–113.
Barder, L. (2013, March 30). *Why is a ship a she?* [Blog post]. Retrieved from: https://www.glosso philia.org/?p=1411.
Bates, J. C. (2004). Names, numbers, and nomenclatures. *Army Logistician. Professional Bulletin of United States Army Logistics, 36*(5), 18–21.
Blumberg, A. (2019, January 4). Death of Legendary Confederate General J.E.B. Stuart. In *Warfare History Network*. Retrieved from: https://warfarehistorynetwork.com/daily/civil-war/death-of-legendary-confederate-general-j-e-b-stuart/.
Boyd, C. W. (1985). Point of view: Alpha-numeric brand names. *Journal of Advertising Research, 25*(5), 48–52.
Cidlinský, K. (2018a). Pojazdy opancerzone Jego Królewskie Mości. *Wojna Revue,* numer specjalny, 83–84.
Cidlinský, K. (2018b). Z białą gwiazdą na pancerzu. *Wojna Revue,* numer specjalny, 36–39.
Collins COBUILD English dictionary for advanced learners (3rd ed.). (2001). Glasgow: Harper Collins Publishers.
David, B. (2014, June 2). Little Willie. In *Tank encyclopedia*. Retrieved from: http://www.tanks-encyclopedia.com/ww1/gb/little_willie.php.
Deighton, L. (1979). *Blitzkrieg. From the rise of Hitler to the fall of Dunkirk*. London: Jonathan Cape Thirty Bedford Square.

Edward, the Black Prince (1330–1376). (n.d.). In *BBC—Historic Figures*. Retrieved March 30, 2019 from: http://www.bbc.co.uk/history/historic_figures/black_prince.shtml.

Forty, G., & Livesey, J. (2017). *The World Encyclopedia of Tanks*. London: Lorenze Books.

Hall, C. (2001). *An introduction to language and linguistics. Breaking the language spell*. London and New York: Continuum.

Hickey, C. (2010). *From coal pit to leather pit. Life stories of Robert Semple*. (Unpublished doctoral dissertation). Massey University, New Zealand. Retrieved from: https://mro.massey.ac.nz/bitstream/handle/10179/1696/02_whole.pdf.

Kall, J. (2001). *Silna marka. Istota i kreowanie*. Warszawa: Państwowe Wydawnictwo Ekonomiczne S.A.

Kosyl, Cz. (2001). Chrematonimy. In J. Bartmiński (Ed.), *Współczesny język polski* (pp. 447–452). Lublin: Wydawnictwo Uniwersytetu Marii Curie-Skłodowskiej.

Kotler, Ph., & Armstrong, G. (2001). *Principles of marketing* (9th ed.). Upper Saddle River, New Jersey: Prentice Hall International.

Little Willie (E1949.322). (n.d.). In *The Tank Museum Online*. Retrieved March 30, 2019 from: https://www.tankmuseum.org/museum-online/vehicles/object-e1949-322.

Mamet, P. (2008). The linguistic aspect of a brand name. Case study based on branding strategy of Opel. *Linguistica Silesiana, 29,* 51–65.

McDowall, D. (1991). *An illustrated history of Britain*. Harlow: Longman.

Ogorkiewicz, R. M. (2019). Tank. Military vehicle. In *Encyclopaedia Britannica*. Retrieved from: https://www.britannica.com/technology/tank-military-vehicle.

Ogorkiewicz, R. (2016). *Czołgi. 100 lat historii*. Warszawa: Wydawnictwo RM.

Oliver, D. (2011). *Czołgi Sherman*. Warszawa: Bellona SA.

Pavia, T. M., & Costa, J. A. (1993). The winning number: Consumer perceptions of alpha-numeric brandnames. *Journal of Marketing, 57*(3), 85–98.

Pershing, J. J. (2018). In *Encyclopaedia Britannica*. Retrieved from: https://www.britannica.com/biography/John-J-Pershing.

Polański, K. (Ed.). (1999). *Encyklopedia językoznawstwa ogólnego (wyd. 2 popr.)*. Wrocław: Zakład Narodowy im. Ossolińskich.

Richards, J. C., Platt, J., & Platt, H. (1999). *Longman dictionary of language teaching and applied linguistics*. London: Pearson Education Limited.

Ricketts, C. (2018). 3 Important Roman Military Tactics. In. *History Hit*. Retrieved from: https://www.historyhit.com/roman-military-tactics.

Sorley, L. (2018). Creighton Williams Abrams, Jr. In *Encyclopaedia Britannica*. Retrieved from: https://www.britannica.com/biography/Creighton-Williams-Abrams-Jr.

Stingray Symbolism. (2015). [Blog post]. Retrieved from: https://www.spirit-animals.com/stingray-symbolism/.

Tetrarch. (1998). In *Encyclopaedia Britannica*. Retrieved from: https://www.britannica.com/topic/tetrarch-ancient-Greek-official.

Trewhitt, P. (2006). *Panzer. Die wichtigsten Kampffarzeuge der Welt vom Ersten Weltkreig bis heute*. Klagenfurt: Keiser.

Usunier, J. C., & Shaner, J. (2002). Using linguistics for creating better international brand names. *Journal of Marketing Communications, 8,* 211–228.

Zasieczny, A. (2006). *Czołgi II wojny światowej*. Warszawa: Oficyna Wydawnicza Alma-Press.

Zboralski, M. (2000). *Nazwy firm i produktów*. Warszawa: Polskie Wydawnictwo Ekonomiczne.

Piotr Mamet is Professor at the Institute of Communication and Education Research of Silesian University of Technology, is engaged in the research on LSP, especially discourse, genre and register analysis, including the Plain language issues, and the linguistic aspect of a brand name. He is the author of two monographs, i.e. "Język negocjacji handlowych (2004) and "Język w służbie menedżerów—deklaracja misji przedsiebiorstwa (2005) as well as 30 articles and two monographs in this area. His recent research covers the language of film characters, e.g. the monograph *Licence to Speak. The Language of James Bond* (2014) as well as conference participation and articles (in print) in which he analyses the translation of the language of 007 and its translation into Polish. Prof. Piotr Mamet was one of the founders and managers of the Business Language College, University of Silesia (1991–2005). Before starting his teaching and research work Prof. Piotr Mamet worked in the international trade sector, including Polish Chamber of Foreign Trade (1995–1991). His considerable experience in international trade is a strong basis for his research and teaching activities in ESP, especially Business English.

Socializing at Work—An Investigation of Small Talk Phenomenon in the Workplace

Adam Pluszczyk

Abstract The purpose of the paper is to focus on spoken discourse—more specifically *small talk* and how it is reflected in various communicative exchanges in working environments—in the workplace. The following study attempts to analyze the social interaction of small talk among people at work—that is in the workplace. This study makes a comparison of how Polish people interact with each other during small talk in the workplace. The various objectives and functions of small talk, the attitudes the respondents have towards this allegedly insignificant and trivial phenomenon and the preference to engage in small talk on the part of men and women and the circumstances which either favour or impede the occurrence of small talk will be investigated and discussed. To investigate the phenomenon and portray the features, various functions of small talk and the attitudes, the informants will be exposed to a number of questions in the form of a questionnaire. The responses will enable us to determine the significance and perception of small talk by the informants at work in selected professional settings.

Keywords Business · Small talk · Functions · Attitudes · Interaction · Gender · Questionnaire

1 Introduction

Although small talk covers a number of topics, it pertains to brief exchanges which are regarded as trivial, non-serious, superficial and unimportant. Moreover, regardless of its alleged insignificance, triviality and non-seriousness, small talk is a phenomenon which is ubiquitous and unavoidable as it serves a number of various functions and is used for many purposes. On the other hand, the perception and attitudes we have towards the phenomenon of small talk might vary—depending on the culture,

A. Pluszczyk (✉)
Faculty of Humanities, Institute of Linguistics, University of Silesia in Katowice, Katowice, Poland
e-mail: adam.pluszczyk@us.edu.pl

© Springer Nature Switzerland AG 2020
U. Michalik et al. (eds.), *Exploring Business Language and Culture*, Second Language Learning and Teaching, https://doi.org/10.1007/978-3-030-58551-8_12

interlocutors, circumstances. More specifically, there are many factors which either favour or disfavour the incidence and frequency of small talk.

The paper explores the various functions of small talk and the attitudes the respondents have towards this phenomenon. Moreover, it investigates the significance or insignificance of small talk in selected professional settings—that is in the workplace. In other words, the study attempts to assess and determine how important small talk is in the workplace and what functions it has when used in the workplace. In other words, the study attempts to determine how much attention the workers pay to engaging in small talk in the work place and for what reasons—more specifically what functions small talk has in these contextual settings. Additionally, the study aims at determining the circumstances which either favour or impede the incidence of small talk. With a view to observing the phenomenon of small talk in the workplace—the occurrence, the functions of small talk and the attitudes of the informants, the respondents are exposed to a questionnaire with various questions on small talk.

The paper encompasses theoretical background and the review of the professional literature. It starts from the various definitions of small talk, its objectives and functions. It also discusses the various topics which are normally raised during small talk and finally elaborates on the occurrence of small talk in the workplace. The practical part includes methodology, the questionnaire results and the analysis—that is the discussion of the results, observations, conclusion and limitations of the study.

2   Theoretical Background—Literature Review

The theoretical background encompasses the various definitions of small talk, its objectives and various functions. In addition, it discusses the choice of the topics which are usually raised when engaging in small talk and it also elaborates on the occurrence of small talk in the workplace.

2.1   *The Definition of* Small Talk

Language constitutes an indispensable part of our every life. It serves for communication, exchanging ideas, giving and getting information, informing others etc. Apart from the purpose of communicating and exchanging important information, language also serves for establishing and maintaining interaction, building up solidarity, relationship, making contacts and creating bonds. Thus,

> Language is particularly good at promoting interaction between people… In spite of the widespread view that language is primarily for conveying information, language is not particularly good at this: … Language is particularly good in social roles, at maintaining social ties and influencing others. (Aitchison, 1996, p. 21, p. 25)

Small talk constitutes an informal, a casual, polite and friendly conversation about mundane, ordinary, relatively unimportant or insignificant subjects that people raise in various social settings for various reasons. There are various definitions of the phenomenon of small talk:

- *small talk* is defined as phatic communion, casual conversation, gossip, social talk, etc. (Jaworski, 2000);
- "Small talk is characterized as "brief talk", i.e. in contrast to technical, informational, problem-solving or conflict discussions, with small talk, the conversation remains superficial; the selected or appropriate topics are less controversial and are not discussed in depth" (Watzke-Otte, 2008, p. 13).

As can be observed, there are various definitions of *small talk*. In order to understand the real nature of *small talk*, one must concentrate on various objectives and functions it has in everyday communication in various contextual settings.

2.2 The Objectives, Advantages and Functions of Small Talk

One of the most important functions of language is to communicate with other people—to understand them and be understood, to exchange information with each other, etc. Through language, we are also able to express our feelings, needs, emotions, etc. There are also a number of other objectives where why we use a language, for instance to persuade people, to make our interlocutors feel good or bad, comfortable or upset, etc. At other times, we use a language to get on with others, to maintain good relationships according to certain social and cultural norms—this is refereed to as a phatic function:

> The focus is not on the exchange of important information, on a discussion result or the resolution of a problem. Instead, the point is to make a congenial impression on the other party and to give them the feeling of being pleasantly entertained: the things that count are an enjoyable, relaxed discussion atmosphere and the build-up and maintenance of relationships. (Watzke-Otte, 2008, p. 13)

Small talk is often associated with politeness and naturalness. In some situations, both formal and casual, it is useful or even necessary to know how to initiate a conversation. The art of small talk is based on the rules of making such dialogues, such as how to start a conversation or what topics should be discussed and what topics should be avoided. Once we start a conversation, the dialogue should go smoothly and naturally, but it is also important to know how to maintain a conversation; in other words, how to make it natural and at the same time make sure that the interlocutors feel comfortable (albeit it is not easy at times). Thus, "Preparation may make the difference between a stimulating, low-risk conversation and an awkward exchange of words. To prepare for small talk, minimize distractions and reduce anxiety" (Wakefield, 2016, p. 16).

According to Schneider (1988), small talk is usually characterized by negative connotations—it is perceived as trivial and unimportant, etc. Hence, one might think that it is unnecessary as it is associated with a waste of time. Similarly, according to Fleming (2018), small talk is generally considered to be insignificant, superficial and aimless. Nevertheless, it must be stressed that there are a number of advantages of small talk. Regardless of its alleged insignificance, small talk is a phenomenon which is ubiquitous as it occurs in both formal and informal contextual settings. As a result, regardless of the alleged trivial and insignificant nature of small talk and all the negative connotations it evokes, such as non-seriousness, insignificance, etc., it seems that it is ubiquitous as it occurs in a number of non-serious interactions or it might accompany the "more serious" interactions and thus constitute a preliminary stage of a real, necessary conversation. Hence, "Small talk provides communicators with simple, often mundane topics to discuss until the conversation turns towards a more stimulating topic" (Wakefield, 2016, pp. 13–14). Similarly, stresses Wakefield (2016, p. 104), "People also use small talk as a way to bridge the gap between topics of importance". As a result, one can observe that small talk is regarded as trivial, insignificant and non-serious although definitely in a positive sense. Moreover, it has a positive impact on the interlocutors who participate in the interaction and the situation in which a particular conversation takes place provided that one does not exaggerate with the amount of small talk as "In the right dosage, small talk contributes to a relaxation and loosening up of the conversational atmosphere, and to your discussion partner opening up. It reduces distance and promotes trust" (Watzke-Otte, 2008, p. 13).

Through small talk, one can make one's connections with others (Wakefield, 2016, p. 10). Moreover, by engaging in small talk, one makes the situation of our interaction comfortable, pleasant and friendly. In addition, through small talk, we can reduce the uncertainty we might have towards our interlocutors. Finally, by engaging in small talk, one can evade uncomfortable silences which occur when we have nothing to talk about at times and which make us feel ill at ease (Wakefield, 2016, p. 13).

However, it is necessary to highlight that the potential openness for small talk might be misinterpreted or wrongly perceived. Oftentimes the possible misinterpretations or misunderstandings are associated with various stereotypes, cultural differences and national features. Thus, "For example, Americans are more likely than those from many cultures to smile at strangers and to engage in personal discussions with people they hardly know…. Later, when the Americans don't follow through on their unintended offer, those other cultures often accuse them of being "fake" or "hypocritical" (Meyer, 2014, p. 174).

Thus, it is worth pointing out that the importance of small talk depends on a culture; for instance it is much more important for the British rather than Polish to small talk: whereas Polish people focus on exchanging concrete information, British people small talk in order to make new contacts and maintain relationship. As we can see, the occurrence and the frequency of small talk are culture-dependent. Thus, for instance, "In Delhi, where I grew up, commerce is brusque. You don't ask each other how your day has been. You might not even smile" (Mahajan, 2016).

Undeniably, small talk plays an important part in both professional life—that is at work and in private life. In other words, small talk enables us to build relationships and create bonds socially and professionally. Moreover, it also builds community

(Fleming, 2018). In institutional settings small talk facilitates building rapport among workers and establishes solidarity (Coupland, 2003).

Holmes (2000, p. 37) makes a distinction between *business talk* and *phatic communion* by enumerating certain important criteria which differentiate between the former and the latter. Whereas the former encompasses "on-topic" talk, is maximally informative, context-bound and transactional, the latter pertains to atopical talk, is minimally informative, context-free and social (Holmes, 2000, p. 37).

It is worth emphasizing that small talk can have several important functions and these functions are undeniably positive and beneficial for the interlocutors. These are the following:

- to break the ice, especially when we talk to someone we do not know well or at all;
- to maintain relationships (Watzke-Otte, 2008, p. 13);
- to make our interlocutors feel comfortable, to cause a friendly atmosphere;
- to exchange ideas about common interests, hobbies;
- to kill an uncomfortable silence;
- to be polite, to be kind to others when avoiding silence;
- to build solidarity and rapport, i.e. in institutional settings (Pullin, 2010);
- to formulate an opinion about our interlocutors (Watzke-Otte, 2008, p. 13);
- to cause a relaxing atmosphere (Watzke-Otte, 2008, p. 13);
- to make the distance smaller (to reduce distance) and to create trust (Watzke-Otte, 2008, p. 13);
- to facilitate interpersonal relationships between people in social and professional settings, i.e. on a street, at a bus stop, at a party, at school, at work;
- to get to know others, to meet new people (Wakefield, 2016).

The attitude which we have towards the phenomenon of small talk is also associated with our personality. How much we wish to engage in small talk might also depend on our personality features—i.e. introverts are reluctant to small talk since they might be afraid or anxious, they could feel ill at ease. There are those who consider small talk to be pointless and artificial. On the other hand, there are a lot of people for whom small talk comes naturally as it constitutes an important element in everyday life.

Admittedly, small talk can be quite easy and natural. It is usually spontaneous and occurs naturally without making much effort. However, making small talk does not have to be easy at times. Moreover, how successful we can be in making small talk also depends on the very interlocutors—i.e., how well we know them (Valev, 2015). Moreover, small talk is a complicated phenomenon and can be quite problematic at times. Similarly, "Anyone who's been caught at a wedding reception or a cocktail party discussing recent precipitation knows that making small talk isn't as easy as it sounds. On the contrary, conversing with strangers can be awkward, stilted, even painful" (Tung, 2004). As can be observed, small talk does not always have to be so natural, pleasant and easy. Hence, it can also be artificial, difficult, cumbersome and can make the interlocutors feel uncomfortable or uneasy at times.

2.3 What Topics Are Raised and What Topics Should Be Avoided?

Taking into consideration the suitability of the topics for small talk and the possible sensitivity of the interlocutors, there are a number of topics which can be raised. Nevertheless, there are also other topics which should definitely be avoided. Therefore, the choice of topics is strictly related to social norms which are established and observed. Depending on a culture, certain topics might be regarded as appropriate or inappropriate. The choice of sensitive and controversial topics might be associated with the violation of certain social and cultural norms. "Norms are then the guides of predictable, coordinated behavior in society. Norms allow persons to expect, recognize, and evaluate actual behavior" (Terpstra and David, 1985, p. 144). In other words, it is crucial to know what topics should be avoided as they can be annoying, controversial, embarrassing, provocative or simply dangerous (Watzke-Otte, 2008, p. 132). Therefore, continues Watzke-Otte (2008, pp. 114–139), there are a number of topics which are regarded as neutral and safe, such as journeys, professional matters, shopping, film and TV, hobbies, family life, music, the news, eating habits, animals, transport, the weather, goals and dreams. However, there are also many other topics—referred to as taboo topics which should be avoided or which do not simply appear on the list of small talk topics, such as family problems, money, illnesses, politics, religion, sexuality and many others (Watzke-Otte, 2008, p. 114–139). There are topics which are acceptable but there are also other topics which should be avoided in certain cultures as they might lead to embarrassing situations, uncomfortable silences or even conflicts (Tomalin and Nicks, 2007, p. 16). For instance, whereas it is all right to talk about families in Italy, in China it can be a more delicate topic for discussion. Similarly, there are certain topics of conversation which are acceptable in Britain or the US, but which do not necessarily have to be raised so willingly or frequently elsewhere (Tomalin and Nicks, 2007, p. 16).

2.4 Small Talk at Work

Making small talk at work is also common, but it must be remembered that there are also certain subjects which should not be raised in the workplace in order not to provoke or contribute to unnecessary conflicts or disagreements. Thus,

> The job is usually a good small talk subject, but certain things are simply no-go areas: these include stories about clients, even if they're genuinely funny, as well as internal matters of working conditions, wages, new products or company management mistakes. (Watzke-Otte, 2008, p. 133)

It must be stressed that small talk at work is a common phenomenon: "... there is a wealth of opportunities to make small talk during the average workday" (Watzke-Otte, 2008, p. 133). However, how willing people are to engage in small talk and how important small talk is at work is also culturally-oriented. In some countries the use of small talk in the workplace is common, expected, recommendable or even necessary; in others it is simply limited, less important or peripheral. For instance, in business settings, whereas for some nationalities, engaging in small talk comes easily, for others it is not necessarily so natural or common (Lewis, 2006, p. 88). Hence, for instance, in the Arab world, it is expected to devote relatively much time to small talk and raise various topics, such as hobbies, family, current affairs, economy. Even during business talk in professional settings, some aspects of small talk can easily be incorporated. Similarly, in Japan, small talk during business meetings is quite common in order to create and facilitate personal trust (Carté and Fox, 2008, p. 71). As a result, for instance, "In more functional cultures, on the other hand, people expect to start on the business agenda within minutes of sitting down. With Germans, Swiss, Scandinavians and Finns, for example, small talk is often no more than a couple of sentences" (Carté and Fox, 2008, p. 71).

It is also necessary to stress that even though we do not like small talk at times, it is usually expected in certain situations. In other words, there are a number of situations where small talk should not be avoided since otherwise, it would be impolite or simply badly-seen (Watzke-Otte, 2008, p. 133). At other times, in certain situations in the workplace, the ability to engage in small talk might also influence the career development. "Many organizations consider the ability to get along with coworkers an important skill. Interpersonal relationships with other workplace staff can often play a role in determining how far one's career advances" (Wakefield, 2016, p. 61).

It should be stressed that the choice of topics is really important as some of them might be risky or dangerous and might contribute to unnecessary disputes, arguments or even hostility. As Wakefield admits (2016, p. 63), "Neutral topics are unlikely to cause heated disagreements among coworkers and office staff... certain topics do not make for appropriate small talk. This is especially true in the workplace. Many topics lend themselves to unwanted disagreements and controversy" (Wakefield, 2016, p. 64). Thus, it is always recommendable to adjust the topics to the interlocutors and a particular situation in order to avoid unnecessary problems, such as conflicts in the workplace.

It is also undeniable that just as small talk brings forth a number of advantages in general, it also causes many positive aspects in the workplace. It contributes to the creation of a friendly environment and to the maintenance of good relationships among workers. It might also facilitate interpersonal relationships when meeting new people. Hence,

> Engaging in small talk is an effective way to establish positive relationships with coworkers. By giving friendly greetings, remaining positive, discussing neutral topics, and adhering to the code of conduct, workplace inhabitants can develop long-lasting friendships and interpersonal relationships with one another. (Wakefield, 2016, p. 65)

Thus, as can be observed, small talk is characterized by a lot of advantages and other positive aspects. On the other hand, there are a number of factors which should be taken into consideration in order to make small talk a nice, successful and pleasurable experience.

3   Methodology

3.1   The Objectives of the Study

The aim of the study is the analysis of the function of small talk and its alleged significance among the workers of 3 selected business companies. Based on the questionnaire, it will be observed if small talk is a common phenomenon in the workplace. In other words, the questionnaire will help us determine how important small talk is in the workplace and what attitude workers have towards small talk (the various attitudes which the respondents might have towards small talk will be investigated and discussed). Additionally, the questionnaire will help us reveal the reasons why people might want to engage in small talk in the workplace.

Moreover, the purpose of the study is to pay attention to the circumstances which either facilitate or hinder the occurrence of small talk, such as different contextual settings (formal, informal), the interlocutors (males, females), how frequently small talk occurs at work in these settings and who engages in it more often.

3.2   Participants

The questionnaire has been conducted among 80 participants aged between 23 and 57 from three different workplaces.

Workplace 1:

- The name of the company: Blue Idea Accounting—Limited Liability Company in Katowice, Poland.
- The company deals with rendering services of business outsourcing in the area of staffing and payroll.
- Premises: Katowice, ul. Korfantego 2.
- The number of respondents: 48 females.

Workplace 2:

- The name of the company: 3S Data Center SA.
- The company deals with data collocation and storing sensitive data of high degree security, especially medical companies.
- Premises: Katowice, ul. Gospodarcza 12.
- The number of respondents: 12—7 males and 5 females.

Workplace 3:

- The name of the company: Fiat Chrysler Automobiles.
- The company deals with the production of cars.
- Premises: Bielsko-Biała, ul. Węglowa 10.

- The number of respondents: 20—4 males and 16 females.

3.3 Tools

In order to investigate the phenomenon of small talk, the informants were exposed to a number of questions in the form of a questionnaire. There are 17 questions in the questionnaire (see appendix). It is necessary to stress that the respondents were exposed to the questionnaire in their native language—that is in Polish.

3.4 Procedure

The respondents were requested to respond to 17 questions in a questionnaire devoted to the phenomenon of small talk. The results of the questionnaire constitute the basis for the discussion and the observations of the ubiquity of small talk in the workplace, its various functions and objectives and the circumstances which either favour or impede the occurrence of small talk in professional settings—in the workplace.

3.5 Presentation of the Results of the Questionnaire

These are the results of the questionnaire conducted in three different workplaces:

(1) In your opinion, why do people practise *small talk*? What role does *small talk* play at work?
(a) to be sociable, to get on with others, to maintain good relationships - **60**
(b) to be polite—**48** (c) to avoid silence—**6** (d) other—**1**

According to 60 informants, which is 75%, small talk is necessary in order to maintain good relationships with other people. 48 respondents, which constitutes 60% of the informants claim that people make small talk in order to be polite. Only 6 informants, which is 7.5%, claim that people engage in small talk in order to kill an uncomfortable silence.

(2) Why do you practise *small talk*? What role does *small talk* play for you at work?
(a) to be sociable, to get on with others, to maintain good relationships—**64**
(b) to be polite—**6** (c) to avoid silence—**6** (d) other—**3**

64 informants, which is 80% of the respondents engage in small talk with a view to getting on with others (more specifically with their colleagues). Only 6 informants, which is 7,5% engage in small talk for politeness. Similarly, only 6 of them practise

small talk in order to avoid silence. These last two aspects are connected with each other as those who are polite feel the necessity of keeping a conversation going.

(3) In your opinion, how often do people engage in *small talk* at work?
(a) always—**27** (b) sometimes—**47** (c) never—**0** (d) other—**9**

According to the respondents, small talk is a common practice and thus 27 informants (33.75% of the informants) state that people always engage in small talk and 47 informants (58.75% of them) claim that people sometimes practise small talk. By circling option d, 9 informants indicated that small talk is made quite often.

(4) How often do you engage in *small talk* at work?
(a) always—**24** (b) sometimes—**44** (c) never—**2** (d) other—**2**

Similarly, 24 informants, which constitutes 30% of the respondents always engage in small talk whereas 44 respondents (55%) sometimes practise small talk. Only 2 respondents (2.5%) never engage in small talk.

(5) In your opinion, do men or women mostly engage in *small talk*?
(a) women—**35** (b) men—**3** (c) both—**40** (d) other—**0**

35 informants, which is 43.75% of the informants think that it is women who engage in small talk. Similarly, 40 informants (50%) claim that small talk occurs in the speech of men and women. Only 3 informants (3.75%) think that small talk can only be identified in the speech of men.

(6) How important is *small talk* for your colleagues?
(a) very important—**13** (b) quite important—**57** (c) not very important—**9**
(d) other—**2**

It appears that small talk is quite important for the informants' colleagues. 13 informants (16.25%) claim that small talk is very important for their colleagues in the workplace and 57 respondents (71.25%) think that small talk is quite important for their colleagues. Only 9 informants (11.25%) admit that small talk is not very important for their colleagues.

(7) How important is *small talk* for you?
(a) very important—**9** (b) quite important—**55** (c) not very important—**14**
(d) other—**0**

For 9 respondents (11.25%), small talk is very important and for as many as 55 informants (68.75), small talk is quite important. Conversely, for 14 informants 17.5%), small talk is not very important.

(8) How important is *small talk* for women at work?
(a) very important—**15** (b) quite important—**50** (c) not very important—**6**
(d) other—**1**

Whereas 15 informants (18,75) claim that small talk is very important for women, 50 informants (62.5%) think that small talk is quite important for women. Only 6 informants, which constitutes 7.5% are of the opinion that small talk is not very important for women at work.

(9) How important is *small talk* for men at work?
(a) very important—**6** (b) quite important—**36** (c) not very important—**33**
(d) other—**6**

Whereas 6 informants (7.5%) think that small talk is very important for men, 36 of them (45%) claim that small talk is quite important for men. At the same time, 33 respondents (41.25%) claim that small talk is not very important for men.

(10) How often do people engage in *small talk* in formal register?
(a) always—**8** (b) sometimes—**66** (c) never—**0** (d) other—**7**

8 informants (10%) say that people always engage in small talk in formal register. 66 informants (82.5%) claim that people sometimes engage in small talk in formal register. By circling option d, 7 of them (8.75%) indicated that people often engage in small talk in formal register.

(11) How often do people engage in *small talk* in informal register?
(a) always—**37** (b) sometimes—**39** (c) never—**0** (d) other—**5**

37 informants (46.25%) say that people always engage in small talk in informal register. 39 respondents (48.75%) claim that people sometimes engage in small talk in informal register. By circling option d, 5 of them (6.25%) indicated that people often engage in small talk in informal register.

(12) How important is *small talk* for your colleagues in formal register?
(a) very important—**10** (b) quite important—**51** (c) not very important—**15**
(d) other—**5**

10 informants (12.5%) claim that small talk is very important for their colleagues in formal register. 51 informants (63.75%) claim that small talk is quite important for their colleagues in formal register. 15 respondents (18.75%) are of the opinion that small talk is not very important for their colleagues in formal register.

(13) How important is *small talk* for you in formal register?
(a) very important—**11** (b) quite important—**47** (c) not very important—**21**
(d) other—**2**

11 informants (13.75%) claim that small talk is very important for them in formal register. 47 respondents (58.75%) claim that small talk is quite important for them in formal register. 21 informants (26.25%) are of the opinion that small talk is not very important for them in formal register.

(14) How important is *small talk* for your colleagues in informal register?
(a) very important—**13** (b) quite important—**52** (c) not very important—**13**
(d) other—**2**

13 respondents (16.25%) claim that small talk is very important for their colleagues in informal register. 52 informants (65%) claim that small talk is quite

important for their colleagues in informal register. 13 informants (16.25%) are of the opinion that small talk is not very important for their colleagues in informal register.

(15) How important is *small talk* for you in informal register?
(a) very important—**12** (b) quite important—**54** (c) not very important—**15**
(d) other—**0**

12 informants (15%) claim that small talk is very important for them in informal register. 54 informants (67.5%) claim that small talk is quite important for them in formal register. 15 informants (18.75%) are of the opinion that small talk is not very important for them in informal register.

(16) When engaging in *small talk*, do you usually feel:
(a) very comfortable—**22** (b) quite comfortable—**53** (c) not very comfortable—**4**
(d) uncomfortable—**2**

22 informants (27.5%) admit that they feel very comfortable when they engage in small talk in the workplace. 53 respondents (66.25%) claim that they feel quite comfortable when they make small talk at work. Only 4 informants (which constitutes 5%) admit that they do not feel very comfortable when they practise small talk in the workplace.

(17) If you engage in *small talk*, what topics do you usually raise and why?
Neutral topics, such as the weather, everyday life, work, health, leisure time, holiday, travelling, shopping, music, important events, the news, films, series, sport, school, children, animals, clothes, cars, humour, jokes. Political, religious issues, personal matters – less frequently.

4 Discussion and Observations

Apparently, small talk is not as insignificant, unimportant or trivial as it might seem. Regardless of the trivial, insignificant and non-serious nature of the phenomenon of small talk, it turns out that it is common and ubiquitous and that it plays a very important role in the workplace. In fact, even in such settings as the workplace where everyone is busy, small talk constitutes an integral part of a working day among workers. Thus, it is not only something positive, but also something needed in this environment as it has a lot of advantages and positive aspects. Thus, small talk is also a common phenomenon in the workplace.

First and foremost, there are many reasons why people engage in small talk and thus, one can state that small talk has many different functions. For instance, according to the results, the informants want to get on with other people and to maintain good relationships. There are also those who think that people engage in small talk because they want to be polite. However, at work not many respondents engage in small talk only to be polite - the respondents do not engage in small talk out of politeness. Similarly, it turns out that engaging in small talk so as to avoid an uncomfortable silence in the workplace is not very common. In other words, there are only few people who feel the need to engage in small talk even though they do not want to because of an uncomfortable silence which is undesirable.

Moreover, the respondents engage in small talk frequently and at the same time, they admit that small talk is important for their colleagues as well as for themselves. More specifically, the respondents sometimes engage in small talk and there are also those who always engage in small talk, which indicates that small talk occurs very frequently in the workplace.

Similarly, small talk is equally important for both genders—males and females and both men and women engage in small talk in the workplace although small talk apparently seems a little bit more important for women than men. There are a number of the respondents who think that small talk is important for both men and women or that it is important for women rather than men.

In addition, small talk takes place in both formal and informal situations—the respondents' colleagues and the respondents themselves engage in small talk regardless of the formality of language (official vs. unofficial). In other words, both formal and informal situations are equally favorable for the occurrence of small talk—the respondents feel comfortable when they engage in small talk.

Moreover, the respondents feel rather comfortable when they engage in small talk. In other words, the respondents' attitudes are mostly positive and friendly—the informants feel comfortable when engaging in small talk and are very willing to participate in small talk. Thus, small talk evokes positive feelings.

Finally, the topics which are raised during small talk vary considerably; however, most of the topics are regarded as "safe" or "neutral" although. Therefore, there are a number of topics which are raised when engaging in small talk, such as the weather, everyday life, work, health, leisure time, holiday, travelling, shopping, music, important events, the news, films, series, sport, school, children, animals, clothes, cars, humour, jokes. As one can observe, the topics are quite safe and do not violate people's privacy. The informants raise such topics because they are interesting and safe to be discussed. In other words, they have a good time talking to each other in the workplace as this is a form of relaxation and most of the topics which are raised do not provoke any possible conflicts. Nevertheless, there is also some room for raising less safe topics, such as political and religious issues and even personal matters, which admittedly are more sensitive topics in nature and thus there is a risk of bringing forth unnecessary conflicts. Even though the more "dangerous" or "provocative" topics are also raised in the workplace, they do not occur very often in these circumstances.

5 Conclusion

The objective of the study was to determine the alleged significance of small talk in the workplace. The study attempts to determine to what extent small talk is important for people at work. Moreover, it examines the various functions of small talk and the attitudes the respondents have towards small talk. Finally, the study also attempts to determine how frequently small talk is made and by whom it is made more often—men or women.

According to the results and the observations, there are many reasons why people might want to engage in small talk. The respondents are involved in small talk in order to get on well with other colleagues. Small talk does not occur in the workplace in order to be polite and kind. In addition, small talk is used very often in the workplace. Small talk is also commonly used by both men and women although it is even more popular amongst women. It is also used favourably in both formal and informal situations. Similarly, small talk apparently occurs naturally and is used willingly in the workplace as it evokes positive feelings amongst the workers.

Nevertheless, there are a number of other factors which might influence the occurrence and the incidence of small talk. In other words, these are the factors which might be crucial in determining the importance and the incidence of small talk.

5.1   Limitations of the Study, Implications

There are a lot of other aspects which have not been dealt with and which, at the same time, would be worth researching. In other words, there are a number of other research areas which would contribute to the development of the current knowledge on the mater. However, if they had been encompassed in this research study, there would be too many objectives and the whole study would definitely have become blurred.

There are several other research studies which would be interesting in the area of small talk. It would also be a good idea to analyze the occurrence and importance of small talk in various languages/cultures, taking into account the fact that there have not been many research studies on small talk regarding different cultures and as was mentioned above—there are many cultures in which the attitude to small talk varies considerably.

Apart from that, it would be recommendable to analyze the occurrence and importance of small talk based on the different positions workers hold in the workplace. More specifically, it would be worth investigating the attitudes people have to small talk if they were to interact with their superiors—that is people of a higher position at work, such as managers, bosses, executives, etc. The results of such an investigation would help us get a better understanding of the nature of small talk in the workplace in terms of the factors which either facilitate or impede the occurrence of small talk.

Finally, it would definitely be worth researching the incidence of small talk during interactions with the people we do not know. In other words, another research study which would contribute to increasing our knowledge on small talk would be the attitudes we have to small talk in the workplace during interactions with strangers. It would be necessary to determine to what extent we are willing to engage in small talk with strangers. It would also be interesting to identify some differences during the interactions with both people we know and those we do not know.

Appendix

The aim of the study is the analysis of the function of "small talk" and its significance among the workers of a business company. Based on the questionnaire, we wish to observe if "small talk" is common and if yes—why. Moreover, the purpose of the study is to pay attention to the circumstances which either facilitate or hinder the use of "small talk", such as the register, gender etc. The theoretical background, the results of the survey, the observations, the conclusions and the implications will be presented in the form of the presentation" Socializing at work—an investigation of small talk phenomenon in the speech of men and women: a questionnaire study" at a conference *Dimensions of Business Language and Culture*—DOBLAC (*Wymiary Języka i Kultury Biznesu*), which will be held in CINIBA in Katowice.

Before you start doing the questionnaire, provide the following information, please.

A. GENDER: _____

B. AGE: _____

(1) In your opinion, why do people engage in *small talk*? What role does *small talk* play at work?

(a) to be sociable, to get on with others, to maintain good relationships (b) to be polite

(c) to avoid silence (d) other

(2) Why do you engage in *small talk*? What role does *small talk* play for you at work?

(a) to be sociable, to get on with others, to maintain good relationships (b) to be polite

(c) to avoid silence (d) other

(3) In your opinion, how often do people engage in *small talk* at work?

(a) always (b) sometimes (c) never (d) other

(4) How often do you engage in *small talk* at work?

(a) always (b) sometimes (c) never (d) other

(5) In your opinion, do men or women mostly engage in *small talk*?

(a) women (b) men (c) both (d) other

(6) How important is *small talk* for your colleagues?

(a) very important (b) quite important (c) not very important (d) other

(7) How important is *small talk* for you?

(a) very important (b) quite important (c) not very important (d) other

(8) How important is *small talk* for women at work?

(a) very important (b) quite important (c) not very important (d) other

(9) How important is *small talk* for men at work?

(a) very important (b) quite important (c) not very important (d) other

(10) How often do people engage in *small talk* in formal register?

(a) always (b) sometimes (c) never (d) other

(11) How often do people engage in *small talk* in informal register?

(a) always (b) sometimes (c) never (d) other

(12) How important is *small talk* for your colleagues in formal register?
(a) very important (b) quite important (c) not very important (d) other
(13) How important is *small talk* for you in formal register?
(a) very important (b) quite important (c) not very important (d) other
(14) How important is *small talk* for your colleagues in informal register?
(a) very important (b) quite important (c) not very important (d) other
(15) How important is *small talk* for you in informal register?
(a) very important (b) quite important (c) not very important (d) other
(16) When engaging in *small talk*, do you usually feel:
(a) very comfortable (b) quite comfortable (c) not very comfortable
(d) uncomfortable
(17) If you engage in *small talk*, what topics do you usually raise and why?

References

Aitchison, J. (1996). *The seeds of speech: Language origin and evolution*. Cambridge: Cambridge University Press.

Carté, P., & Fox, C. (2008). *Bringing the culture gap. A practical guide to international business communication* (2nd ed.). London/Philadelphia: Kogan page.

Coupland, J. (2003). Small talk: Social functions. *Research on Language and Social Interaction, 36*(1), 1–6.

Fleming, C. A. (2018). *The serious business of small talk. Becoming fluent, comfortable and charming*. Oakland, CA: Berrett-Koehler Publishers, Inc.

Holmes, J. (2000). Talking English from 9 to 5: Challenges for ESL learners at work. *International Journal of Applied Linguistics, 10*(1), 125–140.

Jaworski, A. (2000). Silence and small talk. In J. Coupland (Ed.), *Small talk* (pp. 110–132). London: Pearson Education.

Lewis, R. D. (2006). *When cultures collide. Leading across cultures* (3rd ed.). Boston/London: Nicholas Braeley International.

Mahajan, K. (2016). *My struggle with American Small Talk*. Retrieved from http://www.newyorker.com/culture/culture-desk/my-struggle-with-american-small-talk.

Meyer, E. (2014). *The culture map: Decoding how people think, lead, and get things done across cultures"*. New York: Public Affairs.

Pullin, P. (2010). Small talk, rapport, and international communicative competence. *International Journal of Business Communication, 47*(4), 455–476.

Schneider, K. P. (1988). *Small talk: Analysing phatic discourse*. Marburg: Hitzeroth.

Terpstra, V., & David, K. (1985). *The cultural environment of international business*. Cincinnati, Ohio: South-Western Publishing Company.

Tomalin, B., & Nicks, M. (2007). *The world's business cultures: And how to unlock them*. London: Thorogood Publishing.

Tung, J. (2004). *The 10 big rules of Small Talk. Know what to say in a social situation—And when and how to say it*. Retrieved from https://www.realsimple.com/work-life/work-life-etiquette/manners/10-big-rules-small-talk.

Valev, N. (2015). *6 ways to avoid small talk, because life is more meaningful than the weather*. Retrieved from http://www.bustle.com/articles/120864-6-ways-to-avoid-small-talk-because-life-is-moremeaningful-than-the-weather.

Wakefield, M. (2016). *Small talk. The definite guide to talking to anyone in any situation*. Wrocław: Golden Road Publishing.

Watzke-Otte, S. (2008). *Small talk. Jak prowadzić swobodną rozmowę towarzyską.* Warszawa: BC Edukacja.

Adam Pluszczyk Ph.D., is employed at the Institute of Linguistics, Faculty of Humanities, University of Silesia in Katowice. He is interested in English and Spanish linguistics, mainly in sociolinguistics, pragmatics, humour studies and dialectology. His research focuses mainly on sociolinguistics, both regional dialects (especially American dialects) and social dialects, linguistic variation, speech styles, registers, genres, gender differences and verbal humour.

Business and Academic Cultures in Contact: Some Insights from Academic Communication Practices and Research

Krystyna Warchał

Abstract At first glance, the world of business and the world of academia could not be wider apart. The former is typically associated with money and profit, the power of persuasion, and various mechanisms of self-promotion; the latter, if somewhat illusively, with a selfless pursuit of truth, data which speak for themselves, and the priority of disciplinary development over personal achievement. Still, a closer look at some discourse patterns shows that, at least in terms of communication practices, business and academia do have strong points of contact. The aim of this chapter is to draw attention to some of those shared discourse mechanisms, referring primarily to the research article. It refers to the Create-a-Research-Space model of rhetorical moves in research article introductions proposed by Swales (1981) and Swales (1990) to show that this traditional, canonical academic genre is not incompatible with rhetorical tools which are more readily associated with business discourse, and that its structure and function of some of its segments may actually invite their use.

Keywords English for Academic Purposes · Business English · Rhetoric · Research article introductions

1 Introduction: Common Roots and Shared Traits

This chapter aims to demonstrate some essential links between two discourse domains: academia and business. Although the two cultures may appear quite incompatible at first glance, it will be shown that, in terms of communication practices, they do have strong points of contact. Moreover, the chapter will argue that some central forms of academic communication actually invite the use of rhetorical tools that are more readily associated with business than with the traditional model of academic communication.

K. Warchał (✉)
Institute of Linguistics, Faculty of Humanities, University of Silesia in Katowice, Katowice, Poland
e-mail: krystyna.warchal@us.edu.pl

© Springer Nature Switzerland AG 2020
U. Michalik et al. (eds.), *Exploring Business Language and Culture*,
Second Language Learning and Teaching,
https://doi.org/10.1007/978-3-030-58551-8_13

   This introductory section outlines the origins and some of the most noticeable shared characteristics of Language for Academic Purposes (LAP) and Language in/for Business (LB). Section 2 opens with a short discussion of the traditional view of academic communication, where language is construed as a transparent tool for representing facts and relationships, a model which appears quite remote from the nature of business discourse. Next, it presents an alternative approach, founded on the view that knowledge is socially constructed and that it is based in a social consensus that can only be achieved through interaction. Section 3 illustrates the process of consensus-seeking with examples drawn from introductions to linguistics research articles, where the authors negotiate the research space using a variety of strategies that help them introduce new claims, display the necessary respect for the contribution of others, and present themselves as competent, fair, and polite members of the discourse community. Section 4 offers some concluding remarks.

   Both LAP and LB evolved from Language for Specific Purposes (LSP), whose orientation was primarily pedagogic. LB, as Johns (1986) observes, was one of its earliest developed branches, boasting the greatest number of teaching materials designed specifically for those who were to use English in business settings. In an overview of the development of research into business discourse, Bargiela-Chiappini, Nickerson and Planken (2007, pp. 151–152) report that since the mid-1990s, the initial vocational and normative approach to business communication has shifted to a more descriptive, critical, and contextualised approach, aimed at a better understanding of the whole variety of communication practices in business settings rather than direct language instruction. As for LAP, or, more precisely, English for Academic Purposes (EAP),[1] Paltridge (2001, p. 55) places its early, strictly teaching-oriented beginnings in the mid-1940s, which, according to Hutchinson and Waters' (1987, p. 9) dating, actually predates English for Specific Purposes (ESP) by almost twenty years. However, the linguistic inquiry into the nature of academic discourse began later, in the 1960s, and, as Swales points out (2001, pp. 42 ff), very soon emphasis was firmly placed on description, representativeness, and contextualisation of real-life textual material. Thus, both LAP and LB can be traced back to LSP, evolved quite early into recognisable fields with their own well-defined objects of study, were initially dominated by the pedagogic approach, and, in their own time, have developed more descriptive, critical, and contextually situated perspectives on the type of communication they investigate. According to Flowerdew and Peacock (2001, p. 11), they represent the two main divisions of LSP: one focused on academic purposes, and the other on occupational purposes (EAP and EOP, respectively, if one focuses specifically on English). This distinction, however, as the authors admit, is not clear-cut:

> A lot of work conducted in the academy is in fact preparation for the professional occupations students are likely to go into when they graduate and might therefore be classified as EOP. If we take the example of English for Business in the university, aspects of the course designed to assist learners in their studies would clearly be EAP, but university business courses,

---

[1] The dominance of English in early LAP studies reflects its (at that time) growing popularity as the language of science and technology and the language of international academic communication.

like other vocationally-oriented courses, usually seek to prepare their students for business careers. English support for the more vocationally-oriented aspects of the Business course could perhaps be described as EOP as much as EAP. (Flowerdew and Peacock 2001, p. 11)

This fuzzy border shows that there are contexts in which the two branches are naturally interconnected and that it may not always be necessary—or possible—to keep them neatly apart.

Apart from the common roots, an important shared characteristic of LAP and LB is the role of English. In both discourse domains, business and academia (as indeed in many others; see Crystal, 2003), English is a medium for international communication, used not only between the non-Anglophone part of the world and native English speakers, but also for cross-cultural contacts between users for whom it is a second or additional language, often the only one they share. This rise of English as an international language is well visible in the field of pedagogy, where courses and materials for teaching EAP and English for Business (EB) are more popular than those representing other languages, and in the field of research, dominated—again both in the case of academic discourse and business discourse studies—by investigations into English-language practices (both by native and non-native speakers) and contrastive analyses which choose them as a point of reference. In the academia, as Young (2006, p. 3) observes, "English has now become the Rosetta Stone of science, the language used to translate the science of the world into communication for the whole world". In the world of business, in turn, Bargiela-Chiappini et al. (2007, p. 16) comment on the role of English pointing to "an undeniable bias towards English in the research carried out in business language over the past two decades". The authors further explain this situation by referring to the status of English as an international business language on the one hand, and to the influence of ESP on the other.

In both discourse domains, the dominance of English brings benefits and problems. While the former are self-evident—a commonly shared code enables fast transfer of information, access to data, and direct contact between speakers—the latter may be less obvious. In the case of academia, English can be seen as "a tool of linguistic hegemony" (Hyland 2009, p. 180), pushing research in national languages far into the peripheries. As Hyland observes, "[w]ith libraries increasingly subscribing to online versions of journals, the impact of English becomes self-perpetuating, since it is in these journals where authors will be most visible on the world stage and receive the most credit" (p. 180). In the case of business, it poses the threat of imposing an ethnocentric framework which neglects cultural diversity and prevents a deep understanding of what is going on in specific contexts, in extreme cases precluding successful communication (Bargiela-Chiappini et al. 2007, pp. 41 ff).

The third important feature academic communication and business communication share is internal diversity. In either case, it would be difficult to speak of homogeneous discourse; rather, there are various discourses falling within the academic or business spectrum. In the field of academic communication, there is disciplinary variety, with each discipline having evolved features best suited to meet its specific needs, such as distinctive lexis and collocational patterns, typical genres, characteristic argumentation styles, and varying degrees of interpersonal involvement. The range of such discipline-related differences—and similarities—has been investigated, among others, by Dahl (2004), Flottum et al. (2006a, 2006b), Hyland (1999, 2000, 2002, 2005, 2008), Hyland and Bondi (2006), Melander, Swales, and Fredrickson (1997), Vold (2006a, 2006b) and Yakhontova (2006).

Next to this disciplinary variation, academic practices involve a variety of genres, such as research and other professional faculty genres (Johns 1997), including the research paper, the academic book review, the monograph, the abstract, the conference paper, and the multimedia presentation; pedagogical genres, such as the textbook, the lecture, and the office hours; and "school genres", including the essay examination response, the term paper, and the master's thesis, (Johns 1997; Johns and Swales 2002). This list can be extended with occluded genres[2] which accompany the research process, support the publication of other genres, and, more generally, foster individual academic development, such as the submission letter (Swales 1996), the research grant proposal (Connor & Mauranen, 1999; Connor, 2000; Feng & Shi, 2004), the peer review report (Fortanet, 2008a, 2008b), or the MBA thought essay (Loudermilk 2007). Unlike with disciplinary variation, which in most cases does not pose additional challenges to individual academics (the majority of them will probably identify themselves with not more than two or three disciplines throughout their lifetime, and possible disciplinary shifts are more likely a matter of evolution of interests and passions than rapid turns in the academic career), generic diversity usually calls for more individual effort, as a member of academic community is normally expected to achieve a reasonable level of fluency in multiple academic genres, and to do so in a relatively short period of time. Adding to this already complicated picture of academic communication is cultural and linguistic diversity. In the course of their evolution and consolidation, national academic discourses have developed features which may be peripheral or dispreferred in other academic communities. These differences may reflect various attitudes to knowledge (such as egalitarian or elitist), to writing (viewed as a skill that must be learnt, or art, which requires a talent), to the researcher (who may be seen as a fellow expert engaged in sharing and generating knowledge or as a solitary sage who transmits it), and, finally, to communication, with the responsibility for successful interaction falling, in various proportions, with the speaker/writer or with the receiver (Clyne, 1987; Čmejrková, 1996; Čmejrková & Daneš, 1997; Duszak, 1994; Flower, 1979; Hinds, 1987; Mauranen, 1993). Such culture-specific features may and often do persist in international contacts, making it more difficult for those who use English as an additional language to successfully share their research. There is also some evidence, especially from spoken corpora, that thanks to the plurilingual character of the academic discourse community, English as an academic lingua franca has developed its own distinctive features that mark it

---

[2]While part of the publication process, promotional procedure, or administrative routine, occluded genres are not normally available to the public. Access to them is usually limited to individuals or groups of people on the basis of their job duties; they are, to quote Swales (1996, p. 46), "'occluded' from the public gaze by a veil of confidentiality".

off from native speaker English (Mauranen, 2010; Mauranen, Hynninen, & Ranta 2010).

If one turns to business communication, the disciplinary variation is similar, with the core disciplines, such as accounting, finance, marketing, management, business technologies, and business law, recognised by the majority of schools and universities, and, as Bhatia (1999, p. 129) points out, with related areas, such as psychology, public policy, and social administration, systematically gaining recognition in academic curricula. As Bhatia (1999) demonstrates, this essentially multidisciplinary character of business is reflected in the preferred rhetorical patterns, preferred conceptualisations, and the degree of intertextuality even within the same genre. To this strictly disciplinary division, Bargiela-Chiappini et al. (2007) add generic diversity, with oral genres, such as, for example, negotiations, meetings, (tele)conferences, and business presentations in highly variable settings (Bülow-Møller, 2005; Charles & Charles, 1999; Crawford Camiciottoli, 2006); written genres, including a variety of business reports, sales letters, application letters, business faxes, email correspondence, mission statements, and business magazines (Akar & Louhiala-Salminen, 1999; Bhatia, 1993, 1999; Garzone, 2006; Mulholland, 1999; Mamet, 2005; Nickerson, 1999); and multimodal genres, such as websites and podcasts (Luzón Marco, 2002). Finally, in terms of cultural and linguistic diversity and various challenges connected with the use of English as an international language, the situation in business parallels that in academic settings. On the one hand, there are important differences in the assumptions, expectations, and interpretations of what is going on by the parties involved in intercultural business encounters—studied, for example, within the rapport management framework developed by Spencer-Oatey (see Bargiela-Chiappini et al., 2007, pp. 41 ff)—which may lead to the sides forming very different pictures of the situation and evaluating the effect of the interaction differently. On the other hand, used as the language of business around the world, English as an International Language seems to be acquiring features which are highly genre specific and which are being introduced by users who are not native speakers of English but who use English in international professional settings. As Malavasi (2006, p. 121) concludes on the basis of an analysis of banks' annual reports, there is "evidence of the enriching influence exerted by contact languages on international communicative practices and their lexis".

This brief overview has shown that the early developments in the fields of LAP and LB proceeded in a parallel way and that the two discourse domains share many important characteristics, such as internal diversity (generic, disciplinary, and cultural), the status of English as a lingua franca, and some consequences of the dominance of English. The next section presents the traditional model of academic communication and continues with a discussion of a major change that has taken place in thinking about the role of language in the generation of knowledge, a change that has put communication between scientists in a different light.

2 Drawing the Line and Closing the Gap

In a fascinating intellectual history of EAP-related research, Swales (2001) presents the beginnings of the linguistic interest in the discourse of science as a stage dominated by the broader academic and philosophical milieu. He writes:

> This milieu… was predominantly characterised by beliefs in objectivity and the experimental method in both natural and social sciences…. The sociology of knowledge and social-constructionism had yet to make their mark. As a result, the view prevailed that scientific and academic languages were *rhetorically simple* and *transparent* linguistic mechanisms for the *display* and *transmission* of knowledge, hypotheses, methods and experimental results. (Swales, 2001, p. 43; emphasis mine)

Thus, language used for science was construed as a tool for transferring a ready-made product (knowledge) to others. Under this view, it played no role in the formation of knowledge; knowledge was there regardless of the language or linguistic structures used. Swales (2001, p. 43) illustrates this situation with an extract from Bloomfield's "Linguistic aspects of science": "We say that scientific discourse is *translatable*, and mean by this that not only the difference between languages but, within each language, the difference between operationally equivalent wordings has no scientific effect". This perspective on academic discourse makes it very far from what is typically associated with business settings, where the search for consensus, persuasion, evaluation, and self-promotion often require a careful planning of argumentation and adopting a rhetorical strategy best suited to the immediate context, and where, in general, success depends largely on communication skills.

The display-and-transmission-of-knowledge attitude to academic language fitted very well with the positivist view of knowledge as a process of accumulation of data in the form of propositions about empirical facts. This model of knowledge and generation of knowledge, however, has been shown not to be the only model of scientific development, and apparently not the one best suited to explain the world and the human situation in it (Berger & Luckmann, 1967; Kuhn, 1970; Quine, 1975). Among others, Berger and Luckmann (1967) have argued that knowledge is relative to the social contexts in which it is produced, that it consists in the process of legitimation of a socially shared vision of the world, and that it "objectifies this world through language and the cognitive apparatus based on language… [ordering] it into objects to be apprehended as reality" (p. 84). This view puts the role language plays in the generation of knowledge in a slightly different light: rather than aim at representing faithfully an objectively given state of affairs, it co-creates it in social interactions between members of a community, who try to explain this reality which is available to them. These efforts to explain and to understand consist in "the linguistic activity of the members in debating, revising, and legitimizing the 'paradigms' that make sense to them" (Canagarajah, 2002, p. 30). On this view, rather than merely a tool for reporting knowledge, language appears to be its building substance, the matter of which it is formed in the social negotiation of reality.

This new perspective on knowledge and the role of language brings to the fore the dialogic rather than monologic nature of academic communication. Doing science is construed as an essentially dialogic and collaborative activity, involving the researcher, fellow specialists, and the broader academic community. As Hyland (2000, p. 6) notes, "knowledge is not a privileged representation of non-human reality, but a conversation between individuals and between individuals and their beliefs". Thus, the production of new knowledge implies a search for a certain common ground, a point of reference in the negotiation of meaning on which both sides, the author and the reader, would coincide. This involves, among others, making room for different viewpoints, displaying respect for the contribution of others, and disarming criticism. For instance, it has been shown that authors use epistemic markers, reporting verbs, and rhetorical questions as a strategy of "opening up the heteroglossic space" (White, 2000, p. 78; see also White, 2003) in which competing perspectives can be acknowledged, discussed, or contradicted; apply face-saving strategies to show deference to the academic community and to present themselves as "humble servants of the discipline" (Myers, 1989, p. 4); and anticipate criticism by addressing potential objections or doubts before they are voiced, thus turning what might appear a simple account of the research process into a complex dialogue with the readers (Swales, 1990). In the same vein, Hyland (2000, 2001, 2005, 2010) speaks of the interactive nature of writing up research and the need to construct a shared understanding, negotiate concepts, and argue for a claim. These processes are facilitated by establishing proximity (Hyland, 2010)—a relationship with the readers which creates optimum conditions for acceptance of the author's ideas and which brings to mind the notion of rapport, widely discussed with reference to business settings. These elements are part and parcel of academic communication and have long been recognised as essential aspects of business discourse.

If knowledge is to be socially constructed, it must be based on a shared under-standing, a consensus as to what constitutes scientific inquiry, what the present state of disciplinary knowledge is, and what counts as legitimate academic practice. To enter the academic dialogue, a researcher must try to fit in with the existing consensus and thus present him- or herself as a competent member of the community. As Myers (1989, p. 5) points out, "the writer must stay within a certain consensus to have anything to say to members of his or her discipline". The search for consensus is therefore an important motivation for a scholar's linguistic and rhetorical choices.

At the same time, academic authors must strive to go beyond the disciplinary state of the art to convince the reviewers that their contributions deserve sharing with other members of the community, and readers that the texts are worth their time. To do so, they create a research space (Swales, 1990) by indicating a gap in or criticising previous research (as shown, e.g., by Hyland, 2000; Hunston, 2005; Myers, 1989; Martín-Martín & Burgess, 2004) or by providing new data which may lead to a revision or reassessment of previous knowledge. In this way, while in prin-ciple staying within the established disciplinary consensus, they set themselves apart from other researchers and previous literature. Potentially face-threatening (Warchał, 2014), this act of creating and capturing the research space is recognised as one of the most salient rhetorical moves taken by Anglophone academic authors in research genres. The search for consensus and the need to reach beyond whatever is already accepted as given by the discourse community provides academic communication with its characteristic rhetorical profile (Hunston, 2005; Łyda, 2007; Myers, 1989; Swales, 1990; Warchał, 2010, 2014). This characteristic tension between whatever is acknowledged as facts and whatever aspires to this status turns an act of communicating research results into negotiation, another concept firmly associated with business settings.

In fact, negotiation has often been invoked to capture the essence of academic communication. For example, Hyland (1998) speaks of "the negotiation of academic knowledge" and "the negotiation of knowledge claims" (Hyland, 2009, p. 57); in his analysis of stance in academic discourse, Silver (2003, p. 365) refers to "the way the writer attempts to anticipate and redirect the reader's potential rejection of her/his claim, to negotiate or dialogue with her/his idea of the reader's position"; in the context of spoken academic discourse involving experts and novices, Crawford Camiciottoli (2007, p. 183) points to the need to "negotiate knowledge and establish... social identities"; Tang and John (1999, p. 23) demonstrate that "there is room for negotiation of identity within academic writing"; and Vandeyar (2010) speaks of "constructing and negotiating academic identities". Negotiation may thus be an effective metaphor for capturing the essence of academic communication as construed now.

In "Persuasion in business negotiations", Bülow-Møller (2005, p. 34) refers to Fisher's term "a yesable proposition", a helpful tool of successful negotiators. A yesable proposition is one that is attractive, that is, one that can be seen to offer a solution to a problem or, as Bülow-Møller puts it, "to meet some important need or goal" (p. 34); legitimate, that is, one that rests on some shared norms or values; and credible, a quality achieved by "competence-face building exactitude and reasoning" (p. 35). Transferred to academic contexts, an acceptable claim must offer something important and therefore novel, must fit with the general disciplinary consensus, and must be convincing—offered in a way that presents the author as a competent member of the academic community, who displays a necessary amount of expertise on the one hand, and respect for academic values, on the other, including regard for others' achievements and contribution.

3 Negotiation of Academic Contributions: An Illustration from Research Article Introductions

3.1 Journal Article Introductions

In academic discourse research, journal articles are privileged as an object of study because, in numerical terms, they dominate publication, they have huge impact on the development of the discipline, and they play a special role in individual academic career development (Swales, 1990, 2004). Of the standard sections of research articles, the introduction has received special attention (e.g., Abdi & Sadeghi, 2018; Duszak, 1994; Golebiowski, 1998, 1999; Lu et al., 2018; Swales, 1981; Samraj,

2002). It is a section where the authors introduce their research—its subject matter, scope, methodology, and key theoretical concepts—and attempt to win their readers, from first reviewers to the community of fellow specialists. Thus, it is a section of strategic importance for the article's publication, readership, and, ultimately, citability.

Probably the most widely cited and applied model of introductions to English language research articles is the CARS model of rhetorical moves proposed by Swales (1981, 1990). Swales (1990, pp. 140 ff) identifies three moves, further divided into steps. Move 1, Establishing a territory, introduces the topic and establishes its significance by Claiming centrality (Step 1), Making topic generalisations (Step 2), and Reviewing items of previous research (Step 3). Move 2, Establishing a niche, indicates the need for the current research by pointing out some omissions, misinterpretations, or faults in previous studies, and is realised by Counter-claiming (Step 1A), Indicating a gap (Step 1B), Question-raising (Step 1C), or Continuing a tradition (Step 1D). Finally, Move 3, Occupying the niche, announces how the need introduced in Move 2 is going to be satisfied by the current research. This is done by Outlining purposes (Step 1A) or Announcing present research (Step 1B), Announcing principal findings (Step 2), and Indicating research article structure (Step 3). While there is evidence that not all moves are obligatory, that their order may vary, and that they may be realised in cycles rather than linearly, the model proposed by Swales has proved most effective and stimulating as a framework for analysing the ways in which academic authors introduce their research.

The original motivation for this model was ecological, following from

> the need to re-establish in the eyes of the discourse community the significance of the research field itself; the need to 'situate' the actual research in terms of that significance; and the need to show how this niche in the wider ecosystem will be occupied and defended. It follows that the amount of rhetorical work needed to create such a space depends on the existing ecological competition, on the size and importance of the niche to be established, and on various other factors such as the writer's reputation. (Swales, 1990, p. 142).

Biological metaphor has frequently been applied to explain or demonstrate language phenomena (see, e.g., Nettle, 1999). However, the CARS model reads equally well if one applies business metaphor: it is necessary to find a niche for a product or service by introducing the product, demonstrating that there is a need for it, and convincing the potential client that the product offered satisfies the need in a better way than any other product currently available. This shows that apart from correspondences between LAP and LB that follow from their origins, development, and international context in which they operate, there is also some room for similarity on the level of discourse organisation, which, in the case of research articles, not only does not preclude, but actually invites the use of rhetorical patterns known from business discourse.

3.2   Material Used

Examples used to illustrate the process of negotiating academic contributions in the introductory moves are drawn from a corpus of 50 introductions to journal articles published between the years 2001–2006 in five English-language linguistics journals: *Journal of Pragmatics, Language and Communication, Language Sciences, Lingua,* and *Linguistics and Philosophy* (about 41 thousand running words). The corpus was compiled by the author and served as the basis for other studies (Warchał, 2014, 2018). The following sections focus on the following elements: face-saving strategies accompanying Move 2 and Move 3, academic criticism associated with Move 1 and Move 2, and presentation of the self, facilitating Move 3.

3.3   Face-Saving Strategies

Establishing the niche and occupying it constitute a threat to face (Bargiela-Chiappini, 2003; Bogdanowska-Jakubowska, 2010; Goffman, 1967). To indicate a research gap, the writer must point out what has been missing in previous research, that is, what other researchers have so far ignored. To capture the research space, in turn, the writer presents his or her own contribution as one which, in the context of a specific research problem, is superior to others. Indispensable to make research publishable, these moves are often accompanied by strategies that aim at reducing their face-threatening potential and display the necessary amount of deference to the academic community.

Establishing a research space may take a very elaborate and cyclical form, with precise and straightforward statements of what has been missing in the literature so far intertwined with references to valuable studies which (partially) address these omissions. This is shown in (1), which offers an elaborate justification of the research need by indicating a gap (*rarely addressed, rarely subjected to fine-gained analysis, largely ignored*) and the existing asymmetry in research (*other forms of communications overrepresented*). This, however, is accompanied by an ample acknowledgment of authors who have worked in this area, which is a form of showing due respect for the contribution of others, even if some problems have remained unresolved.

> (1)   However, <u>sociolinguistic research has rarely addressed the question of</u> how medical knowledge is constituted (Sarangi and Roberts, 1999: 22)… the linguistic processes by which medical judgment is developed and exercised <u>have rarely been subjected to fine-grained analysis</u> (but see Pettinari, 1988)… oral physician–patient communications are over-represented in the literature, while physician–physician communications, including the medical record itself, <u>have been largely ignored</u> (but see Hobbs, 2003, 2002; Atkinson, 1999; Cicourel, 1999, 1983; Erickson, 1999; Anspach, 1988; Rees, 1981). (JP2004-3)

Example (1) illustrates a strategy that Feng and Shi (2004) in their analysis of research grant proposals call "a niche-centered tide-like structure" (p. 24). The authors explain it as follows:

the recurrences of the "territory" and "niche" should not be considered simply as "recycling of moves". Rather, the running of the text is like the tide, one wave after another, washing up, washing back, and ensuing with washing up again, pushing the discussion of the topic forward. (Feng & Shi, 2004, p. 24).

Move 2 (Establishing the niche) may follow the statement of goals (Move 3), as in (2). In this case, abundant citations in which the author recognises the important input of other scholars prepare the ground for a strong claim that follows (*has not been previously noted*), demonstrating that it is based in a thorough study of available literature. At the same, the author is very precise in indicating the scope of her claim (*the connection between the syntactic structure and interpretation*) and adds a limitation to prevent the reader from overinterpreting it.

(2)   Whether or not these researchers are correct about English, I will show that their arguments apply very elegantly to the Malagasy data. That clefts are in fact pseudo-clefts in some Austronesian languages is not a new claim. Other researchers have come to the same conclusion about Chamorro (Chung, 1998), Madurese (Davies, 2000),Malay (Cole et al., to appear (henceforth WA)), Maori (Bauer, 1991), Palauan (Georgopoulos, 1991) and Tagalog (Kroeger, 1993; Richards, 1998): What has not been previously noted is the connection between the syntactic structure and interpretation.... This paper does not make any claims about the universality of the proposed analysis of clefts. (L2001-5).

Apart from limiting the claim, academic authors may also mitigate it, especially if in Move 2 they refer to some important shortcomings of previous approaches. In (3), the writer makes a concessive remark (*although I am sympathetic to the methodology*), a strategy which allows to uphold a view without denying another, apparently conflicting view (although often denying its possible implications; Łyda, 2007). In this way, he (partly) aligns himself with other researchers before, finally, he opts for an alternative solution (*the former view may in fact be correct*). The verb *suggest* additionally reduces the force of the statement.

(3)   In this paper, I will explore the issue of whether the distinction between tacit and non-tacit awareness of linguistic features is correlated with the distinction between syntactic and semantic features of language. ... Although I am sympathetic to the methodology that supports this latter view, in this paper I will argue that the former view may in fact be correct in some important respects. ... I will suggest that this underlying semantic structure is accessible by us. (LP2004-2)

Example (4)—a fragment that follows a polemic with another author—illustrates a different face-work strategy. In this case, positive comments about her work (*new and insightful, quite interesting*) act as a counterbalance for criticism used in Move 2. The change of perspective—from criticism to praise—is signalled by a concessive marker (*nevertheless*). In this way, the writer makes his critical point, at the same time acknowledging that the discussed approach does make an important contribution to the field, and denying possible but unwanted conclusions (e.g., that the approach is worthless).

(4)   Nevertheless, the variable-free approach has something new and insightful to say about crossover... Given the standard crossover explanation in terms of long-distance LF

movement and co-indexation, the fact that it is possible to formulate a local cross-over constraint is quite interesting in its own right and a large plus in favor of Jacobson's program. (LP2005-7)

A reversed situation can be observed in (5) and (6), which also refer to concession, but in which positive comments act as a lead-into criticism used to establish a niche.

(5) However, these works, while they do appeal to actual discourse-based utterances, still center their analyses on examples with one to two turns or sentences, and thus do not capture the fullness of the interactive potential of the forms in question. (LS2002-1)

(6) While highly thought-provoking, the analysis she proposes suffers from some of the inadequacies of Relevance Theory. (LS2003-8)

Whether acting as a counterbalance or a lead-into Move 2, positive comments help to avoid challenging the professional status of other scholars and to maintain the image of the writer as an objective, unbiased, and fair researcher.

3.4 Academic Criticism

In introductions, criticism is often associated with reviewing literature (Move 1) but, interestingly, exact references are rarely given, although they are inferable to experts, as in (7). The decision to avoid references to concrete texts can be interpreted as a face-work mechanism: the critical point is established, but there is no specific target who might feel attacked; moreover, by refraining from direct criticism, the author presents himself as a polite, socially competent member of the discourse community.

(7) Because the identities of these entities depend so much on relationships among other entities, they are often characterized as abstract, distinct from concrete entities, whose identities depend primarily on continuity of material composition. This characterization has its drawbacks, however, since some of these entities share in more of the prototypical properties of abstract entities than others. (L2003-3)

In (8), the author uses a rhetorical question (*Could anyone look at such a model seriously…*), thus inviting the readers to draw the conclusion on their own and soliciting agreement. In this case, severe criticism is negotiated between the writer and the reader rather than merely stated, with the responsibility for negative evaluation shared between both parties.

(8) There has even been considerable research embracing a model where things start out in one place, move, and then get put back by 'reconstruction' for the purpose of the semantic interpretation. Could anyone look at such a model seriously and not suspect that something is being missed? (LP2002-8)

The responsibility for negative evaluation may also be transferred to other experts, as shown in (9). Here, criticism is cited rather than stated (*as Kulick points out*), with the writer implicitly subscribing to the opinion of another scholar rather than developing his own critical point.

> (9) But, <u>as Kulick points out, there is a central flaw in much of this work,</u> drawing as it does
> on a tautology: people who are lesbian and gay speak in a way that is defined as 'gay
> language'; and people who talk a 'gay language' are, thus, gay. (LC2003-4)

An interesting strategy to mitigate a negative comment is shown in (10), where the author adds a defensive footnote lest her remark should be misunderstood (in this case, the main text is given in square brackets before the text of the footnote). More examples of defensive comments will be discussed in Sect. 3.5 (19–24).

> (10) [An approach to humor grounded in interactional sociolinguistics starts not with reified
> abstractions such as 'humor', 'wit', or 'irony', (cf. Alexander, 1997; Barbe, 1995; Clift,
> 1999),2 but rather with the situated interpretation of joking as a speech activity (cf.
> Davies, 1986; Norrick, 1993; Tannen, 1984).]
>
> <u>I do not mean to suggest that Barbe (1995), Alexander (1997), and Clift (1999) are not</u>
> <u>concerned with interaction in context;</u> what I want to emphasize is that each of them
> starts from one of the reifications, gets caught in definitions, and then either explores
> a range of interaction classifiable under the reification (Barbe and Alexander), or uses
> examples of interaction in context to challenge current assumptions and definitions
> (Clift) <u>but still works within a definitional framework.</u> (JP2003-9)

As noted in Sects. 3.1 and 3.3, a natural occasion for academic criticism is Move 2, creating a research space. As in Move 1, plain negative comments, such as in (11), are rather infrequent, with the majority of writers using concession to counterbalance the negative evaluation (as in example 5 above) or providing only vague reference to prior research rather than quoting concrete authors (12).

> (11) Traugott and Konig (1991), for example, feel that… In the view of Heine et al. (1991,
> p. 1). … And Paul Hopper (1987) goes so far as to claim that… In this paper I
> will put grammaticalization under the microscope and <u>conclude that such claims are</u>
> <u>unwarranted.</u> (LS2001-5)
>
> (12) Up to now, <u>investigations of syllable weight have focused on the nature of</u>
> <u>cross-linguistic variation</u> in weight criteria and the phonological representa-
> tions capturing this variation <u>without examining possible motivations behind the</u>
> <u>language-specific adoption of a particular weight criterion.</u> It thus remains unknown
> whether the language specific setting of the coda weight parameter is at all predictable
> from independent properties of the languages concerned. (L2002-3)

The examples above show that criticism of others provides justification for the research and for the potentially face-threatening act of capturing the research space, but it is rarely direct or unmitigated.

3.5   Presentation of the Self

Presentation of the self is an element that facilitates capturing the research space. It often takes indirect forms, such as evaluative comments on the introduced research, often associated with the importance of the topic or with the adopted methodology. In

(13), they refer to the subject matter *(a key training tool, the record of the resident's acquisition and exercise of clinical judgment)* rather than to the research itself, and thus represent a very indirect strategy of building a positive image of one's own work as a significant contribution.

> (13)   This paper examines the role of physicians' progress notes in the professional social-
>   ization of medical residents. These notes … constitute a key training tool by means of
>   which residents experience and internalize the cognitive processes which constitute
>   medical reasoning and analysis, through the application of general principles to specific
>   individual cases. They thus represent the record of the resident's acquisition and
>   exercise of clinical judgment. (JP2004-3)

Another, more direct strategy of building the image of the self as an expert is positive evaluation of the applied methodology and significance of the research. It is often associated with announcing the purpose of the research (Move 3), as in (14), where the paper (modestly referred to as *essay*) is introduced as *a detailed account*. In this case, positive comments on the methodology are combined with remarks on the subject matter, which is presented as exceptionally complex and demanding *(complicated, overlapping commitment events)*.

> (14)   This essay provides a detailed account of the morphosyntax, semantics, and pragmatics
>   of modal clitics in Q'eqchi'-Maya. … It details the complicated types of commitment
>   events that are encoded and implicated in various contexts. … And it shows the ways
>   in which these complicated, overlapping commitment events may be understood in
>   terms of intentional states—from desire and worry to belief and hope. (LC2006-2)

Example (15), in turn, draws attention to new data and methodology *(new lines of evidence)* applied by the author, and merges this remark with Move 2, indicating that the results call for a reassessment of some earlier findings. As in some other examples (3–6), the act of counter-claiming *(arrives at different conclusions)* is made less face-threatening by concessive contrast: the author states explicitly that many of the earlier findings are actually confirmed by his study.

> (15)   The resulting investigation uses new lines of evidence to substantiate many of the
>   results of Asher (1993), but arrives at different conclusions from those of Asher on a
>   number of key points. (L2003-3)

An explicit comparison with previous studies is also invoked in (16). The strengths of the analysis are highlighted by the disadvantages incurred by the use of alterna-tive approaches *(unrelated formalisms)*. No exact reference is given in this niche-establishing move, a practice observed also in other cases which involve criticism (see 7 and 12)

> (16)   Under our analysis, where each disharmonic sequence is subject to a distinct constraint,
>   the morpheme structure constraints follow from the structure of the grammar. Under an
>   analysis positing a general agreement constraint, the morpheme structure constraints
>   must be expressed by unrelated formalisms. (L2005-9)

A positive image of one's work can also rest on direct references to the obtained findings (Move 3), in (17) presented as *intriguing* (that is, novel and inspiring further research), and in (18) as *substantial* and conclusive *(a final piece of evidence)*.

(17) Another <u>intriguing result</u> is that the crossover constraint proposed below makes crucial reference to linear order. (LP2005-7)

(18) Reference to entities introduced in coordinate structures, examined in Sect. 3, <u>provides substantial further evidence</u> regarding the semantic nature of the expressions involved. … In Sect. 4, results regarding quantification by amount quantifiers over the associated denotation domains <u>provides a final piece of evidence for the nature of these domains</u> and their semantic types. (L2003-3)

A different approach to self-presentation consists in assuming a defensive attitude, for example, by additionally clarifying intentions and concepts, as in (19), where the comment (*is not meant to imply that*) prevents misinterpretation. In (20), by referring to external authorities (*my informants*), the comment provides explanation for the author's potentially disputable decision.

(19) Saying that DMs do not change grammaticality judgments or truth conditions <u>is not meant to imply that they do not carry meaning</u>. (JP2003-1)

(20) The inclusion of 'drag queen' in this list is a particular choice on my part, and not one that all transgender-identified people —or drag queens —might agree with. <u>Indeed, I include it here, somewhat reluctantly, only because many of my informants do so in their explanations of what 'transgender' encompasses</u>. (LC2003-4)

Another defensive strategy is limiting the scope of the research by indicating explicitly what the author does not intend to do or establish. This is shown in (21), where the negative statement of purpose (*my purpose… is not to provide*) functions as a lead-into the proper claim (*my purpose is to make the point that*). Such limiting remarks may also narrow down the topic, as in (22), where the authors resign from discussing more complex or problematic cases (*we cannot illuminate these issues here*), and in (23), where the writer avoids an accusation of oversight (*possible but left for future occasions*).

(21) <u>My purpose in this piece is not to provide detailed empirical arguments for or against any particular conception</u> of this (although I will not try to hide what I believe – or at least hope – is correct). Rather, <u>my purpose is to make the point that</u> acceptance of a complex view does need to be argued for if a simpler view is available. (LP2002-8)

(22) However, <u>we cannot illuminate these issues here</u>, and we will therefore concentrate on underlying sentences such as (1) where the event-structure is clear. (LP2001-5)

(23) Further extensions, such as an application to epistemic indicatives (see below) and conditionals with conditional antecedents, <u>are possible but left for future occasions</u>. (LP2005-3)

Finally, defensive comments may provide a justification for possible imperfections, for instance, when they emphasise the difficulty of the task. This is illustrated in (24), where the remark (*this is not an easy task*) provides the reason for the noncanonical structure of the paper.

(24) <u>This is not an easy task</u> because, as we will see, their starting points and theoretical priorities are rather different, which makes it difficult to compare them in terms of a single set of parameters or issues… For this reason, the paper has a somewhat "fugue-like" structure, considering first some similarities, then differences, then returning to similarities, and again to differences. (LS2003-4)

By emphasising the importance and difficulty of the subject matter, highlighting innovative aspects of the methodology, stressing advantages of the adopted approach, and formulating the claim in a way that prevents misunderstanding, academic authors present themselves as expert members of the community, thus increasing the likelihood of a favourable reception of their research by the readers.

4   Concluding Remarks

The purpose of this chapter was to identify links between two discourse domains: academia and business. It has been shown that there are important similarities that follow from their common origin (LSP) and parallel development, are related to the circumstances in which the two discourse domains have been evolving (namely, the rise of English as an International Language and the need to teach), stem from their internal diversity (a variety of genres and disciplines or areas), and result from the intercultural nature of academic and business contacts. Other shared characteristics follow from the very aim of the interaction: to provide information in a way that makes it acceptable and credible to the target audience, a goal which, in the case of academic authors, goes beyond "presenting research results". In order to achieve it, academic authors establish a dialogic perspective, seek consensus, establish a research space, and present themselves as fair, competent, and unbiased members of the community; in other words, they negotiate their contribution to the field. The structure of the research article introduction reflects these complex needs, and, as this chapter has tried to demonstrate, invites the use of strategies that are well known from business discourse.

This discussion has focused on the research article, a canonical academic genre, which boasts a long tradition both as a text format for sharing research results and as an object of study, but similarities between business communication and academic discourse certainly do not stop here. Strategies familiar from business settings may also be found in such academic genres as the research grant proposal, which, although much younger, has grown into a pivotal text type, enabling further research and development, or the university mission statement, an overtly promotional academic genre (Atai & Asadnia, 2016).

References

Abdi, J., & Sadeghi, K. (2018). Promotion through claiming centrality in L1 and L2 English research article introductions. *International Journal of English Studies, 18*(1), 53–70. https://doi.org/10.6018/ijes/2018/1/297381.

Akar, D., & Louhiala-Salminen, L. (1999). Towards a new genre: A comparative study of business faxes. In F. Bargiela-Chiappini & C. Nickerson (Eds.), *Writing business: Genres, media and discourses* (pp. 207–226). Harlow, Essex: Longman.

Atai, M. R., & Asadnia, F. (2016). The prestigious world university on its homepage: The promotional academic genre of overview. *Iranian Journal of Applied Linguistics, 19*(1), 1–34.

Bargiela-Chiappini, F. (2003). Face and politeness: New (insights) for old (concepts). *Journal of Pragmatics, 35,* 1453–1469.

Bargiela-Chiappini, F., Nickerson, C., & Planken, B. (2007). *Business discourse.* Basingstoke, Hampshire: Palgrave Macmillan.

Berger, P. L., & Luckmann, T. (1967[1966]). *The social construction of reality. A treatise in the sociology of knowledge.* London: Penguin Books.

Bhatia, V. K. (1993). *Analysing genre: Language use in professional settings.* London: Longman.

Bhatia, V. K. (1999). Disciplinary variation in Business English. In M. Hewings & C. Nickerson (Eds.), *Business English: Research into practice* (pp. 129–143). Harlow, Essex: Longman.

Bogdanowska-Jakubowska, E. (2010). *FACE. An interdisciplinary perspective.* Katowice: Wydawnictwo Uniwersytetu Śląskiego.

Bülow-Møller, A. M. (2005). Persuasion in business negotiations. In H. Halmari & T. Virtanen (Eds.), *Persuasion across genres: A linguistic approach* (pp. 27–58). Amsterdam: John Benjamins.

Canagarajah, S. (2002). Multilingual writers and the academic community: Towards a critical relationship. *Journal of English for Academic Purposes, 1,* 29–44.

Charles, M., & Charles, D. (1999). Sales negotiations: Bargaining through tactical summaries. In M. Hewings & C. Nickerson (Eds.), *Business English: Research into practice* (pp. 71–82). Harlow, Essex: Longman.

Clyne, M. (1987). Cultural differences in the organization of academic texts. *Journal of Pragmatics, 11,* 211–247.

Čmejrková, S. (1996). Academic writing in Czech and English. In E. Ventola & A. Mauranen (Eds.), *Academic writing: Intercultural and textual issues* (pp. 137–152). Amsterdam: John Benjamins.

Čmejrková, S., & Daneš, F. (1997). Academic writing and cultural identity: The case of Czech academic writing. In A. Duszak (Ed.), *Culture and styles of academic discourse* (pp. 41–61). Berlin: Mouton de Gruyter.

Connor, U. (2000). Variation in rhetorical moves in grant proposals of US humanists and scientists. *Text, 20*(1), 1–28.

Connor, U., & Mauranen, A. (1999). Linguistic analysis of grant proposals: European Union research grants. *English for Specific Purposes, 18*(1), 47–62.

Crawford Camiciottoli, B. (2006). Rhetorical strategies of company executives and investment analysts: Textual metadiscourse in corporate earnings calls. In V. K. Bhatia & M. Gotti (Eds.), *Explorations in specialized genres* (pp. 115–134). Brno: Peter Lang.

Crawford Camiciottoli, B. (2007). *The language of business studies lectures: A corpus-assisted analysis.* Amsterdam: John Benjamins.

Crystal, D. (2003[1997]). *English as a global language* (2nd ed.). Cambridge: Cambridge University Press.

Dahl, T. (2004). Textual metadiscourse in research articles: A marker of national culture or of academic discipline? *Journal of Pragmatics, 36,* 1807–1825.

Duszak, A. (1994). Academic discourse and intellectual styles. *Journal of Pragmatics, 21,* 291–313.

Feng, H., & Shi, L. (2004). Genre analysis of research grant proposals. *LSP & Professional Communication, 4*(1), 8–30.

Fløttum, K., Dahl, T., & Kinn, T. (2006a). *Academic voices across languages and disciplines.* Amsterdam: John Benjamins.

Fløttum, K., Kinn, T., & Dahl, T. (2006b.) 'We now report on...' versus 'Let us now see how...': Author roles and interaction with readers in research articles. In K. Hyland & M. Bondi (Eds.), *Academic discourse across disciplines* (pp. 203–224). Bern: Peter Lang.

Flower, L. (1979). Writer-based prose: A cognitive basis for problems in writing. *College English, 41*(1), 19–37.

Flowerdew, J., & Peacock, M. (2001). Issues in EAP: A preliminary perspective. In J. Flowerdew & M. Peacock (Eds.), *Research perspectives on English for academic purposes* (pp. 8–24). Cambridge: Cambridge University Press.

Fortanet, I. (2008). Evaluative language in peer review referee reports. *Journal of English for Academic Purposes, 7,* 27–37.

Fortanet Gómez, I. (2008). Strategies for teaching and learning an occluded genre: The RA referee report. In S. Burgess & P. Martín-Martín (Eds.), *English as an additional language in research publication and communication* (pp. 19–38). Bern: Peter Lang.

Garzone, G. (2006). The use of discursive features expressing causal relations in annual company reports. In J. Flowerdew & M. Gotti (Eds.), *Studies in specialized discourse* (pp. 81–107). Bern: Peter Lang.

Goffman, E. (1967). *Interaction ritual. Essays on face-to-face behaviour*. Harmondsworth: Penguin Books.

Golebiowski, Z. (1998). Rhetorical approaches to scientific writing: An english-polish contrastive study. *Text, 18*(1), 67–102.

Golebiowski, Z. (1999). Application of Swales' model in the analysis of research papers by Polish authors. *International Review of Applied Linguistics, 37,* 231–247.

Hinds, J. (1987). Reader versus writer responsibility: A new typology. In U. Connor & R. B. Kaplan (Eds.), *Writing across languages: Analysis of L2 text* (pp. 141–152). Reading, Massachusetts: Addison-Wesley.

Hunston, S. (2005). Conflict and consensus: Construing opposition in Applied Linguistics. In E. Tognini-Bonelli & G. Del Lungo Camiciotti (Eds.) *Strategies in academic discourse* (pp. 1–15). Amsterdam: John Benjamins.

Hutchinson, T., & Waters, A. (1987). *English for specific purposes: A learning-centred approach.* Cambridge: Cambridge University Press.

Hyland, K. (1998). Boosting, hedging and the negotiation of academic knowledge. *Text, 18*(3), 349–382.

Hyland, K. (1999). Disciplinary discourses: Writer stance in research articles. In C. N. Candlin & K. Hyland (Eds.), *Writing: Texts, processes and practices* (pp. 99–121). London: Longman.

Hyland, K. (2000). *Disciplinary discourses: Social interactions in academic writing.* Harlow, Essex: Longman.

Hyland, K. (2001). Bringing in the reader: Addressee features in academic articles. *Written Communication, 18*(4), 549–574.

Hyland, K. (2002). Specificity revisited: How far should we go now? *English for Specific Purposes, 21,* 385–395.

Hyland, K. (2005). *Metadiscourse: Exploring interaction in writing.* London: Continuum.

Hyland, K. (2008). Disciplinary voices: Interactions in research writing. *English Text Construction, 1*(1), 5–22.

Hyland, K. (2009). *Academic discourse: English in a global context.* London: Continuum.

Hyland, K. (2010). Constructing proximity: Relating to readers in popular and professional science. *Journal of English for Academic Purposes, 9,* 116–127.

Hyland, K., & Bondi, M. (Eds.). (2006). *Academic discourse across disciplines.* Bern: Peter Lang.

Johns, A. M. (1986). The language of business. *Annual Review of Applied Linguistics, 7,* 3–17. https://doi.org/10.1017/S0267190500001616.

Johns, A. M. (1997). *Text, role, and context: Developing academic literacies.* Cambridge: Cambridge University Press.

Johns, A. M., & Swales, J. M. (2002). Literacy and disciplinary practices: Opening and closing perspectives. *Journal of English for Academic Purposes, 1,* 13–28.

Kuhn, T. S. (1970[1962]). *The structure of scientific revolutions.* 2nd ed. Chicago: University of Chicago Press.

Loudermilk, B. C. (2007). Occluded academic genres: An analysis of the MBA Thought Essay. *Journal of English for Academic Purposes, 6,* 190–205.

Lu, X., Yoon, J., & Kisselev, O. (2018). A phrase-frame list for social science research article introductions. *Journal of English for Academic Purposes, 36,* 76–85.

Luzón Marco, M. J. (2002). A genre analysis of corporate home pages. *LSP & Professional Communication, 2*(1), 41–56.

Łyda, A. (2007). *Concessive relation in spoken discourse: A study into academic spoken English.* Katowice: Wydawnictwo Uniwersytetu Śląskiego.

Malavasi, D. (2006). Evaluation in banks' annual reports: A comparison of EL1 and EIL texts. In M. Gotti & D. S. Giannoni (Eds.), *New trends in specialized discourse analysis* (pp. 109–123). Bern: Peter Lang.

Mamet, P. (2005). *Język w służbie menedżerów: Deklaracja misji przedsiębiorstwa.* Katowice: Wydawnictwo Uniwersytetu Śląskiego.

Martín-Martín, P., & Burgess, S. (2004). The rhetorical management of academic criticism in research article abstracts. *Text, 24*(2), 171–195.

Mauranen, A. (1993). *Cultural differences in academic rhetoric: A textlinguistic study.* Frankfurt am Main: Peter Lang.

Mauranen, A. (2010). Features of English as a lingua franca in academia. *Helsinki English Studies, 6,* 6–28.

Mauranen, A., Hynninen, N., & Ranta, E. (2010). English as an academic lingua franca: The ELFA project. *English for Specific Purposes, 29,* 183–190.

Melander, B., Swales, J. M., & Fredrickson, K. M. (1997). Journal abstracts from three academic fields in the United States and Sweden: National or disciplinary proclivities? In A. Duszak (Ed.), *Culture and styles of academic discourse* (pp. 251–272). Berlin: Mouton de Gruyter.

Mulholland, J. (1999). E-mail: Uses, issues and problems in an institutional setting. In F. Bargiela-Chiappini & C. Nickerson (Eds.), *Writing business: Genres, media and discourses* (pp. 57–84). Harlow, Essex: Longman.

Myers, G. (1989). The pragmatics of politeness in scientific articles. *Applied Linguistics, 10*(1), 1–35.

Nettle, D. (1999). *Linguistic diversity.* Oxford: Oxford University Press.

Nickerson, C. (1999). The use of English in electronic mail in a multinational corporation. In F. Bargiela-Chiappini & C. Nickerson (Eds.), *Writing business: Genres, media and discourses* (pp. 35–56). Harlow, Essex: Longman.

Paltridge, B. (2001). Linguistic research and EAP pedagogy. In J. Flowerdew & M. Peacock (Eds.), *Research perspectives on English for Academic Purposes* (pp. 55–70). Cambridge: Cambridge University Press.

Quine, W. V. O. (1975). The nature of natural knowledge. In S. Guttenplan (Ed.), *Mind and language* (pp. 67–81). Oxford: Oxford University Press.

Samraj, B. (2002). Introductions in research articles: Variations across disciplines. *English for Specific Purposes, 21,* 1–17.

Silver, M. (2003). The stance of stance: A critical look at ways stance is expressed and modeled in academic discourse. *Journal of English for Academic Purposes, 2,* 359–374.

Swales, J. M. (1981). *Aspects of article introductions.* Birmingham: The University of Aston.

Swales, J. M. (1990). *Genre analysis: English in academic and research settings.* Cambridge: Cambridge University Press.

Swales, J. M. (1996). Occluded genres in the academy: The case of the submission letter. In E. Ventola & A. Mauranen (Eds.), *Academic writing: Intercultural and textual issues* (pp. 45–58). Amsterdam: John Benjamins.

Swales, J. M. (2001). EAP-related linguistic research: An intellectual history. In J. Flowerdew & M. Peacock (Eds.), *Research perspectives on English for academic purposes* (pp. 42–54). Cambridge: Cambridge University Press.

Swales, J. M. (2004). *Research genres: Explorations and applications.* Cambridge: Cambridge University Press.

Tang, R., & John, S. (1999). The "I" in identity: Exploring writer identity in student academic writing through the first person pronoun. *English for Specific Purposes, 18,* 23–39.

Vandeyar, S. (2010). Shifting selves: Constructing and negotiating academic identities. *South African Journal of Higher Education, 24*(6), 914–934.

Vold, E. T. (2006a). Epistemic modality markers in research articles: A cross-linguistic and cross-disciplinary study. *International Journal of Applied Linguistics, 16*(1), 61–87.

Vold, E. T. (2006b). The choice and use of epistemic modality markers in linguistics and medical research articles. In K. Hyland & M. Bondi (Eds.), *Academic discourse across disciplines* (pp. 225–249). Bern: Peter Lang.

Warchał, K. (2010). Moulding interpersonal relations through conditional clauses: Consensus-building strategies in written academic discourse. *Journal of English for Academic Purposes, 9*, 140–150.

Warchał, K. (2014). The face of a scholar: Selected interpersonal strategies in journal article introductions. *Linguistica Silesiana, 35*, 305–326.

Warchał, K. (2018). The place of the purpose statement in linguistics article introductions: An English-Polish perspective. *Linguistica Silesiana, 39*, 327–346.

White, P. R. R. (2000). Dialogue and inter-subjectivity: Reinterpreting the semantics of modality and hedging. In M. Coulthard, J. Cotterill, & F. Rock (Eds.), *Dialogue analysis VII: Working with dialogue* (pp. 67–80). Tübingen: Max Niemeyer Verlag.

White, P. R. R. (2003). Beyond modality and hedging: A dialogic view of the language of intersubjective stance. *Text, 23*(2), 259–284.

Yakhontova, T. (2006). Cultural and disciplinary variation in academic discourse: The issue of influencing factors. *Journal of English for Academic Purposes, 5*, 153–167.

Young, P. (2006). *Writing and presenting in English: The Rosetta Stone of science*. Amsterdam: Elsevier.

Krystyna Warchał, Ph.D., is an associate professor at the Institute of Linguistics, Faculty of Humanities, University of Silesia in Katowice, Poland. She works in the area of text linguistics, pragmatics, and corpus linguistics. Her research interests include academic discourse and Polish-English contrastive studies, genre analysis, and linguistic modality. She has recently been involved in research projects related to epistemic modality, rhetorical change, and the development of academic identity. She has published *Certainty and Doubt in Academic Discourse: Epistemic Modality Markers in English and Polish Linguistics Articles* (Katowice: University of Silesia Press, 2015).

Always Be Closing: An ABC of Business in English Language Feature Films

Anthony Barker

Abstract For the most part, the world of work is missing from feature film representation. Films are not made about librarians, plumbers and quantity surveyors, or if they are, their work is tangential to what they do or signify in their respective films. Even cowboys are rarely seen with cows. The only work that is routinely explored is that of cops/detectives, doctors and lawyers—the staples of television serial drama. The pursuit of business goals, the designing, making and selling of products, constitutes daily experience for many if not most on this planet, yet this area of life remains seriously under-represented. This presentation looks at the instances of doing business that do make it into film culture and the kinds of statement films make about commercial enterprise. It will mostly represent the American scene, because for every *Il Postino* in Europe delivering letters, there are 10 postmen in America, perhaps knocking twice, but rarely delivering them. The broad movement of film representation, I will argue, is to move trade from concerns about the soul of man in commerce and corporate life towards the realization (or imposition?) that business is near allied to crime. In general terms, it is the change from *Death of a Salesman* (1949) to *Glengarry Glen Ross (1983)*, when a man who had to work himself to death to turn a buck finds himself having to screw workmates and customers alike in order to survive. In addition, the pressures of work of the little guy (I will briefly inspect the humbler world of salesmanship and marketing, two activities which have taken on a higher profile since the mid twentieth century) have largely given place to the unbridled opportunism of Reaganomics and deregulation in high finance. The general discontents associated with the financial crises of the 1980s and 2000s have created their very own film genre, the corporate scam exposure movie, as well as a number of important feature-length documentary films.

Keywords Business · Representation · Cinema · High finance

A. Barker (✉)
University of Aveiro, Aveiro, Portugal
e-mail: abarker@ua.pt

© Springer Nature Switzerland AG 2020
U. Michalik et al. (eds.), *Exploring Business Language and Culture*,
Second Language Learning and Teaching,
https://doi.org/10.1007/978-3-030-58551-8_14

1   Introduction

> Money is a singular thing. It ranks with love as man's greatest source of joy. And with death
> as his greatest source of anxiety.
> John Kenneth Galbraith,
> *The Age of Uncertainty* (Galbraith, 1977, p. 161).

The purpose of this article is to offer an overview of how commercial cinema has,
over a number of years, come to represent the activity of doing business. At its
fullest extension, this means what sort of attitude it has taken towards the full-blown
capitalist system as it has operated in the United States. On the smallest scale, cinema
has also explored the travails of *homo economicus*, the little guy who just has to make
his way in the world. The first approach is clearly political in scope and the latter
more existential. But I would not like to claim that cinema (the art form) has a defined
or definable position on this subject. Films invariably signify more than just approval
or disapproval, and they often contain mixed messages. This has a great deal to do
with the nature of authorship of movies, but also with the nature of movie production
as themselves businesses. Peter Biskind explains:

> a conservative director may work with a liberal writer, or vice versa, and both…may be
> overruled by the producer who is only trying to make a buck and thus expresses ideology in
> a different way, not as a personal preference or artistic vision, but as mediated by mainstream
> institutions such as banks and studios, who transmit ideology in the guise of market decisions:
> this idea will sell, that one won't… Hollywood is a business, and movies avoid antagonizing
> significant blocs of viewers: they have no incentive to be politically clear. (Biskind, 2001,
> p. 5)

Beyond the institutional politics of narrative film, there is the question of what it
means to deliver general truths through mimetic art. It is necessary to offer the caveat
that not every business transaction expresses the nature of business and that not every
businessperson is necessarily representative of all businesspersons. However, it is part
of the way we read films that these types of essentialist interpretation come to bear.
This how Andrew Light explains the responses of popular audiences:

> Films do not merely represent individuals and groups but also help to actually create under-
> standings of who we think we are, how we regard others, and how members of groups identify
> and understand their group membership and their obligations to that group. We empathize
> with the characters we see on screen… But more than this, we can come to accept the picture
> that a film offers of some bit of the world as true and then come to react to those inhabiting
> that world as a unified whole. It is astonishingly difficult to appreciate every individual as an
> individual, and films encourage us, sometimes for good and sometimes not, to group people
> together as part of a larger category that we can more easily understand. (Light, 2003, p. 9)

There is also another important distinction to make before discussing the ways that
business is depicted in film culture. This has to do with the nature of work on film.

Generally speaking, after sleep, the world of work is the human activity we engage
in which is most seriously under-represented in films. Many necessary forms of

labour receive almost no attention (delivery work, plumbing, traffic management) while other activities seem almost an obsession of narrative cinema. Law enforcement (cops and detectives), for example, is over-represented, as are other branches of legal activity. The practice of medicine and journalism, where the journalist is detective, lawyer and avenger rolled into one) is also very readily dramatised. The work of soldiering features heavily in genre films, as does the representation of the performing arts (*Black Swan, A Star is Born, Turner*, etc.) when creativity is depicted as a form of work as opposed to the fruits of spontaneity. This degree of selectivity is not difficult to explain—it is related to the potential for crisis and conflict that these professions throw up. Cinema is inimical to the lived experience of work— the drudgery, the repetition, the tolerance of tiredness, the self-abnegation. Unlike cinema, work requires your active engagement rather than your passive enjoyment. Patrick Lencioni, in his *Three Signs of a Miserable Job* (2007), recognizes anonymity (not having your distinctive merit recognized), irrelevance (not being able to make any significant headway) and immeasurement (being unable to assess your contribution in terms of palpable outcomes) as the three main indices of dissatisfaction with one's work. Contrast that with the movies. In the movies, there is a clear social hierarchy of identification and your avatar is picked out for you. Movie characters clearly "make a difference" by their actions. Movie stories are all about plot outcomes that are demonstrable. Think about films on teaching. Movie teachers always establish rewarding rapports with their classes and their selected pupils go on to "find themselves" or achieve academic and/or life success. Real teachers are aware that many, if not most, of the benefits of their work are invisible to them, as are the effects they have on their pupils.

With these general considerations in mind, we can turn to reviewing the kinds of attitudes and postures towards the practice of business that can be identified. What will be offered are some fairly broad categorizations. I need to stress at the outset that the films discussed are works that address business and work directly. The indirect treatment of the subject in genre cinema can be very interesting and has produced many great films, but it is not part of my prospectus here. Just to clarify. Comedies can clearly be seen to address the subject in films like *The Man in the White Suit* (1952) or *I'm Alright Jack* (1959), about the suppression of a consumer-friendly product for reasons of profit or the turbulent and irrational nature of labour relations respectively. But Penny Marshall's *Big* (1988), for example, offers an oblique critique of business management by putting a child in the role of an executive. Science fiction films like *Blade Runner* (1984) and *Robocop* (1987) have anti-corporatist subtexts but they do not overwhelm the film's other themes. In the horror genre, *American Psycho* (2000) could be thought of as anti-capitalist but as with Romero's *Dawn of the Dead* (1978) or Carpenter's *They Live* (1988), it is the impression of *grand guignol* rather than critique that lingers. Moreover, to incorporate films with anti-consumer and anti-managerialist subtexts would be to make this piece over-extensive.

It has to be said that most representations of business are in the context of the detection of criminal activity. This is particularly true of the representation of big business or high finance, areas we do not come in much contact with but which feel have an impact on our lives. When business dealings migrate to the front pages of the newspapers from the business sections, that is when they become note-worthy. Similarly, business affairs become a hot topic when a clear interface is found between big money and political power. A perennial conspiracy theory of popular culture concerns the way politicians and entrepreneurs are corruptly benefitting each other in the shadows. Would that this were just a theory. My concern in this article however is to review the films that deal with business as a legal and legitimate activity, even if there is often a fine line drawn, and some form of immorality is implicit. Indeed, even when the business-themed film is the right side of the law, there is often a desire to measure the distance between what business promises and what it delivers. In particular, American film has sought to test the affirmation of Abraham Lincoln:

> Labour is prior to and independent of capital. Capital is only the fruit of labour and could never have existed if labour had not first existed. Labour is the superior of capital and deserves the much higher consideration. (Lincoln, inaugural address, quoted in Brogan, 2001, p. 384)

Is it money or is it people that drives America? Which indeed deserves the higher consideration? These questions really matter when "by 2002 General Motors sales returns were higher than Denmark's gross domestic product, Walmart's than Poland's and Exxon Mobil's than South Africa's", according to Dickenson (2006, pp. 124–5).

It is therefore proposed to deal with the topic according to scale, starting with micro-aspects and building to macro ones. The five categories of film -and a selection of examples of the type (with some overlap[1])—are therefore: *The Salesman (and Salesmanship)*—*Death of a Salesman* (1951), *Used Cars* (1980), *Cadillac Man* (1990), *Glengarry Glen Ross* (1992), *The Pursuit of Happyness (2007), Joy* (2015); *The Office Worker (or the Factory Floor Worker)*—*9 to 5* (1980), *Working Girl* (1988), *Office Space*(1999), *The Devil Wears Prada* (2006), *Horrible Bosses* (2011), *The Intern* (2015); *The Industrial Leader/Visionary*—*Citizen Kane* (1942), *The Fountainhead* (1949), *Tucker* (1988), *The Aviator* (2004), *The Social Network* (2010), *Saving Mr. Banks* (2013), *Jobs* (2013), *Steve Jobs* (2015), *The Founder* (2016); *The Documentary Exposure of Business Malfeasance*—*Roger and Me* (1989), *Enron: the Smartest Guys in the Room* (2005), *I.O.U.S.A.* (2008), *Capitalism: a Love Story* (2009), *Collapse* (2009), *Inside Job* (2010) and *The World of High Finance*—*Rollover* (1981), *Trading Places* (1983), *Wall Street* (1987), *Boiler Room* (2000), *Wall Street: Money Never Sleeps* (2010), *Margin Call* (2011), *Too Big to Fail* (2011), *Arbitrage* (2012), *The Wolf of Wall Street* (2013), *The Big Short (2015), Equity* (2016).

(All the business-related films cited in this article, together with a number of others not used, are listed in an appendix of films designed as a tool for those who wish to carry forward research on this theme).

---

[1]For example, *The Founder* (2016), the biopic of Ray Kroc of MacDonald's, is an example of salesmanship as much as it exemplifies visionary business practice).

2   The Salesman (and Salesmanship)

The defining text on the American little guy's subordination to the marketplace is Arthur Miller's play, *Death of a Salesman* (1949), of which many film versions have been made. Miller's Willy Loman is driven to exhaustion and then self-destruction by his inability to break through and achieve sales success. His valuation of himself is inextricably bound up with his sense of his commercial worth. Scott Sandage expresses the left-liberal view of business eating the soul of man:

> a century and a half ago we embraced business as the dominant model for our outer and inner lives. Ours is an ideology of achieved identity; obligatory striving is its method, and failure and success are its outcomes. We reckon our incomes once a year, but audit ourselves daily… Willy Loman speaks this way. Choosing suicide to launch his sons with insurance money, he asks, "Does it take more guts to stand here the rest of my life **ringing up a zero**?" He insists that a man is not a piece of fruit to be eaten and the peel discarded, but does not see that a man is not a cash register. (Sandage, 2005, pp. 264–5)

We never find out what it is Willy is so desperately trying to sell, because it is not important. In the update of Miller's play, David Mamet's *Glengarry Glen Ross* (1984), (1983), published by Penguin 1985, we do. Our lone salesman is replaced with an office of salespeople all attempting to offload worthless tracts of swamp and desert as desirable real estate. Mamet makes it clear that although despicable, this trade is legal. "Marks" purchase at their own risk. The office is however a feral environment, where the company sets salesman against salesman in a competition to "get on the board". High-selling staff are rewarded and underperformers are sacked, hence the necessity to "always be closing" (clinch a sale). The predatory nature of both the salesmen and the company is implicit in their cynical exchanges. Mamet upgrades his play in the screen version (1992) directed by James Foley when he interpolates a new character Blake, played by Alec Baldwin, who comes from downtown to give the sales staff a motivational talk. This consists of a tirade of abuse and threats. Mamet differs from Miller in that the world he represents is partly admiring of the energy and raw power of the American business machine. Its indifference to the private lives of its operatives is part of its dynamism. If Miller sees Loman's delusions as masochistic, Mamet's world is clearly sado-masochistic. His salesmen, when they are not feeling sorry for themselves, relish the chance to best each other.

The political right, whose values are evidenced in the curious respect that the ideas and works of Miller's contemporary Ayn Rand enjoy, does not share this left-liberal ambivalence about the American way of business. The ideology that Sandage critiques is fully laid bare in the fiction of Horatio Alger (1832–1899) and the moral exhortations of Dale Carnegie (1888–1955). These two apologists of the much-vaunted American Dream believed that effort, integrity, determination and tireless self-improvement would bring material success and the self-worth that rests upon it. The optimistic belief that will and hard work can overcome the handicaps of life is prevalent in all walks of American life and finds its finest exposition in the recent movie *The Pursuit of Happyness* (2007), direct by Gabriele Muccino from the bestselling book *The Pursuit of Happyness* (2006) by Chris Gardner. The film is also a vehicle for the popular talents of Afro-American actor Will Smith. Smith as Gardner progresses from penniless hustling salesman through serious set-backs to millionaire stockbroker; he manages this transformation by boundless energy, optimism and the ability to charm and influence people. The unusual element in this case is that he is a black, single parent, that is, coming from a demographic often presumed to be shiftless and incapable of success. The theme of parental care and responsibility is reinforced by casting Smith's own son as the child for whose benefit all this effort is marshaled. What the unsuccessful Gardner is selling is bone density measuring machines (some of which don't work and all of which are admitted to be of dubious use in the medical profession). Through an unpaid intern programme with an intake of 20 aspirants, Gardner works long hours and hustles indomitably selling stock until he is given a permanent paid job. The other 19 interns are dismissed after 6 months of effortful unpaid labour and the cycle begins again with 20 more interns. The film (and Gardner) can see nothing wrong with this, because Gardner goes on to become a millionaire.

The release date of the film was incredibly fortuitous—it slightly preceded the launch of Obama's campaign for the Presidency, with its upbeat slogan of "Yes we can", and it came less than a year before the financial crisis which brought the selling of stock into disrepute. In retrospect, it is hard not to see the office where Gardner rose to fortune as a rosy-tinted version of the office in *The Wolf of Wall Street* (2013), a chop-shop brokerage where worthless penny stocks were sold to unsuspecting small investors by lies and subterfuges. Indeed, Gardner's charm is hardly different from the guile of Mamet's salesmen, where only Shelley Levene's love and concern for his daughter humanizes him. However, in the 2007 film we are not allowed to discover the value of the stock Gardner peddles. In the leftist model of capitalism, you can only get rich at the expense of someone else; in the rightist version, individual advancement is either not at anyone else's expense or the competitive nature of the system justifies the generation of winners and losers.

The Pursuit of Happyness, with its title suggesting the constitutionally-sanctioned nature of aggressive individualism,[2] is unusually sanguine about the road to success in a progressively troubled and divided America under the forces of globalization. Perhaps only Tom Hanks in *Larry Crowne* (2011), who is thrown out of work in his forties and forced to retrain, accepts his place and fate with such good grace. The Carnegian salesman is a triumpher over adversity in a system that rarely fails to reward merit. There are occasional side-glances at the toilers who fall by the wayside, but concern for them is often made to look like the "sour socialism" that Chaplin was accused of in the 1930s and 1940s.

---

[2]The misspelling is deliberate—the quotation comes not from a sacred national text but from a piece of graffiti.

3   The Office Worker (or the Factory Floor Worker)

To some extent, the salesman can be a representative American hero because he(she?) is, like Willy Loman, a figure 'on the road'. But what of the office worker, the company drone, the Dilbert? The office worker is trapped in a defining space (the cubicle) and within a corporate hierarchical structure where initiative and American individualism are thwarted at every turn. They have to face the oppression of the boss on a daily basis and the unelected companionship of office colleagues. Whether experiencing the *anomie* of isolation or the irritations of enforced socialization, the office worker is a pitiable figure of discontent. The film comedy (what else could it be?) of office life is caught in Mike Judge's 1999 *Office Space*, starring Ron Livingston and Jennifer Aniston. Contemporary cubicle life consists of officious micro-management, mindless repetition, endless bureaucratic procedures, petty humiliations and hostilities and, worst of all, precariousness of employment. Peter and two of his anonymous colleagues start stealing from the firm in tiny amounts in order to relieve their boredom and to assert their individuality. Peter undergoes some sort of crisis and open displays his contempt for his job. In a system where the worker's sycophancy is expected, ironically the less Peter cares about his job, the more it starts to value him. An insurrection ensues in which revenge is taken on office equipment (a scene where the three colleagues destroy the office printer uses a celebrated rap song to give it the proper note of *gansta* violence).[3] Milton, the ultimate office inadequate obsessed with his stapler, eventually burns the company down. Jennifer Aniston stages a parallel rebellion in the fast food place where she works. The comedy drama of worms turning carries a powerful emotional charge, as it does in the two *Horrible Bosses* comedies (2011 and 2014), where workers entertain the fantasy of murdering their troublesome bosses. But this is essentially gestural; the prospect of self-employment is chimerical for most. Bosses cannot be murdered and corporations will not be done away with.

The ensemble workplace comedy became a staple of the new millennium on television. *The Office* (BBC 2001–3; NBC 2005–13) enacts the daily life of a paper merchant's office, (Wernham Hogg, Slough, in the British version and Dunder Mifflin, Scranton, New Jersey, in the American one). Employing a documentary film aesthetic (with no laughter track), the professional lives of office workers are explored for their delusions and frustrations. The tedium of work is mitigated by the playfulness and eccentricity of the characters, led by a boss who has no head for business at all but who imagines himself both talented and popular when he is neither. As in *Office Space*, there is an air of truancy and wish-fulfillment about these shows.

---

[3]Geto Boy's "Still", also used in similar parodic mode in *Family Guy*, series seven, episode "I Dream of Jesus".

4   The Industrial Leader/Visionary

The Pursuit of Happyness differs from the tale of the struggling salesman insofar as it is also the biopic of a real person. Stories of fictional uplift are more like that of *Joy* (2015), where for once the businessperson is a woman. The traditional biopic usually celebrates success on a larger scale. The biopic of business success is that of the industrial leader or visionary whose tale is an inspirational one. It partakes of the dream of fame and fortune open to all but it also wishes to make claims of an extraordinary nature for its subject. And, more interestingly, it also raises the question of the cost of success. The biopic understands that people want to identify with business success and believe that it rests upon talent, drive and self-belief. They also want to believe that the driven pay a heavy price for their fortune in terms of their personal lives. Another cliché of the form is that talent always goes unrecognized at first and that the gifted are blocked and abused by the mediocre and the shortsighted. In the case of the business visionary, the obstacle is usually entrenched commercial interests. Brian Winston argues that the innovative in business rises to meet some "supervening social need" (Winston, 1998, p. 8), but nearly always faces the resistance of existing commercial and social interests, which he calls "the law of the suppression of radical potential" (11–12). The automobile industry had to outface the interests of the horse-powered transport industry with its hundreds of thousands of operatives. When these forces are too strong, we have the tale of the genius ahead of his time. Such a tale is that of *Tucker—the Man and His Dream* (1988) dir. Francis Ford Coppola. Preston Tucker designed and produced a radically new type of automobile, but despite a flair for publicity failed to produce more than 50 models of his car. The other car manufacturers were threatened by him and conspired to drive him out of business. Then, by slow degrees, they incorporated the innovations of his car into their vehicles. Many commentators have read the story as a parallel to Coppola's own failed attempts to run a studio as an executive and also be a creative filmmaker. The film equivocates on whether Tucker is a genius or a showman—part of his problem is that the engineering never quite matches the hype. He can never quite put the full package together.

The real business visionary gets a similar treatment. There have been two recent film treatments of the life of Steve Jobs, following his death from pancreatic cancer in October 2011. The first *Jobs* came out in August 2012 and the second, based on the Walter Isaacson biography *Steve Jobs* (2011) appearing 19 days after his death, was directed by Danny Boyle from an Aaron Sorkin screenplay in October 2015. *Jobs* (2013) is a conventional eulogizing biopic touching all the bases of boardroom conflict, product innovation and personal heartache and success. It hints at sacrifices and inner demons but skates over what form they might take. The second film, *Steve Jobs* (2015) is more unusual; it attempts to snapshot a life in three product-launches—in 1984, 1988 and 1998—which is a clever way of putting the businessman before the family man. It also dramatizes his life in association with five figures, his personal assistant Joanna, his technical wizard Andy, his ex-partner Steve Wozniak, his former boss and boardroom adversary John Scully and his estranged daughter Lisa. Jobs is shown to be bullying and insensitive and disinclined to give credit where it is due: a man in love with the limelight. Sorkin has Jobs say *"The very nature of people is something to be overcome"*, suggesting an intensity which sees humanity as a design fault. Although disjointed temporally, this back-stage structure capturing the moments before Jobs meets his adoring public highlights the degree of contrivance and showmanship which goes into the construction of the myth of astral business success. Heroes for our wired generation, like Jobs here and Mark Zuckerberg in *The Social Network* (2010) are shown to carry a sharp personal edge with their talent.

5   The Documentary Exposure of Business Malfeasance

More innovative than the biopic, which struggles to avoid Great Man clichés, is the documentary feature about the state of capitalist America. The pioneer of this form of investigative and expository journalism is Michael Moore. Moore managed to carry the documentary film across the divide between worthy television production and commercially viable theatrical release. His first film was the darkly whimsical *Roger and Me* (1989) about the betrayal of his home town, Flint, Michigan, by General Motors, the main employer which was laying off workers by the thousand. After a career in television in the 1990s, Moore broke through with his particular brand of outrage in films in 2002 (addressing gun control) and 2004 (responsibility for 9/11), both of which caught the public mood and generated box-office revenue as no feature documentary had done previously. He then turned to the perversity of the national healthcare system in 2007, before taking on the recent financial crisis in *Capitalism: A Love Story* (2009). In the latter, according to Roger Eberts, Moore.

> believes that capitalism is a system which claims to reward free enterprise but in fact rewards greed. He says it is responsible for accumulation of wealth at the top: The richest 1 percent of Americans have more than the bottom 95 percent combined. At a time when America debates legalized gambling, it has long been practiced on Wall Street. (Eberts, 2009)

However, by this time Moore himself had become a dangerously polarizing figure (gestures like standing in front of the New York Stock Exchange with a bullhorn shouting "Give us our money back!" were not always rhetorically effective) and so it was left to other filmmakers to carry forward the effort of exposure. Perhaps the best of a crop of documentaries exploring the financial excesses originating in the period of the George W. Bush presidency is Charles Ferguson's *Inside Job* (2010)[4] Dark irony is the order of the day in this film, where it is stated, "What used to be called a conflict of interest is now called a synergy". The film starts in the country of Iceland but fairly soon this becomes the metaphor "Iceland". Iceland, with a population of 300,000, had a financial services sector 30 times bigger than its real economy (which is based on fishing and geothermal power). Three tiny Icelandic banks began issuing

---

[4]The advertising for which carried the tagline: "The film that cost over $20,000,000,000,000 to make".

loans on a totally gargantuan scale. This included the creation of financial products bundling and selling on debt ("derivatives") and was effectively a Ponzi scheme run on a national scale.

The size of the US economy made it harder to see that Wall Street was running a very similar scam. *Inside Job* (2010) addresses the behavior of five investment banks (Goldman Sachs, Morgan Stanley, Lehman Brothers, Merrill Lynch, Bear Stearns), two financial conglomerates (Citigroup and J. P. Morgan), three securities and insurance companies (AIG, MBIA and AMBAC) and three rating agencies (Moody's, Standard and Poor's and Fitch). Ferguson's film makes the point that the financial sector has grown since the 1980s to constitute some 45% of all US growth and profitability. The returns that Wall Street had hoped to sustain since the dot.com companies bubble of the 1990s proved to be impossible with conventional investment and stock broking. Those returns now depended on leverage; the key was deregulation which resumed apace under Bush. Deregulation was what enabled the financial services industry to grow exponentially; new and complex financial instruments and accountancy fraud are what helped to conceal malpractice The industry, de facto, renounced its duty of care to its customers, selling "junk", because bonuses and personal incentives were so generous. Nothing much has changed since 2008—unregulated risk, humbled for a while by the scale of its errors, is once again a prevalent danger. Why should it not be? Virtually no one was prosecuted and no one went to prison. No bonuses were returned and no impropriety has been admitted.

There is plenty of evidence here to support the greed interpretation of the nature of modern capitalism. *Inside Job* shows that Wall Street simply bought favourable interpretations of their practices by paying for speeches and articles from so-called experts, and by including professional economists on the boards of investment banks (heads and senior academics from leading Business Schools). Academics took tens of millions of dollars for writing that CDOs (Collatralized Debt Obligations) and CDSs (Credit Default Swaps) made the market more stable when the exact opposite was the case. One of the more depressing conclusions of this documentary is that bankers may not be any more corrupt than the rest of us: the evidence suggests that scholars and economists are just as greedy and their professional judgments are just as easily bought when the sorts of pecuniary incentive Wall Street can provide are on offer. The ratings agencies, whose only task it was to investigate and attest to credit-worthiness, defended their AAA ratings of bundles of worthless bad debts by saying that their ratings were just "opinions". Again, nothing fundamental changed under Obama, who trod water on regulation, and a policy of rampant de-regulation once again has been introduced under Trump. If capitalism holds that you invest or borrow at your own risk, it does not intervene or otherwise comment on institutions which go out of their way to conceal the true nature of things for their own profit. We are back with Mamet's salesman, just on a national trillion-dollar scale.

The villains of *Inside Job*, Hank Paulson (Secretary of the Treasury under Bush), Ben Bernanke (Chairman of the Fed), Timothy Geitner (President of the New York Fed and Secretary of the Treasury under Obama) and others were all former heads of investment banks who had pushed for deregulation. When later made heads of public bodies, they were charged with essential regulatory functions but either by inadvertence or design were asleep at the wheel. *Inside Job* shows that these and other political appointees had in their former careers laboured to facilitate the credit bubble that wiped out life savings, cost 8 million job and untold home repossessions, and in so doing had enriched themselves.

But America is nothing if not the land of pluralism of opinion. The villains of *Inside Job* are the heroes of *Too Big to Fail* (2011), directed by Curtis Hanson. This made-for-TV movie of doughty public officials saving the nation from economic meltdown is a tense exercise in crisis management but it has little or no sense of context. Paulson (William Hurt) bangs corporate heads together to get the current chiefs of investment banks to buy up their infirm competitors and stabilize the market. There is no mention of his personal fortune obtained at Goldman Sachs, nor his alleged tipping off of hedge fund managers about the impending collapse. The message of *Too Big to Fail* is that the system works and that although mistakes were made, no apple was rotten enough to merit prison. The film is a collective jeopardy movie like *Earthquake* or *Towering Inferno*—quakes and fires happen and are facts of life. We should all breathe a collective sigh of relief that they do not happen to us.

6 The World of High Finance

Too Big to Fail is of course not a documentary feature; it is a fictionalized reconstruction of events between March and October 2008. The last category of films dealing with popular understandings of business is exactly the story of rise and fall in high finance. Although business success and failure recurs in hundreds of pictures made before the 1980s, it was the Age of Reagan that made high finance seem like a topic ripe for exploration. And as with *Death of a Salesman* (1949) in the first category, so we have a foundational text here in the form of Oliver Stone's *Wall Street* (1986)—Jack Boozer (2007, p. 176) calls it a "landmark film". The New American cinema films of the 1970s had been hostile to the boardrooms of corporations, seeing conspiracies everywhere, but they were too ignorant of the world they sought to criticize (see Scott 2011, pp. 137–57) for an account of the classic paranoia/conspiracy movie of the 1970s). The thrillers that exposed boardroom skullduggery were easily convinced that the manoeuvrings of bankers and executives were a response to threats to the international position of America represented by the Soviets and by Arab petrodollars. This is what softens the capitalist critique of Lumet's *Network* (1976) and Pakula's *Rollover* (1981). The 1983 comedy *Trading Places* understands the stock exchange as a place where the rich get richer and poor get left behind. It shows stock being manipulated for personal profit by insider trading, but its outrage is not systemic. It is appalled that the trading classes are a closed shop. As long as a wider social slice of Americans can get rich that way, it is okay. *Wall Street* (1987) was the first film to suggest that the financial services sector is essentially parasitic (I say suggest because, as with Mamet, there are mixed feelings about the aggression, intelligence and vitalism of asset stripping and arbitrage). Constantin Parvulescu's *Global Finance on Screen* (2017) shows that both the de Palma *Bonfire of the Vanities*

(1991) and the follow-up *Wall Street: Money Never Sleeps* (2010) found it easy to soften and extenuate the rogue trader.

The banks and the stock market are where one must go to raise capital for investment in productive industry and agriculture. It should serve the making of things that people need. An over-mighty financial services sector means that, having less productive capacity to serve, it tends to serve itself. *Wall Street* is the first commercial film to show this. Brokers and investment bankers are gamblers playing the system *as a system*, exploiting their familiarity with it to defraud legitimate investors and working businesses. Wall Street contrasts Bud Fox's buying and selling of stock with the gainful running of an aviation company of his father Carl. Only the latter serves a wider public. And with the spectacular gains of insider trading on offer, corruption is the inevitable consequence. *Wall Street* makes no bones about the fact that the stock market runs on greed.

There were sufficient warnings in the 1980s that the economy could not go on expanding at that rate. There was Black Monday on 19th October 1987, there was the Savings and Loans Scandal in America throughout the late 1980s and 1990s, when, due to unsound real estate lending policies, hundreds of thousands of homes were repossessed (the estimated losses of the sector were of 160 billion dollars, 132 billion of which was absorbed by the state i.e., the general taxpayer). The 1990s were a period of solid economic growth and low inflation for the US—but trouble was brewing in the form of the dot.com bubble. Internet trading was a huge growth area but the profits reflected in the rise of the Nasdaq stock market composite (where these stocks traded 400% up in the period 1995–2000) were not sustainable. 2000–2002 saw a swathe of accountancy scandals as auditors colluded to hide financial realities. The Enron collapse of October 2001 brought down not only this energy giant but also Arthur Andersen, the accountancy firm, and resulted in the loss of over 20,000 jobs. WorldCom, the telecommunications corporation, collapsed in July 2002 and was exposed as having concealed its weakness by accountancy fraud. It was the largest filing for bankruptcy in US history until Lehman Brothers six years later. The documentary *Enron: the Smartest Guys in the Room* (2005) was able to assemble footage of the cast of executives (Ken Lay, Jeff Skilling, etc.) who were steering this titanic of a company and to show them incriminating themselves, as well as the many public figures who endorsed and protected them.

This was the background to the approaching Millennium but film was largely silent on corporate misdeeds because of the perceived prosperity of the 1990s. Only Ben Younger's *Boiler Room* (2000) returns to the territory of *Wall Street* to rehash the story of a young ambitious gambler prepared to engage in fraudulent trading to get ahead. Once again, it is a street-smart backslider rebelling against his upright disapproving father (this time a judge). And once again, it is very much a boy's club, with a gang mentality that is on show. It is not until *Equity* (2015) that we see any of these boardroom dramas from a woman's perspective; in this film, we can add endemic sexism to the other flaws of corporate raiders and investors.

The financial crisis of 2007/8 kick-started a spate of films about investment banking and stock-broking, subjects that would normally scare off movie-makers and the public alike. *Margin Call* (2011) is essentially an office and boardroom crisis drama, *Too Big to Fail* (2011) looks at the politics and mechanics of the bailout, *Arbitrage* (2012) and *Equity* (2016) are business-context thrillers, and *The Wolf of Wall Street* (2013) is a study in collective over-confidence and excess. Scorsese takes the interesting tack in his financial drama of suggesting that the pursuit of money is like an addiction. The wolf, Jordan Belfort, is quite unable to control or contain his pursuit of fortune and the trappings of success. In that sense, Scorsese carries on the theme of Tom Woolf in *Bonfire of the Vanities* (1987), that stockbrokers came to think of themselves as "Masters of the Universe", quite beyond the laws of man and Nature. It is no surprise therefore that his brokers resemble the gangsters of his 1990s crime films, who felt similarly untouchable and who succumbed fatally to the same temptations and excesses.

But the best of this crop is perhaps *The Big Short* (2015), directed by Adam McKay and written by Charles Randolph from the book *The Big Short* (2010) by financial journalist Michael Lewis. *The Big Short* bridges the divide between documentary and fictional accounts of the financial crisis by finding an innovative way to dramatise it. Lewis's book has some of the elements of a detective story. Various investment insiders come to understand that the mortgage market is a house of cards, ready to fall at any moment. They improvise ways to bet on this happening but it does not. All the institutions of Wall Street are conspiring to keep an aberrant financial nonsense afloat. The world of finance is both deeply delusional and deeply cynical. The book and film follow the lives of four groups of investors who want to expose this folly. At the same time, they seek to exploit it for the grotesque levels of reward that can ensue from these speculations. They are heroes for their clear-sightedness and persistence, but they are also tainted by a strong whiff of profiteering. The cynical Vennett (Ryan Gosling) doesn't care too much, the young traders Charlie and Jamie take it as their foothold in the business, but the older hands, Burry and Rickert (Christian Bale and Brad Pitt), feel it is time to get out of investing. The trading maverick Mark Baum (Steve Carell) takes to public forums to expose the greed and hypocrisy of corporate executives. Very late in the film, the sub-prime mortgage market collapses, CDOs are shown to be the junk bonds they were all along, and our financial Cassandras are proved to have been right. The entities buying this junk were in many cases the parent companies employing our rebels. Yet the film finishes on a sad note: lives have been destroyed, homes and jobs lost, America has courted ruin. We see the same crazy spirit of abandonment as in Scorsese's film, but we have a much better understanding of how it came to happen.

The film does a very creditable job making high finance intelligible. Its characters are either thinly disguised or the real financial personnel from Lewis's book—the claim is made that nothing is made up. Vennett narrates the film in the hard-boiled jump-cut style of *Wolf of Wall Street*. Splashy visuals, irony, direct address to camera (breaking the fourth wall), even a false ending where all corrupt bankers go to jail, the financial system is righted, the exploited receive restitution and the regulatory system is restored ("Just kidding… no one went to jail except this poor schmuck…") are employed to keep us informed and entertained. Its most amusing trope however is the use of celebrities as experts. In a series of cutaways, the financial system is laid bare. A naked Margot Robbie in a bubble-bath, the lead actress from *The Wolf of*

Wall Street, explains America's mortgage market. Chef Anthony Bourdain explains CDOs as unsold out-of-date fish repackaged as gourmet fish stew. Singer Selena Gomez at the blackjack table explains synthetic CDOs. However the fun is only a means to get over the harsh significance of it all. Five trillion dollars in pensions, real estate value, savings and bonds was wiped out by the sub-prime and CDO financial crisis of 2008, driving businesses into bankrupcy and leading to the biggest taxpayer bailout in history. Nowhere in the world was unaffected. Credit Suisse, UBS, HBOS, Royal Bank of Scotland, Northern Rock, Deutschebank were European banks either greatly embroiled in or destroyed by the crisis.

As a consequence of 2008 and its aftermath, there was (and remains) in the general population a widespread suspicion of big business, and of financial services in particular. The globalization of capital has led to the belief that few countries control their own destinies or are able to protect their populations from systemic speculation. Much of today's populist politics derives from the sense that global market factors can destabilize any nation, and drive down living standards. Governments impose the policies we have come to know as "austerity" and suggest this is the consequence of living beyond our means or failure to work hard enough. This is extremely hard to stomach when we learn of the behavior of our captains of finance.

7 Conclusions

The effects of the fallout from the crisis are not as commonly related in film. Apart from *Larry Crowne, The Company Men* (2010) is one of the few films to attempt to see the crisis from both a management and a worker perspective. Despite a strong cast including Tommy Lee Jones and Ben Afleck, it rarely strays from a conventional treatment of shock, disillusionment and recovery. For this reason, it failed roundly at the box office. Television treatments of the entrepreneurial spirit have been generally more successful. A smash success of the crisis period and after was the show *Mad Men* (2007–15), which looked with great detail at the Madison Avenue advertising industry. *House of Lies* (2012–16) does the same for the management consultancy business and *Halt and Catch Fire* (2014–17) for a computer tech start-up. The appeal of many of these shows was precisely that they were set before the loss of faith in American finance, in the 60s and the 80s, when America was clearly a top industrial producer. Period detail and the social naiveties of the past smooth over any critique that might appear of cutthroat business.

To conclude, insofar as we can find a consistent attitude to business in commercial cinema, it would be in line with the following broad observations. Films find it difficult to hold focus on work. The making of a living is a means to an end for many, and it is those ends (the affective and private parts of life) that are generally centre-stage. The business of business (trading, negotiating, selling, building, exchanging, and delivering) only tends to come into focus when businesspeople approximate to criminals and fraudsters. The exception to this is when commercial success is so spectacular that the businessperson can either be an avatar for our own material hopes or is an iconic figure whose life history provides us with both inspiration and a cautionary tale. It is as if the spectacular business success of today is a modern equivalent of the Greek mythical hero ("Those whom the gods wish to destroy they first make mad"). The business visionary can be a classic Promethean over-reacher, but they deserve our awe because, like Tucker and Jobs, they "make things"—normal business practice exists to thwart them by putting "the bottom line" before serving the public. As a rule, success-worship in cinema impedes due respect for common labour. Women in business have become much more visible in the last decade [cf. *Made in Dagenham* (2010), *Joy, The Intern* (both 2015) and *Equity* (2016)], although there is still a movie glass ceiling as well as a boardroom one. By far the biggest change in the last decade has been the identification of corporate finance is a nest of vipers. What in the 1980s were the nefarious activities of a few greedy hustlers (*Other People's Money, Wall Street*) has become the systemic rapacity of a privileged clique that has no fellow-feeling for the common people they exploit (*Margin Call, Arbitrage, Inside Job, The Big Short*). Populist politics, moral panics and fears of "the deep state" flow from the erosion of confidence in state institutions and their ability to serve the whole commonwealth and not just those sectors that staff the higher echelons of government and business. This fear finds a perfect expression in Adam McKay's follow-up film *Vice* (2018) about still-living Vice President Dick Cheney, the Chairman and CEO of Haliburton (a company with a history of malpractice and bribery). Financial scandal on the screen, for so long absent and resistant to film treatment, is now thematically big business.

Appendix

Select Filmography of Business-themed English Language Films.

9 *To 5* (1980) Dir. Colin Higgins. Twentieth Century Fox.

Arbitrage (2012) dir. Nicholas Jarecki. Lionsgate.

Barbarians at the Gate (1993) dir. Glenn Jordan. HBO Films & Columbia.

Bonfire of the Vanities (1990) dir. Brian De Palma, Warner Bros.

Boiler Room (2000) dir. Ben Younger. New Line.

Cadillac Man (1990) dir. Barry Levinson. Orion Pictures.

Capitalism: a Love Story (2009) dir. Michael Moore. The Weinstein Co.

Citizen Kane (1942) dir. Orson Welles. Mercury Co. and RKO.

Collapse (2009) dir. Chris Smith. Bluemark Productions.

Death of a Salesman (1951) dir. Laslo Benedik, Stanley Kramer Productions.

Death of a Salesman (1985) dir. Volker Schlondorff. Roxbury Productions.

Enron: the Smartest Guys in the Room (2005) dir. Alex Gibney. Jigsaw Productions.

Glengarry Glen Ross (1992) dir. James Foley. New Line.

Horrible Bosses (2011) dir. Seth Gordon. New Line.

Horrible Bosses 2 (2014) dir. Sean Anders. New Line.

I'm Alright Jack (1959) dir. John Boulting. British Lion Film Productions.

Inside Job (2010) dir. Charles Ferguson. Sony Pictures Classics.
I.O.U.S.A. (2008) dir. Patrick Creadon. O'Malley Creadon Productions.
Jobs (2013) dir. Joshua M. Stern. Open Road Films.
Joy (2015) dir. David O. Russell. Fox 2000 Pictures.
Larry Crowne (2011) dir. Tom Hanks. Universal Pictures.
Made in Dagenham (2010) dir. Nigel Cole. BBC Films.
Margin Call (2011) dir. J.C. Chandor. Before the Door Pictures.
Office Space (1999) dir. Mike Judge. Twentieth Century Fox.
Roger and Me (1989) dir. Michael Moore. Dog eat Dog Films.
Rollover (1981) dir. Alan J. Pakula. IPC Films.
Steve Jobs (2015) dir. Danny Boyle. Universal Pictures.
Sunshine State (2002) dir. John Sayles. Anarchist's Convention Films.
The Aviator (2004) dir. Martin Scorsese. Forward Pass.
The Big Short (2015) dir. Adam McKay. Paramount Pictures.
The Company Men (2010) dir. John Wells. The Weinstein Co.
The Devil Wears Prada (2006) dir. David Frankel. Fox 2000 Pictures.
The Founder (2016) dir. John Lee Hanckck. The Weinstein Co.
The Fountainhead (1949) dir. King Vidor. Warner Bros.
The Insider (1999) dir. Michael Mann. Touchstone Pictures.
The Intern (2015) dir. Nancy Meyers. Waverly Films.
The Man in the Gray Flannel Suit (1956) dir Nunnally Johnson. Twentieth Century Fox.
The Man in the White Suit (1951) dir. Alexander Mackendrick. Ealing Studios.
The Man who Sued God (2001) dir. Mark Joffe. AFFC.
The Office (2001–3) dir. Ricky Gervais & Stephen Merchant. BBC TV series.
The Office (2005–13) dir. Greg Daniels. NBC TV series.
The Pursuit of Happyness (2007) dir. Gabriele Muccino. Columbia Pictures.
The Wolf of Wall Street (2013) dir. Martin Scorsese. Red Granite Pictures.
Too Big to Fail (2011) dir. Curtis Hanson. HBO Films.
Trading Places (1983) dir. John Landis. Paramount Picture.
Tucker (1988) dir. Francis Ford Coppola. Lucasfilm.
Up in the Air (2009) dir. Jason Reitman. Paramount Pictures.
Used Cars (1980) dir. Robert Zemeckis. Columbia Pictures.
Vice (2018) dir. Adam McKay. Annapurna Pictures.
Wall Street (1987) dir. Oliver Stone. Twentieth Century Fox.
Wall Street: Money Never Sleeps (2010) dir. Oliver Stone. Twentieth Century Fox.
Working Girl (1988) dir. Mike Nichols. Twentieth Century Fox.

References

Biskind, P. (2001). *Seeing is believing: How hollywood taught us to stop worrying and love the fifties.* London: Bloomsbury.

Boozer, J. (2007). Movies and the closing of the Reagan era. In S. Prince, ed. American Cinema of the 1980s. Oxford: Berg.

Brogan, H. (2001). *The penguin history of the USA* (2nd ed.). London: Penguin Books.

Dickenson, B. (2006). *Hollywood's new radicalism*. London: I.B. Tauris.

Ebert, R. (2009). Review of *Michael Moore's Capitalism: A love story (2009),* RogerEbert.com, 30th September 2009. Retrieved January 30, 2019 from https://www.rogerebert.com/reviews/cap italism-a-love-story-2009.

Galbraith, J. K. (1977). *The age of uncertainty*. London: BBC-Andre Deutsch.

Gardner, C. (2006). *The pursuit of happyness*. New York: Amistad.

Isaacson, W. (2011). *Steve jobs*. London: Little Brown, Book Group.

Lencioni, P. (2007). *Three signs of a miserable job: A fable for managers*. San Francisco, CA: Jossey-Bass.

Lewis, M. (2010). *The big short*. London: Penguin.

Light, A. (2003). *Rseel arguments: Film, philosophy and social criticism*. Boulder. Co: Westview Press.

Mamet, D. (1985). *Glengarry glen ross*. London: Penguin Books.

Miller, A. (1949). *Death of a salesman*. New York: Viking Press.

Parvulescu, C. (2017). *Global finance on screen: From wall street to side street*. London & New York: Routledge.

Sandage, S. (2005). *Born losers: A history of failure in America*. Cambridge Mass.: Harvard UP.

Scott, I. (2011). *American politics in hollywood film* (2nd ed.). Edinburgh: Edinburgh UP.

Winston, B. (1998). *Media, technology and society*. London & New York: Routledge.

Anthony Barker is an Associate Professor in the Department of Languages and Cultures at the University of Aveiro and the Coordinator of a Cultural Studies research group. He obtained a D. Phil at Oxford in 18th-century literature and was Munby Fellow in Bibliography at Cambridge University. He was director of the Master course on Languages and Business and is director of the Doctoral Programme in Cultural Studies, as well as coordinator of his research centre. He now teaches film, literary and cultural disciplines and publishes in these areas. Publications include collections on *Europe: Fact and Fictions* (2003) and *Stereotyping* (2005), and articles on televisualising the 50s, Henry James on Film, the American and the British road movie, and British film and television comedy. He has edited a volume on *Television, Aesthetics and Reality* (2007) and another on *Success and Failure* (2009). Recent works include articles on zany film and television comedy, political satire, ultra-violence in the cinema of the 1970s and a book on *Identity and Cultural Exchange in Travel and Tourism* (2015). He has recently co-edited volumes on the First World War and on cultural transformations of body and text. He is preparing a volume on Fake News, Censorship and the Unsayable.

The Language of M—A Female Manager (as Played by Judi Dench)

Anna Majer and Piotr Mamet

Abstract This paper examines the language of M—a fictional character in Ian Fleming's *James Bond* series, as played by Judi Dench in seven *James Bond* movies. The study is an attempt to answer the question whether (or to what extent) the language of M played by this actress is the language of women, whether its characteristics are closer to women's language or to men's language, or else whether it evinces characteristic features of institutional discourse, including the managerial language specificity and power relations in the workplace. The researchers investigate the language of M in terms of selected linguistic features, according to an established methodological framework based on previous studies in the field of discourse and gender (Lakoff (1975); Coats (1993); Wareing (2004); Kendall & Tannen (2003); Cameron (2005); Scollon & Scollon, 2003), and of institutional discourse (Tannen (1990); Mayr (2008); Koester (2010)).

Keywords Institutional discourse · Men's and women's language · Female managers

1 Introduction

The language of M, as played by Judi Dench, is expected to display specific features. On the one hand, the studies of men's and women's language differences allow to assume that the language of the character of M played by a woman will manifest the characteristics of women's language. On the other hand, the institutional context and the arrangement of power relations within it will probably considerably influence her language specificity.

A. Majer (✉)
Institute of Linguistics, Faculty of Humanities, University of Silesia in Katowice, Katowice, Poland
e-mail: anna.majer@us.edu.pl

P. Mamet
Silesian University of Technology, Gliwice, Poland
e-mail: p.mamet@gmail.com

© Springer Nature Switzerland AG 2020
U. Michalik et al. (eds.), *Exploring Business Language and Culture*,
Second Language Learning and Teaching,
https://doi.org/10.1007/978-3-030-58551-8_15

The paper explores the language of M with the aim to discover if it manifests the characteristics of men's and/or women's speech, and also to what extent it has been influenced by institutional and managerial context. The fundamental question is, therefore, what the specificity of the language of this woman manager is. The assumption is that the language of M cumulates the features of men's and women's speech as well as the features of institutional talk in terms of register, style and the pragmatic aspect.

This paper includes an analysis which is a continuation of the research concerning the language of the main characters of the James Bond series. The language of 007 and/or M has also been discussed in Mamet (2014), Mamet, Gwóźdź, and Wilk (2017), Mamet and Wilk (2019), and Mamet, Miś, and Wilk (2020).

2   Theoretical Background

The theoretical background to the study embraces two primary issues. The first one concerns the difference between women's language and men's language. The other one pertains to the characteristics of institutional talk. These two aspects shape the specificity of the language of M—a female manager.

2.1   Women's Language Versus Men's Language

It is not a novelty to claim that gender differences are reflected in language. They manifest themselves in various aspects, such as psychological, social and cultural. One of the factors which contributes to the shaping of gender identity of an individual is the process of socialisation to gender roles. According to Giddens (2004), both boys and girls gradually acquire the roles, cultural values, norms and behaviours typically ascribed to a particular sex through their contact with people and institutions responsible for socialisation, and the phenomenon is inevitably reflected in men's and women's speech (Giddens, 2004, pp. 128–129).

Although the very set of differences does not arouse controversy, Cameron (2005) points out that the attitudes towards possible causes of this linguistic differentiation vary among scholars, some of whom represent a 'dominance' approach to the language-and-gender issue, whereas others represent a 'cultural difference' approach (Cameron, 2005, p. 285).

To name the most prominent and influential stances on the subject matter, Lakoff (1975), who is a representative of the first approach mentioned above, views the linguistic differences as an effect of gender inequality and a strong polarisation of male dominance and female subordination. This implies that while the process of socialisation, the language girls are taught is different from the language boys are supposed to acquire. Therefore, women's language is characterised as uncertain, weak and ingratiatory. Women's speech is indirect, tentative and it expresses subordination and lower social rank. Tannen (1990), on the other hand, relates linguistic differences between men and women to the social arrangement of reality, which profoundly contributes to the diversification of genders during childhood and adolescence.

Whatever the reasons for the differences in speech might be, the following study primarily focuses on the linguistic features typically ascribed to men and women, with the intention to reveal the language specificity of a woman manager, i.e. to what extent it manifests the features of men's and women's language.

2.2   Institutional Discourse

The concept of institutional discourse immediately evokes the association with an institution or an organisation. As Mayr (2008) claims, although the terms may be used interchangeably in some contexts, 'organisation' seems to be more frequently used in reference to commercial units, whereas 'institution' tends to be more often ascribed to units of public character (Mayr, 2008, p. 4).

Within the studies of discourse and institutional communication, an institution may be defined as suggested by Agar (1985), as "a socially legitimated expertise together with those persons authorized to implement it" (Agar, 1985, p. 164). Therefore, institutions are not determined only by their physical conditions or material locations, but they essentially constitute social constructs characterised by a specific system and arrangement of roles and social identities. Furthermore, institutions appear to inevitably and inextricably involve power and asymmetry in terms of institutional roles.

Similarly, Benwell and Stokoe (2006) define the notion of institution as a social category which manifests a set of essential features (Benwell & Stokoe, 2006, pp. 87–90). Firstly, institutions are "structures that embed power relations within them" (Benwell & Stokoe, 2006, p. 87), they are "intrinsically bound up with *power*, and are often seen to serve the interests of powerful groups" (Benwell & Stokoe, 2006, p. 88; italics in the original text). Secondly, institutional talk differs from ordinary, everyday talk mainly due to the necessity to comply with a specific bureaucratic communicative order. This conversational constraint, however, as well as the coercive imposition of power, do not have to involve any oppression exercised by a dominant party over another. It may well be "achieved by persuasion, consensus and complicit cooperation" (Benwell & Stokoe, 2006, p. 89). The essence of institutional dominance and power consists in a possibility to control and shape social life and the life of individuals by influencing them.

In terms of discourse and conversational analysis, institutional context enforces a number of features which characterise institutional talk. These have been identified and labelled, among others, in the research by Drew and Heritage (1992), Nelson (2000), Nelson (2006), Heritage (1997), and Koester (2010). The ones which have been of particular importance to this study are described in the subsequent, analytical part of the paper.

2.3   The Language of Female Managers

Does a woman manager have to use men's language to be effective in professional terms? Is it men's or women's language that prevails and dominates in institutional discourse? Is it still possible to even speak of men's and women's language while considering institutional discourse? Should a manager speak women's language if, according to the theory of management, a model managerial profile is, in fact, consistent with female nature? And, eventually, what is the language of M—a woman manager?

Probably, no unequivocal answers can be given here. Partly due to the overlapping of different aspects and contexts. Partly because of the dynamics of discourse itself. But most importantly, perhaps, because of the need to negotiate, or rather comply to, one's identity, be it social, personal or institutional. As Holmes (2015) aptly points out,

> (i)ndividuals are constantly engaged in constructing aspects of their interpersonal and inter-group identity, including their professional identity and their gender identity. The discourse strategies we adopt, the words we select, and the grammatical structures and pronunciations we favor all contribute to the construction of particular aspects of our social identity. Any particular utterance may thus be analyzed as contributing simultaneously to the construction of more than one aspect of an individual's identity, whether social (enacting gender identity), institutional (their professional identity as a manager), or personal (their wish to be considered friendly, well-informed, and so on). (Holmes, 2015, p. 887)

It seems interesting, however, to what extent at least the variables mentioned contribute to the specificity of female managers' discourse, and which of the characteristics show more than others.

Surprising though it may seem, as Baskiewicz (2013) claims, in the theory of management and business studies, women's nature has been proved to be more consistent with the model characteristic of a manager than men's is (Baskiewicz, 2013, p. 35). Apparently, women gain advantage thanks to their interpersonal skills in the first place. They encourage their employees to involve in and devote to internal business matters, they are willing to share their knowledge and they delegate duties in order to create the atmosphere of creative work and cooperation, and to enable them to derive satisfaction from a cooperative effort. Women more often implement mentoring and coaching, which evinces itself in mutual trust, assistance in the development of their personnel's skills, and openness in terms of listening to one another, enquiring and cooperative task solving, rather than simply instructing and restricting their managees. Women tend to define roles and establish goals clearly. They do not normally avoid counselling or informal information exchanges. In comparison to men, women attach less importance to the organisational hierarchy, which may contribute to their forming new relationships more easily and to their ability to sustain them. Women would rather cooperate than compete. A woman manager rarely resorts to competition for power and exclusive dominance in the organisation. They achieve success due to managing through cooperation, collaboration as well as partnership within their professional team.

The research into gendered talk in the workplace, such as the studies conducted by Tannen (1994), Holmes (2006), Mullany (2007), Schnurr (2009) or Baxter (2010), has provided evidence that effective communicators, no matter if men or women,

> typically draw from a wide and varied discursive repertoire, ranging from normatively "feminine" to normatively "masculine" ways of talking. They skilfully select their discursive strategies in response to the particular interactional context, and their effectiveness derives from this discursive flexibility and contextual sensitivity. (Holmes, 2015, p. 887)

3 Corpus Description and Methodology

The research has been conducted in three stages, each of which concentrates on the issues described in the theoretical part above respectively.

The first stage constitutes an analysis of the features of the language of M in terms of the specificity of women's and men's language. The linguistic studies made by Lakoff (1975), Coats (1993), Wareing (2004) as well as Kendall and Tannen (2003) have been adopted in order to construct a typology which would allow to describe the research corpus in regard of the aspects of men's and women's speech.

The second stage of the research procedure focuses on the qualities of institutional discourse in M's utterances. The typology used has been designed on the basis of the research conducted by Drew and Heritage (1992), Nelson (2000), Nelson (2006), Heritage (1997) and Koester (2010). For more convenient reference, both typologies mentioned above constitute introductions to subsequent parts of the paper respectively.

The third stage involves a pragmatic analysis of the research material, with the primary objective to classify M's utterances in compliance with the aims she intends to achieve while being immersed in the institutional discourse of MI6.

The research material embraces the transcription of all M-Bond encounters from eight (out of twenty-four) James Bond movies, i.e. the ones in which Judith Dench played the role of M. And these are as follows: *GoldenEye* (1995), *Tomorrow Never Dies* (1997), *The World Is Not Enough* (1999), *Die Another Day* (2002), *Casino Royale* (2006), *Quantum of Solace* (2008), *Skyfall* (2012) and *Spectre* (2015).

4 Results

The below description of the research results follows the stages mentioned in the corpus description and methodology part. The material is discussed according to the suggested typologies, and a few examples are cited to illustrate the findings. Also, some statistical data is provided to show the extent of particular linguistic phenomena within the corpus.

4.1 The Language of M in Terms of Men's and Women's Speech Characteristics

Gender specific language has been subject to lots of research. For the purpose of this analysis, a few studies have been chosen, and the criterion for the selection of typologies was to establish a set of features which would be linguistically verifiable and broad enough to provide a sufficient picture of supposed differences. The results of the studies by Lakoff (1975), Coats (1993), Wareing (2004), and Kendall and Tannen (2003) are the basis for the following typology of aspects distinguishing the language of men and women:

1. the use of swear words, expletives and words enhancing the emotional character of an utterance
2. empty, trivialising adjectives
3. discrimination in naming colours
4. question tags
5. (in)direct requests and the use of polite forms
6. tentativeness of utterances and hedges
7. the use of intensifiers[1]
8. the degree of familiarity and intimacy of utterances, and the subjects touched[2]
9. taking on the role of authority or expert.[3]

To begin with, swear words only started to be uttered by M in *Casino Royale* (2006), with one exception only—when she "introduces" herself to Bond in Gold-eneye (1995) by saying *If you think for one moment I don't have the balls to send a man out to die, your instincts are dead wrong.* Apart from curse words, M also weaves weaker expletives into her utterances. Such evolution of M's language is probably a sign of the passing time, of the changing contemporary reality, which happens to be reflected to some extent in the series. Expletives are supposed to enhance the emotional character of what M says, and she usually makes use of such expressions when she criticises Bond's actions, or her supervisors', or when she gives direct orders. The expletives, both weaker and stronger, as well as expressions used to increase the emotional character of utterances, used in the corpus, are as in Table 1.

---

[1] The first seven points have been adopted from Lakoff's (1975) studies. However, it has to be pointed out that not all of Lakoff's observations are included in the above typology. The omitted ones are concerned with intonational patterns (rising intonation on declaratives), hypercorrect grammar and pronunciation, or the use of emphatic stress. The reason for excluding segmental and suprasegmental issues of phonetics is that the research material has been decided to be investigated in the form of a transcribed text, without the consideration of visual or auditory aspects. The hypercorrectness of grammar, on the other hand, may hardly be verified in a pre-arranged script.

[2] This aspect refers to the studies by Coats (1993) and Wareing (2004), according to which women tend to talk more about personal issues, subjects concerning people and feelings, in order to sustain friendly relationships, whereas men in their conversations have the tendency to focus on non-personal subjects, usually coming down to an exchange of information and facts.

[3] Kendall and Tannen (2003) claim that taking on the role of authority or specialist is typically a feature of men's discourse.

Table 1 Swear words and weaker expletives in the corpus

Word	Number of occurrences	Word	Number of occurrences
bloody	6	bastard(s)	2
hell	6	fucked	1
Christ	2	balls	1
for God's sake	2	damn	1

Here are some examples of M's utterances in which expletives are used:

(1) *Doesn't mean that they've got somebody…working for them inside the **bloody** room. What **the hell** is this organization, Bond?*

(2) *Take the **bloody** shot.*

(3) *Where **the hell** have you been?*

(4) *What do you expect, a **bloody** apology?*

(5) *If you think for one moment I don't **have the balls** to send a man out to die, your instincts are dead wrong.*

(6) *Bond! Push that **damn**button!*

(7) *I **fucked** this up, didn't I?*

The use of trivialising adjectives is limited in the corpus. M does not apply many of them in her utterances. The words that can be regarded as empty adjectives, though, are listed in Table 2.

Apparently, this aspect of women's language is restricted to a minimum in M's speech. And so is the next one, i.e. colour discrimination. The only colour names found in the corpus are by no means sophisticated (Table 3).

The above-mentioned words appear in the following contexts:

(8) *Push the **red** button now, Bond!*

(9) *Well, I don't have the luxury of seeing things as **black and white**.*

Table 2 Trivialising adjectives in the corpus

Adjective	Number of occurrences
brilliant	2
exceptional	1
mysterious	1
lovely	1
inconsolable	1
extreme	1

Table 3 Colour names in the corpus

Adjective	Number of occurrences
red	1
black and white	1

Table 4 Intensifiers in the corpus

Intensifier	Number of occurrences	Intensifier	Number of occurrences
too	6	ever	2
so	4	absolutely	1
very	4	at all	1
really	2		

As one can see, not only are colour words used sporadically in M's utterances, but they also belong to the basic colour palette.

In comparison to colour words, intensifiers appear more often. Please consider Table 4.

The use of intensifiers in M's speech is not restricted to any particular contexts within the discourse in question. Here are a few examples:

(10) *They were **very** much in love.*
(11) *Well, we never **really** know anyone, do we?*
(12) *But sometimes you're **so** focused on our enemies we forget to watch our friends.*
(13) *I think you are **so** blinded by inconsolable rage that you don't care who you hurt.*

Another aspect of language to be considered is the use of tentative constructions. These cause utterances to be less direct. They lessen the authoritativeness and firmness of a message. In the analysed corpus, a few ways of making utterances sound tentative have been identified. One of them is the use of modal verb, such as *may* or *might*. Please see the sentences below:

(14) ***May** I remind you that you're the reason I'm here, 007.*
(15) *Bond, this **may** be too much for a blunt instrument to understand that arrogance and self-awareness seldom go hand-in-hand.*
(16) *You **might** like to tell her your theory about there being no oil.*
(17) *And a shower **might** be in order.*

Hedges give a similar effect. Evasive utterances, including expressions such as *I think* (2 occurrences in the corpus), *I suppose* (2 occurrences), *I believe* (1 occurrence), weaken the overtone of a given message and make it sound less direct. Without them, the utterances would be direct statements. Here are some examples:

(18) *Because **I think** you're a sexist, misogynist dinosaur, a relic of the Cold War, whose boyish charms, though wasted on me, obviously appealed to that young woman I sent out to evaluate you.*
(19) ***I think** you are so blinded by inconsolable rage that you don't care who you hurt.*
(20) *Oh, and **I suppose** that's completely inconspicuous.*
(21) ***I suppose** it is too late to make a run for it?*

Another type of utterances which may be considered as tentative by nature is the one beginning with *I need you (to)* (5 occurrences in the research material) and *I want you to* (3 occurrences). These may sound less direct in comparison to imperatives, for instance. Please study the undermentioned sentences:

(22) ***I need you to*** *come in and debrief.*
(23) *Bond.* ***I need you*** *back.*
(24) ***I need you to*** *do something.*
(25) ***I want you to*** *find GoldenEye.*
(26) *007,* ***I want you to*** *go to Electra.*
(27) ***I want you to*** *take your ego out of the equation and to judge the situation dispassionately.*

As a matter of fact, the use of imperative mood in the research corpus is very frequent. Thirty-nine occurrences have been identified. So, on the one hand, the above-mentioned instances of tentativeness may reflect the characteristics of the woman's language, but there are also contradictory features which would be typically classified as male, on the other. It also seems crucial to mention that such structures are very likely to be used in business and professional settings. Therefore, it is reasonable to assume that, in fact, expressions such as *I need you to* and *I want you to* have been forced by the institutional context of MI6, and do not happen to be a linguistic manifestation of tentativeness.

The analysis of the corpus allowed to identify seven instances of question tags in M's speech. In comparison, only two instances of the use of tags have been found in Bond's talk within the research sample. M applies tags in her speech as follows:

(28) *I would ask if you can remain emotionally detached, but I don't think it's your problem,* ***is it Bond****?*
(29) *You don't trust anyone,* ***do you James****?*
(30) *Well, we never really know anyone,* ***do we****?*
(31) *They'll do anything for you,* ***won't they****?*
(32) *Run out of drink where you were,* ***did they****?*
(33) *It's not very comfortable,* ***is it****?*
(34) *I fucked this up,* ***didn't I****?*

The subjects of conversations reflect to some extent the degree of familiarity and intimacy of M's utterances. They are mostly imposed by professional space and the institutional context of events. The utterances may be classified according to the topics they touch, as *professional talk*, *semi-professional talk* and *personal talk*. The first category includes utterances concerning Bond's tasks, the functioning of the MI6 institution, or an exchange of information and facts. In regard to Bond's insubordination as an operative, they are usually emotionally loaded. Semi-professional talk enters the personal sphere (e.g. concerning a character's private life), but it still preserves a rather official character (e.g. a given fragment of Bond's life is supposed to help to resolve a professional problem in MI6, to complete a task). The manager-operative relationship is not infringed. Truly personal talk, in turn, cannot really be observed in the corpus.

The role of an expert or an authority that M has accepted, is connected with three major acts, which are either illocutionary or perlocutionary by nature. The first category of utterances includes commanding and giving orders, which is a necessary consequence of M being the manager in MI6. Please see the examples below:

(35) *I want you to find GoldenEye. Find who took it, what they plan to do with it, and stop it.*

(36) *I'm sending you to Hamburg, 007. We've arranged for you to be invited tonight to a party at Carver's Media Centre.*

M holds the authority to give orders to her operatives, and so she does by giving clear instructions and by using grammatical structures which enable doing this in a direct and explicit way, such as present tenses or the imperative mood.

As an institutional authority, M has the knowledge necessary for instructing her operatives so that they complete institutional missions successfully. Such messages are informative and technical by nature, and they aim at delivering essential details concerning a particular task. Here are some exemplary fragments:

(37) *When they analysed the stock market after 9/11, the CIA discovered a massive shorting of airline stocks. When the stocks hit the bottom on 9/12, somebody made a fortune. The same thing happened this morning with Skyfleet—or was supposed to.*

(38) *After Robert came to me, I sent 009 to kill Renard. Before he completed the mission, Electra escaped. A week later our man caught up with the target. He put a bullet in his head. That bullet's still there. The bullet will kill him but he'll grow stronger every day until the day he dies.*

As one can see, both messages demonstrated above are similar in the sense that they describe a particular context which happens to have led to the present state of affairs in the film. Furthermore, the construction of these fragments of discourse is also alike—the messages have a cause-and-effect structure. Both fragments consist of rather short sentences, which allows to comprehend the message more easily. Even grammatically complex sentences seem to be quite concise.

Adopting the role of authority also entails the necessity to supervise and evaluate the actions of operatives. Although M does on some occasions express her appreciation for Bond's skills and actions, her evaluation of these predominantly comes down to criticising him, accusing him of insubordination. The following examples illustrate how M expresses her disapproval or dissatisfaction:

(39) *Because I think you're a sexist, misogynist dinosaur, a relic of the Cold War, whose boyish charms, though wasted on me, obviously appealed to that young woman I sent out to evaluate you.*

(40) *I will not tolerate insubordination, 007.*

(41) *You disobeyed a direct order and left that girl alone.*

(42) *You stormed into an embassy! You violated the only absolutely inviolate rule of international relationships. And why? So you could kill a nobody. We needed to question him, not to kill him. For God's sake, you're supposed to display some sort of judgement.*

M's criticism of Bond's actions is always point-blank and explicit. There is no place for courtesy or ambiguity. Messages of this kind are often accompanied with an enumeration of reasons for the negative evaluation and criticism, such as in the two last examples.

However, M does have doubts occasionally. This uncertainty usually concerns instances of situation assessment, or searching for solutions and answers to operational problems. Such dilemmas happen to constitute part of professional domain though. Caution in situation assessment and decision-making is typical for organisations and institutions. Doubts and careful analyses seem to be an integral part of any decision-making process, which, in turn, results from a goal-oriented approach of the institution. Please consider the following utterance:

(43) *She kills her father and attacks her own pipeline. Why? To what end?*

Towards the end of M's leadership (of which she is not aware at that point), she also has doubts concerning her overall work at MI6 and the effectiveness of her own actions and decisions as manager. She utters the following sentence:

(44) *I fucked this up, didn't I?*

This one sentence seems to cumulate in itself some typical aspects of men's speech, of women's speech, and of institutional discourse. On the one hand, as typical of men's language, a strong expletive is used. On the other hand, the use of the question tag construction may be considered to be a characteristic of women's language. Additionally, the emotional tone of the confession may be viewed as stereotypically ascribed to females. Finally, in reference to the institutional discourse in question, the sentence happens to be a self-evaluation—an integral part of institutional reality.

4.2 Features of Institutional Discourse in M's Utterances

The second stage of the analysis also requires a typology. The one presented below uses the studies by Drew and Heritage (1992) and Heritage (1997), in which the scholars describe the most prominent features of institutional discourse:

1. Goal orientation (at least one discourse member is task-/goal-/identity-oriented, which task, goal or identity is formally related to the institution in question).
2. Special and particular constraints, requirements and discourse frameworks (limitations and patterns concerning the choice and use of language, of what is considered to be suitable to say or write within a specific institutional context or in a particular professional reality).
3. Special inferential frameworks and procedures (ways of interpreting discourse, as pre-established for the context of an institution or a place of work).[4]

---

[4]The first three points concern the characteristics of institutional discourse as suggested by Drew and Heritage (1992).

4. Asymmetry of institutional interactions (differences resulting from an asymmetry of knowledge and power relations in a given institution).[5]

In terms of goal orientation, a few linguistic aspects may be observed. Firstly, the members of the discourse in question concentrate on professional matters and not the personal and subjective ones. This is clearly visible when considering the topics of these conversations. Secondly, whenever emotive language appears in M's utterances, it accompanies the issues which are in a more or less direct way connected with the functioning of the institution, with Bond's tasks or with the criticism of his actions as an MI6 operative. Even the use of emotive speech, therefore, may be to some extent regarded as a manifestation of an emotional involvement of M in accomplishing institutional goals, rather than, for instance, an indication of stereotypically perceived female emotionality or susceptibility.

Institutional goal orientation may also be reflected in the use of the personal pronoun *we*, which may involve an association with one's institution and its aims, and group identity. In the research corpus, it has a very high frequency, i.e. 48 occurrences, which locates the word at the ninth position in the word frequency list. The legitimacy of the above assertion may be supported by the fact that the same pronoun shows a very high frequency of use both in the Cambridge Business English Corpus (BEC) and the Cambridge and Nottingham Business English Corpus (CANBEC). It may imply that members of a given institution identify with it and involve in achieving its goals.

Another linguistic aspect connected with goal orientation is the use of action-oriented language. This manifests itself in frequent occurrences of deontic modal verbs, expressing obligation or necessity. The word *need* appears 14 times in the corpus, and its frequency results from the institutional context and goal orientation. Other examples are the verbs *have to* (3 occurrences in the corpus) /*had to* (2 occurrences), *must* (4 occurrences, but only two instances of deontic character), and *should* (4 occurrences, including three occurrences of deontic use).

As far as special and particular constraints as well as discourse frameworks are concerned, both lexis and grammar are to some extent determined by the institutional context of MI6. This involves the use of fixed collocations on the one hand and specific linguistic choices on the part of discourse participants, correlating with their position in the institutional hierarchy, on the other. Examples of collocations more restrictively complied with, found in the research material, are *active service, further instructions*, or *standard procedure*. Linguistic and interactive choices, in turn, are mostly motivated by power relations within the institution, by the institutional and discursive roles of the characters, although it has to be pointed out that throughout the series of movies, some linguistic choices have evolved and altered, which may be a symptom of the changing times and, of course, an indication of the changing relationship between M and Agent 007. Therefore, for instance, Bond sometimes addresses M with *Madam*, whereas on other occasions, he tends to call her M, without adding any title.

---

[5] Adopted after Heritage (1997).

Special inferential frameworks and procedures involve specific lexis, collocations, and reappearing expressions—the so-called chunks, which have specific functions. One of the most striking examples reappearing in the corpus is the use of *need* (14 occurrences). The word happens to have a very high frequency in BEC and CANBEC corpora as well. It is, therefore, typical in business environment, and likely to be used in specific situations, such as ordering to accomplish a task, or expressing a necessity to achieve particular institutional or organisational goals. These two functions are surely served with the use of *need* in the analysed corpus.

Table 5, in turn, demonstrates 2-word, 3-word and 4-word chunks which most frequently appear in business and professional settings according to CANBEC. The data is juxtaposed with the number of occurrences of the same phrases in the analysed corpus.

Although no 4-word chunks have been identified in the corpus out of the four listed in CANBEC as most frequently used in business, the above figures show clearly a congruity between the analysed material and the general business English corpus, which, in turn, proves a typically institution-driven character of M's speech.

The last characteristic of institutional discourse is concerned with an asymmetry of institutional interactions, which results from a pre-established institutional hierarchy, i.e. from the professional relationship between M (manager) and Bond (operative). As an example, please consider the following conversation:

M: *You said you weren't motivated by revenge.*
Bond: *I'm motivated by my duty.*
M: *No. I think you are so blinded by inconsolable rage that you don't care who you hurt. When you can't tell your friends from your enemies, it's time to go. You might like to tell her your theory about there being no oil. Her lungs are full of it.*
Bond: *It was Greene.*
M: *No doubt. But why?*
Bond: *It's just misdirection.*
M: *I mean, why her, Bond? She was just supposed to send you home. She worked in an office, collecting reports. Look how well your charm works, James. They'll*

Table 5 Occurrences of highest-frequency CANBEC chunks in the corpus

2-word chunks in CANBEC	Number of occurrences in the analysed corpus	3-word chunks in CANBEC	Number of occurrences in the analysed corpus	4-word chunks in CANBEC	Number of occurrences in the analysed corpus
you know	8	I don't know	1	at the end of	0
I think	2	a lot of	0	the end of the	0
of the	7	at the moment	0	have a look at	0
I mean	1	we need to	1	a bit of a	0

do anything for you, won't they? How many is that now? You're removed from
duty and suspended pending further investigation. You'll give whatever weapons
you have to these men and leave with them now.

M criticises Bond's actions and their consequences in a very explicit way. Simultaneously, the message seems to be rather emotional. M also resorts to sarcasm
to emphasise the seriousness and the dramatic nature of the situation. Her evaluation of Bond's behaviour is considerably longer than her operative's responses. Bond
appears to counter M's judgement and criticism by expressing his perspective shortly.
To be more precise, in the fragment cited above, M uses 122 words, whereas Bond's
responses comprise only 11 words altogether (contracted forms counted as one).
All the same, M's arguments unequivocally unmask Bond's fault and violation of
institutional and operational rules. The manager decides, therefore, to suspend Bond
and remove him from duty, punishing him in this way for his insubordination.

The contrast between the characters' roles in the institution, and their place in the
organisation's hierarchy, is well reflected in the fragment. It also turns out that the
asymmetry of institutional interactions can be observed in different aspects, including
the linguistic complexity of utterances, the emotional load, and power relations seen
at the discourse level.

4.3   The Pragmatic Dimension of M's Utterances

M's utterances are mostly determined by the aims which she intends to achieve as the
manager in the institution she happens to be in charge of. In her encounters with James
Bond, and in order to achieve specific objectives, M (1) gives orders and manages,
(2) assesses and criticises, (3) expresses concern, (4) supervises and requires reports,
(5) cares for maintaining high standards and employee's professional preparation,
and (6) creates interpersonal relationships.

M gives orders and manages the work of Agent 007 by providing clear instructions,
in a direct manner, which is demonstrated in the following examples:

1. *I'm sending you to Hamburg, 007. We've arranged for you to be invited tonight*
   to a party at Carver's Media Centre.
2. *As long as I'm the head of this department, I'll choose my own operatives.*
3. *Find a man called Marco Sciarra. Kill him.*

The first example shows how M informs Bond about the task he is supposed to
accomplish—by saying what she is doing, or else what she is causing him to do.
She also provides some essential information on what has already been arranged to
enable 007 to initiate and complete the mission. In the second example, M in an
outright manner points out the authority of hers to make decisions. In the last of the
examples, on the other hand, M commissions a task to Bond, using the imperative
form, which, again, is a very direct way of making dispositions.

On many occasions, M assesses Bond's performance, which is inextricably connected with her function in the institution. This is often done by citing what Bond has done wrong, by giving him a warning, or by informing about her standpoint. Consider the below examples:

4. *You stormed into an embassy! You violated the only absolutely inviolate rule of international relationships. And why? So you could kill a nobody. We needed to question him, not to kill him. For God's sake, you're supposed to display some sort of judgement.*
5. *Utter another syllable and I will have you killed. I knew it was too early to promote you.*
6. *I will not tolerate insubordination, 007.*

In example (4), M seems to distance herself as representing the MI6 institution from Bond's actions—a clear opposition of *you* versus *we*, which she introduces, proves it. Although this part of the message appears to present substantive information of what Agent 007 did as opposed to what MI6 had expected, the utterance is not void of elements which expose emotionality of it. The expression *for God's sake*, even though it belongs to the category of rather weak expletives, reveals a somewhat emotional character of this criticism. The same aspect is manifested by the use of an exclamation mark.

Example (5) is an earthy warning, combined with stating possible consequences if disobeyed. And this is not the end—M also seems to regret having trusted and promoted Bond, which may be seen as self-evaluation. Example (6), on the other hand, is an *I* statement, including an accusation of insubordination.

Although M frequently criticises Bond, she also expresses care on some occasions. Please see the following utterances:

7. *Bond… Come back alive.*
8. *007, are you all right?*
9. *You look like hell. When's the last time you slept?**
9. *And a shower might be in order.**

M expresses care for her operative and communicates her concern to Bond, which can be observed in the first two example utterances, (7) and (8). The other two examples mentioned are presented with an asterisk because they can also be interpreted in terms of criticism. Example (9) starts with an abrupt criticism of Bond's appearance and follows with a milder question which might suggest M's concern with Bond's physical and mental condition. Similarly, the last instance may be regarded as clinical criticism or as relativised concern.

As manager, M has to supervise her operatives, and in order to comply to this duty, she requires reports concerning their actions. She does it in the following manner:

10. *I want an update. Where do we stand?*
11. *What else do we know about Janus syndicate?*
12. *What's going on? Report!*

M demands updates and reports in a straightforward way, either by stating what she wants to get or by asking questions concerning a specific situation, or by giving an order to dispatch in an imperative mood.

One of M's responsibilities as the manager of MI6 is to care for and ensure high standards of service and possibly best preparation of her operatives for active service. This can be seen in the following utterance:

13. *You'll have to be debriefed and declared fit for active service. You can only return to duty when you've passed the tests. So take them seriously.*

M informs, therefore, what Agent 007 has to accomplish in order to return to active service. She gives him clear instructions and makes him aware of the requirements and the seriousness of the task.

Yet on other occasions, M tries to build up positive relations. She usually does it by creating pleasant atmosphere, or at least some semblance of a friendly attitude or partnership arrangement. It is also clearly visible that M really cares about the sense of trust in her professional relationship with Bond. Consider the following:

14. *Would you care for a drink?**
15. *Care for a drink?**
16. *I have to know I can trust you and that you know who to trust. And since I don't know that, I need you out of my sight.*
17. *But I do need to know, Bond. I need to know that I can trust you.*

Offering a drink in professional settings may be viewed to some extent as a culturally grounded custom. This is why an asterisk appears next to the first two sentences quoted above. This practice may be viewed as something that is typically done in particular contexts since it is considered to be appropriate, expected or advisable. However, customs of this kind may contribute to, or be intended to, create the atmosphere of hospitality and friendliness, to build positive relationships with people, no matter if genuine or superficial.

Trust, on the other hand, is what M truly cares a lot about. She emphasises the significance of mutual trust in her institutional team, especially in her relationship with James Bond.

5   Discussion and Conclusion

The language of M as a woman manager manifests features of both the language of women (e.g. tentative language, empty adjectives) and men (e.g. swear words). Some of the features of women's language specified by Lakoff (1975) do not occur in the analysed material, which might be due to the function M has in the institution and an overall institutional context, the need to adjust her identity, and, therefore, to adjust her talk, to particular contexts.

Indeed, the language of M demonstrates the characteristics of institutional discourse, some of which seem to coincide with the features of men's language (e.g. enacting the role of authority/expert, the use of some modal verbs, including the ones of deontic character, such as *need*). As for the pragmatic aspect, M's utterances comply with the purposes which she intends to fulfil as the manager. Here, also, the institutional context seems to play a predominant role.

Since M's language manifests features of men's speech, women's speech and institutional talk, it is difficult to say unequivocally which of the features predominantly built it up. However, the results allow to conclude what has been suggested by Holmes (2015) that effective communicators have the skill to adopt different discourse features in their speech in order to achieve their goals. The research has also shown a consistency with Holmes's (2015) claim that individuals are constantly engaged in constructing their identities. Therefore, it can be concluded that it is exactly what M does. She simultaneously enacts her gender identity and her identity as the manager of MI6.

The investigation also shows that there is a consistency between M's interactional and communication skills and the model managerial ones mentioned by Baskiewicz (2013). She communicates institutional goals clearly, she does not refrain from listening to her operative and from asking questions. She supervises and actively monitors her operatives' actions by requiring reports and evaluation. Lastly, as a women manager, M expects and opts for mutual trust in her professional team.

References

Agar, M. (1985). Institutional discourse. *Text, 5*(3), 147–168.
Baskiewicz, N. (2013). Kobiety W Zarządzaniu Organizacjami. *Studia Ekonomiczne, 161,* 27–35.
Baxter, J. (2010). *The language of female leadership.* Hampshire, New York: Palgrave Macmillan.
Benwell, B., & Stokoe, E. (2006). *Discourse and identity.* Edinburgh: Edinburgh University Press.
Cameron, D. (2005). Language, gender and sexuality: Current issues and new directions. *Applied Linguistics, 26*(4), 482–502.
Coats, J. (1993). *Women, men and language.* London, New York: Longman.
Drew, P., & Heritage, J. (1992). *Talk at work.* Cambridge: Cambridge University Press.
Giddens, A. (2004). *Socjologia.* Warszawa: Wydawnictwo Naukowe PWN.
Heritage, J. (1997). Conversation analysis and institutional talk. In D. Silverman (Ed.), *Qualitative research: Theory, method and practice* (pp. 161–182). London: Sage.
Holmes, J. (2006). *Gendered talk at work: Constructing gender identity through workplace discourse.* New York, Oxford: Blackwell.
Holmes, J. (2015). Discourse in the workplace. In D. Tannen, H. E. Hamilton & D. Schiffrin (Eds.), *The handbook of discourse analysis* (pp. 880–901). Chichester: Wiley Blackwell.
Kendall, S., & Tannen, D. (2003). Discourse and gender. In D. Shiffrin, D. Tannen, & H. E. Hamilton (Eds.), *The handbook of discourse analysis* (pp. 548–567). Malden, MA: Blackwell Publishing.
Koester, A. (2010). *Workplace discourse.* London, New York: Continuum.
Lakoff, R. (1975). *Language and woman's place.* London, New York: Harper and Row Publishers.
Mamet, P. (2014). *Licence to speak. The language of James Bond.* Częstochowa: Wydawnictwo im. Stanisława Podobińskiego Akademii im. Jana Długosza.
Mamet, P., Gwóźdź, G., & Wilk, G. (2017). (Nie)śmiertelny humor Agenta 007. In J. Lubocha-Kruglik & O. Małysa (Eds.), *Przestrzenie przekładu 2* (pp. 169–188). Katowice: Wydawnictwo Uniwersytetu Śląskiego.

Mamet, P., & Wilk, G. (2019). "Miłosne" gry słowne Agenta 007 w tłumaczeniu na język polski i rosyjski. In J. Lubocha-Kruglik, O. Małysa, & G. Wilk (Eds.), *Przestrzenie przekładu 3* (pp. 115–129). Katowice: Wydawnictwo Uniwersytetu Śląskiego.

Mamet, P., Miś, A., & Wilk, G. (2020). Agent 007 i M w ocenach wzajemnych – polski i rosyjski przekład wybranych fragmentów filmów. In J. Lubocha-Kruglik & O. Małysa (Eds.), *Przestrzenie przekładu 4*.

Mayr, A. (2008). *Language and power. An introduction to institutional discourse*. London, New York: Continuum.

Mullany, L. (2007). *Gendered discourse in the professional workplace*. Basingstoke: Palgrave Macmillan.

Nelson, M. (2000). *Mike Nelson's Business English Lexis Site*. Retrieved May 28, 2018 from https://users.utu.fi/micnel/business_english_lexis_site.htm.

Nelson, M. (2006). Semantic associations in business English: A corpus-based analysis. *English for Specific Purposes, 25*, 217–234.

Schnurr, S. (2009). *Leadership discourse at work: Interactions of humour, gender and workplace culture*. Houndmills, Basingstoke: Palgrave Macmillan.

Scollon, R., & Scollon, S. W. (2003). Discourse and intercultural communication. In D. Schiffrin, D. Tannen, & H. E. Hamilton (Eds.) *The handbook of discourse analysis* (pp. 538–547). Blackwell Publishing.

Tannen, D. (1990). *You just don't understand: Women and men in conversation*. New York: William Morrow.

Tannen, D. (1994). *Talking from 9 to 5: Women and men at work*. New York: Harper Collins.

Wareing, S. (2004). Language and gender. In L. Thomas, S. Wareing, I. Singh, J. S. Peccei, J. Thornborrow, & J. Jones (Eds.), *Language, society and power: An introduction* (pp. 76–92). London, New York: Routledge.

Anna Majer, Ph.D., is an assistant professor in the Institute of Linguistics, Faculty of Humanities, University of Silesia in Katowice, Poland. In her research, she predominantly adopts a socio-cultural-linguistic perspective. Her work and research interests centre on discourse analysis, the study of myths and stereotypes, the language of values, gendered discourse, and recently also on specialised discourse issues. In her socio-linguistic investigations, she mostly applies a critical paradigm.

Piotr Mamet is Professor at the Institute of Communication and Education Research of Silesian University of Technology, is engaged in the research on LSP, especially discourse, genre and register analysis, including the Plain language issues, and the linguistic aspect of a brand name. He is the author of two monographs, i.e. "Język negocjacji handlowych" (2004) and "Język w służbie menedżerów – deklaracja misji przedsiebiorstwa" (2005) as well as 30 articles and two monographs in this area. His recent research covers the language of film characters, e.g. the monograph Licence to Speak. The Language of James Bond (2014) as well as conference participation and articles (in print) in which he analyses the translation of the language of 007 and its translation into Polish. Prof. Piotr Mamet was one of the founders and managers of the Business Language College, University of Silesia (1991–2005). Before starting his teaching and research work Prof. Piotr Mamet worked in the international trade sector, including Polish Chamber of Foreign Trade (1995–1991). His considerable experience in international trade is a strong basis for his research and teaching activities in ESP, especially Business English.

Printed by Printforce, the Netherlands